GLOBAL LITERACIES AND THE
WORLD-WIDE WEB

The World-Wide Web has transformed the way that information is distributed. Increasingly it is touted as a global literacy system, a technology-rich environment within which information is distributed, received and acted upon. *Global Literacies and the World-Wide Web* provides a critical examination of the new online literacy practices; authoring, designing, interpreting and enacting change, especially as these activities are affected, both directly and indirectly, by various cultural and national contexts.

Global Literacies and the World-Wide Web is written by scholars from around the world including Mexico, Japan, Greece, Hungary, Australia, Palau, Cuba and the United States. Each chapter represents and examines online literacy practices in their specific cultures, providing critical commentary on how these literacies are determined by national, cultural and educational contexts.

Gail Hawisher and Cynthia Selfe resist a romanticised vision of global oneness and instead celebrate the dynamic capacity of these new self-defined literacy communities with their continuing redefinition of ethnicity and difference. *Global Literacies and the World-Wide Web* is a lively challenge to conventional notions of the relationship between literacy and technology.

Gail E. Hawisher is Professor of English and Director of the Center for Writing Studies at the University of Illinois. **Cynthia L. Selfe** is Professor of Humanities in the Humanities Department at Michigan Technological University.

LITERACIES
Series Editor: David Barton
Lancaster University

Literacy practices are changing rapidly in contemporary society in response to broad social, economic and technological changes: in education, the workplace, the media and in everyday life. The *Literacies* series has been developed to reflect the burgeoning research and scholarship in the field of literacy studies and its increasingly interdisciplinary nature. The series aims to situate reading and writing within its broader institutional contexts where literacy is considered as a social practice. Work in this field has been developed and drawn together to provide books which are accessible, inter-disciplinary and international in scope, covering a wide range of social and institutional contexts.

SITUATED LITERACIES
Edited by David Barton, Mary Hamilton and Roz Ivanič

MULTILITERACIES
Literacy Learning and the design of social futures
Edited by Bill Cope and Mary Kalantzis

GLOBAL LITERACIES AND THE WORLD-WIDE WEB
Edited by Gail E. Hawisher and Cynthia L. Selfe

Editorial Board:

GLOBAL LITERACIES AND THE WORLD-WIDE WEB

Edited by

Gail E. Hawisher and Cynthia L. Selfe

London and New York

ACI - 9003

First published 2000
by Routledge
11 New Fetter Lane, London EC4P 4EE

Simultaneously published in the USA and Canada
by Routledge
29 West 35th Street, New York, NY 10001

Routledge is an imprint of the Taylor and Francis Group

Typeset in Baskerville by
The Florence Group, Stoodleigh, Devon
Printed and bound in Great Britain by
TJ International Ltd, Padstow, Cornwall

British Library Cataloguing in Publication Data
A catalogue record for this book is available from the British Library

Library of Congress Cataloging in Publication Data
Global literacies and the World-Wide Web : postmodern identities/
[edited by] Gail E. Hawisher and Cynthia L. Selfe.
p. cm. – (Literacies)
Includes bibliographical references (p.) and index.
1. Communication and culture.   2. Communication and technology.
3. World Wide Web (Information retrieval system) – Social aspects.
4. Written communication–Social aspects.
I. Hawisher, Gail E.   II. Selfe, Cynthia L., 1951– .   III. Series.
P94.6.G58 2000   99–25166
303.48′33–dc21   CIP

ISBN 0–415–18941–1 (hbk)
ISBN 0–415–18942-X (pbk)

TO THOSE WOMEN WHO TAUGHT US HOW

"Sug" McCune Cornelius
Helen McCune
Eleanor Caples
Elizabeth Peterson
Hilda Pettrich
Elsie Seisz
Dayle Benson
Julie Carlson

CONTENTS

PLATES, FIGURES, AND TABLES

Plates

Figures

Tables

CONTRIBUTORS

Enikő Csomay, Eötvös University.

Elizabeth W. de Huergo, American Institute of Monterrey.

Aliki Dragona, University of California, Davis.

Victor Fernandez, Trabajadores, Havana, Cuba.

Barbara Field, Simon & Schuster.

Sibylle Gruber, University of Northern Arizona.

Carolyn Handa, University of Southern Illinois, Edwardsville.

Gail E. Hawisher, University of Illinois, Urbana-Champaign.

Cynthia Haynes, University of Texas at Dallas.

Jan Rune Holmevik, University of Bergen.

Jason Johnstone, University of Puget Sound.

Karla Saari Kitalong, Central Florida University.

Tino Kitalong, Chad er a Belau, Orlando, Florida.

James A. Levin, University of Illinois, Urbana-Champaign.

Sean Lewis, University of the Western Cape.

Cathryn McConaghy, University of New England.

Elaine Richardson, Pennsylvania State University.

Susan Romano, University of Texas at San Antonio.

Cynthia L. Selfe, Michigan Technological University.

Sarah Sloane, University of Puget Sound.

Ilana Snyder, Monash University.

Taku Sugimoto, University of Tokyo.

Laura Sullivan, University of Florida.

INTRODUCTION:
TESTING THE CLAIMS

Gail E. Hawisher and Cynthia L. Selfe

The Web as an environment for global literacy practices

The past two decades have yielded enormous and far-reaching changes in the way information is created and exchanged and used – with sophisticated computer networks like the Internet and the Web[1] figuring centrally as environments for global communication. But how "world-wide" a literacy environment is the Web? How do cultural contexts affect the communication that occurs within this globally networked system of computers which appear to be culturally transparent? In what ways is the system itself culturally determined, structured, and ordered? How does the ordered space of the Web affect the literacy practices of individuals from different cultures – and the constitution of their identities – personal, national, cultural, ethnic through language? What literacy values characterize communication practices in this ordered space?

In the United States, in particular, and the western industrial nations, in general, the Web and the Internet have been touted – in the popular press, in trade presses, in the public imagination (see, Gore, 1994; Negroponte, 1995; Rogers, "Global Literacy"; Rheingold, 1993) – as a culturally neutral literacy environment: a technology-rich medium within which messages, documents, reports, words and images can be authored and distributed by writers; read and received by end-users; and acted upon by individuals in businesses, corporations, schools, or government settings, regardless of cultural differences. Given their potential as a medium for information exchange and distribution, such networks have also been hailed as an environment that supports the related spread of democratic ideals and the expansion of world markets based on a global set of consumer wants and needs.[2]

In America, one of the cultural narratives that serves as the basis for this representation – the global-village narrative – is shaped by American and western cultural interests at the level of ideological production (Selfe, 1999). According to this utopian and ethnocentric narrative, sophisticated computer networks – manufactured by far-sighted scientists and engineers educated within democratic and highly technological cultures – will serve to connect the world's peoples in a vast global community that transcends

1

current geopolitical borders. Linked through this electronic community, the peoples of the world will discover and communicate about their common concerns, needs, and interests using the culturally neutral medium of computer-based communication. When individuals within the global community discover – through increased communication – their shared interests and commonweal, they will resolve their differences and identify ways of solving global problems that extend beyond the confining boundaries of nation states.

Increasingly, this representation has been criticized by technology studies scholars who question its accuracy and point to the specific national and cultural interests that determine its ideologic valences. Such scholars, for example, have pointed out the limitations of international computer connectivity, noting that large segments of the world's population have little or no access to the Web (Wresch, 1996; Braman, 1995) and have thus called into question the sobriquet *world-wide* as an accurate descriptor of reality. Other scholars have also noted that the culturally specific nature of literacy practices clearly influence communications on the Web and the use of the Internet in fundamental ways (Skreslet, 1997; Mitra, 1997), thus, belying myths of cultural neutrality. Still other scholars have pointed out the ideologically interested nature of the global-village narrative (Selfe, 1999) as constructed specifically within the framework of American and western politics, economics, and culture.

Unfortunately, although such critical takes on the Web and the related narrative of the Global Village, are increasingly common, very little research has been conducted to trace culturally specific literacy practices online in ways that might offer additional perspectives on the myth of a culturally neutral global network. Only limited work has addressed, for example, the literacy practices of different cultural, ethnic, national, and racial groups who communicate – or choose not to communicate – within such electronic environments. Little or no work has been done to trace the ways in which specific, culturally-determined literacy practices serve to constitute the Web as a communication medium. Nor has there been significant and systematic study of the cultural identities individuals create through their literacy practices on the Web.

Given the lack of culturally specific projects of this kind, the claim – that the Web forms a global literacy environment in which peoples from all over the world can communicate with one another without significant barriers posed by geopolitical location, language, culture, and everyday social practices and attitudes – has retained a significant level of potency within the national consciousness of United States and other highly industrialized western nations, often with the embarrassing results that one might expect to accrue from such international ignorance (Selfe, 1998).

This situation means, further, that even as increased communication, commerce, research, and negotiation is taking place in Web environments (see, del Gado and Nielson, 1996; Hoft, 1995; Andrews, 1996), individual writers, readers, and communicators – especially in the West – have been provided little help in understanding important culturally determined literacy differences that shape such environments. This is true even while literacy scholars have become increasingly clear about their understanding that literacy attitudes and practices are determined within, and shaped by, culturally specific contexts, and that the different ways in which communications are authored, received, or used, fundamentally affect the production, reception, and understanding of information (Gee, 1990; Graff, 1987; Myers, 1996; Street, 1995).

Importantly, until culturally specific investigations and examinations of culturally determined literacy practices on the Web are undertaken, we are no closer to understanding the truth – or the real complexity – of the *internationalness* of the literacy environment offered by the Web, or to identifying the many small inaccuracies so effectively masked by the global-village narrative.

This book, then, begins the examination of such culturally specific literacy practices – authoring, designing, reading, analyzing, interpreting – on the Web, especially as these practices are shaped, both directly and indirectly, by concrete contexts for language and language use. The over-arching goal of the volume is to test the commonly accepted premise that the Web provides individuals around the globe with a common and neutral literacy environment within which international communications are authored, read, and exchanged.

The audiences we envision making use of this collection span several different disciplines: literacy studies, the study of world Englishes, linguistics, composition studies, technical communication, graphic design and representation, international studies, and communications. Faculty and students at advanced levels of study who specialize in these fields and related areas of study may find the book to be of immediate interest.

But even as we introduce the volume, we must acknowledge its limitations. First and foremost, we recognize the extent to which our own national, political, cultural, social, and ideological positions – as two white, American women scholars – shape and limit the perspectives we can provide. In this sense, the two of us have similar national backgrounds (although one of us has lived in Germany and sojourned in Brazil and the other has taught school in Scotland and lectured at the Chinese University of Hong Kong), and similarly limited understandings about the ways in which individuals from other countries use technology (although we have observed such use in Norway, Egypt, Zimbabwe, the Netherlands, and New Zealand). We both speak and write fluently only in English (although we both have the ability to read and speak an additional language at a level below fluency). Further, as is the case with most academic scholars, we are able to maintain contact only with a geographically limited group of professional colleagues – mostly based within the United States (although we have met and continue to correspond with colleagues who study computer use in Japan, Egypt, Sweden, Africa, England, Guam, Puerto Rico, Mexico, Brazil, and Greece). Given our backgrounds, we have designed this collection to extend our shared understandings and resources while acknowledging, in realistic terms, our limits as culturally determined citizens.

As a part of this approach, we have assembled ten teams of writers to contribute to this volume. Each team is composed of at least one person who lives in, or was born in, a country other than the United States. Drawing on the talents of these teams, the volume provides a series of culturally specific snapshots and examinations of literacy practices on the Web – in Hungary, Greece, Australia, Palau, Norway, Japan, Scotland, Mexico, Cuba, South Africa, and the United States. These snapshots are not intended to be exhaustive or representative. They provide, most simply, a series of beginnings: incomplete, momentary, fragmentary assemblages of culturally specific information on Web literacy practices.

In addition to websites of these contributors' own choosing – selected according to the focus of each particular chapter – each team was also given a common set of websites to use, when appropriate, as touch-stones for their analyses. Teams were also asked to focus their chapter on commentary about their own culturally determined literacy practices when encountering these sites, and to discuss how their own literacy practices have been shaped by (and, in turn, shape) the national, cultural, and educational contexts within which individuals participate and enact literacy. Each set of contributors was asked to discuss the extended implications of their experience – and the experiences of some of the other citizens in their country/culture/locale – within the context of the expanding Web and the claims for its effectiveness as an international literacy and communication environment.

Finally, all writing teams read Brian Street's *Social Literacies: Critical Approaches to Literacy in Development, Ethnography and Education* (1995). Although Street does not specifically discuss computer technology as a topic in this book, he does outline a series of key assumptions about literacy practices that help ground the studies of Web literacy contained in this volume in realistically complex cultural contexts. Among these important assumptions, we count the following:

- literacy practices are affected by the social and material conditions of particular cultures – we add that this is especially true of literacy practices in media contexts;
- the nature of literacy, as a social construct, is ideologically determined by individual cultures and this ideological content is deeply sedimented in a society's understanding and determines, to a great extent, what it means to be literate or illiterate in a particular culture;

- literacy practices in individual cultures are determined by multiple social groups and for multiple purposes;
- because literacies are determined within specific ideological frameworks, the acquisition of literacies does not automatically lead to social mobility, educational progress, or effective involvement on the part of citizens.

From the contributions that have grown out of these strategies for working with authors, readers are encouraged to draw their own conclusions about culturally specific literacy practices on the Web. We hope, as well, that readers will use these preliminary efforts to undertake their own, more extensive, investigations of similar topics. For it is only through collective action, and the sharing of our findings, that we can hope to understand more fully the extent of culturally determined literacy practices on the Web.

A word about this Introduction and its organization

Before introducing the chapters that follow, we consider it important to provide a bit more background related to the global-village narrative and the reasons this myth exerts such force on the western imagination. In providing such background material, we do not mean to suggest that the American cultural perspective is somehow privileged in terms of its interpretive perspective. Rather, we hope to recognize the limits of that perspective, while acknowledging its continuing influence.

Certainly, the development of computer technology, while benefiting from the contributions of many peoples and countries, remains essentially flavored by exported American economic and cultural values. These complex social formations, moreover, continue to exert a great deal of influence on the literacy practices that characterize the Web today. They do not, however, comprise the whole of the story, nor do they offer satisfactory representations of the literacy practices in other cultures.

The Web and the global-village narrative:
an American perspective

In part, the depiction of the Web as a neutral international communication environment represents the latest manifestation of the global-village narrative – a particularly American image first introduced by Samuel Morse, the inventor of the telegraph, when he petitioned the United States Congress to support the development of his invention (Braman, 1995). The representation of the global-village was later popularized and further romanticized by Canadian scholar Marshall McLuhan (1964) and other technology advocates in connection with computer networks. The narrative articulates the popular American belief that technology will serve to join the various peoples in the world in a global network, a cyberlandscape that will diminish current geopolitical boundaries and erase differences among cultures even as it restores a shared community of international spirit.

For Americans,[3] at least, this representation is an easy one to subscribe to. The majority of citizens in the United States like to think that computers have been continually refined in their design by scientists and engineers, committed to making technology serve the needs of human beings, and carefully legislated by a democratic federal government committed to looking after the best interests of citizens. According to this potent, culturally specific representation, American technological know-how, as it has been fostered and encouraged within this country's system of education, has resulted in the knowledge and skills required to create such a global information infrastructure that now links people around the world in productive ways. This global network supports ongoing and much needed research on health, scientific puzzles, and other projects, as well as encouraging the vital and democratic involvement of citizens in decisions of global importance.

The linkage of technology with the social formations of science, economic prosperity, education, capitalism, and democracy lends this story potent cumulative power in the collective imagination of citizens in the United States. Within this narrative context, computers are understood as the latest technological invention in a long line of discoveries that will contribute to making the world a better place by extending the reach and the control of humankind, most specifically the reach of America and its related system of free-market capitalism and democracy. Operating from such a belief structure, for example, many Americans hope and believe that computers will help unravel the mystery of human genes and, thus, help identify a cure for diseases that have plagued humankind for centuries; that computers will help humans develop an improved understanding of the natural world as they support efforts to travel in space and map the floor of the oceans; that computers will help humans unravel the mysteries of natural events like hurricanes, tornadoes, earthquakes, and volcanoes and, thus, allow us to predict and avoid the danger posed by such phenomena; and that computers will help make education more effective and efficient and will thus help prepare literate citizens who are capable of increased democratic involvement.

Two American books – Negroponte's *Being Digital* (1995) and Rheingold's *The Virtual Community* – provide more elaborated illustrations of this representation. In *Being Digital* (1995), Negroponte portrays a world-wide digital revolution that is all but accomplished, all but complete. He writes:

> Did you ever know the childhood conundrum of working for a penny a day for a month, but doubling your salary each day? If you started this wonderful pay scheme on New Year's Day, you would be earning more than $10 million per day on the last day

of January. . . . When an effect is exponential, those last three days mean a lot. We are approaching those last three days in the spread of computing and digital telecommunications.

(p. 5)

Negroponte then goes on to explain that computers are similarly entering our everyday lives – that 35 percent of families in the US and 50 percent of teenagers in the US own personal computers; that 30 million Americans are on the Internet; and that these figures ignore the millions of micro-processors in answering machines, toasters, automobiles, CD players, and so forth (p. 5). He sums up his recounting of statistics by stating, simply: "Computing is not about computers any more. It is about living" (p. 6).

The tone of Negroponte's recital suggests the cumulative power of tech-nology's growth and implies that the pace and direction of its expansion within American culture is less a matter for individuals and groups to shape, determine, or control than it is for them to observe, enjoy, and revel in. For Negroponte, the continuing efforts of the computer industry, a fortunate child of the marriage of science and capitalism, will supply new products to fuel the desires and the dreams of consumers. Such electronic products will include right and left cufflinks or earrings that communicate with one another; a telephone that responds like a well-trained British butler; and schools modeled on electronic museums where children communicate with other children all over the world (p. 6).

As might be expected from this enthusiastic commentary, Negroponte makes no suggestion about limiting the growth and expansion of tech-nology and technology markets, even on a world-wide scale. Indeed, he describes how computer technology – informed by the American projects of science and fueled by the engine of multinational capitalism – will estab-lish a global network that will transform the values of the US and others into a harmonic whole, erase meaningless geopolitical borders, and create of the world a global village in which all members are cooperating part-ners. According to Negroponte,

> The user community of the Internet will be in the mainstream of everyday life. Its demographics will look more and more like the demographics of the world itself. . . . The true value of a network is less about information and more about community. The infor-mation superhighway is more than a short cut to every book in the Library of Congress. It is creating a totally new global social fabric.
>
> (p. 183)

For Negroponte, the harmonizing effects of computer technology will also extend to education and literacy efforts. He sees students crossing tradi-tional disciplines and collaborating with one another rather than competing.

7

New computer programs will be such that they will encourage teachers and students to move away from linear modes of teaching and learning to one which embraces all of art and science as one. He continues in this visionary vein by predicting that

> [t]omorrow people of all ages will find a more harmonious contin-uum in their lives, because, increasingly, the tools to work with and the toys to play with will be the same. There will be a more common palette for love and duty, for self expression and group work.
>
> (p. 221)

Similar claims issue forth from Howard Rheingold (1993) in *The Virtual Community: Homesteading on the Electronic Frontier* in which he sketches a world of connected individuals and groups. He tells us that online participants "exchange pleasantries and argue, engage in intellectual discourse, conduct commerce, exchange knowledge, share emotional support, make plans, brainstorm, gossip, feud, fall in love, find friends and lose them, play games, flirt, create a little high art and a lot of idle talk" (p. 3). For Rheingold, virtual community denizens behave and converse just as they do in real life (IRL) but leave their bodies behind. In describing life in such virtual communities, Rheingold also identifies the links between computer-supported networks and the ongoing projects of American democracy, economic prosperity, and literacy education. He argues that such computer networks can give power to ordinary people, enabling even a 10-year-old to "instantly obtain a bully pulpit; the Library of Congress, and a world of potential coconspirators" (p. 5). Computer-mediated communication, according to Rheingold, is capable of re-invigorating public discourse and revitalizing the public sphere (p. 14).

These representations of technology and literacy describe the overlapping system of social effects, cultural formations, practices, and attitudes within which Americans – and the inhabitants of countries influenced by American belief systems and economic systems – have come to understand and order the Web. The cultural elements associated with this framework are formulated to appeal to inhabitants of technologically developed countries that might benefit – economically and politically – from the global expansion of computer networks. Given this context, however, the interested nature of the Web cannot be revealed to citizens of western cultures. Rather – to justify the expense and investment associated with building the Internet infrastructure and to appeal on an ideological level to a sense of fair play and inclusion – the global network is portrayed as a culturally-neutral medium that has been built to support a larger global community, one that transcends the problems of race, geopolitical borders, national interest, and culturally specific values that hinder communication, free exchange, and shared understanding.

The global-village myth, then, provides a convenient and ideologically effective way of making efforts to expand free-market economic development, provide active support of fledgling democratic political efforts, and intervene militarily in the affairs of non-western countries (Deibert, 1997). This narrative also helps citizens explain the effects of overdetermined social formations that support the rapid, and often confusing, pace of technology change; the barrage of new chip-based products; and the increasingly high degree of technological specialization necessary to support patterns of national economic success in competitive world markets. The potency of the story can be gauged by the fact that American computer users seldom notice or question the use of English as the primary language of the Web, or the widespread and culturally specific features of the Web that reveal a western perspective (e.g., a reliance on westernized instantiations of authorship, visual design, text, and representation), or the economic and political ordering of Web resources at the service of capitalism, democracy, and other free-market forces.

To citizens of other countries, however, the global-village myth is far from culturally neutral and understandably much less appealing. The inhabitants of countries traditionally identified as less technologically "developed," for example, may interpret the global expansion of the Web within the historical context of colonialism. As technology scholars, Constance Penley and Andrew Ross (1992) note, the "struggle for self determination" that such countries must undertake is often "waged under technological conditions produced elsewhere" (p. ix) – within the frameworks, for example, of American-designed computer networks, computer-based educational environments, or economic and political systems. It is within such exported or colonial frameworks, then, that the citizens of such countries may interpret the establishment of off-shore factories that exploit inexpensive labor; a local government's continuing and unwelcome reliance on foreign investment; or the devaluation or erasure of culturally specific linguistic, social, political, and religious practices that sometimes occurs in some electronic sites. To citizens in these countries, the Web may seem less a neutral and welcome medium for global communication than a disturbing and unwelcome system for broadcasting western colonial culture and values.

In some cases, given this interpretive framework, investing time and resources in such a culturally marked communication environment may be associated with an ideological surrender to foreign interests or colonial values. As a result, many cultural groups may place considerably less value on computer technology and access to the Web, may not incorporate the Web within the fabric of their literacy practices, or may consider computer technology a negative influence on the quality of their lives, language use, identity formation, and cultural practices. Further – given that such groups may have, or choose to encourage, less access to computer technology for

9

Web development, and less technologically-rich educational opportunities – local and national websites, resources, and culturally specific representations and texts may remain unrealized.

Of course, attitudes toward the Web as a medium for communication and literacy practices are far from monolithic. As an alternative to the global-village myth, for example, some national, ethnic and racial groups, among them Palauans (Kitalong and Kitalong, Chapter 4, this volume), Scots (Sloane and Johnstone, Chapter 7, this volume), and the diasporic peoples of the Indian sub-continent (Mitra, 1997) – understand the Web as a landscape within which some of their own particular cultural values and literacy practices can be expressed, extended and enriched.

Culturally specific literacy practices on the Web: difference and identity on the Web

The chapters contained within this collection are designed to contribute culturally specific perspectives on online literacy practices as they are formulated within and shaped by different and related sets of historical, economic, educational, and social values. Rather than elaborating on the Web within the particularly American context of the global-village narrative, these chapters challenge this narrative and, thus, reduce its potency, in part by demonstrating how literacy attitudes and practices adhere more specifically to specific cultural representations, values, and contexts.

To this end, we have organized the main body of this collection into three parts that take subtly different exploratory routes: Part I: Literacy, culture, and difference on the Web; Part II: Literacy, diversity, and identity on the Web; and Part III: Literacy, conflict, and hybridity on the Web. The concluding chapter of this book, "Hybrid and transgressive literacy practices on the Web," relies on the work of Manuel Castells, Donna Haraway, Homi Bhabba, and the collective work of authors in this volume to suggest an alternative perspective to the global-village narrative. This perspective – which admits that identities and literacies are multiplied and freely transgressed in electronic landscapes – denies outdated geopolitical landscapes, but maintains a value on cultural specificity; argues against a romanticized version of global oneness, but for the continuing redefinition of ethnicity and difference in hybrid and multiple forms.

The first part of this book – Part I: Literacy, culture, and difference on the Web – offers three chapters that explore Web literacy practices as they have come to be constituted within specific cultural, historical, and economic contexts. These chapters demonstrate the particular embeddedness of reading and writing as sociocultural activities, and, taken as an ensemble, they suggest that the landscape of the Internet and the Web is far from the promised global village. Rather, they indicate, cyberspace is a culturally interested geography, one designed in ways that differentially supports various peoples and groups around the globe, both in their literacy practices and values.

In "Changing economies, changing politics, and the Web: a Hungarian perspective," for example, Sibylle Gruber and Eniko Csomay note that the use of the Web by Hungarian schoolchildren currently serves as a cultural symbol for "the country's move away from a system closed to outside interference to a system that welcomes not only new ideas within the country but also outside its borders". The online literacy practices of schoolchildren, the authors are careful to add, however, do not "automatically replace or erase previously held attitudes or beliefs" that grow from cultural rootstock – indeed such practices seem to represent a vigorous site of cultural struggle. On one hand, these electronic literacy practices are aligned with sociocultural forces of change – the trend toward modernization of educational systems, the trend toward global marketplaces, or the trend toward international economic and military cooperation as modeled by NATO and the European Union. On the other hand, however, the online literacy practices are also shaped by more conservative forces – among them, economic infrastructure, educational bureaucracy, and social pragmatism. These forces, at times, serve to reduce the amount and frequency of school-age children's access to the Web.

Underscoring Gruber and Csomay's arguments, authors Aliki Dragona and Carolyn Handa in "*Xenes glosses*: literacy and cultural implications of the Web for Greece" maintain that communications on the Web may not carry some of the rich contextual values associated with more traditional literacy practices in Greek culture. In part, this claim is true, the authors observe, because such exchanges, frequently, are articulated in English, which is not the mother tongue of Greek citizens. In part, it is true because the multiple layers of literacy practice as sedimented by history and tradition (based on experiences with family, convention, geography, mythology, and religion) are transmitted, in large part, through face-to-face interaction, both official and unofficial – a highly valued aspect of Greek culture.

Shifting the focus from Europe to Australia, Cathryn McConaghy and Ilana Snyder in "Working the Web in postcolonial Australia" explore how the Web has offered indigenous people in Australia "opportunities . . . to connect, to correct, and to disrupt existing textual enclosures" (Peters and Lankshear, 1996), and, in Anna Yeatman's (1996, p. 91) terms to exercise "voice and choice". McConaghy and Snyder examine the ways in which the Web supports a renegotiation of aboriginal identities as well as the repositioning and transformation that are involved in this effort. The authors focus on various Web-based literacy practices that construct "Aboriginality," not only investigating narratives on the Web that serve to "isolate Aborigines and constitute them as exotic rather than contemporary peoples", but also those that seem to allow indigenous Australians to construct a more productive politics of identity, difference, and representation.

11

Heeding Brian Street's (1995) cautions that literacy practices are variously constructed, manifested, and understood in particular political and ideological contexts, the authors situate the Web practices that they examine within the neocolonial and anticolonial discourses that lend them force and meaning.

The second part of this book – Part II: Literacy, diversity, and identity on the Web – includes four chapters that explore the complex ways in which groups of people from different nations, cultures, and ethnicities have come to constitute complex online identities through their literacy practices on the Web, and have, in turn, been constituted by these electronic spaces.

"Complicating the tourist gaze: literacy and the Internet as catalysts for articulating a post-colonial Palauan identity" authored by Karla and Tino Kitalong, focuses on the ways in which people who live on Palau and Palauans who live elsewhere in the world construct their own cultural identities on the Web. The online literacy practices in which Palauans engage, the authors note, help them create and maintain a sense of community among the dispersed members of this island nation. In this chapter, Kitalong and Kitalong address the concern of Penley and Ross (1992) that – within developing nations technology developed by industrialized nations may be applied inappropriately within the context of "developing nations' economic, social and political needs and their cultural values" (see Chapter 4). The authors provide an example of how Palauans, despite the obvious influence of such factors, have managed to "appropriate and re-contextualize" their national identities in a process of what Mary Louise Pratt (1991, p. 36) calls "transculturation."

Foregrounding the importance of Norwegian cultural identities, Jan Rune Holmevik and Cynthia Haynes in "Norwegian accords: shaping peace, education, and gender on the Web" provide an additional example of a national identity shaped within the landscape of the Web. The authors suggest that Norwegians have used the Web as an environment in which to construct their own culturally embedded political, educational, and gendered identities and reflect these identities outward to the world at large. These authors identify a deep respect for nature and the natural world, peace and international cooperation, a concern for education, and social opportunities for both women and men as the hallmarks of Norwegian culture that are reflected and conveyed in the electronic environments of the Internet and the Web.

Turning to Japan, Taku Sugimoto and James Levin in Chapter 6, "Multiple literacies and multimedia: a comparison of Japanese and American uses of the Internet" use the metaphor of *adaptation* rather than *adoption* to explore how cultural and national values shape both literacy practices and the construction of identity within the Web. The authors note that Japanese uses of the Web and the Internet point to "substantive as well as subtle variations" in the ways that technology is used in Japan, a country that has "imported technology" and the United States, a country that has been a primary exporter of network and web technology. As these authors point out, literacy activities are necessarily shaped by the historical values that inform a culture and by the many ways in which these values are grounded in complex sociocultural contexts.

The final chapter in Part II, "Reading sideways, backwards, and across: Scottish and American literacy practices," by Sarah Sloane and Jason Johnstone, also explores how cultural identities are historically constituted and changed through Web literacy practices. The authors note that literacy practices on the Web, especially in online newspapers, serve both to amplify and alter the national dynamic of a "nervous looking outward beyond the borders of Scotland to frame compositions, critical responses, and even the shape of Scottish identity". As the authors point out, the "cross-cultural character of some Web-based reading," like online newspapers, complicates both the "extra- and intra-cultural understandings of Scotland and Scottish identity" as they are realized in literacy practices.

The final major section of the book – Part III: Literacy, conflict, and hybridity on the Web – includes three chapters that focus on the ways in which cultural, political, and economic values are contested through and within literacy practices on the Web. From these chapters, we glean additional perspectives on the inaccuracies characterizing the global-village narrative. People who practice literacy on the Web and form this networked community have very different interests, histories, priorities, and concerns. Moreover, the differential power exercised within this digital landscape – the tendential force of multinational capitalism and the related effects of poverty, the continuing operation of colonial and racist values, the export of western perspectives and language – ensures that differences based on socio-economic status, color, and power are maintained, exacerbated, and reproduced, rather than eliminated. In these chapters, literacy values and practices – and the cultural, national, and personal identities that these values and practices help constitute – are revealed as contested sites, sites of social struggle and change.

"Web literacies of the already accessed and technically inclined: schooling in Monterrey, Mexico", authored by Susan Romano, Barbara Field, and Elizabeth W. de Huergo, describes how the entrepreneurial forces that have marked Monterrey's economic success since the nineteenth century have been played out and extended within the literacy environments of the Internet and the Web. At the American Institute of Monterrey (AIM), a bilingual school that serves Mexican nationals interested in professional careers that require proficiency in English, for example, teachers and students have come to understand the Internet as a "window to the world" that can help them develop the skills they need to compete in a global marketplace. Using this resource, students now study and learn English online, and come into contact with popular cultural values, materials, and information exported from international sources, primarily those in the industrialized west. Education at AIM, however, also has the goal of "upholding community values and social order" and educating students about Mexican culture. Informed by these sometimes competing educational agenda, a series of "separations" in literacy practices have been exacerbated, the authors note, by an increasing use of the Internet and the Web: separations between younger generations of individuals who use computers to communicate and older generations who do not communicate electronically; between family members who conduct much of their daily communication offline and in Spanish, and those who communicate primarily online and in English; and between individuals whose linguistic practices include talking frequently with strangers via e-mail and those whose most frequent interactions are with known individuals in face-to-face environments.

Moving to another Spanish-speaking culture, Laura Sullivan and Victor Fernandez in "Cybercuba.com(munist): electronic literacy, resistance, and postrevolutionary Cuba," describe the many ways in which – and many levels at which – the literacy practices of Cubans and expatriot Cubans reveal the political and economic contestation characterizing that country's cultural identity. This chapter examines the complexity involved in moving from print literacy to electronic literacy in Cuba; the ways in which multinational political conflict affects this move; and the ways in which gender, class, and power relations complicate the online literacy practices in which Cubans engage.

The constitution of complex and contested identities through literacy practices is also the theme of the last chapter in Part III: Elaine Richardson and Sean Lewis "'Flippin the script/blowing up the spot': puttin Hip-Hop online in [African] America and South Africa." Richardson and Lewis explore how hip-hop – as a shared African and African-American cultural phenomenon – is historically and politically related to the African and African-American literacy values and practices of these two groups. The authors note that both South Africans and African-Americans continue to use hip-hop as a "means of representing, preserving, critiquing, and controlling" cultural values and literacy practices as these groups "struggle for survival, self-definition, and self-determination" and resist the powerful forces of accommodation exerted by multinational capitalism and the related, accumulated power of racism.

Transgressions and hybridty on the Web

For the editors and contributors of these chapters, the project that we have undertaken marks a new kind of scholarship on Web-based literacy practices – one that recognizes the specificity of cultural situatedness within electronic environments, and, at the same time, acknowledges certain cross-cultural, transgressive forces that shape Web literacy practices and the hybrid identities constituted through such practices. In studying the manifestations of specific culturally-based literacy practices – which vary widely in their values, purposes, role, and history – we have also come to understand the broadly influential effects of powerful cultural formations like colonialism, poverty, multinational capitalism, and racism – all of which are exported through the design and the use of the network we call the Web and the Internet.

Thus, what we offer with this collection is a vision of the Web as a complicated and contested site for postmodern literacy practices. This site is characterized by a strongly influential set of tendential cultural forces, primarily oriented toward the values of the white, western industrialized nations that were responsible for designing and building the network and that continue to exert power within it. Hence, this system of networked computers is far from world-wide; it does not provide a culturally neutral conduit for the transmission of information; it is not a culturally neutral or innocent communication landscape open to the literacy practices and values of all global citizens. But the site is also far from totalizing in its effects as the final chapter and conclusion of this volume suggests. The Web also provides a site for transgressive literacy practices that express and value difference; that cling to historical, cultural, and racial diversity; and that help groups and individuals constitute their own multiple identities through language.

Notes

1   The World-Wide Web (Web) is a subset of the Internet – one developed in a linked hypertextual format that allows users to jump from site to site by clicking on designated links and automatically downloading documents at each. In this volume, reference to use of the Web will also sometimes imply reference to use of the Internet, and many of the cultural attitudes and values associated with Web use grow out of closely related attitudes and values associated with the Internet and other earlier computer technologies.

2   From the beginning, policy makers in the United States have linked the concept of the networked global-village to the related projects of opening increasing numbers of international markets to American goods and services, expanding free-market trade, and spreading democratic forms of government around the world. For these purposes, the same computer network that linked peoples of the world in communicative exchanges would also support the export of American perspectives on economic and government issues to developing nations. US Vice President Gore has described this process – in terms of a global information infrastructure (GII) to members of the International Telecommunication Union:

> the Global Information Infrastructure [can be used] for technical collaboration between industrialized nations and developing countries. All agencies

of the U.S. Government are potential sources of information and knowledge that can be shared with partners across the globe ... [T]he U.S. can help provide the technical know-how needed to deploy and use these new technologies. USAID and U.S. businesses have helped the U.S. Telecommunications Training Institute train more than 3500 telecommunications professionals from the developing world many ...

(Gore, VP Remarks – International Telecommunications Union, 1994)

Such a system, it is clear, also sets up the possibility of continued reliance on American goods and services and the opening of new markets to American exports. Technicians trained in the deployment and use of American technology and American-designed operating systems, and American software, and American networks, for example, would tend to continue to rely on – and purchase – those products and components after the initial training.

The Vice President has also laid out the ways in which both the GII and the NII (National information infrastructure) are aligned with American political goals such as expanding the base of global capitalism, encouraging the spread of democracy around the world, and revitalizing the American economy by opening additional world markets:

The GII will not only be a metaphor for a functional democracy, it will in fact promote the functioning of democracy by greatly enhancing citizens in decision-making. And it will greatly promote the ability of nations to cooperate with each other. I see a new age of Athenian democracy forged in the fora the GII will create.

The GII will be the key to economic growth for national and international economies. For us in the United States, the information infrastructure already is to the U.S. economy of the 1990s what transportation infrastructure was to the economy of the mid-20th century.

The integration of computing and information networks into the U.S. economy makes U.S. manufacturing companies more productive, more competitive, and more adaptive to changing conditions and it will do the same for the economies of other nations ...

To promote, to protect, to preserve freedom and democracy, we must make telecommunications development an integral part of each nation's development. Each link we create strengthens the bonds of liberty and democracy around the world. By opening markets to stimulate the development of the global information infrastructure, we open lines of communication.

By opening lines of communication, we open minds.

(Gore, VP Remarks – International Telecommunications Union, 1994)

3   In this Introduction and other chapters within the book, we refer to citizens of the United States as "Americans" in several places, lacking a more specific alternative. We recognize that such a description is overly general and freighted with historically and culturally specific values. We are, however, unaware of any less problematic alternative. The use of term "North Americans" may also create confusion in that it can be interpreted as including citizens of Canada. The alternative, "citizens of the United States," is awkward and resists various stylistic constructions.

References

Andrews, Deborah (1996) *International Dimensions of Technical Communication*, Arlington, VA: Society for Technical Communication.

Braman, Sandra (1995) "Policy for the Net and the Internet," *Annual Review of Information Science and Technology*, 20: 5–75.

Deibert, Ronald J. (1997) *Parchment, Printing, and Hypermedia: Communication in World Order Transformation*, New York: Columbia University Press.

del Gado, Elisa M. and Nielson, Jakob (1996) *International User Interfaces*, New York: John Wiley & Sons.

Gee, James (1990) *Social Linguistics and Literacies: Ideology in Discourses*, Brighton, GB: Falmer Press.

Gore, Albert (1994) "Remarks As Delivered by Vice President Al Gore to the International Telecommunications Union." Speech presented on 21 March 1994 at the meeting of the International Telecommunications Union in Buenos Aires, Argentina. Accessed on 7 March 1995 at <http://Web.whitehouse.gov/WH/EOP/OVP/html/telunion.html>.

Graff, Harvey J. (1987) *The Legacy of Literacy: Continuities and Contradictions in Western Culture and Society*, Bloomington, IN: Indiana University Press.

Hoft, Nancy L. (1995) *International Technical Communication: How to Export Information About High Technology*, John Wiley & Sons.

McLuhan, Marshall (1964) *Understanding Media: The Extensions of Man*, New York: McGraw-Hill.

Mitra, Ananda (1997) "Diasporic websites: Ingroup and Outgroup Discourse," *Critical Studies in Mass Communication*, 14: 158–181.

Myers, Miles (1996) *Changing Our Minds: Negotiating English and Literacy*, Urbana, IL: NCTE.

Negroponte, Nicholas (1995) *Being Digital.* New York: Alfred A. Knopf.

Penley, Constance and Ross, Andrew (1992) "Introduction," in *Technoculture*, Penley and Ross (eds), Minneapolis: University of Minnesota Press.

Peters, Michael and Lankshear, Colin (1996) "Critical Literacy and Digital Texts," *Educational Theory*, 46(1): 51–70.

Pratt, Mary Louise (1991) "Arts of the Contact Zone," *Profession '91*: 33–40.

Rheingold, Howard (1993) *The Virtual Community: Homesteading on the Electronic Frontier*, Reading, MA: Addison-Wesley.

Rogers, Al. Global Literacy in a Gutenberg Culture. Accessed on 7 March 1998 at <http://lrs.ed.uiuc.edu/Guidelines/Global-Literacy-Rogers.html>.

Selfe, Cynthia L. (1998) "Technology and Literacy in the 21st Century: The Perils of Not Paying Attention," Chair's Address to the Conference on College Composition and Communication, Chicago, April.

Selfe, Cynthia L. (1999) "Lest We Think the Revolution is a Revolution: Images of Technology and the Nature of Change," (eds) Gail E. Hawisher and Cynthia L. Selfe, *Passions, Pedagogies, and 21st Century Technologies.* Logan, Utah: Utah State University Press, 1999.

Skreslet, Paula Youngman (1997) "A People of the Book: Information Policy and Practice in the Muslim World," *Libri*, 47: 57–66.

Street, Brian V. (1995) *Social Literacies: Critical Approaches to Literacy in Development, Ethnography, and Education*, London: Longman.

17

Wresch, William (1996) *Disconnected: Haves and Have-Nots in the Information Age*, Piscataway, NJ: Rutgers University Press.

Yeatman, Anna (1996) *Citizenship, Choice, and Voice*, abstracts from the Culture and Citizenship Conference, Australia Key Centre for Cultural and Media Policy. Brisbane, 30 September to 2 October, 1996, p. 91.

Part 1

LITERACY, CULTURE, AND DIFFERENCE ON THE WEB

1

CHANGING ECONOMIES, CHANGING POLITICS, AND THE WEB: A HUNGARIAN PERSPECTIVE

Sibylle Gruber and Enikō Csomay

I believe that we talk not only about a new communication device [the Internet] that is introduced and spread in schools. It is a revolution of our relationship to knowledge.
(Balint Magyar, Hungarian Minister of Culture and Education, February 1997)

The enthusiasm for the new information technologies in Hungary and the perceived changes in the "relationship to knowledge" are an indication of the country's move away from a system closed to outside interference to a system that is receptive to and welcomes new ideas that are forming within the country and outside its borders. It acknowledges the need for changing perspectives on "knowledge" as well as on how knowledge and literacy(ies) are taught and distributed. This shift in approaching knowledge as changing and constantly expanding is partly influenced by Hungary's political and economic changes, and by social and ideological shifts since the late 1980s. Specifically, the perceived need to join other European countries and to become a part of a "global citizenship" has led to serious reconsiderations of political and educational practices in many Eastern European countries. According to Balint Magyar, for example, new technological advances, and new ways to present and disseminate information, make it necessary to look at the world from new angles and to re-evaluate the previously imposed restrictions on knowledge acquisition and distribution (Magyar, 1997).

Implementing change, of course, is not without its problems. Although enthusiasm is necessary, it has to be followed by specific responses to the perceived restriction of existing structures. The Internet, and especially the Web as a largely "borderless" medium, can help in promoting new literacies; however, if the Web is to be implemented successfully, politicians,

Balint Magyar, born in 1952, studied English, history, and sociology at Eotvos University in Budapest. He was involved with the Hungarian Democratic Opposition since 1979; from 1981 to 1986 he was forbidden to travel to Soviet satellite states because of his activities as an opposition proponent. He founded the Alliance of Free Democrats in 1988. He has been a Member of Parliament since 1990, and since 21 December 1995, he has held the post of Minister of Culture and Education.

(Ministry of Culture and Education (March 1997)
"Balint Magyar: Hungary's Minister of
Culture and Education".)

<http://www.mkm.hu/angol/ang.HTM>

teachers, students, parents, and special interest groups have to be aware that current perceptions and uses of technology are influenced by, and often dependent on already existing world-views of a country's citizens. Current users of the Web, then, approach new technologies as a construct based on specific histories, political systems, educational practices, and cultural identities.[1]

To understand how Hungarian users of new technologies are influenced by – and influence – established social, cultural, educational, and political practices, we take a close look at the historical context that influenced current approaches to education and technology. We then discuss the implementation goals for educational technologies put forth by the Hungarian Ministry of Education. Finally, we focus on a situated exploration of actual implementation strategies within specific schools in Budapest and surrounding areas. We conclude with an exploration of how the Internet, and specifically the Web influences students' and teachers' perceptions of educational practices in these institutions.

Hungarian education in context

The uses of new technologies – and of educational strategies – have to be seen within Hungary's historical and ideological framework, taking into account the different forms of government, the different approaches to cultural unity, and the changes in educational policies based on shifting perspectives in political and economic systems. The dissatisfaction with the education system in the eighteenth century, for example, led to a reorganization of then current school practices, focusing on a unified system overseen by an absolutist ruler. In the nineteenth century, instruction started

Hungary – Magyar Koztarsasag (pop. 10 million; 35,919 square miles): located in Central Europe; borders on Austria, Croatia, Romania, Serbia and Montenegro, Slovakia, Slovenia, and the Ukraine. Government: Kingdom since 1000; Republic since 1918; Soviet Style Peoples Republic since 1949; Democracy since 1989.

Population: 89.9% Hungarian, 4% Gypsy, 2.6% German, 2% Serb, 0.8% Slovak, 0.7% Romanian

to focus on advocating the country's culture and national language, paralleling the American school system's shift to teaching English-language arts instead of the classical languages.

The educational climate changed even more dramatically after the end of the monarchy. The Teachers' Union revised the Hungarian curriculum, working toward a democratic society's educational and political needs. After the Socialist Revolution on 21 March 1919, the Party leaders insisted on a complete upheaval of current practices to "allow the masses to rise" (Köte, 1976, p. 206). Quoting from the Document of the History of the Hungarian Workers' movement, Köte points out how education became an interest of the state:

> Education must be a task of the State. . . . Instead of promoting a world view embedding religious–historical beliefs, education should rely on the principles of the scientific world and work. Religious studies are not promoted in the standardized working classrooms. . . . All workers need and have the right to obtain the same basis and degree of knowledge in science and work.
>
> (Book 5, Part 1, Document of the History of the Hungarian Workers' Movement, quoted in Köte, p. 206).

The separation of church and school, and the emphasis on preparing students for future employment shifted literacy practices and knowledge

"There is no more illustrious history than the history of the Magyar nation. . . . The whole civilized world is indebted to Magyarland for its historic deeds."

(Theodore Roosevelt, to the Hungarian Parliament, 2 April 1910)

acquisition from the humanities to the natural and social sciences. Schools focused on hands-on learning and tried to teach students how to become successful workers who would be able to operate the technologies of the workplace.

Despite the efforts of the Socialist–Communist Party, education up to 1949 focused on middle-class values. Kornis, the State Secretary of Education in the 1920s and 1930s, promoted an educational system which excluded working-class students from higher education, mainly because of fears of an intelligentsia forming from this group. Between the two world wars, working-class children rarely continued to secondary school or to higher education. From a total of 56.4 percent of pupils from the working class, for example, only 5.1 percent went beyond mandatory schooling.

"Communist rule was established in Hungary in 1948–49, somewhat above three years after the Soviet Red Army had liberated the country – with much raping of women, looting of the population's belongings, and rounding up of civilian men to boost the number of POWs taken to the levels expected by Stalin – in 1945. It then remained in occupation, augmented with units of the NKVD (the later KGB), initially to supervise the dismantling and removal to the USSR of most of what industrial infrastructure had not been destroyed during the war. At the General Election held in September 1945 the Communist Party had received only 17% of the popular vote, but using salami tactics (move towards power a small slice at a time), and backed by Soviet pressure and assistance, it gradually eliminated (often physically) all non-Communists – and especially those who had been active in the resistance to Nazi Germany – from political life and positions of any consequence."

(Palffy 1998)

<http://www.users.zetnet.co.uk/spalffy/h_hist_0.htm>

After the Second World War, however, Kornis's ideas were considered unacceptable, and the new Communist regime changed Hungary's social, political, and educational climate. Once again, the state system tried to undermine the monopoly that the upper and middle classes held over education, and this time they succeeded in large part. The new eight-year basic primary educational system was the start for a new literacy program which was intended to be accessible to all Hungarian children. Much of the impetus for this change was based on the new industrial development and the new technological advances which could not happen with people who could neither read nor write. For this reason, education moved beyond school-aged children and branched out to evening schools for those working during the day. Vocational and technical schools were expanded and upgraded and provided direct entry into the work force. Furthermore, the Communist regime attempted to provide 50 percent of the seats for higher education to students from working-class backgrounds, thus moving higher education from the élites to those previously excluded from a college education. Hanley and McKeever, however, claim that the proposed reallocation of college seats did not radically change the composition of who attended colleges and universities. Instead, they point out that the Communist regime depended on a larger number of workers during rapid industrialization and was therefore not interested in reinforcing their policies concerning higher education (1997, pp. 6–7). In other words, education was used to provide people with skills for daily life – what C. H. Knoblauch would call the "professional tasks of a complex technological world" (1990, p. 76) – without promoting criticism of the existing regime. In this sense, the functionalist approach to education in Hungary supported "a given social order" while at the same time being "content to recommend the training of persons to take narrowly beneficial places" in society (76).

The new politics and policies, mainly driven by the ideologies of the new political powers and by a perceived need to technologize the workplace, did not lead to the radical educational changes promised by the regime.

[Janos] Kádár held office as General Secretary of the Communist Party and was de facto ruler far longer than anyone else in twentieth-century Hungary. This era dragged on from 1956 until 1988. Kádár may well be regarded as the most successful "people's democratic dictator". He was able to make adjustments to the system out of line with Kremlin policy and to extend the country's Western contacts while avoiding any actual clash with the Moscow leadership. The West, on the other hand, was able to maintain markedly good relations with a "people's democracy", accepting the latter's non-conformity by Moscow's standards, and yet still avoid a confrontation with Moscow.

("Kádár's Pied Piper," *The Hungarian Quarterly*
37.147, autumn 1997)

<http://www.hungary.com/hungq/no147/>

However, the more extensive and easily accessible Soviet pedagogical system helped increase functional literacy levels of most Hungarian citizens. Students' learning was largely restricted to ideas and ideologies supported by the government which promoted excellence in five areas: literacy and intellectual development, technical, moral, aesthetic, and physical development. Technological development, according to this scheme, is necessary to understand the basic principles of the flow of production, and it includes a student's training in how to use technology for an increase in production. This, certainly, does not take into account critical uses of technologies for educational purposes. Nevertheless, it is important to keep the focus on "productive" uses of technology in mind when looking at educational appropriations of computers in the classroom.

Looking at the present

The Hungarian Education Act of 1985 legalized the decentralization of education. However, according to Kaufman, the "lack of experience over the previous 45 years now blocked the implementation of educational decentralization goals" (1997b, p. 30). Because of this lack of experience, no criteria were set up to allocate monies for the different schools, and instead of advancing education, the system was initially paralyzed. In the last few years, however, the situation has been changing, and the administration as well as the whole country are working toward an educational mission statement that follows other European countries and that allows for "international competitiveness" by changing the structure, content, and administration of education. Steps in this direction have been taken since the break with Moscow in 1989. Schools have started to eliminate political ideology from the curriculum and, according to Kaufman, also stress "learning to think" strategies (1997b, p. 36).

Although changes are being made, a lack of instructional resources, economic difficulties, a computer and computer-access shortage, and conflicting visions of the "purpose of schooling" (Kaufman 1997b, p. 38) have slowed down educational reform and the implementation of new technologies in classroom teaching. Instead, the proposed reforms have led to confusion and frustration among teachers, students, and parents. Parents are concerned that teachers do not have the qualifications to deal with the new demands of a democratic country and instead reflect the authoritative Soviet model. One parent, for example, points out that "our children need teachers who teach how to solve problems. They (the students) know only memorized text. They cannot decide anything for themselves. We must have teachers who bring change" (quoted in Kaufman 1997a, p. 90). Teachers, on the other hand, are frustrated by the demands made on them: "While they (parents) say that the schools must serve as a training ground for democracy, they want to dictate what our job will be. How can we lead?

We are being smothered. There is no path open. We are encouraged to expand our teaching methods. How? How? New possibilities? No. Empty possibilities" (quoted in Kaufman 1997a, p. 91).

The frustrations of teachers, students, and parents are widespread in the newly evolving democracy. Educators, however, are making attempts to provide "new possibilities" for their students by expanding their literacy skills in a number of ways. The 1993 Act on School Education with its approval of the 1995 National Core Curriculum is a move in this direction. In addition, the political and economic incentives to cooperate with European countries, and the ensuing need for new educational practices have changed many of the ideologies prevalent during Communist rule. Instead of a centralized perspective on politics, economics, and education, the country is now experiencing a new challenge – a division according to political, social, and educational goals, as well as a division according to cultural groupings. The New London Group's description of the "new age" portrays this development well: "A strong sense of citizenship seems to be giving way to local fragmentation, and communities are breaking into ever more diverse and subculturally defined groupings" (p. 61). Instead of relying on a closed interstate system, people's groups and organizations are starting to reach beyond state borders, often utilizing technologies that encourage "the formation of virtual communities that transcend traditional barriers to understanding" (Brecher, Childs, and Cutler, 1993, p. xvi). In Hungary, for example, organizations and individuals have started to use the Web for disseminating political, personal, and business information to viewers and readers inside and outside the national borders. Eotvos Jozsef Gimnazium provides a Web page in Hungarian and English on its history, classes,

---

"Since it took office, the present government has considered the preparation of an educational policy strategy a priority. Its first version was submitted to public debate in December 1994. Over the last year educational experts, sociologists, practicing teachers, school staffs and a large number of professional and public organisations have discussed the draft for development strategy. Their comments and critical remarks, their questions and recommendations have set the direction for the experts' work to lay a foundation for the strategy and its implementation."

("The Long-Term Strategy for the Development
of Hungarian School Education" (1997))

<http://www.mkm.hu/angol/ang.HTM>

teachers, and students (http://eagle.ejg.hu/ejg). The Hungarian Directory provides an extensive list of cultural events (http://hudir.hungary. com/Events), political sites (http://hudir.hungary.com/Pol), sports events (http://hudir.hungary.com/Sports), and travel destinations in Hungary (http://hudir.hungary.com/Travel), making it easy for viewers to gain more insight into a country previously closed off to global communication.

A recent history of electronic technology

Policy makers in the Hungarian government and the Ministry of Education have expressed their commitment to implementing computer technology into the curriculum to modernize educational practices and to make Hungarian students competitive in an expanding market economy. Statistics from 1986 and 1991 already show a major shift in computer equipment in primary and secondary schools as Table 1.1 shows.

> "During the long history of modern school education a structured and complicated school system has emerged, which undergoes constant changes. Following the development of science and technology the contents of education is continuously changing. The teaching methods and aids reflect the times and their choice is expanding accordingly. Human development makes it necessary for education to be adjusted to the new and repeatedly changing requirements."
>
> ("The Long-Term Strategy for the Development of Hungarian School Education" (1997))
>
> <http://www.mkm.hu/angol/ang.HTM>

Table 1.1 Computer usage in schools

	Primary schools		Secondary schools	
	[1986]	[1991]	[1986]	[1991]
% of schools having computers	21	82	98	98
no. of computers in schools	2.1	7.1	3	15.6
no. of students per computer	323	164	55	31
% of students who received computer education	1.5	5.4	6.7	6.3

Source: Tompa, 1994, pp. 30–34.

To further improve educational access to the Internet and to increase computer literacy, the Hungarian Minister of Education, Balint Magyar, had committed to equip each secondary school with Internet-capable computers by the year 1998 and every primary school by the year 2002 – a promise comparable to Clinton's goal 2000, the year when every child should have a computer in his or her classroom. Specifically, the ministry envisions five implementation phases of the telecommunications efforts (called SULINET <http://www.sulinet.hu>) with a projected cost of three billion *forints* approved by the Hungarian Parliament:

> "The overall goal of the Ministry is to make the Internet accessible to, and to provide technical and professional support for, all institutions of public education and culture, and public collections; to create a means for ethnic Hungarians abroad to keep in touch with culture in Hungary; and to produce public education databases accessible to everyone" (taken from "An Internet Programme for Hungary's Secondary Schools").
>
> <http://www.mkm.hu/angol/ang.HTM>

1 Establish an infrastructure and Internet network among schools.
2 Develop and provide institutions with the necessary equipment and computer labs.
3 Plan, organize and finance materials suitable for the Internet and the schools.
4 Establish teacher development and provide a "human infrastructure."
5 Provide educational materials, information, and continuing educational programs for teachers and for the public.

If SULINET is implemented according to plan, 200 primary schools, 900 secondary schools, and 20 pedagogical institutes will be affected by the

> "If I told my students to go to a particular site there is a danger that they cannot get there. The only way I can imagine using the Web is to select games or poems for them and I print those out."
>
> (Bea, primary school teacher, taped interview, December 1997)

efforts to "technologize" educational institutions within the next five years. However, according to the *Weekly Economist* (Vajna, 1997), by the end of 1997, phase one had only been implemented in some schools in Budapest and in the major cities in Hungary, leaving smaller towns and rural areas without computers and Internet connections.[2] This, of course, is not a new or "local" phenomenon. According to a radio broadcast on National Public Radio, the United States is undergoing similar challenges in terms of computer equipment. For example, 66 percent of affluent school districts have adequate computer equipment whereas only 30 percent of school districts in poor neighborhoods have computers for their students ("Ask the Teacher" 23 December 1997).

To promote the ministry's plans, Balint Magyar focused on the possibilities of the Internet during a computer and software exhibition in February, 1997, held in the Fine Arts Museum (a strategic choice to show how computers and the twenty-first century can operate in harmony with the past and with ancient icons on the walls). He argued that "knowledge" would be revolutionized by the new technology and would become more easily accessible to all. At the same time, Hungary would become a major player in European culture and politics and move to the "middle of the world's mainstream." Furthermore, "users of the Internet can get in touch with each other and will be able to learn from each other, teach each other, and they will establish congenial relationships with the world, with knowledge, and with each other." He foresees a "timeless" and "spaceless" world without geographical and geopolitical borders where collective knowledge can be used in the best interest of all. Similarly, Grepaly sees the Internet as a new space – or microsociety – that fosters cooperation and at the same time teaches tolerance (1995, p. 69). This, of course, assumes a move away from party line thinking – or functional literacy – to new ways of looking at the "word and the world" (Freire and Macedo, 1987, p. 29). The "expansion" of literate behavior could then also include "a critical consciousness of the social conditions in which people find themselves" (Knoblauch, 1990,

> "If the information could come in, it would be very good and of course it would be useful then. But it is difficult to download things, and when people spend hours there waiting for the stuff and it always gets disconnected, then people just spend their time and their money on nothing. So you need much better phone lines, I think, and a good modem."
>
> (Zsuzsa, secondary schoolteacher, taped interview, December 1997)

p. 79), thus allowing for literacies suppressed before the official 1989 break with Russia.

The minister's enthusiasm for new approaches to literacy, and his promise to root out computer illiteracy for the good of all, however, should not deflect from the many problems concerning a successful implementation of these goals. Certainly, the assumption that access to the "world" via the Internet will promote cooperation and tolerance and teach a critical appreciation of easily accessible information neglects to take into consideration decades of "enforced literacy" which often focused on teaching "the canon" of party politics.

> "Those who have qualifications in this area will go somewhere else to work where they get real money. Those who have a degree in computer science will leave in a year or so because they can earn four times as much somewhere else with that degree. We have had teachers who just leave after one or two years."
>
> (Katalin, secondary vocational schoolteacher,
> taped interview, December 1997)

The attrition of qualified educators because of dissatisfaction with the system and constantly decreasing salaries leads to an additional drawback, and as a consequence many students are taught by teachers who adhere to a pre-1989 curriculum and pedagogy. In terms of technological advances, the high expenses of technologies and of Internet access, and the partial elimination of foreign funds for higher education make the success of the Education Minister's promise hard to achieve. What is even more discouraging for educators and students interested in using new technologies, the National Core Curriculum supported and sponsored by the Ministry of Culture and Education, which "shall declare the most important long-term objectives and outline the ways to achieve them" ("The Long-Term Strategy" 1997), does not mention computer use in schools or access to the Internet for its students in its extensive long-term plan. As a consequence, many of the humanities departments at the university level are left without inside or outside support for maintaining and updating the machines donated to them by the World Bank or private organizations. And although the ministry is sponsoring science teachers in secondary schools to learn about the "information technology revolution" in the sciences, these seminars are not accessible to those in the humanities and at the college level. Thus, although there could be a "machine" in every school by the year 1998, the high cost of software and the high cost of telephone lines make actual uses of the machines questionable. As the principal of a high school in Budapest points

31

out, "we have 80 machines in the school. We have heard about the Internet. Neither we, nor the local council have enough money to pay for the various bills" (quoted in "Internet Development," Febuary 1997, p. 94). Similarly, a primary school in a small town far removed from any major cities, is unable to use a Pentium computer and the modem which they bought with grant money because they no longer receive funds for long-distance calls necessary to establish Internet connections.

Additionally, many teachers and students are suspicious of and reluctant to explore the unknown and to acquire new literacies – which also slows down the adoption of new technologies for teaching purposes. Grepaly, for example, points out that users see the systems manager as the police officer who can punish anybody who gets out of line (1995, p. 68). These Internet users, according to Grepaly's comment, see the new technology not as a "liberating" medium but instead as just another way to increase close observation of the country's citizens. Fears of government control and authoritarian treatment of the people are certainly based on historical events – from an absolutist monarchy to the more currently overthrown Communist regime – which many Hungarians still remember.

Although the Minister of Education is enthusiastic about Internet access, teachers and students are still struggling with access issues. Furthermore,

"Other than the horribly slow connection it was actually kind of fun to do the questionnaire. I personally love the Internet and I love browsing. Unfortunately, right now this Internet class is about my only chance to get on the net and do anything with it. It is very time consuming, if not for the slow connection then for the fact that it is very easy to forget about what you're doing and just get 'lost' in it.

I think that the net could be a great teaching device but only if the technical circumstances are given. And I mean a computer for every student and good computers with fast modems. The independence of students in their learning could be improved a great deal if they were given the chance to use Internet sites to look up words, grammar points or even to test their English. There's thousands of ways to bring the net and computers into the classroom. Plus, more computer use would mean a huge relief to the teachers."

(Mercedes, Eotvos University,
personal e-mail, 10/14/97)

many teachers do not have the training to integrate new technologies into a curriculum which has undergone a number of changes over the last eight years. They also lack the experience of adapting the new technologies to their pedagogical goals which in turn can lead to a continuation of literacy practices which do not advance new ways of approaching knowledge acquisition and distribution. The new information technology can thus become a medium that contributes to established power structures instead of providing a means to enrich, expand, or change current literacy practices.

The danger of using the new technology to promote only certain kinds of new literacies in education is apparent in the allocation of resources and the tendency to favor scientific areas over those that are considered less important for production and competition in a growing market economy. From this point of view, students and prospective workers do not acquire new literacies to be more independent and critical of current power structures; instead, they receive their training to promote a rapid move toward a capitalist market economy. Although this new literacy presents a solution to economic problems and is by no means undesirable to many Hungarians, it disregards other literacies that balance consumer-oriented production with a critical focus on how this new integration of western society's ideals affects existing literacy practices. Because the human mind is "embodied, situated, and social" (New London Group 1996, p. 82), teachers who want to include new ways of meaning-making – particularly information accessed through the Web – need to consider the many recent changes, as well as forty years of Soviet rule, which have influenced Hungarian approaches to literacy. In other words, the integration of the Web and the Internet into the curriculum does not automatically change existing values but can instead continue an already existing fascination with the machine as a way to increase worker productivity without promoting worker autonomy.

In some Hungarian schools, however, teachers and students are beginning to trust the recently acquired freedom from stringent rules and regulations and are working with the newly acquired equipment. Teachers are exploring new ways of presenting information and are encouraging their students to take advantage of the information accessible via the Internet. Instead of "empty possibilities," they are trying to create "new possibilities" for their students not only in math and science courses – the areas favored by those trying to implement computer technology – but also in the humanities. Many of them encourage students to reconsider existing perspectives on education which often reflect a top-down, authoritarian approach to meaning-making. Furthermore, the Hungarian Ministry of Culture and Education and various government organizations are starting to encourage the integration of a "multiplicity of communications channels and media," and to promote what the New London Group has called the "saliency of cultural and linguistic diversity" (p. 63) in and outside the classroom. Changing the curriculum to include new languages which students can study is one step in the direction of acquiring new literacies and becoming global citizens; providing access to the Internet is another means of encouraging such globalization.[3]

Exploring the Web: first-hand accounts

The usefulness of the Web and its possible function as a medium which changes or upholds literacy perceptions, of course, can best be judged by those who are trying to use it. For this purpose, we interviewed teachers in primary and secondary schools in Budapest and surrounding areas about their experiences with the Internet, and we asked students at Eotvos University in Budapest and high-school students to fill out a questionnaire we provided. We also asked them to "surf" the Web, letting us know their impressions about the pages they accessed. Their willingness to participate, however, decreased after some frustrating attempts to access the Internet. First, all students who were enrolled in an English Teacher Training program promised to work with us on this project; however, only a few returned the questionnaire after exploring three specific sites.

Although for a researcher, such an attrition rate is rather frustrating, it also tells an interesting story. Unlike in the United States and Sweden – which have the quickest and most advanced systems – Hungarian connections to the Internet are unreliable and slow. Up until 1993, Hungary did not have an Internet provider within its country. Instead, users had to call Vienna long distance to read an e-mail message.[4] Creating a more reliable and easily accessible Internet system is a major struggle in the efforts to modernize the country's technologies. Although George Soros, the Hungarian-American billionaire, has provided $100 million for purchasing Internet-capable computers for educational institutions, these machines either do not get used because they are not connected, or their use is limited because of maintenance costs. Thus, the promise of the Hungarian government to spend between $10 and $20 million to install fiber-optic cables

> "You get addicted to 'accessing information' and there is no end to it. Yes, it's s-o-o-o-o interesting that you cannot stop it. You just watch it and say, oh yes, this interests me, and that interests me too and I have to check out this one. And then you don't realize and you are on for hours, without noticing."
>
> (Mary, primary schoolteacher, taped interview, December 1997)

and satellite hook-ups[5] to make the connections possible is still in its beginning stages.

As a consequence of the unreliable and slow connections, some of the students at Eotvos University gave up on surfing the Web. Furthermore, the teachers we interviewed also pointed out that the technology is still in its beginning stages, and students are not yet used to spending time on the Internet. And because access is so restricted, and only very few students have computers at home, the time they can spend online is also extremely limited. Many schools do not yet integrate technologies into their curriculum on a regular basis, and not all students know computer basics. Furthermore,

> "I think it is an absolutely bad arrangement that this year we have the practical skills class and not the computer science one! I think for all jobs today you need the computer and so I am not sure how I will use what I learned in the practical skills class. Especially how the girls will use it!"
>
> (Eszter, secondary school student, questionnaire)

some of the high-school students who agreed to participate in our project had problems with the sites not only because of insufficient technology but because the sites we chose were in English or a language other than Hungarian. Andrea, a student at Sagvari Endre Gimnazium, admits that she had "language problems" when she tried to access the website for the *International Herald Tribune.*

The participants who did get on the Web and who are included in our study were not completely successful in accessing the information provided online. In their case, looking at the Web as a way to gain or promote new literacies was not overly promising, and their frustrations overshadowed any gains they might have perceived had the hardware been more cooperative. However, the participants did provide feedback on the questions we asked. They navigated the Web as best they could and showed their online literacies despite the many technological impediments.

Anna, Mercedes, and Milas were born in Budapest and went to vocational school before they started at Eotvos University. Anna and Milas became less and less interested in school as the years went by; Mercedes, on the other hand, considered school very important and was very interested in the technological development that went on in her high school during the last years she was there. All three want to be teachers of English, and their educational program includes a course that stresses the need for learning how to use computer-mediated communication in the classroom.

When Anna, Mercedes, and Milas accessed the three Web pages we had chosen for this study[6] we asked them to pay specific attention to the following criteria:

- organization of material on the page;
- navigation (easy/difficult);
- links (do they get you to the places you want to go to?);
- visual presentation (does it enhance or distract from the content?);
- information provided (is it pertinent/comprehensible?);
- what did you really like about this website? What did you find unacceptable?

We also were interested in looking at the broader political and social impact of the Web. The following questions were intended to solicit information concerning the participants' attitudes and changes in attitudes after exploring various websites:

- did surfing the Web influence your perspectives on political, social, and economic issues in Hungary, Europe, or the world at large?;
- did you find the information you accessed newsworthy, trustworthy, and valuable for your career?;
- did you prefer using the Web to reading newspapers or magazines (which of course assumed that participants would not have difficulties with accessing the Web)?[7]

The three students encountered many technical problems and distractions, especially when they tried to load pictures or long files. They finally made the connections and were able to provide us with feedback on the sites we selected for them. The first website they looked at was put together by the Council of the European Unity. Anna and Mercedes thought that the material was organized very well and that the message the designers wanted to convey was easy to understand. And, once it worked, navigation was easy and quite simple. The links were a bit confusing for Anna – she wasn't quite sure where clicking on the picture would take her. But the visual presentation, according to her, was excellent: "I love this perspective. I can really look around in the rooms. It makes the whole thing friendlier, and easier to digest." Mercedes had similar comments to make about this aspect: "It was really nice, and the tours involve nice photographs." Both of them saw the purpose of the website to familiarize browsers with the European Institutions in Brussels; Mercedes, in addition, mentions that "I am not sure if it tries to convey anything – maybe showing the US that we can be cool if we want to be."

Milas, on the other hand, did not like to be bombarded with that much information and that many possibilities for clicking on phrases which then

"Although Hungarian is not an option when choosing the various languages to tour the website, it is still nice to be given an option about which language to choose before plunging into the exploration of the European Union. The first page is simple and very tastefully designed (maybe because I like blue and yellow). Navigation is a problem, though, once you move beyond the first page. For slow machines, it is really bad. You can switch off the pictures, but then you wouldn't really know what is behind because there is no text underneath telling you where you could go next. This makes navigation extremely difficult for those who have slower and older machines. The pages try to communicate factual information, and sometimes the pictures get in the way. I would be happier to read the text on what the Legislation is doing, for example, and not look at the pictures that are so difficult to download. The text is only in a tiny little column on the right hand side and the rest are pictures. What is really distracting is that if you don't have Java Script enabler – which we don't have on our machines – then you miss a lot of what is presented on the pages. That means that although a lot of information is out there, it's hard to access it, and we are again left behind because we don't have the technological advantages that other countries have."

(Enikő Csomay, questionnaire)

got him distracted and lost. He didn't see a clear objective and was disappointed in the website as well as in the slow connection. His computer crashed several times during his efforts to explore the European Community in Brussels.

The second website – the online version of the *International Herald Tribune* – was difficult for Anna, Mercedes, and Milas to access. The slow connection combined with the graphics on the *Herald Tribune*'s page led to comments such as "it was impossible to get beyond the second page" (Anna), "I couldn't see anything after the front page because it crashed" (Milas), and although the links were considered to be "very nice," the problem was that "it just breaks down, I mean the connection, when I tried to enter a link" (Mercedes). Neither one of them, as a consequence, could get to the actual articles. Mercedes, however, was impressed by the interactivity of the Web page. She found out that "you can create your personal portfolio in the market sections." Milas was less gracious. He pointed out that "I cannot accept pages stuffed with unnecessary images!"

"I remember that the *International Herald Tribune* was my favorite foreign language newspaper before 1989. The Web page they created is well done, simple, informative, and eye catching. The main information is on the front page, and I don't have to scroll down to find additional information. Navigation is really easy, and I can follow the links without problems. The pictures do not distract from the content; instead, they actually enhance what's on the page and increase my appreciation of the paper. What is really nice is that you can get the news fast, and you can get news that would otherwise not be easily accessible in Hungary. The front page could be set up a bit differently – providing headlines arranged by content rather than by date. Also, the technology page wasn't very interesting. I only found one article (out of 40) which looked remotely exciting. What is nice, though, is that the online version is free right now, but I am not sure how much longer they will publish an online version for free. What kinds of information will we get for free then, and what kinds of information will only be accessible to a paying audience?"

(Enikō Csomay, questionnaire)

Hotwired, in comparison to the *Herald Tribune*, was much easier to access and provoked more enthusiastic answers from the three participants. Navigation was easy, and the links were readily accessible. Anna and Mercedes thought, however, that the visual presentation was a little overdone, and that there was "a lot of stuff to attract the eye." Milas liked the visual presentation and saw it as enhancing the content of the page. Mercedes mentioned that "it's slightly more vivid than it should be – a lot of strong colors (red background)." She didn't think, though, that it distracted too much from the content. Mercedes liked the intensity of the Web page but did get frustrated when some of the pictures didn't load up. Anna thought that the entertainment value and the resources were the most valuable parts on this web page. Milas found the site very acceptable because it was interactive and linked to other news.

Neither Mercedes, Anna, nor Milas thought that exploring the Web has changed their perceptions of political, social, and economic issues in Hungary, Europe, or the world at large. Mercedes admitted that she might have been influenced by what she had seen if she had spent more time on the Web. However, the bad connections and the frustrations associated with not being able to move from one link to another restricted the usefulness of the Web as a medium which would be influential in forming a "new

"There is something very distracting about this web page, and I don't know what the purpose of it is. It is really hard to understand what the information they provide is supposed to achieve and what the audience is supposed to learn. If it is an alternative approach to presenting information and provide news for its audience, it's not really clear what the focus of this 'newspaper' or 'magazine' is. They did have some interesting links though. One that I really liked provided information on how to set up a newsgroup. That will help me in my professional advancement."

(Enikö Csomay, questionnaire)

literacy." And although they pointed out that the information on the Web is valuable and newsworthy, Anna and Milas also pointed out that they don't trust information that's online, nor do they trust information printed in newspapers because, in Milas's words, "nothing is completely trustworthy." Here, Anna and Milas shows the same distrust in the Web that they have for other kinds of printed information. And although newspapers today are considered reliable sources of information, and although foreign newspapers are now easily available, their reaction can be linked to experiences

"Although I don't think that checking out the different web pages has influenced me in how I see the world, touring the Website put together by the European Union has made me more aware of what is going on in the European Community. Since Hungary is interested in joining, it is really essential to know what the Union presents and what we are getting into. Some bits and pieces from the sites I looked at were really valuable, but there is also a large amount of information that is not that interesting. The reason I like the Web is that you can get updated information and don't have to wait for newspapers or magazines or articles to be published. A colleague of mine once said that the Web provides information when you want it where you want it, and that's true. However, not everything is updated with the same speed. For example, box office hits in the movie industry get updated more often than what's playing in the art theater."

(Enikö Csomay, questionnaire)

when the print media only produced highly selective information sanctioned by the government.

Mercedes's interpretation of the site describing the functions of the European community – "showing the US that we can be cool if we want to be" – and her additional comment that the site was "not that interesting, really," conveys some of the attitudes toward "westernization" of Hungarians' social, educational, and economic lives. Similar to the Minister of Education, Mercedes sees Hungary as an integral part of the European system. On the other hand, the European Community has not yet accepted Hungary as a member, and browsing through a web page that is not yet of immediate relevance seems to lose some of its appeal for Mercedes.

Literacies and the Web

It is certainly true that the "increasing multiplicity and integration of significant modes of meaning-making" (New London Group, 1996, p. 64) influence and change the acquisition of literacies. According to the New London Group, "people are simultaneously members of multiple lifeworlds" and are "members of multiple and overlapping communities" (p. 71). To apply this perspective, Mercedes, Anna, and Milas participated in a number of "lifeworlds," one of which includes the Web. As they pointed out, however, they didn't see the Web as influencing their attitudes toward politics or other events in any way. Of course, we can argue that being able to log on to the Internet and having access to information provided on the Web in itself changes the context in which literacy is practiced. In Hungary, although the Internet is still widely inaccessible or only partly accessible, the move to integrating new information technologies shows a willingness and desire of the government to provide the country and its citizens with the opportunity to acquire literacies censured by the previous government. As the participants' responses to our questions show, though, new technologies do not automatically replace or erase previously held attitudes and beliefs – whether they show themselves in a distrust of newspapers or a distrust of political systems.

To work toward integrating multiple literacies in Hungarian society, educators can help their students understand the importance of becoming critical participants in their communities. The Web can certainly be used

> "It would be miserable if I let the web influence me in my perceptions of political, social, and economic issues in Hungary."
>
> (Daniel, Eotvos University, questionnaire)

to enhance this goal if teachers promote its use as a medium which enhances student learning. Nemes, a participant in an academic writing class at Eotvos University during autumn of 1997 pointed out that "the question is not whether it is good or bad to use this new phenomenon or new device. It is here, and it is here now. We'd better figure out how we could best take advantage of it and make the best use of it for ourselves and for our kids."

If we want to make sure that students and teachers gain from implementing new information technologies in education and can acquire literacies that are meaningful to them in different settings, applications of technologies have to be evaluated critically. Since the goal is to provide every school with Internet access, it is important to ensure that students are introduced to the wide variety of information online. Teachers certainly need to learn how to engage students in meaningful literacy activities which

> "I have always thought that with the internet we are encouraging students to stay only on the surface. They cannot go deep into the problems. They look at it, and they may not be interested in it, or they get interested in something else, and then they go on, spending a lot of time practically doing nothing. They cannot quite show what they produced but spent a lot of time on the computer. So, we really should be careful about what we want the students to do on the net."
>
> (Katalin, secondary vocational schoolteacher, taped interview, December 1997)

include the Web and which move beyond literacies ingrained in Hungarian society. Following the suggestions of the New London Group, teachers can first provide "overt instruction" to provide scaffolding for their students' online activities, then move to "critical framing" to encourage students in their own knowledge making and questioning of knowledge, and finally prompt them to engage in "transformed practice" to help students move beyond existing ideas to ideas that have been changed by their and their communities' practices (pp. 85–87).

Helping students understand how information influences their perspectives on cultural, social, and political issues and at the same time influences their literacies is important if they are to become aware of their multiple subject positions within their communities. To provide Hungarian teachers with the pedagogical and methodological tools to promote students' online literacies, a number of programs for teacher training have started to take shape. At Eotvos University, Enikō Csomay and some of her colleagues are promoting the uses of the Internet to broaden – and in some cases change

– existing literacy practices in their school and also in the country. Several workshops, interest groups, and courses on the uses of the Internet are intended to promote critical appreciation of the new technologies (see Appendix A).

One of the in-service workshops for language teachers, "The CALL of the Information Age," tries to challenge existing forms of teaching and established belief systems about language acquisition and language learning. The participants are asked to use the Internet and other multimedia materials to *explore different perspectives* on language teaching. Instead of the

"What is good about the net is that there is a great variety of possibilities. If there is a system that we could make out, one that we can understand, it will be good. But I am scared that it is a complete jungle for me and I cannot make my way around it. But if we have the keys to this, and if we can help the students to be able to find their own way that gets them closer to acquire a skill, or some knowledge, then we could help them. If we do not have the key, we won't be able to help them."

(Mary, primary schoolteacher, taped interview, December 1997).

predominantly used skill-and-drill approach, teachers are encouraged to promote a more flexible, task-based approach. This certainly implies a radical change in pedagogical goals and how teachers see their role in the classroom. The Internet, with its many resources, is part of opening new venues for language teachers.

In addition to workshops, a number of teachers at Eotvos University are members of a foundation which is working with the Ministry of Culture and Education and which promotes various uses of the Internet for educational purposes (see Appendix B). The goal of this foundation is to help integrate educational technology in any subject area, and to encourage innovative uses of the Internet and the Web. Planned projects include incorporating teacher material on the Web, encouraging students to research and publish online, and promoting cross-cultural exchanges among students. This foundation, then, is expanding existing literacy practices to include global means of communication and to encourage international cooperation among schools and educators.

Although using technology in the classroom is still frustrating, some teachers try to integrate the Internet and the Web in their courses. One of the language-learning courses at Eotvos University, for example, promotes the use of the Internet by encouraging students to use the Web to develop materials connected to language teaching. Students also use online writing labs to look for information on writing skills. In this way, they use the technology for research but also for improving their own writing.

The many changes in the country, the need for economic growth, political diversity, and educational reform create excitement and many challenges; innovative approaches to teaching and to literacy acquisition are encouraged by the administration. However, these efforts are, at the moment, largely dependent on underpaid teachers and on volunteers. Additionally, the unreliable and slow connections make an online course difficult to teach and to take. The Ministry of Education and the National Core Curriculum Committee acknowledge the difficulties of trying to implement new standards while the salary of teachers slowly decreases. The Committee points out: "If the deterioration in the wages and the standard of living of the teachers that began in recent years cannot be held in check we cannot expect the renewal of the profession required by the introduction of the National Core Curriculum to take place. Further, we cannot even expect an adequate standard of work in schools in general." Thus, although programs exist that promote Internet use, Hungary's schools are in the midst of major changes that might include more extensive uses of computer equipment or that might continue the struggle for basic access to the Internet.

Appendix A The CALL of the information age: designing language-learning tasks and the computer (Internet and CD-ROM)[8]

Instructor: Enikõ Csomay
Class: Fridays 2–6 (classroom: 308; complab: 213)
Office Hours: Fridays 12:00 noon to 2:00 pm
Phone: (1) 32 15 947 (office); (1) 264 30 20 (home);
Fax: (1) 25 22 897
E-mail: csomay@ludens.elte.hu;
URL: http://e3.hu//c3.hu/~ecsomay

Aims

This course aims to help participants develop language-learning tasks for the classroom incorporating the use of computer facilities. More specifically, the focus is on how the teaching of communicative competence can be enhanced through employing the Internet and various educational CD-ROMs.

Objectives

In order to be able to design effective and meaningful language-learning tasks, by the end of the course participants will have:

- familiarized themselves with some of the relevant literature related to both task-based learning (especially task design) and issues related to the Internet;
- discussed some of the relevant literature related to the topics above;
- acquired presentation skills in practice;
- explored what various multimedia companies offer concerning educational materials;
- gained further insight into how the four basic language skills, grammar, and vocabulary development can be enhanced through the use of the Internet;
- how to get involved in professional development via the Internet.

Procedures

Participants will:

- take part in professional discussions through the Web and e-mail;
- evaluate and critically review language-learning interactive materials available on the Internet and on CD-ROM;
- learn how to access specific information as well as how to search on the Internet effectively;
- keep a journal of sites visited on the Web;
- present and critically review one or two articles about the Web and/or on CD-ROM materials;
- learn how to create a basic Web page and how to publish it;
- design language-learning tasks;
- try these tasks out through interaction in a virtual classroom with "real" learners online (still under negotiations);
- complete a project and present it to class.

Evaluation

Evaluation will be based on:

- attendance and participation (including accomplishing small assignments) (5 percent);
- journal (5 percent);
- presentation and evaluation of an article (10 percent);
- review – presentation and evaluation of different websites and CD-ROMs (10 percent);
- project (70 percent).

Dates for your diary (available for self-study hours also)

- October 14–18 Computer Fair (BNV) – sulinet + others;
- October 30 at 2 pm Hungarodidact (BNV) – Jakubi Zsuzsa presentation;
- November 6 Premiere – Kókai Tamás presentation.

Specifications

- There is no class on 7th November. For the three contact hour self-study period, the following are the options:
  1. Reading two to three articles related to the two underlying themes of the course with the aim of preparing a short paper combining the two themes into one conceptual framework.
  2. Go to Compfair and complete the task assigned on the evaluation of a CD-ROM.
  3. Go to either Hungarodidact or Premiere and listen to the presentation. Write up the presentation (including inquiries) in the form of a publishable report.
- Each class has a dual face: (a) discussions in real classroom and (b) hands-on practice in the comp lab. 2.5 contact hours are spent at both venues.

Assignments, projects

JOURNAL – ANNOTATED WEBSITES

While accessing the various websites in and outside the framework of the course, participants will take notes in the form of journal entries. Ten of these entries will be assessed. Each entry will contain the following aspects: (a) exact URL address; (b) brief outline of what you can find on the front page; (c) surfing further, find at least one page that is or could be useful for your teaching/learning context; (d) take notes why and in what way it could be useful for you (if so, what modifications you would need to make to be able to use the site).

PRESENTATION AND EVALUATION OF AN ARTICLE

Participants will present one article to fellow participants in the class. The readings will be chosen in advance. The presentation should contain the following two aspects: (a) briefly the content of the article, and (b) a critical view of the content. The presentations last 5 minutes minimum and 10–15 minutes maximum.

REVIEW

Participants will write five reviews (max. one typed page each) in which they further evaluate websites and/or language-teaching/learning CD-ROM materials. The review should be written up in a publishable manner, keeping the audience (fellow professionals) and the purpose (exposition and evaluation) in mind. (Guidelines will be handed out at a later stage.)

PROJECT

Participants will complete a project which will comprise the design and publication of a Web page including language-learning/teaching materials suitable for the participants' own context. The material should show the participants' individual conceptual framework demonstrating their understanding of the issues raised during the course.

Appendix B Foreign-language learning and teaching via the Internet

Project outline for the Hungarian language professionals

Enikő Csomay

The primary purpose of the project is to help foreign-language professionals familiarize themselves with the possibilities the Internet can offer in their profession. The intended audience, more specifically, is foreign-language professionals principally comprising foreign-language teachers in the primary and secondary school context in Hungary.

Based on the project launched by the Hungarian Minister of Education, Magyar Balint, by the year 1998, all secondary schools will have an Internet connection. Parallel to the execution of this plan, it is essential to make language teachers aware of the ways the Internet actually works, and the ways in which the Internet could help language teaching, and teachers in their everyday work.

The project has various stages. The stage described below offers to establish a communication forum for foreign-language professionals in Hungary to "talk" Internet through various sources: (a) professional journals; (b) interaction via the Internet; (c) professional organizations (e.g., IATEFL-H); (d) personal contacts with professionals. Below are the details concerning various aspects of successfully carrying out Stage 1 of the project.

Aims

1   To familiarize foreign-language professionals with the potential use of the Internet facilities.

2   To make teachers aware of how these facilities could serve them in their:
  - professional development;
  - teaching;
  - communications with professionals within and outside of Hungary;
3   To provide ongoing, online information "service" in the above areas.

Objectives

1   To establish a forum for communication/discussion where teachers can ask questions related to any aspect of their use of the Internet.
2   To establish "pages" on the Web containing relevant information for the given audience in four languages (Hungarian, English, French, German, N.B. Cyrillic has not been available yet).
3   To maintain these pages through continuously monitoring the new sites with relevant information and adding them to the already existing ones.

Procedures

Objective 1

I have carried out preliminary research in the forum of a questionnaire asking teachers about their familiarity with issues related to the Internet. Results could be provided upon request. (200 questionnaires throughout Hungary, mainly returned from outside Budapest.)

We have also started giving workshops for language professionals on the basics of Internet use. So far, I, personally, have given two lectures (at Internet.Galaxy and at IFABO (Internationale Fachmesse für Informations-, Kommunikations- und Bürotechnik) and a series of workshops (in pre- and in-service teacher education settings) on how to use the Internet. We have founded a Special Interest Group in IATEFL-H (International Association of Teachers of English as a foreign language – Hungary), called Computer-Assisted Language Learning. Our main focus for the upcoming conference in October this year is the use of Internet in the classroom. There will be at least 9 presentations and workshops related to the issue.

Our newly established foundation called "EduNet" could be a valuable resource in establishing and maintaining web pages, as well as to raise funding, to write out competitions and sponsor talented individuals for various sub-projects.

Alternatively, in order to provide the very basic information, professional journals will be used. Based on preliminary agreement, *Novelty* will start an "Internet corner," edited by men, and starting in the next issue. In this section, materials are focused in two ways; teachers will be reading about (a) some very basic steps on how to use the Internet (e-mail and the Web); and (b) Internet (Web) sites useful for language teaching/learning. The latter is backed up by evaluation of sites and also ideas on how these sites could be used for teaching. The same text would appear in either *Nyelvinfo* or in *Modern Nyelvoktatas*, with the same focus and purpose including other languages apart from English.

Objectives 2 and 3

BASIC STEPS

1 Request sufficient amount of space on the Ministry's server for the Web pages and for communication on the various Listservs (set communication groups via e-mail); it is essential so that these pages can be accessed more quickly within Hungary.

2 Involve colleagues familiar with the languages mentioned above to write introductory texts in four languages for the Web pages.

3 Code these texts into HTML files – based on which they can be uploaded on the Ministry's server; possibly contact Web designers for more sophisticated pages.

4 Continuously expand these pages (adding new items).

5 Establish intranet among schools in Hungary.

6 Establish forum for communication for teachers via Internet and intranet discussion groups among language professionals in the schools so that they can exchange ideas, experiences already from the very beginning of their contacting the Internet (Newsgroup or Usenet).

7 Set up a Listserv through which online courses could be provided for teachers needing help in making their way through the Net.

8 Set up a Listserv through which online help can be provided for foreign-language teachers in their getting around the Net.

PROFESSIONAL ASPECTS IN EXPANDING THE PAGES

1 **Phase 1 The Web as informational resource**
Getting familiar with:
- the basics (e-mail and the Web) (e.g., receiving, sending messages, uploading, downloading messages, printing messages, etc.);
- resources already available on the Web and on e-mail for both professional development and teaching aids (vast area including various sites already existing on the Web; primary aim: to make teachers familiar with them and to provide an information bank easily accessible for them).

2 **Phase 2 The Web as means for communication**
Getting familiar with:
- specific steps to show how the Internet could be used in the classroom (multimedia presentations, display of a project to the world, interactive pages);

- the interactive features of the Web and the e-mail;
- how to use the Web for teaching purposes;
- ways to communicate with the world (professional communication and communication for teaching purposes, e.g., sources for setting up cooperative projects among schools within and outside of Hungary).

3 **Phase 3 The Web as means for self-expression**
Getting familiar with:
  - the basics of HTML writing;
  - how to upload/download files for/from the Web;
  - how to make designs with CGI/Java.

4 Setting up a Listserv (through e-mail) for professional exchange of ideas.

5 Setting up a newsgroup (through the Web) for professional exchange of ideas.

Notes

1 See Street, 1995, for a detailed discussion on the social construction of literacy.

2 Although the Ministry of Education has been working toward this goal in 1998, many schools are still without Internet access at the end of 1998. And according to the *Nepszabadsag*, a Hungarian daily newspaper, the Education Department has stopped further development of SULINET because of high costs (20 November 1998: "Developing SULINET stops").

3 We refer to globalization in the sense of "globalization-from-below." According to Becher, Childs, and Cutler, "globalization-from-below, in contrast to global-ization-from-above, aims to restore to communities the power to nurture their environments; to enhance the access of ordinary people to the resources they need; to democratize local, national, and transnational political institutions; and to impose pacification on conflicting power centers" (1993, p. xv).

4 Although Hungary started to have its own providers in 1997, the connections leave much to be desired.

5 George Soros, before donating his money, received a pledge from the Hungarian government to spend the money on the connections. However, economic and political fluctuations have slowed down Hungary's commitment to providing Internet access to schools.

6 The Council of the European Unity <http://agenor.consilium.eu.int>; *The International Herald Tribune* <http://www.iht.com>; and *Hotwired Magazine* <http://www.hotwired.com/frontdoor>

7 Enikő Csomay, born in Budapest and co-author of this piece, also explored the Websites included in this study and answered the questions we posed to the participants.

8 Copyright Enikő Csomay 1997.

References

"An Internet Programme for Hungary's Secondary Schools" (1997). Ministry of Culture and Education. <http://www.mkm.hu/angol/ang.HTM>

Bajkó, Mátyás (1977) "The Development of Hungarian Formal Education in the Eighteenth Century," *Studies on Voltaire and the Eighteenth Century*, in The Voltaire Foundation at the Taylor Institution, Oxford: Oxford University Press, pp. 191–221.

"Balint Magyar: Hungary's Minister of Culture and Education" (1997). Ministry of Culture and Education: <http://www.mkm.hu/angol/ang.HTM>

Brecher, J., Childs, J. B. and Cutler, J. (1993) "Introduction", in Brecher, J., Childs, J. B. and Cutler, J. (eds) *Global Visions,* Boston: South End Press.

"Developing SULINET stops" (20 November 1998), *Nepszabadsag.*

Faludi, Szilárd (1976) "A korszerü müveltség követelmenyei az új tantervben," in Horváth, M. and Zibolen, E. (eds), *30 év neveléstudomány és müvelödéspolitika.* Magyar Pedagógiai Társaság Pécs: Táncsics, pp. 121–130.

Forgo, Sandor, and Koczka, Ference (1996) "The Use of Multimedia in Distance Education," *Educational Media International* 33(1): 16–19.

Freire, Paulo, and Donaldo Macedo (1987) *Literacy: Reading the Word and the World,* South Hadley, MA: Bergin and Garvey Publishers.

Grepaly, Andras (1995) "Internet: The World Wide Web and the Schools," *New pedagogy* 5: 64–70.

Gutsche, Márta. (1993) "The Hungarian Education System in the Throes of Change," *European Education* 25(2): 5–11.

Gyula, Simon (1976) "Felszabadult nevelésügyünk huszonöt évéröl," in Horváth, M. and Zibolen, E. (eds), *30 év neveléstudomány és müvelödéspolitika,* Magyar Pedagógiai Társaság Pécs: Táncsics, pp. 215–224.

Hanley, Eric, and McKeever, Matthew (1997) "The Persistence of Educational Inequalities in State–socialist Hungary: Trajectory–Maintenance versus Counterselection," *Sociology of Education* 70: 1–18.

Horváth, M. and Zibolen, E. (eds) (1976) *30 év neveléstudomány és müvelödéspolitika,* Magyar Pedagógiai Társaság Pécs: Táncsics.

Jódoru, Madga (1976) "Az ellenforradalmi neveléspolitika alapelveinek megfogalmazása," in Horváth, M. and Zibolen, E. (eds), *30 év neveléstudomány és müvelödéspolitika,* Magyar Pedagógiai Társaság Pécs: Táncsics, pp. 239–248.

"Kadar's Pied Piper," *The Hungarian Quarterly* 37.147 (autumn 1997): <http://www.hungary.com/hungq/no147/>

Kaufman, Cathy (1997a) "Transforming Education in Hungary," *Social Education* 61(2): 89–92.

Kaufman, Cathy (1997b) "Educational Decentralization in Communist and Post-communist Hungary," *International Review of Education* 43(1): 25–41.

Knoblauch, C. H. (1990) "Literacy and the Politics of Education", in Lunsford, Andrea, Moglen, Helen and Slevin, James (eds) *The Right to Literacy,* New York: MLA, pp. 74–80.

Köte, Sándor (1976) A Tanácsköztársáság közoktatása és pedagógiája. In Horváth, M. and Zibolen, E. (eds), *30 év neveléstudomány és müvelödéspolitika,* Magyar Pedagógiai Társaság Pécs: Táncsics, pp. 205–214.

Magyar, Balint (1997) "The Possibilities of the Internet", unpublished talk at the Fine Arts Museum, February.

Ministry of Culture and Education (March 1997) "Balint Magyar: Hungary's Minister of Culture and Education" <http://www.mkm.hu/angol/ang.HTM>

New London Group (1996) "A Pedagogy of Multiliteracies: Designing Social Futures", *Harvard Educational Review* 66(1): 60–92.

Palffy, Stephen (1998) "An overview of Hungary's history," <http://www.users.zetnet.co.uk/spalffy/h_hist_0.htm>

Selfe, Cynthia L., and Richard J. Selfe Jr. (1994) "The Politics of the Interface: Power and its Exercise in Electronic Contact Zones," *College Composition and Communication* 45: 4.

Street, Brian (1995) *Social Literacies: Critical Approaches to Literacy in Development, Ethnography and Education*, New York: Longman.

SULINET (1998) <http://www.sulinet.hu>

"The Long-term Strategy for the Development of Hungarian School Education" (1997). Ministry of Education. <http://www.mkm.hu/angol/ang.HTM>

Tompa, Klára (1994) "The Transferability of Information Technology", *Educational Media International* 31(1): 30–35.

Vajna, T. (23 August 1997) "Suli Buli", *Weekly Economist* XIX/34: 63–94.

2

XENES GLOSSES: LITERACY AND CULTURAL IMPLICATIONS OF THE WEB FOR GREECE

Aliki Dragona and Carolyn Handa

> In Greece, where every enterprise that involves language –
> publishing, entertainment, journalism, tourism – is dependent
> on the roughly nine million who speak Greek, knowing
> one or more foreign languages is a professional necessity.
> Businessmen, politicians who deal with European Community
> officials, doctors who must keep abreast of foreign research,
> writers who here largely make their living on translations, all
> need foreign languages in order to survive.
>
> (Storace, 1996: p. 6)

The Web cannot and does not provide a completely common and neutral environment for global international communication between all cultures. To participate actively in the informational exchange offered by the Web, the people of different cultures must obviously speak the dominant language of the Web and be able to read its alphabetic characters. At the moment that language is English. But, while many Greeks today do speak English, this particular strand of bilingualism is not a given; the ability to read and write both Greek and English fluently characterizes primarily the professional and intellectual classes.[1]

Even for Greeks of these classes who do speak English, the Web with its attendant demands – using only English for participating in most of its activities, learning hypertextual search skills, mastering the cognitive functions of navigating successive layers of apparent specificity in order to gather information, being savvy to the rhetorical implications of the Web's graphic elements, and possibly learning HTML (Hypertext Mark-up Language) and JAVA – does not constitute a neutral environment. Learning the "language" of the Web becomes more like mastering a foreign language, another in a series of foreign tongues that most Greeks already learn as part of a cultural heritage of polylingualism. As Patricia Storace (1996) has noted in the epigraph above, the Greeks' emphasis on learning foreign languages seems unusual, even startling, to a non-Greek observer, and probably more so to a citizen from the United States where foreign-language study has gradually diminished over the last few decades. Describing her first trip to Athens, Storace comments: "It takes no more than a drive from the airport to realize how critical the study of foreign languages is in Greece. One of the most common neighborhood sights is the colorful signs offering the teaching of 'xenes glosses'" (p. 5).[2]

Cultural imperialism can take the form of one culture's indirect demand that another culture operate in a certain linguistic arena that the first culture is more versed in. Certainly such linguistic demands have caused volatile and highly political situations in some countries. Linguistic cultural imperialism may be less obvious, however, when the language under discussion combines graphic elements, multimedia, and one primary language, all in the form of a hypertextual medium. Hypertext may not reflect a universal mode of cognition; it may, instead, be a mode of thinking that reflects cognitive constructs and connections that are particularly English. The simple act of "clicking on" a word to receive more specific detail to reach more specific levels of generalization, for example, may not reflect a connection common to all languages. That specificity can be established by working through layers of concreteness within a given collection of sentences called in English a paragraph may be a culture-specific, socially situated practice rather than a universal language component. Finally, the visual literacy and skills needed for analyzing the combined effects of language, sounds, images, and video clips, may not be operating on a critical level in any culture, Greek included, because of this medium's novelty, with the result that this multimedium appears more as "pure" information and "pure" entertainment rather than a medium fraught with cultural baggage. We must always remember, however,

> that the human mind is not, like a digital computer, a processor of general rules and decontextualized abstractions. Rather, human knowledge, when it is applicable to practice, is primarily situated in sociocultural settings and heavily contextualized in specific knowledge domains and practices. Such knowledge is inextricably tied to the ability to recognize and act on patterns of data and experience, a process that is acquired only through experience, since the requisite patterns are often heavily tied and adjusted to context, and are, very often, subtle and complex enough that no one can fully and usefully describe or explicate them.
>
> (New London Group, 1996, p. 84)

For a Greek, then, the action of immersing oneself in the literacy environment of the Web could bring with it the following situations which we are tempted to label "dangers": (a) Greeks may be subjecting themselves to a cultural imperialism in the form of rhetorical structures of ideas and images that may not be native to the Greek language; (b) giving precedence to English as the linguistic medium of exchange emphasizes and places "value" on speaking English as opposed to speaking other foreign languages: "around the world, English is already the Windows of languages – you need to have it because everybody else does" (Hamilton and Rhodes, 1997, p. 15) (although English in the last thirty to forty years has gained ground over French, the dominant foreign language which literate Greeks once learned, English will now become even more necessary to learn);[3] and (c) the Web leaves little place for, and may be competing with, the cultural web that so highly characterizes Greek culture and literacy, except through the use of gate-keepers who, as they have done for so many centuries with other foreign languages, will facilitate access to the Web and interpret its language for non-English-speaking Greeks.

Before moving into a discussion of Greek history and culture, we feel we must describe our literacy situations and, to a degree, our personal cultural histories which obviously shape and skew the way we have approached this project, view literacy, and interpret both culture and technology. As Street (1993) recommends, "Since all approaches to literacy in practice will involve some [ideological] bias, it is better scholarship to admit to and expose the particular 'ideological' framework being employed from the very beginning: it can then be opened to scrutiny, challenged and refined in ways which are more difficult when the ideology remains hidden" (pp. 7–8). Problems arise when intellectuals do not realize or admit to their rather privileged status in society and their particular ways of viewing the world: "The problem for the intellectual is not so much . . . mass society as a whole, but rather the insiders, experts, coteries, professionals who in the modes defined earlier in this century . . . mold public opinion, make it conformist, encourage a reliance on a superior little band of all-knowing men in power. Insiders promote special interests, but intellectuals should be the ones to question patriotic nationalism, corporate thinking, and a sense of class, racial or gender privilege" (Said, 1996, p. xiii). We cannot help but approach this subject of technology, literacy, and culture in Greece from the limited perspective of intellectual "insiders" ; however, we do hope that explaining our literacy situations will work to keep us as honest as possible, to steer us clear of the type of "corporate thinking" that nearly always arises among a group of like-minded individuals, and to help us to recognize situations of race, class, and gender in which one group retains more privileged than another.

We do have a common literacy situation: our families are middle-class and of average means. They have both, however, always valued education and have permitted us to pursue higher academic studies; we have each earned Ph.D.s in literature, we both teach writing and literature classes in higher education, we often teach in computer classrooms and make use of both traditional and technological methods of research; we also live in the same college town, one having a large international community and amenities particular to a location catering to highly literate citizens who have reached an above-average financial status. We both grew up during a time when communications media were not so widespread as today. Personal computers did not yet exist in the form we are familiar with today; MTV was not even an idea in the back of someone's mind. Movie theaters were not as ubiquitous, and VCRs playing videotapes of all the latest movies were decades down the road. Even the television was not an appliance present in either co-author's home until after her early formative years. The primary forms of literacy for us both were books and children's magazines. These facts are important because they explain our preference for a certain type of literacy document based on a linear, book-type format; they also explain why, despite taking care to guard against such oversights, we might more easily overlook certain types of unofficial literacies such as oral storytelling, oral family histories and legends, and the rhetoric of graphic arts. Furthermore, our philosophy about pedagogy, student literacy, and the educational problems presented by a stratified social structure, derives from a common set of readings and acquaintances who view education as a tool which teachers give their students so that these students not only read the word but also the world (see, Freire, 1970 and Berlin, 1993; 1996). Ethnically, we both come from non-mainstream American backgrounds. One of us is a Japanese-American, the other a native of Greece, born in France and raised in a polylingual household which encouraged its offspring to learn foreign languages.

Valuing foreign languages, however, is not uncommon for all social classes in Greece. One can see foreign-language schools even in the smallest islands. For most Greeks – who come into daily contact with other languages and cultures through tourism, movies, music, advertising, television, and mass media in general – knowing a language other than Greek means financial survival and social ascendancy. Not only can a Greek earn more money by knowing English or German (most white-collar jobs require proof of English at least in the form of a certificate such as "Lower" or "Proficiency" granted in the form of written and oral examinations administered by agencies representing the universities of Oxford, Cambridge, and Michigan); he or she can also ascend to the ranks of the "scientist" or "scholar" (*"epistemon"*), and become a "literate" person who is not semi-literate (*"imimathis"*) and definitely not "illiterate" (*"agrammatos"*).

Aware of our own biases, we are equally aware of and concerned about certain assumptions that English-speaking people, most particularly ones living in the United States, might unconsciously hold about the Web. Such assumptions, if left unexamined, merge into a type of ideology working to undermine the classless, unhierarchical environment for global communication which the Web has often, erroneously we feel, been portrayed as. We want to emphasize that we cannot speak for an entire nation of Greeks. We speak mostly about those Greeks who are middle or upper class, bilingual, well educated: their financial status can afford them personal computers, the latest software, and Internet access. This is a limited part of the population. There will always be variations and individual differences even within the small subgroup.

We list below some of what we feel are the literacy and cultural presumptions of the Web. We follow each point by describing a situation in Greece which reveals why these are assumptions, not universals, and how not realizing the assumption as such could keep forever at bay any ideal of the Web as a place for neutral global communication.[4]

- **Many of us assume that people own computers that can access the Web in color and sound. We also assume that people can purchase and continually update technological equipment.**

  In reality, in Greece, personal computers are not so widespread in the home as they are in the United States. Only those few Greeks who do have computers and have subscribed to a local Internet carrier can access the Web. Even for those who do, updating their equipment continually can be an economic challenge. One of our Greek correspondents said, "I must admit I am rather upset with the 'ekviastiki' ["blackmailing"] behaviour of the companies which have the databanks through which we communicate. They support their programs (in my case a program called Europa) for about three years and then you must change [your] computer or you are out of the Web. Another problem is [the] computer's memory, of course. Using the Web has been an extremely slow process and all the new programs require Windows 95. I must say [that we] who don't have powerful machines but are able to do [our] own work with the computer [have found] it very frustrating and feel sometimes we want to resist this continuous demand of the market."

- **Many of us assume that dial-in charges and phone bills are similar everywhere to the relatively inexpensive rates common in the US.**

  The telecommunication situation in Greece is quite different. Phone bills and dial-in charges are high; Greeks pay for each local phone call, and the average Greek phone bill is much higher than the average American phone bill. Phone bills are not itemized unless Greeks request a new digital phone line, a very recent phenomenon. Phone bills for the old lines cannot be itemized, as in the United States, so Greeks have no idea how much calling a foreign or local number costs; the bill is simply one lump sum. And even though Greeks can use a local Internet carrier to access the Web, local calls are not inexpensive. A phone bill with a few calls to the United States from Greece, plus local Greek calls and a few hours on the Web, can run from $100.00 to

$200.00 in US currency. This expense in the context of average Greek salaries is unaffordable. Furthermore, if the bills are not itemized, the callers do not know how long each call lasts; obviously this situation can cause problems for those who might wish to spend more than a few minutes online connected to the Web. In fact, many Greek Web users take advantage of a device called a "spider" to access the Web quickly without incurring huge phone costs.

- **Many of us also assume that people have an interest in the Web and can benefit from it as a literacy tool.**

We believe that the Web addresses an English-speaking audience. The sheer number of English Web pages compared to Greek pages is staggering. Many Greek pages we located are written either all in English or offer a combination of Greek and English. One of our contacts explained that he does not check Greek Web pages because they are so few and he finds their links unhelpful. Typical pages originating from an English-speaking country do not contain a Greek version for those Greek citizens who do not read English. In addition, some pages written in Greek need (at least in the US) a special application that can translate characters into Greek letters. Without this special application, pages written in Greek appear as gibberish (see for instance http://www.ee.gr/ especially farther down on the page, or http://www.hri.org/news/greek/apegr/1998/98–01–15.apegr.html [Substitute the current date for the date above]).

This application aside, the average citizen of the US and other English-speaking countries speaks no Greek so has no urgent cause to access information from a Greek Web page. For a few reasons we could think of, such as travel to Greece, foreign study in Greece, and research on Greek history or customs, we did find pages in English. These pages seemed, to us, to have more to do with advertising and offering stereo-typical pictures of Greece and its people rather than with literacy. In a communication to one of the co-authors, one Greek contact says: "The Web [in Greece] is used extensively nowadays as a marketing tool. Most major corporations and businesses have a website. Bearing in mind the tendency of the Greeks to be 'with it,' 'modern,' 'European,' 'advanced,' etc. and the advertisers' knack of finding ways to sell services and products, it may be that 'literacy' in this area will come by way of advertising (or may not go far beyond this level). Advertisers will find ways of overcoming the language problem (by making websites 'user-friendly,' i.e., using pictures, cartoon characters, and other such gimmicks)."

- **Many of us assume that today practically any kind of information we want might be found on the Web.**

For Web users, however, this situation does not fully apply. Specialized information pertaining to Greek literature, music, and art, is not widespread on the Web. Even Web pages for major Greek universities are either under construction, difficult to access, minimally informative, or non-existent. We did find some Greek pages on politics, news, sports, and government, and with the help of Panos Phillipakos, we were able to locate Web pages for Greek elementary and high schools.[5]

Working with the designated Web pages chosen by this volume's editors, we looked the pages over cursorily at first with the following reactions: the pages seemed to be culturally specific, that is, pertinent or interesting to a particular class of English speakers, namely those educated, technologically savvy, and aware of various aesthetic perspectives and art movements. As we considered Greek audiences we thought that, for the most part, the pages addressed no issues of Greek interest, with the exception of the European Union and the *International Herald Tribune* sites. These two sites, we felt, might address current political and economic issues particular to Greece as the tenth member of the European Union and as a member of the international community. In fact, however, when we logged on to the site (http://agenor. consilium.eu.int/) for further analysis on 29 July 1997, we were surprised to find no Greek link although a space had been marked for Greece. When we queried the EUROPA Mail Box Service, the e-mail address given at the bottom of the page, we received a message reassuring us that: "the Greek language version of the homepage has not at all been forgotten and that Greece is still very much a member of the EU," but that "final technical problems with using Latin and Greek characters simultaneously are still being resolved." This message seems to contain an apologetic undercurrent which perhaps reflects the situation in Greece regarding the European Union: when one co-author traveled to Greece during the summer of 1997, she spoke with friends about the EU, discovering that many Greeks felt marginalized and ambivalent about long-term benefits for Greece as a member of the EU. The EU page seemed to reflect this ambivalence.

We also asked contacts in Greece to give us their reactions to these pages as well as their general reaction to the Web. (See Appendices 1 and 2 for the list of questions we forwarded to our Greek correspondents.) Some of our contacts expressed similar complaints and impressions upon visiting the site. One said that the EC site was interesting despite the lack of the Greek language; another bookmarked it without second thought, believing that it would be packed with relevant information, but when he returned to explore it further, he felt as if it were "a tourist site-seeing tour" with "no information given." It was, to him, "more like the tour of the White House."

Along these lines, these same contacts felt no attraction to the graphics of the *HotWired* page. One felt that while the ultimate contents were useful, the front page graphics were off-putting: "Shame for the site," he says. "It's like having to enter a mansion through a dirty men's room. What I mean is: The 'frontdoor' doesn't come close to describing the contents of the site." About the *Graffiti* site one contact stated: "Not interesting. It is beyond me or I am beyond it. I just don't care for such stuff."

On the contrary, the pages of the *International Herald Tribune* proved more interesting for our contacts. At first one of us felt that the *International Herald Tribune* did not contain much Greek news, and that what it did contain, again, would only be accessible to a narrow audience of Greek Web users who read English. The other of us felt, however, that because many Greeks constantly keep abreast of international news, the site would pique some interest. The average educated Greek reads newspapers daily, often more than one paper, and follows the news through radio and television; politics and international news are much beloved topics of everyday discussion for all social classes. For those Greeks who could access and read this site, then, it did offer a more satisfying experience than the other assigned Web pages, as far as ease of access, clear links, and understandable language. One of our correspondents says, regarding this site, that it is "the kind . . . that you always remember to go back to, to see what's new . . . [the *IHT*] covers in depth many different topics. It gives links to other sites which are equally interesting . . . [O]f course the *IHT* name counts. It stands up as a reliable source of information. Something important: it uses easy to understand language."

- **Many of us assume that people see the Web in a positive light, as something good and useful.**

  This point does seem to be true for the most part. Much of the Greek media and many Greek Web users portray the Web as a source of information and interest. In fact, Internet terminology has seeped into Greek culture so much that average Greek newspapers encourage readers to use the Internet and provide them with marketing guides for computer shopping and Internet carriers (Kotsikopoulos, 1997). Moreover, Greek magazines such as *RAM* admire the extent to which Greek lower schools in rural areas have joined the world of technology (Dimopoulou, 1997). The magazine *RAM* has also printed results of a Nielsen survey of Greek Internet users which concludes that although the survey cannot give exact numbers, unofficial numbers point towards between 85,000 and 110,000 users. This figure, however, is approximately only one percent of the current Greek population. This survey also predicts that the number of Greek users doubles every 14 to 16 months (Tombras, 1997).

- **Many of us also assume that the commercial aspects of the Web are more or less culturally neutral or that the ideology imparted by advertising and mass consumerism can easily be ignored.**

If any English or US cultural vestiges are transported through this medium, many Greeks will not so much be influenced by these values as they will "Hellenize" them, or, in other words, appropriate and weave them into the fabric of daily Greek existence. We must remember that for centuries Greece has been invaded as well as influenced by so many various foreign forces that it is savvy to foreign "intrusions," benevolent or otherwise. (See below for a brief history of foreign invasions of Greece and the Greek ability to recover from such intrusions.)

- **Those of us who are familiar with the Web assume that people will go to a *machine* for information and entertainment instead of to other *people*, or other means of information and entertainment.**
  We have found that many Greeks are interested in the Web, but the majority of Greeks we talked to most likely access their cultural web first. Many networks of family and friends take up the time of the average Greek, time that would not normally be spent alone with a computer. In a private e-mail message, one of our Greek contacts said: "Greek cultural upbringing has resulted in a modus operandi that can best be described as 'networking,' i.e., Greeks are more likely to turn to fellow human beings for information rather than to machines, for they want and value the interaction. Thus, within the culture, there is a resistance to machines as sources of information. (This is probably true of most Mediterranean people who, I would guess, would prefer human interaction rather than human–machine interaction.) This resistance may also be a matter of trust, which can be explained in terms of Greek history, politics, etc." The Greeks who are computer and Web literate will access both webs; however, it seems that the Web serves as a source of mostly professional information. Although a recent marketing survey claims that the principal reason for Greeks to access the Web is entertainment (Tombras, 1997), responses to our questions to our Greek contacts confirm that primarily professional reasons underlie most Web use. As a result, we feel the Web caters primarily to one class, the professionals, who again, may or may not be able to access the Web on their own; they may need to go through "gatekeepers" either because they are not computer savvy or literate, or because their English skills are weak or non-existent.

The attitudes and reactions of the Greeks above to the Web arise from Greece's history and that history's pressures in shaping Greek literacy and culture. For the last 400 years Greece has suffered foreign invasions and rules. The fall of Constantinople in 1453 signaled the end of the Byzantine Empire and the beginning of the Ottoman Empire's rule over Greece. Though this Empire did tolerate the Greek language, and to a degree Greek religion, it changed Greek freedom forever and affected Greek literacy practices significantly. "Schools of a kind existed throughout the Ottoman rule

... [imparting] a basic knowledge of reading and writing to their pupils" (Clogg, 1986, p. 36). In the eighteenth century, the gradual disintegration of the Ottoman Empire gave rise to a small class of Greek élite called the Phanariots. The Phanariots, who among other duties, acted literally and metaphorically as interpreters between the Ottomans and the western world, in turn helped launch another class of Greeks, wealthy merchants and "noblesse de robe" (Clogg, 1986, p. 32) who fostered the growth of numerous academies. This new class defined the way contemporary Greeks still view and value literacy and overall education as well as upbringing. In stressing this point, Faubion (1993) claims, "A catalyst of social mobility, the school has also been one of the securest means of procuring social and symbolic 'dignity' and . . . both social and symbolic power . . . [This] hypothesis would account in part for the enormous lengths to which the petty bourgeois especially often go in seeing to the schooling of their sons and daughters" (p. 59). He also wonders, "Had Greece somehow been absorbed into the world-systemic core, would the Phanariote precedent be less relevant, polyglossia and polymathy less compelling ideals than they presently are?" (p. 61).

Before we outline official literacy practices as they are specifically defined by formal education, we need to underscore the range of literacy practices that surround and shape the cultural identity of most Greeks. These unofficial literacy practices, in combination with the official ones we will discuss below, forge a strong cultural web that maintains its attraction despite the looming presence of the electronic Web.

When the average young Athenians, for example, go shopping downtown to Hermes or Homer streets, they will "read" their city. "Reading" the Greek past and partaking of what we want to call "Greek-ness" often comes before official schooling. These unofficial practices in the form of stories told by family, in the form of architecture and street naming, in the form of popular songs are confirmed and validated by official education.

Education and literacy have always been a lifelong pursuit of Greeks, both educated and uneducated. Similar to Faubion, George Psacharopoulos (1995) argues, "Education has a long tradition in Greece. . . . Happenings during those four hundred years [of Ottoman occupation] must have stirred the Greeks' appetite for education; it is clear, in any case, that the [secret school] helped to preserve the Greek language and national identity" (p. 169). In the nineteenth century the foundation of academies, or advanced schools, emphasized the Greek classics as well as math and sciences heavily. These schools pushed a literacy that promoted a pure Greek language, a sense of history and heritage, and the Greek Orthodox religion, actions which resulted in a very strong and vibrant national pride, called "ethni(ki)smos or "nation(al)ism" (Faubion, 1973, p. 75).

During the nineteenth century, in the aftermath of Greece's struggle in the war against independence from the Ottoman rule, the language issue came to the forefront: what form of Greek would serve as Greece's national language? The dispute over the identity of Greek language and what it represented at the time started a heated debate that took on political, social, economic, as well as literacy implications. More specifically, a group of erudite Greeks argued that Greece needed a language worthy of its illustrious classical past, one closer to the Attic dialect, and unmarred by foreign intrusions (for example, Slav, Turkish, Albanian, and Italian influences) and corruptions. As a result, a pure, albeit artificial, Greek or "katharevousa" was created, (Clogg, 1986, p. 72). Others felt that the "demotic" Greek spoken by the people was more appropriate as the national language. The struggle and ambiguous co-existence of both "katharevousa" and "demotiki," the so-called issue of "diglossia" or two co-existing languages, continued well into the twentieth century; the debate was resolved to a degree in the 1960s under the ministry of George Papandreou. Even so, "[katharevousa] remained the *modus dicendi* of the Greek government until 1975" (Faubion, 1993, p. 16).

What this all ultimately means in terms of Greek literacy and literacy practices is that Greeks for centuries had to operate in more than one language. The Web, an attractive and useful technology, is yet another foreign language, a *xeni glossa*. The Ottoman Empire and all the previous waves of foreign intruders had always forced the Greek nation to operate linguistically and culturally in more than one system, in literacy practices both official and unofficial as would be the case with any nation suffering under a foreign yoke, any nation suffering through the imperialist expansions of other nations. The issue of diglossia, although it focused on the rebirth of Greece as a descendant of the classical Greece of Homer and the "katharevousa" as representative of a pure, "cleansed" Greek past, simply reinforced the long national tradition continually having to operate within more than one cultural and linguistic system, always acknowledging that, as a nation, Greeks would be schooled, governed, and employed in the official literacy practices, but that they would talk, sing, compose folk poetry, and lead their everyday lives in unofficial literacy practices.

In addition, Greece's mere geographic location at the southern tip of the Balkan peninsula and at Europe's southeastern point dictates its view outward. Part of the Mediterranean, Greece is surrounded by the Ionian and Aegean seas; in the north, Greece's borders include Albania, Bulgaria, the former Yugoslavia, and Turkey at the northeast. Greece's scarcity of raw materials and resources and its resulting long tradition of sea trade have both ensured that the majority of Greeks value the ability to speak, read, write, and operate overall in other languages. Finally, in the twentieth century and especially in the more recent past since the Second World War, even the working classes have realized that to survive and better their social and economic position, in other words, to become "educated," "civilized," and "literate," they have to learn another language enabling them to deal not only with the constant flux of tourists at home – tourism is one of the major financial resources for Greece – but also with the outside world and Greece's participation in the European, and larger, community. To survive and improve means now as much as ever that the Greek nation needs more than its native tongue. And those *xenes glosses*, in turn, signify that Greeks will always exist perched between more than one world, more than one literacy.

Given the extent to which the Internet has entered into everyday Greek life, language, and usage already, advising the Greeks to be cautious and skeptical about the cultural influences and the ultimate impact of the Web would be foolish on our part. The Web and the Internet in general are part of Greek life right now and will continue to grow as both technological and cultural influences. More interesting to observe, however, is the degree to which Greek Web users have already managed to "Hellenize" the Web, as well as to employ those Greeks who speak its language, and to use them as "gate-keepers" (Street, 1995, p. 110). Our observation leads us to define a process we call the "Hellenization" of the Web. This process, rather than chronicling ways in which these users have taken over the Web and changed it in a way that is particularly Greek, instead notes the ways they are beginning to employ the Web as an economic tool and a mask offering the world the "Greek face" it expects while manipulating the Web in a way that preserves Greek privacy from being overrun by yet another in a long series of conquerors, albeit a technological rather than an armed one. Street argues that

> the analysis of the relationship between orality and literacy requires attention to the "wider parameters" of context largely under-emphasized in Anglo-American linguistics. Within social anthropology, for instance, these would be taken to include the study of kinship organizations, conceptual systems, political structures, habitat and economy, etc., which are seen as "systems", and analyzed in terms of function and structure rather than simply of "network" or "interaction". There is little point, according to this perspective, in attempting to make sense of a given utterance or discourse in terms only of its immediate "context of utterance", unless one knows the broader social and conceptual framework that gives it meaning.
>
> (1995, p. 165)

This simultaneous acceptance and manipulation of the Web that we have noted above springs from Greek history and culture. So we will analyze Greek reaction to and use of the Web in terms of the points we outlined earlier in this essay, namely (a) the cultural imperialism of imposed foreign rhetorical and visual structures; (b) technological pressures causing English to emerge as the dominant foreign language; and (c) the relationship between the Web and the Greek cultural web. Cautioning us, however, against believing that we are seeing any cultural situation clearly, even if we account for our own blindnesses, Faubion warns,

> Ethnographers should not overestimate their own impact. They are, after all, relatively few in number and relatively rarely read. On the other hand, they belong together with the journalists, with the authors of guidebooks and the directors of tours, and the droves of other participants and observers from whose selective gaze Athenians have been less and less able to hide. If not always intentionally, [ethnographers] belong together with all the other agents and patients of a late capitalist market in which tradition itself is, as Baudrillard suggested some two decades ago, just another commodity. . . . If the foreign gaze is one from which Athenians are less and less able to hide, the foreign presence is one that they have learned, for all their victimization, to put in its place [through stereotypes].
>
> (1993, pp. 48–49)

The Web will not become, at least not yet, the dominant source of information and resources. So Greeks will use the Web in a variety and/or combination of ways: those who are middle class, have English and technical skills, and can afford the phone bill, will search the Web for specific reasons (professional, research, and entertainment interests); those who may be lacking in one or more of the above categories will ask the gate-keepers to search for them, always conscious of the time and expense such a search will inflict on the gate-keeper who facilitates their participation in the communal life of this global Web (in this sense, while the Web does not operate according to literacy conventions that are as native to Greek culture as they might be to American culture, and while American Web users might think that their Greek counterparts are more "illiterate" in their use of the Web, the latter are as successful in their literate use of it, according to Street's explanation of literacy without schooling (Street, 1995; p. 106); those who know that the Web exists but find that it does not serve their needs will continue their long-standing traditions of cultural networking (they will contact friends and acquaintances, rely on word of mouth, and use such traditional methods as regular mail, phone, and fax). English, then, and a certain financial, economic status, are vital in initiating and maintaining any kind of contact with the Web.

The cultural imperialism of imposed foreign rhetorical and visual structures

As we have indicated earlier in this chapter, underlying grammatical and linguistic structures, as well as graphic design and visual displays, arise directly from specific cultures and bear markers connoting specific classes and ideologies. We point to Hodge and Kress (1993) who have shown how language, which always involves a selection, reflects ideological motivations whether or not the speaker or writer is aware of them. Examining linguistic transformations and utterances, they analyzed the motives underlying such seemingly neutral constructions as passive voice questions, transitive constructions, and two nominalized forms, one which hides actors and the other which hides negativity (pp. 15–29). And addressing the culturally specific nature of discourse from another direction is Brian Street (1993). Describing Besnier's criticism of traditional studies of discourse analysis, Street agrees with Besnier that such traditional approaches are "highly biased" because they focus primarily on western literacy genres and situations and have studied databases consisting only of "the literate activities and output of the intellectual elite" (p. 2).

Visual structures are just as culturally marked as their verbal and written kin. One specific visual example would be the *HotWired* Web page assigned to this volume's contributors. The design of that page directly refers to the hard-copy magazine *Wired*. In addition the design taking our eyes all over the page is one that states a kinship more with hypertext and non-linear reading than it does with standard paper texts. The design is also aimed more at the MTV generation than the older edge of baby-boomers or their parents who were born well before the Second World War. When we import such culture-specific visual displays, we are likely to get responses such as the following: our contacts had a hard time relating to the *HotWired* pages at first because they found the graphics off-putting. One contact said he almost was unable to interpret the layout in order to find what he considered good information. He found the language "far-fetched" and had a hard time making sense of the words in order to follow links. He had to study the links to uncover pages he felt were more meaningful: he wished "they had done away with the zany stuff on the first page" and gone directly to the contents. Another contact thought that visually the site was "very messy and confusing" with "no central subject." Overall, our Greek contacts' reactions parallel those described by Sibylle Gruber and Enikō Csomay in their study of Hungary and the Web in this volume, see Chapter 1.

Even aesthetically speaking, different cultures look differently at the images the world offers, often preferring images of the culturally familiar. The resulting sense of style reflects a culture's preference for color, shape, and arrangement. Greek aesthetics have been forever inscribed by the color of the sea, the grayness of stone, and the ever-present remnants of its several and different historical buildings and ruins, evidence of Greece's past. Images which are distinctly Greek and certain types of aesthetics have arisen directly from Greek geography and history. (See also Slesin *et al.,* 1988.)

Technological pressures causing English to be the dominant foreign language

As we have argued elsewhere, literacy in its official form is highly valued in Greece. Most Greeks perceive going to school – for many earning a college degree – and learning foreign languages to be as vital as getting a driver's license is for the average American. Even during times of great political distress such as the Ottoman rule or the Nazi occupation of Greece during the Second World War, participation in some form of official or unofficial literacy practices provided Greeks with a sense of direction and pride, a form of moral sustenance. For instance, the "secret schools," which operated clandestinely and "illegally" during the Ottoman rule over Greece for nearly 400 years, taught the children basic literacy skills but also instilled in them a strong Greek ethos. Similarly, during the Second World War when official public and private schools were forced to shut their doors to the young Greeks, many were "home-schooled" by relatives or friends. The co-author's mother, a girl of nine in 1940, and her younger brother, were sustained during the entire war by a steady, daily diet of the classics, and arithmetic, as well as French, English and piano lessons. Taught by family friend and well-known University of Athens professor, Ioannis Kakridis, the Decavalla family of children and adults alike studied Homer and history, and read contemporary poetry over meager rations of beans and bread.

Learning official and unofficial versions of one's native language, however, or choosing to learn foreign languages for economic reasons, is a little different from being indirectly pressured to learn one particular foreign language because of an occupying presence, albeit a technological one. Whether they realize it or not, many Greeks, especially professionals, are being pressured and are pressuring each other to master English at a particularly high level that enables them to utilize the Web. For example, a well-known Greek dance troupe, Omada Edafous, feel a great need to hire a Greek publicist fluent in computer skills and *xenes glosses* in every sense of that phrase; among the desired languages are English, French, and HTML. Other Greek professionals have communicated to us that they believe they cannot remain current in their professions without the above skills and languages.

Further testimony of our point occurs in a Greek computer magazine article assessing several websites created by elementary and high schools. The writer continually praises those websites with bilingual access and encourages those who do not to follow their example in implementing English. "The schools have entered dynamically the game of the Internet, "the article enthuses, "and seem to have seriously taken into consideration the function of the Internet. They offer pages as carefully constructed as possible, which are often very interesting. It is especially encouraging, if one considers that the greater majority of the people are not familiar with technology. So, for the schools to have a Web page *and especially in the English language* [our emphasis] is something more than encouraging. Encouraging, but also worthy of praise. Bravo to the students and the instructors who had the audacity, the courage, and the desire to initiate the students into the world of technology and if not initiate, at least make them realize the importance that the function of the Internet has [possessed] for communication and educational purposes" (Dimopoulou, 1997, p. 84). Further on, the article states, "We emphasize, however, for one more time, that it is important for this particular Web page to be enriched quickly *and especially with the help of the English version* [our emphasis] which it has already, so that the roads for international communication and collaboration are opened up more easily (p. 86). The author of this article praises the school of Elliniki Pedia because it "presents a Web site which is immediately impressive with its aesthetics and the many subjects of its Internet map. Much color, many possibilities of surfing, in a site that can be characterized as 'enviable.' A very correct move to include a page with further links to the Internet, an event which we believe that the student surfers will appreciate and will also utilize appropriately. A unique way, *especially if they are looking not only for more knowledge, but also to improve their English*" [our emphasis; our translation for all Dimopoulou passages] (p. 86).

The relationship between the Web and the Greek cultural web

Because Greece has always been so open to outside cultural forces through trade, foreign occupation and wars, tourism, and now the media and foreign products, as well as the return of many Greeks who had immigrated to such countries as Germany, Canada, Australia, and the United States, Greek culture is both distinctly Greek and distinctly international. Greek culture, as we have shown, is defined by its history, geography, economy, and beliefs. One unique cultural feature is the obligation several Greeks feel to their parents and their country. Unlike Americans, they do not just "pick up" and "go west" painlessly. Although in the last century many poorer Greeks had to emigrate for economic reasons, they often tried to keep in close touch with their country and have suffered over this separation. The ones remaining in Greece have continued to live in extended family households for the most part, and rely on this extended cultural network for moral and economic support. As a result, Greeks usually go through these human channels first, when dealing with everyday life situations, asking for help, or obtaining information. Going to college and establishing a family of one's own are examples of the differences between American and Greek family networks. In the US, children expect to go away to college and find their own lives, set up their own households, and establish their own families. In Greece, children expect to attend local universities and continue their lives with their families until they are married, then during and after their marriages. If divorced, they usually return to their parents. Extended families often occupy the same house or live in the same building or neighborhood.

Consequently, for most Greeks, their sense of literacy includes a multi-layered knowledge of the world transmitted through unofficial and official means. Grandparents and extended family members as well as a sense of geography, history, mythology, and religion act as unofficial literacy events, whereas schools, texts, and museums provide them with an official literacy experience. As a result, the culturally narrow parameters of the Web may not provide as rich and complex a literacy environment as Greeks are accustomed to.

And because human interaction is valued highly, important knowledge is passed down through the mouths of persons who, though not teachers or history and literature experts, have stories to tell, stories unrecorded in the country's textbooks. Such unofficial literacy practices have shaped and, we believe, will continue to shape many Greeks as long as life within the wider cultural web of family and friends continues to be valued in Greece.

In the words of one such superb (hi)storyteller, Yiorgos Prikas, who, as a family friend and unofficial literacy instructor has shaped the co-author, her friends, and her family, "One has to tell what has befallen this place. Because in this place people have struggled, tried to better their lives, fought hard, and suffered humiliations." In narrating his experiences as a young schoolboy living near the Jewish neighborhood of Salonica during the Second World War, then as a young man during the Greek civil war of the late 1940s, and later his views on the military junta of the 1960s and early 1970s, he exclaims: "I would like these things I have to say, from the point of view of a simple man, to be heard outside, because the information that people have today comes from the official history, and in general from the official dissemination of information."

Even at this time of peace and political stability in Greece, many Greeks continue to value the lessons of the past imparted by the members of their cultural web as well as other sources, official and unofficial. Perhaps because the past is so much an official presence – the Parthenon sits in the midst of contemporary Athens next to Muslim mosques and Byzantine churches – as well as an unofficial one, Greeks have become accustomed to knowledge received from diverse media.[6] Consciously or subconsciously, Greeks partake of a multi-layered literacy experience. Many Greeks will access the Web but they will always look at it and use it from the standpoint of this double identity. They are Greeks.

They are Greeks. But they are also Europeans and members of the larger European community. Ultimately, because of their cosmopolitan nature and acceptance of and interest in other cultures, they are active and interactive members of the global community in every sense. We believe that the rest of the global community will follow their example. As Richard Pells says, "In the future, Americans and Europeans may have to maintain a dual sense of loyalties – one to their own traditions and institutions, the other to an international culture and a global economy . . . This acceptance of a double identity is a way for Europeans and American to live more comfortably in what is still, for all the fears of 'globalization,' a decidedly pluralistic world" (1997, p. B5).

The Web, at this point in time, is not a neutral space, either rhetorically or culturally. Perhaps some day such a utopian vision of the Web might be realized. After all, no explorer, of the Internet or otherwise, ever leaves from or returns to a pure culture and a single national identity. "Nationality is a fiction" (Trend, 1994, p. 225).

> "Simply put, there is no such thing as a single national culture that remains the same year after year. Nations are constantly assimilating, combining, and revising their national "characters." Moreover, even spatial boundaries rarely correspond to the demarcations between racial and ethnic groups, speakers of various languages, and even families. Thus, the heterogeneous and changing nature of nations raises the question of who is authorized to speak on behalf of a national identity and when.
>
> (Trend, 1994, p. 229)

Although Greece is a small country geographically, its unique position at the crossroads of east and west and the fact that three-quarters of its geographical borders are sea have always directed the curiosity of the Greeks outward and dictated a lifestyle characterized by an ever-present sense of the other. In the final analysis, however, this interest and learning about the other will return to the Greek community. Like Odysseus, the archetypal cultural seafarer who pines for the faintest wisp of smoke from his hearth, Greeks will brave the ocean of the Web in order to satisfy their centuries-long curiosity about the other.

Until the time that people recognize the dominance of English with its attendant rhetorical and visual pressures and work to balance them, the Web cannot be a space for neutral global communication. Some day, perhaps. But not now, not yet.

Appendix 1

Questions

1   How familiar are you with the Web?

2   What do you normally look for on the Web?

3   Do you know of any Greek Web pages that you like? If so, could you tell us why and give us some addresses?

4   Do you know of any English-language Web pages that you like? If so, could you tell us why and give us some addresses?

5   Do you find that you help or have helped other Greeks who do not have a computer or access to the Web or English-language skills?

6   How much time do you spend on the Web per week or per month?

7   How does getting information from the Web compare (positively, negatively, or somewhere in between) to getting information from: (a) libraries; (b) people; (c) other sources such as (here fill in what sources you might use).

8   Apart from yourselves, who do you find is interested in the Web and why? Indicate age, language skills, education level, financial status, technical (computer) skills.

9   Would you like to help us in our research by further looking at some Web pages we have in mind? We would like your reaction and brief feedback.

Appendix 2

1   Would you please give us your initial response in five sentences (or more hopefully) to each website? Do not be afraid to freewrite and free associate and don't censor yourself. We are looking for your emotional as well as more logical, analytic reaction.

2   Would you normally look at these pages or pages similar to these on your own (i.e. if we hadn't asked you)?

3   Are they of interest or use to you? If yes, please tell us why in some detail. If not, again tell us in as much detail you can manage.

4   Do you know of any Greeks who would be inclined to look at these pages? Why would they be interested, if that is the case?

Notes

1 We wish to thank Helen Dendrinou-Kolias, Yiannis Kolias, Stavros Karageorgiou, Panos Philippakos, Hariclea Zengos, and Bessie Mitsikopoulou, who kindly answered questions for us about their use of the Web. And we are especially indebted to Yiorgos Prikas for the time he spent reconstructing his invaluable historical narration; he is a living illustration of the power and extent of Greece's cultural web.

2 This phrase has a double meaning in Greece, both of which we feel applicable to the language of the Web that we are discussing in this chapter: (a) foreign languages; (b) a language that all do not understand, thus needing to be "glossed," or translated.

3 As a case in point, when we were communicating via e-mail with our Greek contacts regarding this project, we used English only. We had no way to discuss the Web and the Internet in Greek; in addition, we had no access to e-mail programs that use the Greek alphabet. Further confirmation that English is the language privileged on the Web can be found in the chapter by Susan Romano, Barbara Field, and Elizabeth W. de Huergo in this volume, see Chapter 8.

4 Since we started writing this chapter in July 1997, technology in Greece has been constantly changing. For example, one can now ask for an itemized phone bill because more and more digital phone lines have been installed.

5 See:

   a Eleventh Elementary School of Glyfada. Last accessed on 29 November 1998 at
     http://users.forthnet.gr/ath/fotgous/
   b Ellinogermaniki Agogi. Last accessed on 29 November 1998 at
     http://www.ellinogermaniki.gr/
   c High School of Lavrion. Last accessed on 29 November 1998 at
     http://www.techlink/gr/schools/lavrio/
   d Second Elementary School of Microthebes. Last accessed on 29 November 1998 at
     http://www.tol.hol.gr/business/microth/index.html
   e Moraitis School. Last accessed on 29 November 1998 at
     http://www.di.uoa.gr/~globe/Moraitis/Moraitisen.html
   f Project Alexandros International Program Globe. Last accessed on 29 November 1998 at
     http://www.di.uoa.gr/~globe/

6 Evgenia Facinou's recent novel (1997) addresses this form of literacy and is evidence of the Greek preoccupation with the past and its bearing on the 'modern' Greeks. Similarly, family histories like [*The Family of Michalaki Isigoni of Smyrni*] by Eleni and Margarita Isigoni and [*The difficult years (a testimony)*] by Drakos Stamatakos attempt to explore, understand, and reconstruct for the younger generations an important part of the Greek past.

References

Berlin, James A. (1993) "Composition Studies and Cultural Studies: Collapsing Boundaries," in Gere, Anne Ruggles, (ed.) *Into the Field: Sites of Composition Studies*, New York: The Modern Language Association, pp. 99–116.

Berlin, James A. (1996) *Rhetorics, Poetics, and Cultures: Refiguring College English Studies,* Urbana, IL: NCTE.

Besnier, Niko (1993) "Literacy and Feelings: The Encoding of Affect in Nukulaelae Letters," in Street, Brian (ed.) *Cross-cultural Approaches to Literacy,* Cambridge: Cambridge University Press.

Clogg, Richard (1986) *A Short History of Modern Greece,* (2nd edn), Cambridge: Cambridge University Press.

p 72   72

Clogg, Richard (1992) *A Concise History of Modern Greece,* Cambridge: Cambridge University Press.

Dimopoulou, O. (1997, November) ["Though small to look at, capable on the Net"], *RAM,* pp. 84–89.

EUROPA Mail Box Service. [EUROPA@DG10.cec.be] (29 July 1997), Greek Links – EEC Web Pages, [Private e-mail].

Facinou, Evgenia (1997) [*One hundred roads and one night*], Athens: Kastaniotis.

Faubion, James D. (1993) *Modern Greek Lessons: A Primer in Historical Constructivism,* Princeton: Princeton University Press.

Freire, Paulo (1970) *Pedagogy of the Oppressed,* trans. Myra Bergman Ramos, New York: Continuum. (Original work published 1968.)

Hamilton, Kendall and Rhodes, Steve (20 October 1997) "So I'm like, 'Who needs this grammar stuff?'" *Newsweek,* p. 15.

Hodge, Robert and Kress, Gunther (1993) *Language as Ideology,* (2nd edn), London: Routledge.

Isigoni, Eleni M. and Isigoni, Margarita I. (1995) [*The family of Michalaki Isigoni of Smyrni*], Athens: Trochalia.

Kotsikopoulos, Nikos (5 September 1997) "Computers for beginners," *Ta Nea, Agora,* [*shopping*], 5–8.

Kress, Gunther and van Leeuwen, Theo (1996) *Reading Images: The Grammar of Visual Design,* London: Routledge.

New London Group (1996) "A Pedagogy of Multiliteracies: Designing Social Futures," *Harvard Educational Review* 66(1): 60–92.

Pells, Richard (1997, May 2) "The Local and Global Loyalties of Europeans and Americans," *The Chronicle of Higher Education* 43: B4–5.

Prikas, Yiorgos (1997) [An oral testimony: taped narrations], personal communication.

Psacharopoulos, George (1995) "Education in Greece Today: Contributions to the Perennial Debate," Introduction, *Journal of Modern Greek Studies* 13: 169–179.

Said, Edward W. (1996) *Representations of the Intellectual: The 1993 Reith Lectures,* New York: Vintage. (Original work published 1994.)

Slesin, Suzanne, Cliff, Stafford, Rozensztroch, Daniel, and de Chabaneix, Gilles (1988) *Greek Style,* New York: Clarkson N. Potter, Inc.

Stamatakos, Drakos (1996) [*The difficult years (a testimony)*], Athens: Vivliopromitheftiki.

Storace, Patricia (1996) *Dinner with Persephone,* New York: Pantheon.

Street, Brian (1993) "Introduction: The New Literacy Studies," in *Cross-cultural Approaches to Literacy,* Cambridge: Cambridge University Press.

Street, Brian (1995) *Social Literacies: Critical Approaches to Literacy Development, Ethnography and Education,* New York: Longman.

Tombras, Christos (1997, November) ["The identity of the Greek users,"] *RAM*, 290.

Trend, David (1994) "Nationalities, Pedagogies, and Media," in Giroux, Henry A. and McLaren, Peter (eds) *Pedagogy and the Politics of Cultural Studies*, New York: Routledge.

3

WORKING THE WEB IN POSTCOLONIAL AUSTRALIA

Cathryn McConaghy and Ilana Snyder

In recent years, the use of new forms of cultural production by Indigenous Australians has made an important contribution to their changing status in relation to the political, social, and economic structures of the nation. Noted Indigenous academic, Marcia Langton (1994, p. 90), describes the rise of Indigenous film, television, music and art as a "cultural efflorescence" which is enabling Indigenous peoples to renegotiate their identities and relations with white Australians. The flowering of new media forms is also enabling the transformation of Indigenous Australians from colonial objects to post-colonial subjects. Aboriginality, Langton argues, "is a field of intersubjectivity in that it is re-made over and over again in a process of dialogue, of imagination, of representation and interpretation." Further, she writes, "both Aboriginal and non-Aboriginal people create Aboriginalities" (1994, pp. 99–100).

In this chapter, we consider a new media form of cultural production, the Web, as a site for the renegotiation of identities, and for social repositioning and transformation. Our focus is on the Web-based literacy practices which are used by both Indigenous and non-Indigenous people to construct "Aboriginality." We are interested in examining the Web as a site for the production of rhetorical narratives that isolate Aborigines and constitute them as exotic rather than contemporary peoples, or otherwise depict them in ways Aborigines themselves judge to be negative. But we are particularly interested in examining the Web as a site offering opportunities for people to connect, to correct, and to disrupt textual enclosures (Peters and Lankshear, 1996), and, in Anna Yeatman's (1996, p. 91) terms, to exercise "voice and choice." In other words, we see the Web as constituted by both neocolonial and anticolonial forces, but our emphasis is on its potential as a site for oppositional work.

Integral to our investigations are several key understandings about Indigenous peoples and the Web. First, even though we use the term "Indigenous peoples," we are aware of the danger of presenting a monolithic vision of Aboriginal people in Australia. We emphasize the importance of acknowledging the multiplicity inherent in Indigenous cultures – manifest in the many language groups, diverse histories, and different experiences of Indigenous peoples, for example, the distinctive experiences of Australian colonialism held by Indigenous women and men, and the distinctive experiences of those who live in cities and those who live in more isolated regions. In relation to the issues of gender, place, and diversity, we recognize that Web-based cultural productions take place within a politics of location in which both subjectivities and struggles are constituted spatially. What this suggests for the possibilities of engaging local struggles in the global arena of the Web is of considerable interest to our analysis of the uses of the Web in postcolonial Australia. Second, we know that the Web is a complex literacy and communication space, enabled by technology, yet at the same time linked to social, political, cultural, and economic formations. The Web is often read as a purely technological space and, in that sense, as self-contained and neutral. Such a reading, however, represents a partial account because it leaves out the understanding that the Web is embedded in the larger dynamics organizing society. Such a reading fails to recognize that the Web is not only inscribed and shaped by openness and decentralization, but also by power structures and cultural contestations (Sassen, 1997).

It follows that the literacy practices associated with the use of the Web, as all literacy practices, are specific to particular political and ideological contexts, they are constructed, and their consequences vary situationally (Street, 1995). Using the Web for literacy purposes does not in itself promote cognitive enhancement, social mobility, progress or, for that matter, Indigenous peoples' advancement, for literacy cannot be defined, understood, learned, studied or acquired independently of social context without sensitivity to ideology and without taking account of the cultural and political formations which imbue literacy events and practices (Richardson, 1997). Thus our analysis of Web-based literacy practices associated with neocolonial and anticolonial impetuses in Australia includes descriptions of the broad cultural context in which these practices assume meaning (Street, 1995).

Our investigations are framed by a number of questions: in what ways is the Web being used to disrupt the representations of Indigenous Australians that have been a significant aspect of their constitution as colonial subjects? To what extent and in what ways are Indigenous Australians engaging with the new medium? What are the new forms of text which are being produced? What are the politics of identity, difference and representation being played out on the Web? And, finally, what does our exploration of these issues reveal about the connections between Web-based literacy practices and power relations both within Australia and in a broader global context?

We explore some of the issues raised by these questions. We also identify key theoretical resources which throw light on the complex connections between new literacy practices, electronic information and communications media and contemporary Australian colonialism. Further, our investigations seek to contribute to the broader debates in relation to the Web as a universal communications medium. We ask, to what extent, if at all, is the Web a neutral environment, a "literacy utopia" (Pratt, 1987), and to what extent is it an "interested" environment in which old oppressions are remade? We also discuss the extent to which Web-based literacy practices reflect specific social and historical conditions and the extent to which they resonate with new globalized practices.

Our analysis of Web-based literacies is located within a broader theoretical discussion of the relationship between literacy practices and the production of colonial texts. Specifically, it is located within a critique of "Aboriginalism," the term used to describe the complex processes by which Indigenous Australians are represented as colonial "others." Using this critical frame, we reflect on the extent to which Web-based literacy practices represent a continuation of a tradition of writing against Aboriginalism as a strategy of Australian decolonization.

We then look at the emergence of critical social literacies in Indigenous Australian education, including an examination of the ways in which a variety of technologies have been used progressively to subvert colonial representations. This is followed by a brief overview of current Web-based literacy practices in Indigenous Australia. We also consider the extent to which the Web provides opportunities for the development of new literacy practices and new textual representations. We suggest that the ways in which the Web works simultaneously to exclude and include Indigenous Australians may be characterized as an embodiment of Bhabha's (1995a) notion of colonial ambivalence. Overall, we observe that there is much to celebrate about the emergence of Indigenous voices on the Web. However, the local struggles for self-determination and social justice are taking place within a global context characterized by the rapid and exponential growth of information and communications networks, a resurgence of racism and the spread of transnational capitalism. An environment, at least at first glance, inhospitable to the promotion of Indigenous rights.

While our discussion concentrates on the material and cultural conditions of contemporary Australia, we suggest that the local–global tensions described are echoed in many other sites around the world. The ambivalent play between the celebration of Indigenous voices and the trend towards greater social disadvantage for certain groups in Australia and elsewhere requires a critical and reflexive approach to analyses of Web-based literacy practices. Moreover, our research suggests the need to identify and promote Web-based literacy practices able to transform, rather than simply reproduce, particular social and cultural formations.

Literacies, texts, and colonial relations

An analysis of Web-based literacy practices in Australia necessarily begins with an understanding of the relationship between literacy practices, colonial texts, and relations of colonial domination. The colonization of Australia, which began in 1778, was part of the larger project of the expansion of the British Empire and the spread of western liberal modernity (Goldberg, 1993). Although Australian colonialism has a history of more than two hundred years, we are only beginning to understand the complexities of what continues to be a significant force in the shaping of contemporary Australian social relations.

Several factors help explain new understandings of the enduring effects of colonialism. The recent publication of a number of testimonies by Indigenous Australians have revealed many examples of injustice and suffering (Sykes, 1997). Further, a number of Royal Commissions and National Inquiries, most notably the Royal Commission into Aboriginal Deaths in Custody (Johnston, 1991) and the National Inquiry into the Separation of Aboriginal and Torres Strait Islander Children from their Families (Human Rights and Equal Opportunity Commission, 1997) have exposed the often sinister and brutal elements of Australian colonialism.

The work of Edward Said (1978) has also contributed to our understanding of Australian colonialism. In his analysis of western imperialism, Said observes that domination was achieved not only by guns and aggressive mercantilism, but also through the rendering as "other" of peoples deemed inferior. Said's critique of orientalism emphasizes the material and symbolic power of textual representations in the domination of the colonized by the colonizers. In Australia, textual representations of Indigenous Australians have played a similar role. Recognizing the power of certain kinds of textual representations of Indigenous Australians helps us understand the complex connections between Web-based literacy practices and specific projects of contemporary Australian colonialism.

A tradition of textual representations, described as constituting the discursive regime of "Aboriginalism" (Hodge, 1990; Attwood, 1992), has been particularly effective in the colonization of Indigenous Australians. Drawing on Said's (1978) notion of orientalism, "Aboriginalism" refers to the production of texts about Indigenous Australians which emerge as integral to the imposition of authority and power over them. The Aboriginalist project is described by Bain Attwood (1992) as taking three interdependent forms: researching and speaking about Indigenous people; constructing "them" as oppositional to "us"; and maintaining institutions for disciplining, administering, and ruling over Indigenous Australians. One of the central projects of Aboriginalism is the construction of normative and prescriptive statements of what it means to be "a real Australian Aborigine" or a "real Torres Strait Islander." These constructions of Indigenous identity and subjectivity contain and limit the possibilities for the multiplicity of Indigenous Australians to be self-determining and self-representing. They also allow cultural stereotypes to remain deeply embedded in social structures. Further, certain fictions about "Indigenous culture" and "Indigenous identity" are produced and reproduced as part of the material investment in Aboriginalist representations that sustain many of the institutions of Australian society. Overall, the discourses of Aboriginalism tend to impose identity rather than allow Indigeneity and subject positions to be negotiated.

Not surprisingly, it seems that the Web, like its technological forerunners, is playing an increasingly important role in the perpetuation of Aboriginalist representations. But, at the same time, it seems there are also possibilities to use the Web to challenge such representations. For, although influential, the texts of Aboriginalism are fragile constructs that may provide opportunities for oppositional work.

It is with these understandings of contemporary Australian colonialism and the possibilities for transformation that we approach our analysis of Web-based literacy practices within postcolonial Australia. We do not use the term "postcolonial" to suggest that Australian colonialism is an event of the past. Rather, we use it to emphasize the possibilities for critical engagement with colonialism and its consequences (McClintock, 1995; Hall, 1996). Australia is "postcolonial" to the extent that we may now subject contemporary colonial forces to the important processes of critique.

Critical social literacies and Australian colonialism

Our analysis of Indigenous literacy education and the associated use of a range of communication technologies is located within the broad context of popular narratives about Indigenous education which continue to have currency. These narratives have been informed in great part by Aboriginalism and its representations of "the essential Aboriginal subject." A resilient construction of "the essential Aborigine" has been "Indigenous incapacity" (Hodge and Mishra, 1991, p. 27). A direct consequence of this construction has been pedagogical efforts to deal with what is generally perceived to be lacking among Indigenous Australians. Hence, literacy education becomes a project aimed at redressing the "lack" of literacy. Not surprisingly, the absence of written records within Indigenous Australian material culture was used to explain apparent illiteracy, despite many examples of symbolic representations and forms of communication. But as these examples did not support the narrative of the lack of something they were conveniently erased.

Following the Second World War, as in many other nations, a new focus on the importance of (print-based) literacy emerged in Australia. Literacy was considered a basic human right and a key to social and economic development. It was regarded widely as one of the important ways in which people could escape the "poverty cycle" and create a better life. Improved literacy standards were thought to lead to superior jobs, higher incomes, and enhanced standards of living. In this period, Indigenous literacy education policy was dominated by assimilationist ideologies. The aim of assimilationism was to remake all Indigenous Australians in the image of the capable white self (McConaghy, 1997a, p. 144).

By the 1970s, cultural relativist pedagogies began to challenge these policies and influenced Commonwealth government support for the development of bilingual literacy practices in selected remote-area Indigenous communities in the Northern Territory. In this changing literacy environment, children were given "readers" in a local language and adults were taught to read using local bilingual newspapers. As editor of a bilingual newspaper, *Galiwin'kupuy Dhawu*, from 1984–86, McConaghy (1997c, p. 32) observed that people enjoyed the photos but took little interest in reading the printed texts. She also ran small literacy classes for adults who could not read or write. These adults wanted to learn to write their signatures but when they developed this skill often lost interest in the class.

Influenced by Paulo Freire's (1972) notion of literacy consciousness-raising, McConaghy developed versions of Freire's "problem-posing, problem-solving" workshops in a remote Aboriginal community of the Northern Territory. Literacy programs for collective political action and self-empowerment proved an attractive goal for her and other adult educators in the mid-1980s. However, on reflection some ten years later, McConaghy concludes that the approach was inherently problematic, at worst, constituting another form of white supremacy (forthcoming, p. 32). She points out that consciousness-raising approaches to literacy education depended on "facilitators" who assumed they knew more about oppression than those who actually experienced it. Moreover, in the spirit of liberal individualism, such approaches rested on the belief that the problems of structural inequality would be solved when the oppressed started to take action for themselves. We see the same ideology manifest today in liberal celebrations of Indigenous voices on the Web.

A more recent influence in Indigenous literacy education is the development of "critical social literacies" (Walton, 1993). Integral to this position is a critique of the notion of a literate/illiterate continuum. Often linked to the written/oral dichotomy, the literate/illiterate polarization works to sustain beliefs in Indigenous incapacity, poverty of expression and general primitiveness. Martin Nakata's (1991) analysis of the placement of "the Torres Strait Islander" on this literate/illiterate continuum is useful here. He explains how constructions of literacy and illiteracy were used as a technology for colonial subjugation – for the degeneration and dehumanization of Torres Strait Islanders.

A form of cultural relativism provides the basis for arguments that certain cultures exhibit different forms of literacy and that each is to be recognized and valued. Hence, we now speak of literacies, rather than literacy. Further, there is a recognition that peoples' literacy practices are located in particular social and historical contexts and are therefore variable and multiple (New London Group, 1996). Moreover, it is argued, the dynamic nature of literacies is better understood when literacy practices are seen as closely connected to other social practices, including economic and political (Gee, 1996).

The notion of the critical in "critical social literacies" owes much to the early work of Freire. Drawing on Freire's work, Peters and Lankshear (1996) describe critical social literacy as a social practice in which "meta-level understandings" of literacy are combined with "moments" of critique. In these moments, evaluations and judgements are made in relation to certain social phenomena. To make these judgements, the critically literate person needs to have sufficient knowledge of the phenomena to undertake an analysis. The metalevel understandings of literacy include an awareness that literacy practices, such as the reading, writing and viewing of texts, are never value neutral. They also include an understanding of the socially constructed and interested nature of knowledge. The inference is that when individuals acquire these metalevel understandings, they are able to engage with or intervene in the processes. However, this link between the development of critical social literacy practices and social transformation is both problematic and complex.

We see some of these complexities in the ways in which Indigenous Australians have used different technologies for literacy purposes. Although certain Indigenous people have used print technologies to great effect through the production of submissions, reports, policy documents and novels, plays and poetry (Narogin, 1990), many remote-area Indigenous people have not actively pursued print technology skills. Other forms of technology have held greater attraction, despite decades of print-based adult literacy efforts by missionaries and governments.

We describe two such non-print literacy projects. The first used video in the mid-1980s to develop vocational skills with Indigenous health workers in Galiwin'ku, an East Arnhem Land community. Despite many years of literacy and numeracy programs, skills remained inadequate for the tasks required of a health worker and enthusiasm for the weekly classes was absent. By contrast, when the health workers were invited to contribute to the production of community health information videos, they enthusiastically acquired the necessary literacy and numeracy skills. Successive video projects were mounted and training in using the medium was extended to other members of the community for a variety of projects. These included the production of submissions to government agencies, a local video news program (McConaghy, 1985) and, eventually, other programs for local television broadcasting.

The second project operated in the late 1980s and early 1990s. It focused on the development of students' literacy skills in the Adult Education Studies program at Batchelor College, an institution in the Northern Territory of Australia dedicated to Indigenous tertiary education. Many of the students had left school in the early primary years. One of the successful programs emphasized writing for publication, and composing texts using computers equipped with word processing and graphics programs. The students worked collaboratively in a computer laboratory where they created a range of products including some of the first graphic images of Indigenous art. Stories were written to accompany these graphics and were published in a volume of the local Indigenous adult education journal, *Kurlalaga* (McConaghy, forthcoming, p. 35).

These projects, together with others such as Eric Michael's (1986) work at Yuendumu, where video literacy was developed successfully to achieve a range of social, cultural, and economic objectives, suggest that certain literacy practices associated with the use of particular technologies may serve to promote Indigenous voices and transform approaches to Indigenous pedagogies. Cognizant of these possibilities, we now consider the development of Web-based literacy practices in postcolonial Australia.

Determining the extent to which Indigenous Australians are using the Web is difficult as there is little research in the area. Hobson (1997a; 1997b), however, carried out a survey of the websites which have a predominant focus on Indigenous topics. He characterized sites in terms of level of consultation with Indigenous people in their development and degree of Indigenous participation in aspects of their construction. Hobson concludes that Indigenous activity in online services is very limited, with only three of the 174 sites surveyed designed by Indigenous people and 61 percent having no Indigenous involvement. In particular, Hobson notes that there is a dearth of Indigenous personal home pages. The reasons are clear. For Indigenous Australians, the rate of individual computer ownership is very low and private access to Internet services minimal. A few community organizations and individuals have opened accounts with commercial Internet service providers and a small number of these have established a Web presence. The major representations of Indigenous Australians on the Web are as the objects of research interest for universities and other institutions, identified by Attwood (1992) as characteristic of the "Aboriginalist project," or within the commercial sphere, particularly for the promotion and sale of Aboriginal Art and Crafts.

However, our own research indicates that despite the generally low participation of Indigenous Australians in the production of textual representations on websites, there are some notable exceptions. These include the Maningrida Arts and Cultural Centre home page (Maningrida, 1997), which is used to market art and to "correct the information" about

Indigenous cultural practices in the Maningrida area (Danaja and Garde, 1997). The Yothu Yindi home page (Yothu Yindi, 1997) represents a virtual manifestation of the renowned musical group's aim to promote common understandings and "demystify" Indigenous people (Yunupingu, 1993). The Yorta Yorta Clan Group is using its website (Yorta Yorta, 1997) to reconnect the clan and to establish continuity with the land in support of a land-rights claim, and the Indigenet site (Indiginet, 1997) is connecting and promoting the work of Indigenous Australian researchers and establishing a closed discussion group for community activists known as Indigepol. At a new site, Pekin Yalkin, the visitor is greeted with the statement: "While others are talking about telling our story on the Internet, we'll be selling it" (Pekin Yalkin, 1998).

The VICNET Aboriginal Homepage (VICNET, 1998) is part of an Internet resource in the first instance for people living in the Australian state of Victoria interested in Aboriginal issues. It provides links to other pages such as the Indigenous Peoples' Page which is concerned with Indigenous peoples "under threat." In addition, Indigenous people have made effective use of Internet discussion groups (University of Sydney, 1997) to mobilize Australians for particular political causes. Causes include petitions in support of Indigenous land rights and the return from overseas of collections of Indigenous Australian human remains, the organization of rallies to protest funding cuts for Indigenous students, and efforts to bring together all Australians in the growing social movement towards Indigenous and non-Indigenous reconciliation. What these sites have in common is an attempt to use new textual representations to counter existing colonial ones – to construct new legitimating conditions for the production of power and knowledge in postcolonial Australia.

Textual authority, colonial legitimacy and the Web

Issues of legitimation and authority are crucial to our consideration of the ways in which the Web may be used effectively to support anticolonial projects. We are interested in how individuals and groups are able to subvert the authority of particular texts which have been constructed for a range of purposes using different technologies. We have, for example, some understanding of how authority is secured through different types of textual forms: print texts as compared to video texts as compared to hypertexts. Our specific focus here is how textual authority is secured on the Web. At the same time, we are also interested in identifying any opportunities the use of the Web may provide to subvert that authority.

Central to our consideration of these issues are claims about the ways in which hypertext, intrinsic to the Web's landscape, reconfigures our notions of textual authority (Landow, 1992; Snyder, 1996). Hypertext theorists contend that in this new medium: centres and margins disappear; textual hierarchies tend to collapse; texts are generally more unstable; authorial power is dispersed; and there is potential for disruptive behavior on the part of readers. Also relevant are claims about the connections between hypertext and postcolonialism. According to Odin (1997, p. 627), the post-colonial and the hypertextual "represent two manifestations of the topology of postmodern information culture where grand narratives are being replaced by local narratives and local knowledges." She goes so far as to assert that there is sufficient evidence to argue "that the hypertextual is the representational space through which the postcolonial can work most effectively" (1997, p. 627).

However, we ask: are these claims which point to the possibilities for oppositional and disruptive projects in hypertext merely indicative of unmet potentials or do they reflect the reality of literacy practices on the Web? We bear in mind Joyce's (1997) cynical dismissal of the "web." He argues that much of the promise of hypertext has been subverted within the crass, commercialized, multimedia wastelands of the Web, a name he deliberately represents in lower-case letters. Joyce asks us to distinguish between "hyper-text" which, he believes, has great potential for artists and educators (and by implication postcolonial theorists and activists) and "multimedia" which is merely a variety of television. Joyce argues that hypertext had every promise – a medium which makes possible new kinds of stories for new readers – but he sees it as a "passing form" (1997, p. 165).

If not as dismissive as Joyce, we are ambivalent about the potential to disrupt textual authority on the Web. While we are celebratory of examples of Indigenous voices on the Web, we are also aware of the immense hegemonic powers of mass-communications media. Some researchers suggest that all forms of mass media, be it radio, television or the Web, permit little experimentation and only people of enormous influence, resources and sophistication are capable of escaping their binding power. As Katz and Wedell (1977) observed from an international survey of Third World mass-media broadcasting there is "a sameness in the style of television and radio presentations which has come packaged with the technology, almost as if the microphones and cameras come wrapped together with instructions for presenting a news program or variety show" (p. 119). Although Katz and Wedell made this observation more than twenty years ago, it is possible to argue a similar case about the structure, composition, appearance and content of the Web. In the brief period of time since Berners-Lee invented the Web in 1991, certain features have become formalized and institutionalized with the result that any significant departures are extremely difficult to initiate.

When we examine the six sites which provide the touchstone for this volume, we are struck by their similarities: the architecture, design, use of color, relationship of text to image, the content, and, perhaps most importantly, the political and cultural affiliations and influences. The *International*

Herald Tribune site (*International Herald Tribune*, 1997), may have the word "international" in its title, but a truly international voice is difficult to discern. The operating mechanisms of American capitalism are on display at Geocities (Geocities, 1997), while those of transnational global capitalism "materialize" at Samsung (Samsung, 1997). Although the European Council site (European Union, 1997) represents a different part of the globe from the United States, its activities and aspirations are more than familiar. It might appear that *HotWired* (*HotWired*, 1997) is different, with its pulsating grabs of color, an opening screen that changes with each successive visit, numerous buttons, and at least the promise of heightened interactivity, but these features do not add up to a substantial departure from the omnipresence of commercial interests. Similarly, the Graffiti site (Graffiti, 1997) may seem to represent something politically subversive, but in the end its sameness with the other five is overwhelming.

We are also struck by the similarities between the Indigenous Australian sites we have identified, with each other, but also with the touchstones sites. Indeed, distinctions between the two sets of sites become somewhat blurred. Although the Indigenous sites exhibit some diversity, they also share a number of common features. Their architecture and design, and the relationship of text to image do not represent any significant departure from what we now expect from websites. Menus of what is on offer and possible pathways for visitors are indicated by conventions which have become more or less universal. Unlike most of the touchstone sites, except for the Graffiti one, the Indigenous sites are notable for their use of bold color. A striking aqua and orange map of Arnhem Land in the Northern Territory of Australia, dominates the opening screen of the Maningrida site, with an arrow pointing to Maningrida (Maningrida, 1997). The Yothi Yindi (Yothi Yindi, 1997) site foregrounds Aboriginal designs, represented in evocative variations of browns and yellows. Scrolling white text, overlaid on the textured browns and yellows, provides information about the band and further resources available, including a QuickTime movie of the group performing. Red, yellow, and black, the colors of the Aboriginal flag, dominate several of the sites.

The textual content of these sites may at first seem to be more political than the touchstone sites. The Yorta Yorta (Yorta Yorta, 1997) site informs visitors that the "Yorta Yorta struggle for justice continues." It goes on: "Since the European invasion into Yorta Yorta Tribal Lands in the 1840s, the Yorta Yorta people have been continually seeking justice for the dispossession of their land and the destruction of their traditional culture and heritage." The Indigenous People's Page (VICNET, 1998) begins with the banner: "Indigenous People and other cultures under threat." It then explains:

> This page is concerned with indigenous peoples around the world and other cultures that are under threat. It contains links off to

84

all the current sites on the Internet which have information on this very important area. We hope that people in Victoria will find this page a worthwhile starting point in their exploration of this very serious issue in today's world and we would welcome hearing from anyone interested in this page.

Its links include: Aboriginal Youth Network in Canada; a guide to the Great Sioux Nation; and Milarepa – Information on the Tibetan civilization and informing people of what they can do to stop the destruction of Tibetan culture. However, these sites may be no more political or ideological than the touchstone ones: perhaps their political affiliations are simply more transparent.

We have two main responses to the absence of significant differences between the two sets of sites. The first suggests that rather than asking questions about their distinctive features and how they differ, it might be more salutary to concentrate on the conditions of their production and use. To do so would be to acknowledge that "texts come into existence, and must be described, in terms of social relations between institutionally situated audiences and producers, and that meanings arise in these relationships between text and context in ways that require a precise description in each case" (Michaels, 1994, p. 43). Indeed, our investigations indicate that we are not going to discover anything that is uniquely Indigenous simply by looking at the websites. Rather than focusing on the texts which constitute the websites, it would be more generative to ask questions about the subjects and their positioning.

The second response suggests that all the sites visited, both the Indigenous and the touchstone, represent variations of a system of dominant styles, structures and ideologies. What we are observing is a display of particular cultural values in the ways in which many websites are conceived and constructed. These values are predominantly North American, signified more accurately in these "new times" (Hall, 1989) as global ways of communicating, producing images, and commodifying information. Indeed, the commodification of the Web is a well-rehearsed American, if not more broadly western, habit. We have seen it with radio and television. Now we see it with the Web. It comes as no surprise as we observe the homogenizing effects of globalization, enabled, paradoxically, by the very technologies we are examining here for their potential to contribute to anticolonial projects.

When we consider our responses to the touchstone sites, together with our responses to the Indigenous Australian sites, it seems that the homogenizing factor is so prevalent that any oppositional work is severely restricted. Indeed, if the homogenization of the mass media presents an inescapable hegemonic force, we must ask whether the Web can be an authentic site for effective oppositional work. However, the ideas of two theorists, though not writing directly about the Web, suggest that, even if relegated to the margins, there are some ways in which the Web may be used productively in anticolonial projects. First, in his study of resistance to oppressive domination, Scott describes the creation of a social space in which "offstage dissent to the official transcript of power relations may be voiced" (1990, p. xi). Scott calls this place a "social space of a dissident subculture," a space in which "hidden transcripts" (1990, p. xii) may be produced. Dissent is given voice in these hidden transcripts which represent a critique of power spoken behind the backs of the dominant. It may be that the Web could provide a space for the production of Scott's hidden transcripts. We are reminded here of the Indigepol closed-discussion site for Indigenous Australian community activists (Indiginet, 1997).

Second, Odin, invoking Homi Bhabha, suggests that "the borderlands of postcolonial discourse" may indeed constitute "a textual contact zone where the dominant and the marginal cultures meet" (Odin, 1997, p. 615). She points out that Bhabha (1995b, p. 208) terms this zone of interaction as "the enunciation of cultural difference" or the "Third Space" which is marked by hybridity. Bhabha argues that recognizing the existence of the Third Space "may open the way to conceptualizing an *inter*national culture, based not on exoticism or multi-culturalism of the diversity of cultures, but on the inscription and articulation of culture's *hybridity*. . . . And by exploring this hybridity . . . we may elude the politics of polarity" (Bhabha, 1995b, p. 209). Perhaps the Web could provide a site for the enunciation of this Third Space.

We must now ask whether the Indigenous Australian sites, as well as those that relate less directly to Indigenous Australia, can foster the production of Scott's hidden transcripts or recognition of the existence of Bhabha's Third Space, given the oppressive hegemonic constraints of the Web's dominant structures and ideologies. Scott suggests that the strongest evidence for the importance of autonomous social sites in generating hidden transcripts is the strenuous effort made by dominant groups to abolish or control such sites. As far as we know, no such efforts have been made to shut down any Indigenous sites, although this does not preclude the possibility that funding may have been denied those wishing to establish sites.

Our position is, therefore, qualified. Any further exploration of the Web as exhibiting both hegemonic and counter-hegemonic possibilities would need to examine carefully the Web's representational modes – fragmentation, discontinuity, multiplicity, multilinearity, active traversal and active encounter (Odin, 1997). It would also need to examine the threads of the social, the political, and the historical that interweave these modes of representation. A great deal more research is required to understand the links between Web-based literacies and the formation of new relations of social power – how the new textual forms may give rise to new social relations.

Possibilities for social transformation on the Web

In this chapter, we argue that the Web is an interested literacy environment, in much the same way as all social environments are interested, and that on the Web people engage in particular political, moral, and epistemic projects. We base this argument on recent understandings of literacy practices (Gee, 1996; Peters and Lankshear, 1996) and insight into the complex changes to these practices associated with the use of new communication and information technologies (Snyder, 1997).

Literacy practices are irredeemably ideological and implicated in creating and maintaining social hierarchies, differences, advantages, and disadvantages. Furthermore, all literacies, like all D/discourses (Gee, 1996), are historically contingent, socially constructed and, to that extent, *transformable.* (Peters and Lankshear, 1996). At the same time, new media, such as the Web, which are enabled by new technologies, are giving rise to "institutional realignments" that are "shifting the boundaries between what used to be clear-cut divisions between (corporate) producers of media texts and (audience) consumers" (Luke, 1995, p. 16). New media are also creating new languages and symbolic systems resulting in "new dimensions of meaning, knowledge production and sociality" (Luke 1995, p. 14). Further, new media are encouraging greater participation by a more socially diverse population. This diversity "challenges traditional views of "national culture" or even the singular hegemony of American culture as a global benchmark" (Luke, 1995, p. 16). What does all this mean for Indigenous Australians and for those working the Web in postcolonial Australia?

Despite the growing influence of critical social literacies, contemporary Indigenous Australian literacy policies and programs, from beginning school to adult, continue to be dominated by the belief that improved literacy levels will allow Indigenous people to participate more fully in the economic and social life of Australia. This belief, however, is ill-founded. It is impossible to prove a direct relationship between levels of education and the degree of social and economic participation. Other critical factors, such as the economic climate and policy environment (Luke *et al.*, 1993), and enduring racialization practices (McConaghy, forthcoming) continue to intervene with the result that some people and groups remain disadvantaged and excluded.

While we argue that everything possible should be done to enable Indigenous people to make "the voyage in" (Said, 1993), to have a voice that counts, we also argue that *all* Australians have a role to play in the scrutiny of the textual representations evident in social and political structures. Subjecting these representations to close examination is an ongoing process, particularly in the face of a resurgence of racism. We need to be mindful of the influences of both text and context in our anticolonial work – of both the textual and the material projects of oppression. For we know, as the critique of Aboriginalist representations demonstrates, that textual representations have real material consequences.

Understanding the Web's limitations in achieving social transformations is explained in part by a consideration of the Web and the phenomenon of intertextuality. Media texts "cannot be studied independent of their inter-textual connections to other popular cultural discourses, or the social relations and cultural politics within which those texts are consumed and given meaning" (Luke, 1995, p. 15). In Australia today, a vigilant group of white supremacists continues to undermine the gains made in recent decades in relation to a culturally diverse Australia. There are also exam-ples of structural and institutional policies and practices, some of which are a legacy of past ideological assumptions, but some of which represent new initiatives, that collectively constitute new Australian colonialisms. So while we are celebratory of the possibilities for Indigenous representations on the Web, we understand that Indigenous voices alone, whether on the Web or in other locations, are not sufficient to change Australian social, cultural, and political structures (McConaghy, 1997b). While the new racisms in popular discourse continue to flourish, Indigenous Australians will remain ambivalently positioned in Australian society.

We also question the relationship between new technologies and the reproduction of social disadvantage. Not only the Web, but information technologies more generally, are often seen to have the potential to create egalitarian communities based on an increased understanding and accep-tance of cultural difference. Far from the "linguistic utopias" described by Pratt (1987, p. 48), as providing discursive landscapes that are the same for all participants, no matter their class, race, gender, and/or ethnicity, the Web emerges as another site for the production of racist discourses. As Selfe and Selfe (1994) have pointed out, the democratic potential of the new technologies is limited by the types of cultural information that pass along the maps of computer interfaces. These interfaces are sites of racism and sexism in very much the same ways as other communicative contexts are sites of racism and sexism. Further, not all social and cultural groups are similarly advantaged by developments in information and communica-tions technologies. For example, while Yuendumu, an Aboriginal community in Central Australia, can boast a long history of using interactive video for educational programs, down the road, Papunya struggles to maintain basic telephone services.

Engaging the local with the global through the Web

Although a very new form of media, the Web has already generated consid-erable interest within Indigenous Australia. It is viewed with a degree of optimism, as Geoff Harman (1998) explains in relation to establishing his own site: "In the main I have faith in this technology and reckon it's gonna change things for the better." Whereas community television and video production are claimed to promote self-determination, cultural maintenance, and the prevention of cultural disruption (Langton, 1994), the Web provides for a range of alternative possibilities for cultural and economic production, such as "the selling of Indigenous stories" at the Pekin Yalkin (1998) site. But even while observing this optimism and the ways in which the Web provides opportunities for social, cultural, and political acts of resistance, we argue that it also plays an important part in the reproduction of social difference.

Australian colonialism has a 210-year history in which many Indigenous people have been dispossessed, displaced, and disenfranchized. The social disadvantages experienced by many Indigenous Australians are a subject of at least great national shame, if not global. The Web contains possibilities for both redressing and perpetuating this disadvantage. It is not sufficient to support Indigenous voices on the Web. Also required is ongoing vigilance against the lies and distortions of racists as well as concerted efforts to confront the material and structural consequences of a national history which has continued to cast Indigenous Australians as Other. In relation to the latter, we are reminded that Australian colonialism incorporates not only the oppressions resulting from the excesses of the extreme right, but also the more insidious contradictions of Australian liberalism that espouse fairness and freedoms for all, while continuing to contain Indigenous Australians within textual (and other) enclosures. We see evidence of the exploitative and oppressive nature of Australian liberal representations on the Web, together with the more obviously racist, as in other forms of textual representation.

In their fight to self-identify and self-represent, Indigenous Australians are not alone. The struggles of the local are also the struggles of the global. It is something of a paradox that the hegemonic powers of the new globalized media that may serve to thwart local struggles may, when local contests move to the global theatre, actually enhance opportunities for engaging in counter-hegemonic work. Although the struggles of postcolonial Australia are unique, we are aware, through our engagement with the Web, that we are part of a global community within which similar struggles are taking place. The trajectories of peoples previously separated by geographic and historical disjuncture now intersect (Odin, 1997). Perhaps, in the final analysis, the possibilities for engaging the local in the global through the Web represent the new medium's greatest potential.

References

Attwood, Bain (1992) "Introduction" in Attwood, Bain and Arnold, John (eds) *Power, Knowledge and Aborigines*. Special Edition of Journal of Australian Studies, Bundoora, Victoria: La Trobe University Press in association with the National Centre for Australian Studies, Monash University.

Bhabha, Homi (1995a) "Of Mimicry and Man: The Ambivalence of Colonial Discourse" in Bhabha, Homi, *The Location of Culture*, London: Routledge, pp. 85–92.

Bhabha, Homi (1995b) "Cultural Diversity and Cultural Differences" in Ashcroft, Bill, Griffiths, Gareth, and Tiffin, Helen, (eds) *The Postcolonial Studies Reader*, New York: Routledge, pp. 206–209.

Danaja, Peter and Garde, Murray (1997) "From a distance: Aboriginal Music on the Maningrida World Wide Web site," paper presented at the Fulbright Symposium, Darwin, July 22–24, "Indigenous Cultures in an Interconnected World."

European Union (1997, December) http://agenor.consilium.eu.int/ (virtual visit)

Freire, Paulo (1972) *Pedagogy of the Oppressed*, Harmondsworth: Penguin.

Gee, James (1996) *Social Linguistics and Literacies: Ideology in Discourses*, 2nd edn, London: Taylor & Francis.

Geocities (1997, December) http://geocities.com/SiliconValley/5620/

Goldberg, David, Theo (1993) *Racist Culture: Philosophy and the Politics of Meaning*, Oxford: Blackwell.

Graffiti (1997, December) http://www.graffiti.org/

Hall, Stuart (1989) "The Meaning of New Times." in Hall, Stuart, and Jacques, Martin (eds) *New Times: The Changing Face of Politics in the 1990s*, London: Lawrence and Wishart, pp. 116–134.

Hall, Stuart (1996) "When was the 'Post-Colonial'? Thinking at the Limit," in Chambers, Iain and Curti, Lidia (eds) *The Post-Colonial Question: Common Skies, Divided Horizons*, London: Routledge, pp. 242–260.

Harman, Geoff (1998, February 8) [Online]. atsiuni@mail.koori.usyd.edu.au Available E-mail: ghannan@space.net.au [Accessed 09.15, 8 February 1998].

Hobson, John (1997a). "Strategies for Building an Indigenous Australian Cybercommunity: The KooriNet Project" paper presented at the Fulbright Symposium, Darwin, July 24–2, "Indigenous Cultures in an Interconnected World."

Hobson, John (1997b) *"Where are all the Aboriginal Home Pages? The current Indigenous Australian Presence on the WWW,"* paper presented at the Fifth International Literacy and Education Research Network Conference, 1–4 October Alice Springs.

Hodge, Bob (1990) "Aboriginal Truth and White Media: Eric Michaels Meets the Spirit of Aboriginalism," *Continuum* 3(2): 201–205.

Hodge, Bob and Mishra, Vijay (1991) *Dark Side of the Dream: Australian Literature and the Postcolonial Mind*, Sydney: Allen & Unwin.

HotWired (1997, December) http://www.hotwired.com/frontdoor/

Human Rights and Equal Opportunity Commission (1997) *Report of the National Inquiry into the Separation of Aboriginal and Torres Strait Islander Children from their Families*, Canberra: Australian Government Printing Service.

Indignet (1997, December) http://www.indigenet.unisa.edu.au/ [Accessed December 1997].

International Herald Tribune (1997, December). http://www.iht.com/

Johnston, Eric (1991) *National Report: Overview and Recommendations. Royal Commission into Aboriginal Deaths in Custody*, Canberra: Australian Government Printing Service.

Joyce, Michael (1997) "New Stories for New Readers: Contour, Coherence and Constructive Hypertext," in Snyder, Ilana (ed.), *Page to Screen: Taking Literacy into the Electronic Era*, Sydney: Allen & Unwin and New York: Routledge, pp. 163–182.

Katz, Elihu, Wedell, George (1977) *Broadcasting in the Third World*, Cambridge MA: Harvard University Press.

Landow, George (1992) *Hypertext: The Convergence of Contemporary Critical Theory and Technology*, Baltimore, Maryland: Johns Hopkins University Press.

Langton, Marcia (1994) "Aboriginal Art and Film: The Politics of Representation," *Race and Class* 35(4): 89–106.

Luke, Alan, Nakata, Martin, Garbutcheon Singh, Michael, Smith, Richard (1993) "Policy and the Politics of Representation: Torres Strait Islanders and Aborigines at the Margins," in Lingard, Bob, Knight, John and Porter, Page (eds) *Schooling Reform in Hard Times*, London: The Falmer Press, pp. 139–152.

Luke, Carmen (1995) "Multimedia Multiliteracies," *Education Australia*, 30: 14–17.

McClintock, Anne (1995) *Imperial Leather*, New York: Routledge.

McConaghy, Cathryn (1985) "The Use of Video in Aboriginal Adult Education," *East Arnhem Adult Education and Training News* 1(2): 8.

McConaghy, Cathryn (1997a) "Knowing Indigenous Adult Education: A Study of the Production of Disciplinary Knowledges in a Colonial Context," unpublished Ph.D. thesis, University of Queensland, Brisbane.

McConaghy, Cathryn (1997b) "Colonial Desires and the Contradictions of Australian Liberalism," in Soliman, Izabel (ed.), *Does the Body Count?*, Department of Women's and Gender Studies, Armidale, New South Wales: University of New England.

McConaghy, Cathryn (1997c), "The Flexible Delivery of Critical Adult Literacies in Postcolonial Times," in Singh, Michael, Garbutcheon Harreveld, Bobby and Hunt, Nikki (eds), *Virtual Flexibility: Adult Literacy and New Technologies in Remote Communities*, Rockhampton: Central Queensland University Press, pp. 29–41.

Maningrida (1997, December) *http://www.peg.apc.org/~bawinanga/welcome.html* [Accessed December 1997].

Michaels, Eric (1986) *The Aboriginal Invention of Television in Central Australia 1982–1986*. Report of the Fellowship to assess the impact of television in remote Aboriginal communities. Canberra: Australian Institute of Aboriginal Studies.

Michaels, Eric (1994) "Aboriginal content: Who's Got It – Who Needs It?" in Michaels, Eric, *Bad Aboriginal Art: Tradition, Media, and Technological Horizons*, Minneapolis, Minnesota: University of Minnesota Press, pp. 21–48.

Nakata, Martin (1991) "Placing Torres Strait Islanders on a Sociolinguistic and Literate Continuum: A Critical Commentary," *The Aboriginal Child at School* 19: 39–53.

Narogin, Mudrooroo (1990) *Writing from the Fringe: A Study of Modern Aboriginal Literature*, Melbourne: Hyland House.

New London Group (1996) "A Pedagogy of Multiliteracies: Designing Social Futures," *Harvard Educational Review* 66(1): 60–92.

Odin, Jaishree, K. (1997) "The Edge of Difference: Negotiations between the Hypertextual and the Postcolonial," *Modern Fiction Studies* 43(3): 598–630.

Pekin Yalkin (1998, February) http://www.space.net.au/~ghannan/ [Accessed February 1998]

Peters, Michael and Lankshear, Colin (1996) "Critical Literacy and Digital Texts," *Educational Theory* 46(1): 51–70.

Pratt, Mary Louise (1987) "Linguistic Utopias," in Fabb, Nigel (ed.) *The Linguistics of Writing*, Manchester: Manchester University Press, pp. 48–66.

Richardson, Paul (1997) "The New Literacy Studies and Situated Cognition," *The Australian Journal of Language and Literacy* 20(4): 333–340.

Said, Edward (1978) *Orientalism: Western Conceptions of the Orient*, London: Penguin.

Said, Edward (1993) *Culture and Imperialism,* London: Chatto & Windus

Samsung (1997, December) http://www.samsung.com/

Sassen, Saskia (1997) "Electronic Space and Power," *Journal of Urban Technology* 4(1): 1–17.

Scott, James, C. (1990) *Domination and the Arts of Resistance: Hidden Transcripts,* New Haven and London: Yale University Press.

Selfe, Cynthia, L., Selfe, Richard (1994) "The Politics of the Interface: Power and its Exercise in Electronic Contact Zones," *College Composition and Communication* 45(4): 480–504.

Snyder, Ilana (1996) *Hypertext: the Electronic Labyrinth,* Melbourne: Melbourne University Press and New York: New York University Press.

Snyder, Ilana (1997) (ed.) *Page to Screen: Taking Literacy into the Electronic Era,* Sydney: Allen & Unwin and London and New York: Routledge.

Street, Brian (1995) *Social Literacies: Critical Approaches to Literacy in Development, Ethnography and Education,* London: Longman.

Sykes, Roberta (1997) *Snake Cradle,* Sydney: Allen & Unwin.

University of Sydney (1997, Dec) Discussions since May 1997; available e-mail: *atsiuni@mail.koori.usyd.edu.au*

VICNET (1998, December) http://dargo.vicnet.net.au/aboriginal/default.cfm [Accessed February 1998].

Walton, Christine (1993) *Critical Social Literacies,* Darwin: Northern Territory University Press.

Yeatman, Anna (1996) *Citizenship, Choice and Voice,* Abstracts: Culture and Citizenship Conference, Australian Key Centre for Cultural and Media Policy, Brisbane, 30 September to 2 October, p. 91.

Yorta Yorta (1997, December) http://users.mcmedia.com.au/~yorta/yorta.htm [Accessed December 1997].

Yothu Yindi (1997, December) http://www.yothuyindi.com/ [Accessed December 1997].

Yunupingu, M. (1993) "Indigenous Education," in *Voices of the Land,* Boyer Lectures, Sydney: ABC Books.

Part 2

LITERACY, DIVERSITY, AND INDENTITY ON THE WEB

4

COMPLICATING THE TOURIST GAZE: LITERACY AND THE INTERNET AS CATALYSTS FOR ARTICULATING A POSTCOLONIAL PALAUAN IDENTITY

Karla Saari Kitalong and Tino Kitalong

In October 1994, Palau, an island nation in the Western Pacific, gained its independence after a century of colonial rule. In this chapter, we describe how the Internet has contributed to the development of a postcolonial Palauan identity. That story begins, as so many do, with a tragedy.

On Thursday, 26 September 1996, at about 5:45 p.m., in the midst of preparations for the second anniversary of Palauan independence, the Koror–Babeldaob Bridge collapsed. Electricity, water, sewer, and communication lines were severed between Palau's two main islands, Koror, the national capital, and Babeldaob, the larger island on which are located the power and water facilities and the airport. Two people died in the disaster, and several were injured. The 20-year-old bridge had just been repaired; the cause of the collapse remains unclear, although investigations continue. In June 1997, on the eve of the third anniversary of Palauan independence, Palau's bi-weekly newspaper, *Tia Belau News*, reported that a temporary bridge was being installed ("Temporary Bridge," 1997). As the fourth anniversary of independence approached, in the summer of 1998, planning for a new permanent bridge was just underway ("Babeldaob Governors," 1998).

The bridge collapse created adverse political, economic, social, and financial effects for the citizens of Palau, the ramifications of which will be felt for years to come. But with adversity in one realm came synergy in another: within days of the disaster, two electronic spaces built and controlled by Palauans emerged – an e-mail list for discussion of the bridge collapse and a website that displayed scanned images and news reports – that initiated a new era for Palau. For the first time in history, news that previously might have taken months or even years to percolate out to thousands of expatriate Palauans[1] in the Pacific Basin, the US mainland, and elsewhere, was available almost immediately. More importantly, the two sites, and the many others that have followed, provide a significant Palauan-created and -sustained counterforce to the "tourist gaze" that prevails on the Web. As we'll demonstrate in this paper, Palauan-made Internet spaces also enable Palauans – whether or not they live in Palau – to build community, teach and learn about their cultural heritage, and engage in important social action.

Viewed from a global perspective, the stories we tell in this chapter seem insignificant. After all, on a map of the world, Palau is merely a tiny cluster of dots in the western Pacific Ocean just north of the equator, dwarfed by its nearest neighbors, New Guinea to the south and the Philippine Islands to the west. Although search engines make it easy to find Palau on the Web, the tourist gaze – because of Palau's attractiveness as a destination for divers – authorizes the "hits" that are found. The following description, from the "Aggressor Fleet" home page,[2] perennially at the top of search engine hit lists, is typical of the language of the Palau-oriented websites aimed at the tourist market:

> Just 600 miles east of the Philippines drifts a tropical lei of over 300 islands known as Palau (Belau). With its magnificently abundant reef, drift and wall dive sites, Palau garners distinction as another of the "World's Seven Underwater Wonders."

Descriptions such as this call tourists not to a remote-island community but to a kind of uninhabited underwater theme park. True to form, the Aggressor Fleet description continues with the following solicitation.

> No one's better qualified to guide you through its magical melange of caverns and coral gardens, marine lakes and blue holes, shark encounters and caves, and walls and wrecks, than the new, sumptuous Palau Aggressor II.

Considerably further down in the list of search engine hits, another of Palau's claims to fame – its role as a famous World War II battleground – is highlighted in the Discovery Channel's "Beast of Eden" website.[3] In the autumn of 1944, a bloody – and some say unnecessary – Pacific Theater battle, the Battle of Peliliu, was fought on Palauan soil as Japan and the United States struggled for control of the strategically placed islands (see also Sledge, 1991). The Beast of Eden site reveals that during this two-month-long battle over a piece of land the size of 20 football fields, some 10,000 US troops and nearly 11,000 Japanese died.

The "Old Dispatches" section of the Beast of Eden site consists of the Discovery Channel project team's day-by-day chronicle of their work in Palau. Here, we find some evidence that there are Palauans living in Palau. But what kind of people are they? If we believe the Discovery Channel team, Palauans are naïve: "last night we schmoozed the High Chief of Koror with a Discovery Channel Online T-shirt, so we figure we're pretty much untouchable." Palauans are indifferent about schedules: "like late departures – late anything – no explanation is required." Palauans' English-language skills are inadequate, as well, by the Discovery Team's standards. A taxi driver is described as speaking "with a thick pidgin English," while a boat captain's English is rated "good," but "his guttural accent is so thick that sometimes he talks like he's got bugs in his mouth." Finally, Palauans are resigned to whatever fate befalls them:

> When I asked a local woman what had happened to [the Koror–Babeldaob Bridge], she said, "It collapse." "Earthquake?" I asked. "No. Just collapse." She said it is as though these things just happen sometimes. And perhaps in Palau they do.

On the Web, as these offensively ethnocentric examples show, outsiders' representations and interpretations – what anthropologist Jocelyn Linnekin calls the tourist gaze – not only conceal or caricature Palauan people, culture, language, and politics so that outsiders do not see a full picture, but more problematically, offer Palauans themselves "a distorted mirror for viewing their own lifeways" (Linnekin, 1997, p. 216; see also Kincaid, 1989). Fortunately, the tourist gaze is being supplemented on the Internet by Palauan self-representations. In this chapter, we discuss a number of Internet sites created by and for Palauans to illustrate some mostly modest and tentative – but occasionally aggressive – ways that Palauans have been using the Internet to begin to articulate a postcolonial identity and to reshape the literacies they have acquired through a century or more of colonial rule.

As Palauans represent themselves on the Web, they are engaging in a literacy practice that Mary Louise Pratt calls "transculturation," whereby "members of subordinated or marginal groups select and invent from materials transmitted by a dominant or metropolitan culture" (Pratt, 1991, p. 36). This paper provides examples of transculturation in action: instances in which Palauans have appropriated the Internet in general and the Web in particular as spaces within which to teach and learn about Palauan culture, language, and people; to help determine "key issues of community identity" (Street, 1995, p. 110); and to enact important social action for their national development.[4] Although Palauans acquired both their literacy practices and their Web development proficiency within western institutions, governed by western literacy traditions and practices, our analysis of these early examples of Palauan-made Web pages suggests that within a culture's communicative repertoire, a range of coexisting literacy practices and influences typically are employed for different purposes (Street, 1995, p. 44), and that literacy practices imposed by outsiders can be adapted and integrated with local knowledge (Pratt, 1991, p. 36).

Palauans' literacy and subsequent Internet activity are framed within the country's long and tangled colonial history. Not surprisingly, the printed historical record of Palau, like much of the Web content, is written from an outsider's point of view. From the outsiders' histories, we learn that Palau, or Belau, as the natives call it,[5] is a tiny cluster of volcanic islands, located in the Western Pacific Ocean. The histories also tell us that, like many small island nations, Palau has been visited repeatedly by explorers and colonizers, beginning as early as the mid-1500s. The first to arrive were English and then Spanish traders, followed by Spanish Catholic missionaries (Leibowitz, 1996, p. xxi). The Spanish Capuchin missionaries established the first school in Palau in 1891, where they found that "the children were very eager to learn and surprisingly faithful in their attendance" (Hezel and Levin, n.d.).

In 1898, Spain sold Palau to the Germans, but the Spanish Capuchins continued to operate the schools for a few years. By 1907, however, "German Capuchins had replaced their Spanish counterparts" as educators, while Palau's high chief had "built at his own expense a school for his village's high-ranking children." The German government, which usually relegated responsibility for education to the priests, did establish the first government-sponsored school in Micronesia, consisting of a "program to instruct local policemen in the German language and arithmetic" (Hezel and Levin, n.d.). The German colonial period also marked the first attempts to commit the Palauan language to writing. A legacy of this early writing consists in the use of the letters "ch" to represent a glottal stop; in many other languages, an apostrophe serves this purpose. (For example, the Palauan word for "yes," is spelled *ochoi* but pronounced *o'oi.*)

The Japanese occupied Palau in 1914 and officially administered the islands between 1920 and 1945 (Leibowitz, 1996, p. xxi). Within a year after taking over the islands, they instituted an extensive public education system offering three years of Japanese language, as well as arithmetic, singing, drawing, and some vocational instruction to any interested Palauan. Certain Palauans were chosen for up to two additional years of schooling (Hezel and Levin, n.d.). Roman Tmetuchl, a prominent Palauan businessman and political leader, took advantage of the Japanese educational system to learn carpentry, one of the vocations available to Palauans. Following his training, Tmetuchl worked as a reporter for a Japanese newspaper, where he demonstrated sufficient investigative skills to become "the first Palauan in the Japanese Police," and, after further training in Indonesia, served as an assistant to the Japanese chief of police in Palau (Henry, 1997, p. 5).

98

Palau was strategically important to the prevailing superpowers at mid-century; therefore, as the "Beast of Eden" website shows, during World War II, American and Japanese troops battled for control of Palau. The "Beast of Eden" website also makes clear how the outsiders' historical record has, to date, nearly always submerged authentic Palauan voices. Thus, although the historical record clearly states that about 20,000 Americans and Japanese perished during one famous battle fought on Palauan soil, the fact that some 1,000 islanders also died in that fighting, either from injuries or from starvation, is buried in an obscure Micronesian studies journal (George, 1995, p. 335).

The American colonial era began immediately after World War II, lasting longer than any other regime – nearly fifty years. While the Spanish colonizers' imperative came from the Catholic church and the Japanese and Germans owed their allegiance to their respective countries, the Americans were answerable to the United Nations Trusteeship Council. In their role as overseers of the islands, they were charged with preparing the citizens for eventual self-government, a goal that necessitated a substantive educational effort.

Roman Tmetuchl's educational experience is fairly representative of opportunities available to select Palauans during the transition from Japanese to American colonial rule, although, of course, he was not the only Palauan to avail himself of such opportunities. Tmetuchl received his American high-school diploma in 1952, and subsequently became "[o]ne of the first Palauans to attend the Pacific Islands Teacher Training School in Guam," (Henry, 1997, pp. 5, 10). Like many people of his age group, Tmetuchl is fluent in Japanese, English, and Palauan. Over the years, he has been a teacher, a politician, and a businessman – owner of a construction company, a legacy of his Japanese vocational training.

William Vitarelli was charged by the US government with building American schools in Palau in the 1950s. Like the early Capuchin teachers, Vitarelli noted that Palauans were "eager for education" (Van Amburgh, 1996). Personally, Vitarelli wanted to establish "markets and schools with Palauans as owners" so as to help Palauans become self-sufficient (Van Amburgh, 1996). However, his stated goals conflicted somewhat with the United States government agenda, which reportedly called for carefully structured educational systems that would "strengthen ... cultural ties between Micronesia and the United States," as a means of encouraging Palauans and other Micronesians to "choose a closer relationship with the United States over independence" (Wilson, 1995, p. 27). Accordingly,

> U.S. educational policies introduced U.S.-oriented curricula, instituted patriotic rituals of the United States, and enforced English as the language used in all the classrooms.
>
> (Wilson, 1995, p. 27)

The islanders' stories of their literacy acquisition under the American regime remains to be told through future research. We do know, however, that with few exceptions, literacy has functioned as a vehicle for presenting a version of the outside world to Palauans, and for teaching them how they should respond to that outside world (see, Street, 1995, p. 15). In many cases, the outside world became more attractive to Palauans than their own circumscribed world. The introduction of television in the late 1970s, for example, crystallized how the western world was represented to the Palauans and how it should be processed. Furthermore, it changed many social and literacy practices, as Keobel Vitarelli-Sakuma notes, explaining how television affected his early literacy experience.

> It encourages people to stay at home instead of moving around the village talking to each other. For some children, the Palauan language became less important when television was introduced, and they became fluent in American English at an early age. Television also contributed to increased commercialism.
>
> (Keobel Vitarelli-Sakuma, personal communication, 21 October 1997)

US educational policies coupled with the introduction of television, then, did not achieve the degree of Palauan self-determination that William Vitarelli is said to have hoped for (Van Amburgh, 1996). Instead, Palauans, like other colonized people – including their Micronesian neighbors – were exposed to a steadily increasing barrage of signs "produced elsewhere" (Penley and Ross, 1992, p. ix) – primarily in the United States. Indeed, the US educational and technology policies strengthened cultural ties between Micronesia and the US; in fact, of the six Micronesian island groups covered by the United Nations trusteeship agreement, Palau is alone in having chosen independence from the US. Palauans have managed to use the literacy gained through over a century of colonial rule to establish themselves as the world's newest independent nation, in the process squelching westerners' attempts to build supertanker ports and oil depositories in their lagoons (Van Amburgh, 1996) and constructing the world's first nuclear-free constitution.[6]

Palau's independence did not happen as quickly or as deliberately as spelled out by the United Nations Trusteeship Council. Fifty years passed between the beginning of the trusteeship agreement and Palau's independence in 1994. Mary Spencer, Director of the Micronesian Language Institute at the University of Guam, considers Palau to be a bilingual-education success story, reporting that "both Palauan and English are official languages" in Palauan schools,[7] with Palauan being the language of instruction in the early grades and English at the high-school level. She notes that

This attention to providing Palauan reading material and expectations that children will learn to both read and write well in their
indigenous language and that English will be acquired as a second
language seem to have paid off. ... Although the average scores
indicate skill in reading 2nd grade English materials, the range of
skills extends considerably, so that by the 12th grade many students
are reading English text materials from 3–12 grade levels.

(Spencer, 1994, p. 209)

Palauans have, in short, enjoyed some measure of success in appropriating
the colonizers' literacy and in maintaining their own native-language literacy.
Yet, they have been afforded precious few opportunities to use literacy as
a means of representing themselves to the outside world. The Internet has
emerged as a potential vehicle through which Palauans can overcome that
limitation and begin to counter the tourist gaze that defines them.

The Internet is the first major technological innovation to be introduced
since Palau declared its independence in 1994. A prominent, if relatively
new and undertheorized literacy site, the Internet is rapidly joining televi-
sual and print media as components of the vast system of signs through
which the world can be attained (Street, 1995, p. 121). As such, the Internet
has the potential to play a substantive role in organizing and shaping the
culture, politics, and literacy practices of even the world's smallest nations.
Like other mass media, though, the Internet is dominated by western
(primarily American) ideologies, values, and language-use practices. In the
remainder of this chapter, we illustrate three of the strategies employed by
Palauan Web developers to create culturally coherent self-representations
that contribute to the construction of a postcolonial Palauan identity and
help to moderate the aggressive yet insufficient tourist gaze that dominates
the Web. The strategies include community building, cultural pedagogy,
and social action.

The community-building function

We have shown how Web representations of Palau focusing on tourism and
World War II have tended to suppress – or worse, caricature – Palauan
people and culture. Some Internet sites are being created by Palauans, on
the other hand, who stress community in strong and culturally coherent ways.

Early Palauan-made Internet sites served a crucial community-building
function in the weeks following the collapse of the Koror–Babeldaob Bridge.
The importance of one such site, the bridge-l e-mail list, has increased, as
expatriate Palauans have become accustomed to logging on to their e-mail
to see what's new back home and to express their views on a variety of
topics that impact their newly independent nation. A second electronic
space became an important locus of information and community building

for Palauans in the months following the bridge disaster. "KB's Island," a website created by Keobel ("KB") Vitarelli-Sakuma, included news clippings and several scanned photos of the collapsed bridge from the *Pacific Daily News*, a Guam newspaper. Unfortunately, when Vitarelli-Sakuma left college for the summer, his website disappeared, and the one he created the following year did not have the same community-building centrality. During the nine months of its existence, though, the original "KB's Island" served a key community-building role that has since been taken up by other Palauans.

For some Palauans, including the Palauan language on their Web pages functions as a form of community building. Outsiders who happen upon Ikrebai Blesam's page,[8] for example, might not even notice her use of the Palauan language in the title bar of the page, where she writes, "*Olekoooi! Ngkuk ngera soam!*" Because Palauan remains an oral language, despite recent codification by linguists and dictionary makers,[9] context is very important in understanding what is meant. Depending upon the context in which it is used, *olekoi* can express surprise, contradiction, or mild exasperation. In this case, exasperation is implied, such as Blesam might feel if she were repeatedly being interrupted with insignificant but persistent requests. By adding extra o's and an exclamation point (*olekoooi!*), Blesam draws out the final syllable to emphasize the exasperation. Then she reinforces and contextualizes this exasperation by adding, "*Ngkuk ngera soam*," which translates roughly as, "Now what do you want?" For the most part, she writes in English, and her Palauan-links page includes commercial pages aimed at an audience of outsiders. Nonetheless, Blesam's strategic placement of a subtly humorous Palauan expression that cannot be translated out of context suggests to other Palauans a mutual, good-humored tolerance of outsiders. In fact, throughout her Web page, Blesam seems to be trying to discourage visitors from exploring by protesting that the page is unfinished.

> I'm not in the "creating my webpage" mood, so don't expect much. Anyways, this page is "under extreme construction," so come back again later. Thanks for stopping ... You have a good day ... chikung! =)

The Palauan word *chikung* is short for *mechikung*, which means "Goodbye." Blesam seems to be turning visitors away, but she inserts a softening "smiley-face" [=)], welcomes visitors with an animated waving hand, and uses the "Mr Yuck" poison-control cartoon to signify her dissatisfaction with the work she has done. In short, Blesam's Web page indicates an awareness of the larger Internet audience, while addressing her in-group (other Palauans) with subtle linguistic humor.

Quay Polloi, a student at the University of Scranton, also uses the Palauan language to greet visitors to his site,[10] but in a more openly inviting way.

His welcome message, "*Eang, Alii-lii!*" ("Well, Hello, hello!"), expresses pleasure and surprise at finding a visitor at his door. *Eang* is another of those Palauan words that has diverse meanings in different contexts. It can mean "why," as it does in a popular Palauan song in which a spurned lover asks, "Why, why, why did you leave me?" It can also function as an attention-getter, a way of breaking into a conversation, in the way Americans might use "Say" or "Well" to begin a sentence. ("Say, did you see last night's newspaper?" or "Well, I think . . .") The contraction *Alii-lii* mimics an oral greeting (Hello, hello!); instead of the grammatically correct *alii alii*, however, Polloi uses an abbreviated conversational form. Unlike Ikrebai Blesam, Polloi makes no apologies for the condition of his well-appointed site.

The Palauan-created websites that we located appeared to be targeted primarily at an audience of other Palauans, rather than to outsiders; the unexplained use of the Palauan vernacular is an aspect of this, but we found other evidence of this practice, as well. For example, Polloi includes pictures but no explanation of the *ngasech*, the Palauan first-baby ceremony. All Palauans and most outsiders who have lived in Palau have attended a *ngasech*, and would thus require no explanation, although the details of the ceremony's integration into Palauan culture go much deeper than is evident to the outsider (see, for example, Wilson, 1995, p. 115). Polloi's inclusion of the photographs without any explanation suggests that he expects them to be of interest mainly to an "insider" audience.

Lois Remeliik of Eastern Oregon University, a member of the family of Haruo Remeliik, the late first president of Palau, dedicates the Palauan section of her home page[11] to her parents and siblings, without mentioning either the fact or the circumstances of the president's death.[12] She apparently expects members of her family to visit the page, as she uses family nicknames for her siblings. Insiders would not need the dedication to note her membership in a prominent family; outsiders would most certainly not make this connection, although they might admire the family devotion she exhibits.

Polloi, Blesam, and Remeliik make subtle use of insider language and visuals to encourage a sense of Palauanness without specifically excluding outgroup members. Other more interactive community-building strategies call upon visitors to reveal themselves as members of the in-group. One such interactive site is Quay Polloi's Palauan e-mail address directory, which simply provides mail-to links so that Palauans can contact others from their country. Such a feature is especially beneficial to members of the growing Palauan diaspora.

Palauans also interactively build community on the Web through the use of guest books. Visitors are invited to enter comments and feedback, to read others' comments, and to paste in their e-mail and Web addresses, all actions that help Palauans find each other in the vast labyrinth that is the Internet.

Two guest-book applications are particularly interesting. While *Full Moon* magazine's website[13] was active, its guest book became a veritable Who's Who of wired Palauans; visitors not only commented on the magazine, but also left personal and general greetings with their contact information attached. The site is still accessible, but is no longer viable. Return visitors were particularly disheartened to find that the site had stagnated; one Oregon-based Palauan's disappointment was almost palpable: "Is this page ever gonna be updated anytime in the nearer future?? It's been quite a while since I last visited and it's still the same!!!!"

A second community-building guest-book application was created by Palauan Web developer Alexander Asuma. Asuma's special-purpose guest book[14] – essentially an electronic sign-up sheet – was designed to gather demographic information about members of the bridge-l e-mail list while concurrently ascertaining the level of interest in and commitment to planning a Palau Youth Conference. Readers of the guest book might have noticed that many Palauans who signed seemed unwilling to share personal details about themselves, and even chastised themselves when they felt that they had revealed too much. Circumspection is highly valued in Palauan society, and self-revelation is discouraged; we will discuss this Palauan cultural trait in more detail in the next section.

As a further community-building strategy, some Palauans have aligned themselves with a broader Pacific Islander community, something that is becoming possible now that inter-island relations need not be filtered through Palau's colonial association with the United States. For example, Quay Polloi's page includes electronic links to Xavier High School alumni. The Catholic high school, located on the island of Chuuk (Truk), in the Eastern Caroline Islands, educates students from throughout the Micronesian islands. In another kind of broadened community-building move, several Palauans, including Asuma,[15] have chosen to register their websites in the thirty-five-member Pacific Islands Web Ring.[16] A Web Ring groups related sites together, making it possible to navigate from site to site with the click of a button. Registering with the Pacific Islands Web Ring implies a *de facto* affiliation with a diverse group including Samoans, Pitcairn Islanders, and the Vaturangans of Guadalcanal.

In short, Palauans build community on the Internet in several ways: by slyly inserting cultural commentary meant only to be noticed or understood by insiders, by signaling their affinity with other islanders, and by including electronic mechanisms designed to bring wired Palauans together. In so doing, these early Palauan Web developers forge, for the first time in a century, important new alliances that don't require the blessing of a colonial power. In the process of community building, they simultaneously educate themselves and others about Palau and its neighboring islands. In the next section, we will describe more direct educational interventions that are being enacted by Palauans on the Internet.

The cultural-pedagogy function

We define cultural pedagogy as a direct intervention into the cultural knowledge-making practices of an individual or group. This pedagogy is enacted by Palauans on the Internet both as a vehicle for Palauans and interested outsiders to understand the culture, and as a medium for negotiating how traditional cultural values should be integrated into postcolonial ways of life. Both of these cultural-pedagogy functions involve active interpretation of existing knowledge, in contrast to the more passive reception of knowledge that is commonplace in traditional colonial education.

Traditionally, Palauan families and clans were secretive about their affairs, and Palauan cultural interactions themselves were mostly hidden from outsiders (Smith *et al.*, 1990). In fact, the modern-day legislature is called "Olbiil era Kelulau," which means "House of Whispered Decisions," a carryover from the days when traditional chiefs met to plan and negotiate in secret. As we noted in the discussion of guest books in the previous section, this cultural habit runs deep: many Palauans are reluctant to reveal personal information to others. Palau's first female senator, Sandra Sumang Pierantozzi, who is an active participant on the bridge-l e-mail list, commented that the secrecy of Palauan customs may ultimately contribute to their gradual erosion, and suggested that this erosion could be curtailed by using the Internet to make Palauan customs known to as many people as possible (Sandra Sumang Pierantozzi, personal communication, 3 November 1997). Included among the people whom Pierantozzi would like to educate about Palauan customs and cultural values are the growing numbers of expatriate Palauans and their children; she includes herself among this group as she is married to a foreigner, and lived abroad for some time. The following e-mail excerpt reveals a bit of self-deprecating humor.

> Through the Internet, our culture is permanently stored for all future generations to read and learn. Palauans, especially those born and raised outside of Palau, can simply log on to Internet and learn about their own culture so that when they return home, they can "fit" in and behave as Palauans rather than those awkward ones who don't quite know how to fit in, if you get my meaning!
> (Sandra Suman Pierantozzi, personal communication,
> 3 November 1997)

In contrast, Patrick Tellei expressed concern that inaccurate materials posted about Palau on the Internet could be construed as the truth about Palau and its culture. After all, he notes,

> a small journal entry has led many people to believe that the inhabitants of the Marianas were thieves, Chamorro people have

had to live with this entry for centuries. Imagine someone posting
something that will be believed all over the globe.
(Patrick Tellei, personal communication, 26 February 1998)

Seemingly unconcerned about this possibility, Alexander Asuma and
Charlene Ongelungel are two Palauans who have used the Web to create
sites devoted to cultural pedagogy about Palau. Asuma's Palauan-
proverbs link[17] includes a table of thirty Palauan metaphorical sayings,
along with their literal and practical translations, that combine to articulate a set of personal characteristics that Palauans recognize as privileged
in their society. One metaphor provides a sense of the qualities that
Palauans value in a leader: *"Ngkora tengadidik el di melekoi el suebed,"* translates literally as "He's like the kingfisher who chatters loudly when flying
off." In Asuma's translation, the saying describes the type of boss who
"suddenly rattles off a series of directions or instructions and then
leaves." On the other hand, *"A ungil el merreder a ua chull el melemedem
er a daob"*; that is, "A good leader is like rain that calms the ocean," which
Asuma translates to mean, "He can calm down disputes and settle problems easily."

The values of common sense and good judgement are contained in the
saying, *"Kekora rubak era Ngerchelong el omtab era bngel era eabed"* ("You're like
the man from Ngerchelong who uses clouds to mark locations of his fish-
traps"). Asuma translates this as, "You depend too much on people who
are unreliable," suggesting the importance of surrounding oneself with
people who can be counted on. Interestingly, the adage does not directly
chastise those who are unreliable, but implies that the person who relies
upon unreliable people lacks judgement. In other words, clouds cannot
help being unanchored, but only a person lacking in common sense would
expect a cloud to stay in one place.

Using Web space on various Internet service providers' servers, Charlene
Ongelungel's work educates people about Palau through scanned images
of Hans Ongelungel's paintings,[18] an incipient Palauan music archive,[19] and
a spoof on the "you might be a redneck" genre, titled "You Know You're
Really Palauan If . . ."[20] She pokes fun at the heavily layered Palauan govern-
mental system, for example, with "You know you're really Palauan if . . .
You walk into a bar, say 'Hey Governor!' and all the men there turn around
. . ." Palauans' casualness about deadlines, so offensive when mocked by the
Discovery Channel team, becomes a gentle gibe: You know you're really
Palauan if "you borrow someone's pots and pans for your party and return
them three months later . . ." Ongelungel's and Asuma's pages complement
each other, and provide some culturally grounded justification for behav-
iors that might be denigrated by culturally unenlightened outsiders.
Ongelungel's audio archive also raises the possibility of providing samples
of Palauan speech – parhaps even language instruction – on the Internet,

to allow those "awkward ones" living abroad to re-engage with *tekoi er Belau* (the Palauan tongue).

Palau was isolated from the media mainstream for hundreds of years, until television brought the world to these remote islands. Like television, the Internet gives Palauans timely access to world news, business, and culture. But, as the story of the Koror–Babeldaob Bridge collapse illustrates, the Internet provides more than television does – instead of a one-way flow of outsiders' news and values to the islands, the Internet provides for a two-way communication channel that not only carries the outside world to Palauans, but also carries news of Palau to citizens living abroad. Moreover, the Internet permits widely scattered Palauans to effect change, as the next section of this chapter illustrates.

The social-action function

The incident that we wish to discuss in this section began on the bridge-l e-mail list, created, about a week after the bridge disaster, by Richard Salvador, a Palauan doctoral student at the University of Hawaii, as one of two means by which Palauans from around the world could learn about and discuss the tragedy (the other was the "KB's Island" website discussed earlier). Although news reports about the bridge rebuilding are still posted from time to time, once the excitement about the bridge collapse had subsided, the list members turned to other topics. For example, Senator Pierantozzi regularly posts news from the legislature and solicits opinions. Salvador, the list's founder, is an indigenous-rights activist, who posts reports and concerns from the organizations of which he is a member. The list is an active forum for cultural pedagogy, as well. For the most part, though, discussions are restricted to bridge-list members only; a key tenet of the list is that the discussions remain secretive, treated as a "backstage," "hidden transcript" (Scott, 1990, p. 27). This is understandable; since the list provides an essential site for the articulation of a postcolonial Palauan identity, Palauans need to feel confident that their comments in that protected space will be excluded from the public eye and from the public record. Accordingly, although the discussion that we introduce here began on the bridge-l list, we will report only on that portion that was carried out on the Web.

In the spring of 1998, a member of the list reported that the availability of Asian prostitutes in Palau was advertised on the Internet.[21] After confirming the website's allegations and exploring the topic for several days, list members created an electronic petition, which was signed by well over 100 Palauans living both in Palau and throughout the United States.[22] This petition was printed out and hand-carried to Palau, where it was presented to the legislature later that spring. The text of the petition was strong and unequivocal.

107

To: Honorable President Kuniwo Nakamura
Senate
House of Delegates
Fr: Belau Bridge List Members and Other Concerned Palauans!

Subj: PETITION REQUESTING MEASURES NEEDED TO COMBAT PROS-
TITUTION IN PALAU; AND EXPRESSING CONCERN OVER LEADERSHIP
PERFORMANCE AND INTEGRITY

Dear Elected Leaders:

The Belau Bridge List is an Internet forum which was instituted
soon after the collapse of the K–B Bridge. At the time, members
shared information on the conditions back home and other matters
concerning Belau. Since then, the membership of the Bridge has
grown to almost two hundred persons at home and abroad. Its
function as a forum for sharing information and discussing Belau
issues has been very rewarding.

Recently, it was brought to our attention that prostitution is in
fact an issue at home. Our concerns over the issue were further
exacerbated when we were informed of an Internet web site which
not only advertised but also described in offensive detail, how one
institution already operates in Palau less than a mile from where
you are sitting.

This advertisement is found at:
http://www.paranoia.com/faq/prostitution/palau_bits.txt.html[23]
and a copy of it is enclosed for your information. In addition, a
Bridge member was recently informed that there were in fact two
establishments, the other one being Crystal Palace which is also
not more than a mile from where you are sitting. It is a shame for
some, if not all, concerned Palauans.

We are further dismayed by the apparent lack of concern from some
legislators and are puzzled as to why pending legislation combating
prostitution has not been passed. Our concern, therefore, is not
limited to prostitution. We are also concerned about the performance of some of our leaders whom we entrusted with our confidence at the voting polls. Granted you have done much good and
we applaud and thank you. However, we have here an issue the solution of which should not be ambiguous or elusive yet no action has
been taken yet. Why is a pending legislation which addresses and
combats a wrong not passed? Does one actually need time to reflect
on the merits of prostitution if there are actually any? If there are
actual merits to prostitution which any of you are reflecting upon,
we would like to know. For now, we are puzzled and concerned.

Therefore, we the undersigned members of the Belau Bridge List and all concerned Palauans, request the Senate, the House of Delegates, and the President to take all action required in addressing and ridding the threat of prostitution in Palau. It is embarrassing, offensive, and degrading, and we do not appreciate any further delay. We also request that any action taken by the Olbiil er a Kelulau and the President be transmitted to the Belau Bridge List for our information.

Kom Kmal Mesulang.

Tia Belau News reprinted the petition in early June ("Concern," 1998), and in the same issue reported that the Olbiil era Kelulau had passed an anti-prostitution bill ("Anti-prostitution Bill," 1998). There is no clear evidence that the petition drive effected the legislative action; however, it may have accelerated the momentum. As late as April a *Tia Belau News* article stated, "As of this writing, [no one] in or outside the government is doing anything about this budding sex trade" ("Sex Joints," 1998). By June, following the intervention of the petitioners, the bill had passed. Whether or not this specific action made an impact, it showed that, using the Internet, a strong, vocal, and organized Internet presence made up of expatriate Palauan citizens can effect coordinated social action of an unprecedented magnitude.

What comes next?

A story that began with challenge and tragedy ends in hope and optimism. Using the Internet, various educational opportunities, and any other resources available to them, Palauans have begun what Penley and Ross call "the complex process by which Western culture [is] reread and reinterpreted in ways that make sense of local cultures and that intersect with local politics" (1992, p. xi), the practice that Mary Louise Pratt refers to as transculturation (1991, p. 36). Taking charge of their own Internet representations, some of the newly independent Palauans have begun actively to rearticulate individual and national identities; renew key cultural values; and clarify and strengthen Palau's global position as an independent entity decoupled from the US.

The positive forces that the Internet brings together are easy to identify, especially from a world citizenship perspective; we have focused on a number of these forces in the preceding pages. Less self-evident and therefore more difficult to identify are the potential dangers that use of the Internet poses to Palauans' salient cultural values. Like many other world citizens, Palauans are concerned about their children's exposure to unsavory influences such as pornography; the anti-prostitution law articulates a commitment to such protection. Senator Pierantozzi's concern about the negative impact of pornography is not specific to Palauans; her reasoning, however, is pointed and culturally coherent.

> I read about x-rated material and other trash being put into the cyberspace. Exposure to such trash can have negative impact on our young people (especially the younger generations who are logging on to Internet). As you all know, in our culture, sex is another very private matter, not as exposed as you would see in other cultures.

Pierantozzi also expresses concern that the same forces that will bring enlightenment to Palauans and explain Palau and its people to the rest of the world will erode the strong family and community values on which Palauans pride themselves.

> Again, exposure to such different cultures and learning their different ways [may corrode] our own cultural values. Another area that might be affected would be our family values. You know in our culture that family and clan values run deep and strong and such values could be corroded from exposure to other cultures.

The last sentence of this passage crystallizes the ambivalence with which she and others regard the Internet's presence in their lives. The advantages that accrue for Palauans when they control their own self-representations may, of course, be offset to some extent by others' rights to do the same.

This initial investigation has sampled how some Palauans have begun to use literacy practices gained through a century of colonial rule to begin to articulate a postcolonial Palauan cultural identity. Senator Pierantozzi, Keobel Vitarelli-Sakuma, and others note that the Internet, like television, provides a potentially negative "enormous bombardment of foreign influence and values," possibly accompanied by the loss of Palauans' own culture, language, and values (Keobel Vitarelli-Sakuma, personal communication, 21 October 1997). Overall, though, Palauans are optimistic about the Internet's potential for enhancing community, creating opportunities for cultural pedagogy, and enacting social action.

Vitarelli-Sakuma expresses concern for those who can't afford a computer or Internet access and states that the Palau National Communication Corporation (PNCC) now holds a monopoly on Internet access, which elevates the price. He notes, too, that the "communications industry is a very lucrative industry these days and would be a very good addition to Palau's economy" (Keobel Vitarelli-Sakuma, personal communication, 21 October 1997). Palau's remote location, which makes it so attractive to tourists, naturally hinders some industrial development, but information is inexpensive to transport. Using the bilingual literacy of its citizens that

Spencer praises so highly, perhaps Palauan businesses could provide information services, thereby diversifying the tourism economy.

In this chapter, through close readings of Internet-based literacy artifacts, coupled with anecdotal evidence gleaned from published reports and personal interviews, we have attempted to raise some of the issues associated with the complex links among literacy, technology, and culture in a small, newly independent island nation. A comprehensive exploration of these issues remains to be carried out.

Acknowledgement

The authors gratefully acknowledge the contributions of Keobel Vitarelli-Sakuma, Senator Sandra Sumang Pierantozzi, and the Palauan Internet pioneers whose work is presented herein.

Notes

1 Sources disagree on the number of Palauans living abroad: the reported number ranges from 3,000 to 6,000.
2 URL: http://www.aggressor.com/palau-aggressor.html [accessed 10 July 1998]
3 URL: http://www.discovery.com/DCO/doc/1012/world/specials/palau/palau1.html [accessed 10 July 1998]
4 As a side note, in the process of developing this chapter, we've been dismayed by the paucity of work that attends to Palauans' acquisition and use of literacy. The historical record is sparse and scattered, and anecdotal evidence was difficult to gather due to time and distance. Therefore, we present this piece as a prologue to a much larger project.
5 We have opted to use the westernized form "Palau" here, because so many of the published works from which we are quoting use that form.
6 The nuclear-free clause was voted down during the long constitution-ratification process; the issue divided Palauans and arguably resulted in the deaths of Palau's first two presidents, Haruo Remeliik and Lazarus Salii (Kluge, 1991; Wilson, 1995; Leibowitz, 1996).
7 The *CIA World Factbook* (URL: http://www.odci.gov/cia/publications/factbook/ps.html) claims that Palau has six official languages, including Palauan, English, Japanese, and three local languages spoken by only a few hundred people each, and that as of 1980, an estimated 92 percent of Palauans aged 15 and over could read and write.
8 URL: http://www.eou.edu/~blesami/
9 The earliest Palauan–English dictionary appeared in 1948 (Capell), and was revised in 1950 (McManus 1950). The definitive work was published in 1977 (McManus 1977).
10 URL: http://academic.uofs.edu/student/cqpl [accessed 10 July 1998].
11 URL: http://www.eosc.osshe.edu/~remelim/ [accessed 10 July 1998].
12 See Kluge (1991) and Leibowitz (1996) for well-written and factual accounts of the volatile pre-independence years in Palau.
13 URL: http://virtualguam.com/biz/fullmoon/index.html [accessed 10 July 1998]. Only one issue of *Full Moon* was placed on the Web; nonetheless, the page and its guest book remain accessible.
14 http://www.geocities.com/SouthBeach/Palms/6757/bridgebio.html? [accessed 16 July 1998].

15 URL: http://www.geocities.com/SouthBeach/Palms/6757/ [accessed 15 July 1998].
16 URL: http://www.webring.org/cgi-bin/webring?ring = pacandid = landlist (Accessed July 15, 1998)
17 URL: http://www.geocities.com/SouthBeach/Palms/6757/proverbs.html
18 URL: http://members.tripod.com/~medidai/rt-ngal.html
19 URL: http://www.geocities.com/The Tropics/Cabana/7635/
20 URL: http://www.geocities.com/The Tropics/Cabana/3065/palau l.html
21 URL: http://www.worldsexguide.org/palau_bits.txt.html [10 July 1998] (Formerly http://www/.paranoia.com/faq/prostitution/palau_bits.txt.html)
22 http://www.geocities.com/SouthBeach/Palms/6757/petition.html [accessed 10 July 1998].
23 Moved to http://www.worldsexguide.org/palau_bits.txt.html as of 10 July 1998

References

"Anti-prostitution Bill Passes House," (6–20 June 1998). *Tia Belau News*, 7, 11.

"Babeldaob Governors Thank K–B Bridge Designers," (25 April to 9 May 1998). *Tia Belau News*, 7, 4.

Capell, Arthur. (1948) *A jibiki tiagid a babier er a bldekel a togoi 'r a Belau ma Merikel ma Merikel ma Belau.* [Palauan–English/English–Palauan dictionary.] 1948. [CIMA report], no. 6.

"Concern Palauans over prostitution" (1998) *Tia Belau News,* 7(11): 10.

George, Karen R. (1995) "Through a Glass Darkly: Palau's Passage through War, 1944–1945," *Isla: A Journal of Micronesian Studies* 3: 313–337.

Henry, Jackson M. (March–April 1997) "Dreams, Visions and Roman Tmetuchl: A Palauan Statesman." *Full Moon,* pp. 4–5, 10, 24, 26.

Hezel, Francis X. and Levin, Michael J. (n.d.). "Micronesian Emigration: The Brain Drain in Palau, Marshalls, and the Federated States," in *Papers of The Micronesian Seminar.* [Online.] Available: http://www.microstate.net/micsem/PALBRAIN.htm [accessed 12 July 1998].

Kincaid, Jamaica (1989) *A Small Place,* New York: Penguin.

Kluge, P. F. (1991) *The Edge of Paradise: America in Micronesia,* New York: Random House.

Leibowitz, Arnold H. (1996) *Embattled Island: Palau's Struggle for Independence,* Westport, CT: Praeger.

Linnekin, Jocelyn. (1997) "Consuming Cultures: Tourism and the Commoditization of Cultural Identity in the Island Pacific," in Picard, Michel and Wood, Robert E. (eds) *Tourism, Ethnicity, and the State in Asian and Pacific Societies,* Honolulu: University of Hawaii Press, pp. 215–250.

McManus, Edwin G. (1950) *English–Palauan dictionary,* Koror. Mimeograph.

McManus, Edwin G. (1977) *Palauan–English dictionary,* edited and expanded by Josephs, Lewis, S. with the assistance of Masa-aki Emesiochel, Honolulu : University Press of Hawaii.

Mitra, Ananda (1997) "Diasporic Web sites: Ingroup and Outgroup Discourse," *Critical Studies in Mass Communication* 14: 158–181.

Penley, Constance and Ross, Andrew (1992) "Introduction," in Penley, Constance and Ross, Andrew (eds), *Technoculture,* Minneapolis, University of Minnesota Press, pp. vii–xvii.

Pratt, Mary Louise (1991) "Arts of the Contact Zone," *Profession 91*: 33–40.

Scott, James C. (1990) *Domination and the Arts of Resistance: Hidden Transcripts*, New Haven: Yale University Press.

"Sex Joints in Internet and Advertised at Airport," (25 April to 9 May 1998) *Tia Belau News*, 7, 3.

Sledge, E. B. (1991) *With the Old Breed: At Peleliu and Okinawa*, New York: Oxford University Press.

Smith, De Verne Reed and the Society of Historians (1990, March) *Rechuodel*, vol. 1. Koror: Ministry of Social Services.

Spencer, Mary L. (1994) "Language, Knowledge and Development: The Micronesian Way," in Morrison, John, Geraghty, Paul and Crowl, Linda (eds) *Sciences of Pacific Islands People*, Suva, Fiji: Institute of Pacific Studies, University of the South Pacific, pp. 199–212.

Street, Brian V. (1995) *Social Literacies: Critical Approaches to Literacy Development, Ethnography and Education*, London: Longman.

"Temporary Bridge Arrives," (28 June to 12 July 1997) *Tia Belau News*, 6, 1.

Van Amburgh, Todd (7 August 1996) "A Lively Renegade: Ha"iku's Dr. William "Vit" Vitarelli," *Haleakala Times Online!* [Online.] Available WWW: http://www.maui.net/~haltimes/7Aug96/p3.htm/

Wilson, Lynn B. (1995) *Speaking to Power: Gender and Politics in the Western Pacific*, New York: Routledge.

5

NORWEGIAN ACCORDS: SHAPING PEACE, EDUCATION, AND GENDER ON THE WEB

Jan Rune Holmevik and Cynthia Haynes

Plate 5.1 Aurora Borealis: Northern Lights
(http://www.csd.uu.se/~ce96vha/norrsken.html [accessed 20 December 1998]

Norwegians call their country Noreg, which means "the way to the north." In some respects, Norway is synonymous with the north. Other Scandinavian countries adopt the Nordic description, among them the sovereign states of Denmark, Finland, Iceland, and Sweden, plus three autonomous territories (the Faeroe Islands, Greenland, and the Aaland Islands). But when the Northern Lights illuminate the wintry Norwegian skies, it truly feels like one is on "the way to the North," amid tales of Vikings, trolls, and (Ibsen's) Nora. That deep and abiding identification with things northern and journeys northward marks Norwegian culture in a number of ways, among which are how Norwegians perceive their role in the global environment and how they prepare themselves for that role. It is not something that Norway boasts about necessarily, though it has made them a quiet force in diplomatic foreign-policy disputes.

Among its many attributes, Norway has earned a global reputation for negotiating peace (most recently with the Oslo accord) and awarding international peace prizes (Nobel Peace Prize). It is not surprising, then, to find the Norwegian people among the most generous and peaceful in the world. Perhaps contributing to their nature is nature itself. Norway is a land of dramatic landscapes where the flow of glacial water is a beautiful reminder of the cycle of life. Even the language is tightly bound to places and geographical features. Holmevik is an excellent example – "holme" means small island, and "vik" means small bay. Holmevik, therefore, is the name of the farm located where the island sits in the bay. Nideros, the earlier name for the city of Trondheim, means the place where the river "Nidar" meets the sea. Norwegian identity is thoroughly entwined with its geography. Combine this with Norway's mythologies, sagas, and nationalism, and the contexts that constitute its literacies are striking factors that merit deeper analysis.

These constants, like cascading waterfalls into countless fjords, spill over into Norwegian ideologies of politics, education, and gender and the situated knowledges that inform them. According to Brian Street, literacy practices, which encompass more than "literacy events," are shaped by ideology and the cultural contexts in which ideologies are played out. In Street's account, ideology is not conceived in the Marxist "sense of 'false consciousness' and simple-minded dogma, but rather in the sense employed by 'radical' groups within contemporary anthropology, sociolinguistics and cultural studies, where ideology is the site of tension between authority and power on the one hand and individual resistance and creativity on the other" (1995, p. 162). Following the lead of Street's articulation of the factors that affect how literacies are formed and how cultural and political formations are affected by literacies, we begin our chapter with *description* and *inscription*. We describe the Norwegian traditions that inscribe the people of Norway as deeply as Viking runes carved in stone, writing that digs its petro/graphical and petroglyphic images into the technologic literacies of Norway at the turn of the millennium.

In addition to including ideology as a defining influence on literacy practices, we also *subscribe* to a wider hermeneutic scope with which to understand literacy itself. Recently The New London Group explained how to "broaden this understanding of literacy and literacy teaching and learning to include negotiating a multiplicity of discourses" (1996, p. 61) in two ways: first, by extending the context of diverse cultural and linguistic societies, and second by extending the "burgeoning variety of text forms associated with information and multimedia technologies" (p. 61). Keeping these constants in mind, our chapter sets forth a dual purpose and a tri-part focus. First, it is concerned with the intricate and interwoven network of literacies that shape Norwegian culture and the cultural and ideological distinctions that shape literacies in Norway. To exemplify and amplify our discussion, we will employ our Norwegian/American perspectives to analyze several websites and the composition and interpretive protocols that they exhibit. Second, it aims to bring these literacies to bear on other Web literacies and the forces that shape them. Each goal focuses specifically on the political, educational, and gendered contexts that mark Norwegian Web literacies as unique lenses with which to view other global Web literacies. Our challenge is to situate Norway within the international communication environment that makes the Web an exciting new space in which multicultural literacies thrive and flow – where literacy meets the sea of culture.

"Cross-country" culture

Norwegian culture is deeply rooted in the cultural diversity of Norway's rural regions. By cultural diversity we do not mean only ethnic diversity, although Norway has certainly become an increasingly multi-ethnic society over the past thirty years, but rather the multitude of local differences in language dialects, architecture, cuisine, customs and traditions that characterize the various regions of Norway. Most people have strong cultural and personal ties to the place where they were born and grew up, and they continue to speak their dialect and uphold regional traditions even when they move away to other parts of the country for school or work. One of the most important factors behind the strong rural flavor in Norwegian cultural heritage is the fact that, historically, Norway has never really had an aristocracy or a dominant urban elite, as most other European countries have had at one time or another. In this absence, the rural cultures have been allowed to influence and dominate the national culture in a profound way. Another effect of the absence of the typical European continental aristocracy and feudalism is that Norwegian peasants for the most part were allowed to be free owners of their own land. As a result, Norway became a very egalitarian society, something that was reinforced and institutionalized with the social democratic governance and the welfare state system since the early 1930s.

Another important part of Norwegian identity is nature. Outdoor activities like hiking and skiing are among the things that Norwegians treasure the most, and on a winter weekend in Oslo, people carrying skis on the subways and trains going out of the city is a common sight. Popular myth has it that Norwegians are born with skis on, and it's easy to see why. For a country with less than one third of New York City's population to take home twenty-five medals in the 1998 Winter Olympic Games in Nagano, Japan (and finish second in the total medal count) shows the passion and pride that Norwegians share for sports and all sorts of outdoor activities.

Their closeness to nature explains to a large extent the deep environmental awareness you will find among Norwegians. The words "miljøværn," meaning environmental protection, and "bærekraftig utvikling," meaning self-sustained growth and development, are keywords in the Norwegian government's policy, and something that almost all Norwegians understand and support. Because of their affinity with nature, environmental protection and self-sustained development means peaceful and harmonic *coexistence* with nature and a balanced and responsible utilization of natural resources that will preserve and cultivate them for the benefit of coming generations. This is why Norwegians continue to hunt non-threatened species of whales much to the condemnation of the rest of the world, particularly environmental organizations like Green Peace. Contrary to how such groups may view Norwegian bioethics, ultimately one has to visit Norway and get to know the people before making judgements.

Of Norway's many cultural treasures, one of the most beloved by Norwegians and all who visit is Vigeland Park in Oslo, named after the sculptor Gustav Vigeland, who created 192 sculptures and over 600 figures between 1907 and 1943. The astounding full-size figures, representing humanity in all its various stages of life and activity, are a unique testament to Norwegian cultural and spiritual identity. Fountains of water spill over "tree groups" symbolizing the relationship between humans and nature. Children frolic; the elderly sustain one another. Vigeland captured profoundly how Norwegians view the human spirit by depicting each figure in the nude and in the full splendor of joy, sorrow, and death. Unlike

Plate 5.2 Vigeland sculptures in Vigeland Park, Oslo.
(http://home.earthlink.net/~roethe/Vigeland/ [accessed 20 December 1998]

the United States, where the elderly are very often shuffled out of sight, Norwegians exhibit a much more holistic approach to the stages of life, and their attitude of abiding compassion and respect for age stands out among other cultures.

The same holds true for the ways in which children and the physically and mentally challenged members of Norwegian society are treated. It is not uncommon to see groups of children, shepherded by their teachers, skipping and squealing toward the parks, among the Christmas shoppers at the mall, or staring in wonder at paintings or artifacts in museums. In Norway, parental leave makes it possible for fathers and mothers to take time off to be with their families when children are born. Children are also taught at an early age to respect their families (young and old), to protect the environment, and to foster an interest in social and political issues.

In the video, *Crossing the Stones*, Norwegian philosopher Arne Næss discusses "deep ecology," a term he coined "to express a vision of the world in which we protect the environment as a part of ourselves, never in opposition to humanity. Deep sensitivity to nature is the articulation of something that every child understands. And for Næss, knowledge of the deepest kind should bind humanity to nature, and not push us further away from the tactile object of its study" (*Crossing*). On Norway's official government home page, two children introduce other young people to Norway. Kari says, "I like playing football [soccer] and am interested in protecting nature and the environment. It seems strange to me that people are not more concerned about taking care of the world we live in." Øyvind says, "I am interested in working for peace and in helping the developing countries. All human beings have a right to food and education. My greatest hope is that someday there may be real peace in the world."[1]

Shaping peace has become a hallmark of the Norwegian position in global politics. Norway is home to the Nobel Peace Prize, which constitutes a defining perception of Norway as a world leader in the peace process. Attempts to negotiate peace in the Middle East were initiated among world leaders meeting in Oslo in 1993, and the talks resulted in what is now known as the Oslo Accord. Peace at home is also paramount to Norway's political identity. As an occupied country in the Second World War (and the subject of rule under Denmark and Sweden for many centuries), Norwegians share a heightened sense of nationalism and pride in their social democratic government. Similar to Independence Day in the United States, Norway celebrates its national day on 17 May, a date that marks the secession from Denmark in 1814, and the proclamation of one of the first constitutions in the world. Other important dates in Norwegian cultural consciousness are 7 June 1905, when, after 600 years of Danish and Swedish economic and political rule, Norway became a sovereign national state, and 8 May 1945, when the country was liberated from five years of Nazi occupation and government. Norway is a monarchy, and the royal family, King

Harald the fifth, Queen Sonja, Princess Märtha Louise, and Crown Prince Haakon are well loved and respected.

Today, Norway is a powerful and affluent nation, rich in natural resources and industries such as oil, shipping, and fishing. However, life in Norway is quite diverse depending on whether you live in the city or in the country. Thomas Eriksen writes:

> In the essay "Norway out of step" (1984), the German sociologist and student of Norway, Hans Magnus Enzenberger, sketches an ironic but friendly picture of his interpretation of Norwegian characteristics. Enzenberger's Norway is a paradoxical society which in many ways is still a rural community on the outskirts of Europe, but it is also one of the world's most modern and advanced societies with regard to state administration and development of high technology. Enzenberger's diagnosis can be summarised like this: "Norway is currently Europe's biggest folk museum but simultaneously a huge laboratory of the future."
>
> (Eriksen, 1996)

In many ways, then, Norway has managed to preserve its history while also preparing its people for life in the new millennium. In part, we attribute this to the influence of Americanism now so ubiquitous in Norwegian culture. Eriksen explains that, "[a]s in other well-off countries, mass culture in Norway is nearly synonymous with American mass culture: pop and rock, jeans and T-shirts, American films, TV series such as 'Baywatch,' burgers and cola." For example, when asked whether the Web (and specifically the six websites used as touchstones in this volume) expands his sense of being in the world versus being Norwegian, Johan Utne Poppe writes:[2]

> The question implies that I normally walk around feeling part of some specific "Norwegian" culture that is very different from all others, and honestly I don't. I'm not saying that I don't feel like a Norwegian, or I feel like a human, or a citizen of the world, or any such high-flying crap. I'm saying that the Norwegian culture I am a part of is interlocked, and has been for a long time, with the rest of the world. HotWired isn't something alien. It's quite normal and familiar – a part of my culture. And to the degree there is a difference, a feeling of "otherplace" by reading HotWired, it is not something specific for the web. The question suggests that the Internet in general and specifically the web might give me a fundamentally new, and more encompassing, experience with other cultures. But my "norwegianness" has been challenged and influenced by impulses from other cultures all my life – by books, TV, music, films and magazines. The Internet isn't *that* different from these media.

Such comments are most common among latter generations of Norwegians, especially the postwar generations who began studying English from fourth grade on as part of the required curriculum and who have been exposed to American consumer products for many years. Of course, other languages and cultures have influenced literacy practices in Norway as well. Most major news-stands in Norway, for example, carry magazines and newspapers in Norwegian, Swedish, Danish, English, German, French, and Spanish. When asked whether she tends to look at Web pages in English or Norwegian, Torill Mortensen (a teacher at Volda College) replied, "both," and she added German as well. She also selects "all languages" when using search engines on the Web. The fact that she did not begin using a computer until she was 26 years old, and yet now integrates the Web in her teaching and research, indicates a high level of proficiency in multicultural and multilingual literacy practices that preceded her current perceptions of and use of the Web.

Tourists have also influenced the Norwegian sensibility to other cultures. For example, in Geiranger, a small rural community nestled at the end of the most beautiful fjord in all of western Norway (and where Jan Rune Holmevik was born and raised), the local people (some 250 residents) have met and hosted countless tourists in the last 100 years, from those disembarking from the many cruise ships that visit each year, to those who arrive on bus tours or for camping. Many of the tourists are North American, though most are from other Scandinavian countries or elsewhere in Europe and Asia. It is not uncommon to find taco fixings at the only store in Geiranger, a welcome sight for a Texan! In general, when in Norway, as Hilde Corneliussen put it, "English is in the air."

Reading Norway

Given that Norwegian culture is suffused with American and European cultural influences, it is not surprising that reading and writing are deeply ingrained in the people, but Norway also boasts its own lengthy and rich literary history. By 1928, Norway enjoyed the distinction of having two winners of the Nobel Prize for literature (Knut Hamsun in 1920 and Sigrid Undsett in 1928). The literary traditions ranging from the Viking sagas to such twentieth-century notables as Undsett, Hamsun, and Henrik Ibsen are rivaled only by the Norwegian musical and artistic traditions made famous by composer Edvard Grieg and painter Edvard Munch. And since America received a large number of Norwegian immigrants beginning in the nineteenth century, several American websites that feature Norwegian literature have emerged. At a site called Links to Scandinavia we found a succinct explanation of Norwegian literacy:

> Norwegians have one of the world's highest literacy rates, and are second only to Iceland in the number of books they read on an

average basis. Norwegians also are prolific writers, and a number of their authors are world renowned and have been translated to scores of languages. In Norway, Easter Crime (Påskekrim) doesn't mean break and entries in the holiday season but new mystery books available for reading during the Easter vacation. Some attribute it to the national character, another explanation is the climate with long and dark winter nights. During Easter vacation, people go to their cabins, usually equipped without phones or television, relying on a radio (for weather reports) and a selection of the spring crime books for entertainment. One result of the high literacy and reading level in Norway is that authors actually get paid, often well, for writing, unlike their counterparts in many parts of the modern world.

> (http://www.nq.com/nordic/norway/norlitt.html,
> 20/12/98, produced by Tor Rognmo)

Language, it seems, informs everything Norwegian, from the primitive runic inscriptions preserved over hundreds of years, to the pride in dialect discussed earlier. Even Hamsun, Norway's pre-eminent novelist before the Second World War (and many say afterwards as well), harbored the urge to write (to "language") his experience in the form of novels. Following a hearing that judged his association with Nazi officials during Norway's occupation, Hamsun was confined to an asylum and forbidden to write. So driven was he to prove his innocence and to chronicle his sanity, Hamsun wrote his last novel in the margins of a library book he was allowed to read. The following excerpt from an online essay on Hamsun by Lars Frode Larsen attests to Hamsun's courage to write:

> Both during and after the Second World War, many Norwegians would, had they had the power to do so, have exhorted Hamsun to return to the anonymity from which he had once emerged. Yet it was impossible to reduce Knut Hamsun to silence. His need to express himself and his urge to write were too strong. That his talent, too, was unimpaired he showed in *On Overgrown Paths* (*På gjengrodde Stier*) 1949. In this, his last book, he hit back at the director general of public prosecutions and the psychiatrists for their treatment of him. That apart, the work exudes resignation and sadness. Old and new events parade before the incessantly writing man of letters: "One, two, three four – thus I sit and make notes and write little pieces for myself. It is to no purpose, just an old habit. I leak muted words. I am a dripping tap, one, two, three, four – .

The Hamsun connection between literature and politics has tainted, to a slight degree, his legacy, and to this day there are no public monuments to him or his work. It is a sore subject among Norwegians torn between loyalty and pride and the new global political and economic roles they have recently begun to play.

Shaping economic peace

Comparatively speaking, Norwegian politics has played a major role in global peace only in recent years. The Nobel Peace Prize, awarded from the Nobel Institute in Oslo, is a highly coveted honor and no doubt the major factor in the recent Middle East peace effort aptly named the Oslo Accord. Norway is also distinguished as one of the few nations to vote against joining the controversial European Union. Opting instead to join the European Economic Area (EEA), Norway sent a key message to the world market. Chief among the reasons for its decision, Norway is one of the richest countries in the world and distributes its wealth among its people in ways that support their cultural, social, health (a national insurance system), educational, and material needs. Norway's income from the North Sea oil industry is so large that it has less motivation for joining a union that would threaten to control domestic and foreign policies and that could have represented a crippling loss of jobs for vulnerable Norwegian farmers and fishing enterprises in the coastal and rural districts.

The website of the Council of the European Union (EU) is interesting from a Norwegian point of view because Norway is not a member of the EU. The organization that in 1992 became known as the European Union dates back to the early post-World War II period, and grew out of a strong desire to prevent further conflicts and wars in Europe by making the European nations, first and foremost Germany and France, economically and politically dependent on each other. The original members from 1951 (also known as the Six) were Belgium, France, Germany, Italy, Luxemburg, and the Netherlands. Over the years, other European countries also joined the coalition, which in 1998 numbered 15 member states. The Norwegian government has applied for EU membership twice, but accession to the Union has been rejected by the Norwegian people in referendums both in 1972 and 1994.

By looking at the EU website one may almost see why the Norwegians decided not to join the Union. First, the EU entry page greets us with a conservative blue color that signals the capitalist economic basis for the Union. For many Norwegians, who are skeptical of capitalist free-market economies, the EU represents a "Fortress Europe" that is designed to protect narrow European economic, political, and cultural interests against competition and influence from the US and Japan, but even more importantly, from the developing countries of the world. Second, the very organization of the website reinforces the bureaucratic nature of the EU and its centralized, Brussels-based power center. To Norwegians, who hold local

governance and democracy in very high regard, this centralization of political power represents a threat to not only their social democratic welfare state
system, but also to the rural settlement and district development policies that
have been key elements in Norwegian politics for the past twenty-five to thirty
years. Third, the word "Union," which is so prominent in the philosophy of
the EU, does not ring well in the ears of nationalistically oriented Norwegians
who value political, economic and cultural freedom over political directives
and super governance from Brussels. Even though it has been almost one
hundred years since the union with Sweden was dissolved, the very word
Union is something that carries negative associations in Norway.

Another thing that may strike a Norwegian reader is the *apparent* absence
of information about EU family and children policies, Third World development and aid programs, environmental programs and so forth, issues
that feature prominently in Norwegian political consciousness. Information
about these issues can be found inside the EU website, but one must look
around quite a bit to find it. On the positive side, the multilingual EU
website is something most Norwegians will acknowledge and value highly.
The Norwegian culture is small and for this reason Norwegians are very
conscious about the influence of English and the way this affects their own
languages, *nynorsk* and *bokmål*, in the age of globalization and information.

Nordic directions in education

Because of Norway's strong economy, the government is committed to
research and development in areas that greatly affect literacy practices. The
Norwegian Research Council funds diverse projects in the sciences
and humanities, development in educational technologies, and arts and
literature, among other things. These factors have created an educational
environment in which Norwegian literacy thrives on its own traditions, but
also on the importation of other strong traditions. Presently, Norway is also
making a name for its commitment to the use of cutting-edge technology
in education. One prime example is the recent creation of a Department
of Humanistic Informatics at the University of Bergen where both tradi-
tional-aged students (like Johan Utne Poppe, Britt Høyland, and Hilde
Corneliussen) and returning students (like Hanne Leira Knutsen, who
balances her studies with her family obligations) offer examples of students
who have integrated active use of the Web and real-time technologies like
MOOs (multi-user domain, object-oriented) in their daily lives. Within this
department (and with the financial support of the Norwegian Research
Council(NRC)), the authors are involved with several projects that emphasize a blend of the humanities and technology. Our experience shows that
collaborative technologies like MOOs and the Web have contributed greatly
to how we have combined Norwegian and American literacy practices to
further a development of hybrid literacies and technologies.

In the introduction to our recent edited collection, *High Wired: On the Design, Use, and Theory of Educational MOOs*, we articulate new modes of textuality emerging in real-time technologies joined with Web interfaces, what we call the *cyphertextual* conjunctions of text, real-time, and personae. In a similar morphing of such literary modalities, Espen Aarseth, Associate Professor in the Department of Humanistic Informatics, terms it *cybertext*, or ergodic literature. As director of and consultants on The Cyber/Media/ Culture Project[3] (funded by the NRC), Aarseth, Holmevik, and Carsten Jopp (respectively) are now working with MOO and Web technologies to create a language-learning synchronous environment to be used by students like Poppe, Høyland, Knutsen, and Corneliussen as well as students in Germany, Ireland, and the US (Texas) who are part of the pilot study of teaching German as a second language. Yet even the Norwegian students who will graduate from the Bergen program, clearly a cutting-edge proto-type of programs to come all over the world, already view the Web through hyperliterate (though no less ideological) lenses. Poppe sums it up by saying:

> Since I'm not at the net to see "14% of 65KB downloaded," I prefer simple sites with shorter download time. Too many graphics and frames, and thus longer download times, make me leave the site. (*HotWired* is pretty close to that limit, and keeps on the right side just because of the contents.) A few graphics are nice, though.

Another reader, however, is not necessarily drawn to graphics over text, but specifically objects to animated images. Mortensen explains: "I have developed an intense dislike to pages where things move, flickering messages or things demanding my attention." Although Norway is quite Americanized, as we mentioned earlier, one uniquely American trend has not been popular in Norway, namely, the rapid barrage of images that we see in television commercials and websites with splash pages, Java applets scrolling across the page, blinking links, "push" pages set to millisecond delays, and so forth. The Hamsun tradition of cohesive narratives with a purpose is still very important to literacy practices in general and to Web literacy practices and preferences in particular.

Interestingly, several of the students we queried ranked the graffiti website in last place. In recent years, as graffiti grew into a radical form of sub-cultural resistance to the dominant culture in many countries, the Norwegian government quickly responded by making such "tagging" on buildings and structures illegal. In the eyes of many Norwegians, young and old alike, the kind of crime that graffiti represents is unacceptable for the most part, and certainly not to be encouraged as the graffiti site extols. When asked which of the six sites she would recommend to fellow students, not only does Knutsen rank the graffiti site last, she writes that she "would probably not recommend [it] to anyone." Similarly, Høyland ranks it last, but specifies in detail why:

I have been brought up to thinking it bad conduct and not very pretty to smear graffiti on a wall. And usually I don't think it's very nice, except when I occasionally come across a "pretty" one, which happens. I must admit I turned up my nose at it at first, but it is an interesting enough page for those interested in graffiti, I suppose. I followed a couple of links in hopes of finding some really good graffiti; but I didn't stay long.

Perhaps chief among the reasons for the prevalence of this attitude in Norway toward such unseemly images is the fact that it offends a very traditional aesthetic sensibility. It is not unrelated to why surrealism, and other non-representational art, has always been controversial in Norway. This might account for the unpopularity of websites, like the graffiti site, that extol a kind of anti-aesthetic over a more traditional artistic and architectural aesthetic.

On the one hand, it is also possible that since the two students who commented on this site are female we might draw conclusions about how gender affects the attitudes and interpretive strategies of Norwegian women reading and writing the Web. On the other hand, another female reader ranked the graffiti site number one among the six websites this collection examines. Torill Mortensen found that it had "interesting and fun links." She points out that the graffiti site "shows how the web can be used for publishing that which is not said in traditional media." Certainly this is not enough to make assumptions about much more than personal predilections, though the more positive roles that women enjoy in Norwegian culture and politics can at least be said to have influenced the early and continued strong Web presence of Norwegian feminists. In the final section we address how gender politics in Norway have promulgated the cause of feminism in high-tech ways.

"Femina Borealis"

As key components of Norwegian literacy practices, women figure prominently in all aspects of Norway's political and domestic spheres. Women have traditionally enjoyed a major role in Norwegian culture and politics. For example, in the sixteen ministries of Norwegian government (as of 20 December 1998), women currently occupy nine of the eighteen key positions (including some positions that might otherwise be considered masculine spheres):

Minister of Children and Family Affairs
Minister of Justice and Police
Minister of Local Government and Regional Development
Minister of Cultural Affairs

Minister of the Environment
Ministry of Petroleum and Energy
Minister of Labor and Government Administration
Minister of Social Affairs
Minister of International Development and Human Rights
(http://odin.dep.no/html/english/minlist.html, 20/12/98)

It is worth noting that women occupy 50 percent of the ministries' positions, and until recently, this included the office of prime minister (Norway's
first woman prime minister was elected in 1981). On Norway's official
government-sponsored website, ODIN,[4] one may find several links to essays
about the role of women in Norwegian culture and politics. In one such
selection, Irene Engelstad and Janneken Øverland write:

> In society as a whole, women have officially achieved equality with
> men in every sphere of activity. The government of Gro Harlem
> Brundtland [Norway's first woman prime minister] has consistently
> followed a recruiting policy that brings women into the Cabinet
> and the national assembly, the Storting. Despite this, men still hold
> the main positions of power, not least within cultural life, and while
> the number of female authors has increased radically since Camilla
> Collett's time, only a quarter of the members of the Norwegian
> Society of Authors are women. It is therefore, something of a
> paradox that women read more books than men, and women writers
> such as Anne Karin Elstad (born 1938) and Herbjørg Wassmo (born
> 1942) have achieved the biggest sales.

To Norway's credit, at the time of this writing (December 1998) former
Prime Minister Gro Harlem Brundtland is now the Director General of the
World Health Organization. "Dr Brundtland was nominated by WHO's
Executive Board on 27 January [1998] and elected to the post on 13 May
[1998] by Member States of WHO. Her term of office is five years."[5] Among
the essays archived on ODIN, under "social conditions," Pernille Lønne
Mørkhagen's piece on "The Position of Women in Norway" chronicles a
number of significant historical lines of progression for women. Of literary
models, Lønne Mørkhagen writes:

> Forceful personalities among writers, teachers and socially commit-
> ted women were quick to put the disadvantaged position of women
> on the agenda, and to do something about it. One male writer was
> particularly active in the fight for women's rights: Henrik Ibsen's
> contemporary dramas feature strong female characters in leading
> roles who express their need for freedom. And the writer himself
> gave such a thundering speech to the Scandinavian Society in Rome

in 1879 when he failed to get a majority to allow women members into the organization, that a woman fainted. Women writers have also provided poetic descriptions of women's role in society. The first of them was Camilla Collett, with her novel "The Governor's Daughter" ("Amtmandens Døttre") in 1855. The Norwegian author, Sigrid Undset, who won the Nobel Prize for literature in 1928, also described women and the reality they faced in both her contemporary novels and her works set in the middle ages.

Political and literary clout notwithstanding, women's participation in and construction of Internet-based technologies lags behind political gains in gender equality, although there are quite a few websites of online feminist research networks, both official and unofficial (and academic and non-academic), worth noting.

Perhaps the most powerful and well-organized group to establish its presence on the Web is the intergovernmental Nordic Institute for Women's Studies and Gender Research, located at the University of Oslo. Primarily text based, its online newsletter, *News from NIKK* (or *Nytt fra NIKK*) has a wealth of information about the Institute and the various projects it supports. News items like these below indicate the degree of commitment and coordination achieved between the Norwegian government and the other Scandinavian countries participating in the Institute.

The Secretariat for Women and Research in The Research Council of Norway is the Norwegian co-ordinating body for Women's Studies and gender research. The task of the Secretariat is to contribute to increasing the number of women in research, to promote and co-ordinate Women's Studies and gender research and to disseminate information to the research community as well as to the community at large. The Secretariat supports researchers, networks, provides funds for meetings, arranges seminars and conferences, acts as a lobbying agency and publishes the national journal *Kvinneforskning* (Feminist Research). The Research Council of Norway has decided to found an international guest professorship from January 1st 1997. This will be a position held by one international scholar after another, for the term of a year. The idea behind this is to develop and strengthen Women's Studies and gender research in areas where Norwegian competence needs strengthening.

The Board of the Research Council of Norway has supported the proposal to establish a national information and documentation service for Women's Studies and gender research. The work to find good ways to organize, locate and finance this new service has started, aiming to get it launched in 1997.

In November 1995 Norway's northernmost University, and in fact the most northern in the world, The University of Tromsø, established its Center for Women's Studies. So doing, the last of Norway's four universities obtained its centre. The new centre is full of energy and is already planning to host the second circumpolar *Northern Women, Northern Lives* Conference together with The Northern Feminist University in June 1997. The Tromsø centre has also, together with the Nordic Institute for Women's Studies and Gender Research, requested to host the *7th International Interdisciplinary Congress on Women* which is to be held in 1999.

(http://wwworg.uio.no/www-other/nikk/
Institute/newsletters/News961.html, 20/12/98)

As evidenced by these brief excerpts, NIKK went online less than one year after it was founded in 1995, and through the Web a network of communication and conference organizations grew into a thriving group of feminist and gender research networks. On the staff of NIKK is Aino Saarinen, who also initiated the research network "Femina Borealis: Women and Development in the North." A rich source of information, Femina also boasts one of the most interesting graphic logos we found of any site in this study:

Plate 5.3 Femina Borealis: the logo of one of NIKK's research networks.
(http://syy.oulu.fi/fb/index.html [accessed 20 December 1998]

The relation of women to the Northern Lights (aurora borealis) has been one of the defining characteristics of how Norwegians historically perceive the Lights. Asgeir Brekke explains that in western Norway people believed that the Lights were "old maids dancing and waving with their mittens" (1997, p. 43). Further north, among the Sami, "the following jingle was occasionally used about girls and unmarried women when they saw an aurora form a veil between the stars: Girls, girls are running around the hearth/trailing their trousers after them" (ibid., 1997, p. 44). Still other interpretations in Norwegian folk beliefs about the shimmering wave-like phenomenon associate it with the "dancing of the souls of dead virgins" (ibid., 1997, p. 43). In an interesting juxtaposition, one comment made by our reader Torill Mortensen about her general attitudes toward web pages belies the association of the Lights with women (perhaps). As we mentioned earlier, Torill says, "I have developed an intense dislike to pages where things move, flickering messages or things demanding my attention." While her remark is not specifically related to the auroral–feminine link, it does (we think) point to a strong characteristic of Norwegian feminist Web literacies, namely, a desire to maintain historical associations to Norwegian mythologies without trivializing the various domains of power that many Norwegian women like Torill now enjoy. The "Femina Borealis" graphic does not move, though it suggests movement. The icy blue color does not suggest frigidity so much as a cool poetic bridge between Norwegian women and political culture.

Prior to the official financial and political support of the Norwegian government, work among the Nordic feminists had been slowly growing, but "[a]n institutional basis for strengthening the co-operation was established in 1991, when the Nordic Council of Ministers (an inter-governmental body) agreed to finance the position of Co-ordinator for Nordic Women's Studies."[6]

Plate 5.4 "She can do it!" NIKK logo. (http://wwworg.uio.no/www. other/nikk/ Andre-steder/kvinnolinksE.html [accessed 20 December 1998])

The question we asked ourselves, given the online presence we have only been able to briefly represent here, is how this translates into Norwegian female literacy practices on the Web. Against this backdrop and within an academic milieu of feminist technoculture, we were not surprised to hear Høyland describe how studying humanistic informatics has affected her relation to and use of computers:

At the university I have studied languages (German and English) and there I have used computers in grammar and phonetics exercises, but wasn't really comfortable with computers. So it wasn't until I started studying Humanistic Informatics that I learned to be comfortable with computers. Now I actually love computers and computing. Using it as a communication channel brings me in contact with it nearly every day. And now I have bought myself a new and modern computer to communicate with, study with, and play with.

As an only child, Høyland had no siblings to teach her about computers, and her parents are not computer users either. So, her introduction to computers and the Internet has put her in touch with something she describes almost as a person she can "play with." While reading the various websites we asked her to view, she says:

> I followed a link to Korea, which is quite far away . . . [but] it is not so different from viewing a book, because then you also travel in fantasy, but this is still different, perhaps somewhere between tv and a book? Or maybe that is wrong too, it is more like travel than tv, because I decide where to go. And it is more than a book, because it seems much more limitless. . . . But it is not just when travelling to Korea that I feel a bit expanded. I mean, just by viewing the product list I feel sort of "above" it all (hard to explain). . . . Or perhaps I am not above, but *between all countries.* [our emphasis]

We could not have said it better. The Web teleports us into the tiny interstices "between all countries," and perhaps among all literacies. A more

Plate 5.5 View from the authors' living room.
(http://www.ifi.uib.no/student/sd/pekkai/welcome.htm [accessed 20 December 1998])

critical approach to Norwegian literacy practices might (and would) reveal segments of the population who know nothing about the Internet, or (at the very least) understand little about it. As mentioned earlier, the paradox in Norwegian literacy practices hinges on Enzenberger's observation that Norway "is currently Europe's biggest folk museum but simultaneously a huge laboratory of the future." We think this is a good thing. In Geiranger we spend our summers hiking and checking e-mail, surfing the Web and visiting our septuagenarian neighbor, Erling Hole, whose fax machine is hard to hear above the goats and sheep on their way back to the barn. Often we hear their bells jangling as our modem signals it has connected at 56,600 bps (a rate that will seem to travel as slowly as sheep on the road to their mountain pastures by the time this essay sees print). In a final portrait of Norwegian culture and Web literacy, we leave you with the view from our living-room window that can be your view as well with one click of your mouse.

Notes

1   (http://odin.dep.no/ud/publ/96/norway/intro.html, 12/20/98)
2   We want to thank Hilde Corneliussen, Britt Høyland, Hanne Leira Knutsen, Torill Mortensen, and Johan Utne Poppe for generously agreeing to participate in our research for this chapter.
3   See http://www.hf.uib.no/hi/espen/default.html, 20/12/98.
4   http://odin.dep.no/html/english/12/20/98.
5   http://www.who.org/inf-dg/, 12/20/98.
6   NIKK   Newsletter,   http://wwworg.uio.no/www-other/nikk/Institute/newsletters/News961.html, 20/12/98.

References

Aarseth, Espen (1997) *Cybertext: Perspectives on Ergodic Literature*, Baltimore: Johns Hopkins University Press.

Brekke, Asgeir (1997) "Women in the Northern Lights," *The Northern Lights: Science, History, Culture*, (ed.) Knudsen, Anne Merete, Alta, Norway: Alta Museum, pp. 43–47.

Corneliussen, Hilde (1997) personal interview, 18 December, Bergen, Norway.

Crossing The Stones: A Portrait of Arne Næss, produced by the Norwegian Broadcasting Company, http://www.bullfrogfilms.com/catalog/191.html [accessed 20 December 1998].

Engelstad, Irene and Øverland, Janneken (1995) "Norwegian Women Writers," ODIN,   http://odin.dep.no/html/nofovalt/depter/ud/nornytt/uda-423.html [accessed 20 December 1998].

Eriksen, Thomas Hylland (1996) "Globalisation and Norwegian Identity," ODIN, http://odin.dep.no/ud/nornytt/uda-371.html [accessed 20 December 1998].

Haynes, Cynthia and Holmevik, Jan Rune (eds) (1998) *High Wired: On the Design, Use, and Theory of Educational MOOs*, Ann Arbor: University of Michigan Press.

Høyland, Britt [stud2039@student.uib.no] personal interview, (18 December 1997, Bergen, Norway, 1997,) and private e-mail, (13 January 1998).

Knutsen, Hanne Leira [knutsena@online.no], 4 January 1998, Web literacy questions, private e-mail.

Larsen, Lars Frode "Knut Hamsun," ODIN, http://odin.dep.no/ud/nornytt/uda-446.html [accessed 20 December 1998].

Mørkhagen, Pernille Lønne "The Position of Women in Norway," ODIN, http://odin.dep.no/ud/nornytt/uda-147.html [accessed 20 December 1998].

Mortensen, Torill [tm@hivolda,no] 5 May 1998 Web literacy questions, private e-mail.

The New London Group (1996) "A Pedagogy of Multiliteracies" *Harvard Educational Review* 66(1): 60–92.

Poppe, Johan Utne [stud2376@student.uib.no] 9 January 1998 Web literacy questions, private e-mail.

Rognmo, Tor "Links to Scandinavia," http://www.nq.com/nordic/norway/norlitt.html, [accessed 20 December 1998].

Street, Brian V. (1995) *Social Literacies: Critical Approaches to Literacy in Development, Ethnography and Education*, London: Longman.

6

MULTIPLE LITERACIES AND MULTIMEDIA: A COMPARISON OF JAPANESE AND AMERICAN USES OF THE INTERNET

Taku Sugimoto and James A. Levin

This chapter explores the multiple literacies realized by new multimedia, based on case comparisons of Japanese and American uses of the Internet. The analyses of the cases will range from relatively superficial issues like different emoticons (that is, simple character sequences that express emotions) used by Japanese and American users of e-mail to issues raised by Web-based electronic publishing. We will examine some of the ways that uses of the Internet for communications, self-expression, and learning are culturally grounded.

Recently, literacy has been viewed as a complex set of social and cultural practices rather than as a neutral technology of reading and writing. According to Street (1995), the "literacy practices" concept "refers to both behavior and the social and cultural conceptualizations that give meaning to the uses of reading and/or writing" (p. 2). At a time when many new information technologies are being developed, it is important for us to look carefully at how we "behave" when using such technologies and how we conceptualize meaning through our uses. Print literacy has sometimes been viewed as a neutral technology of reading and writing. So too, new information technologies, such as e-mail, the Web, multimedia, and hypermedia, are sometimes viewed as neutral. But this chapter presents evidence that this is not the case.

First of all, new technologies are created in specific cultural and social contexts. The uses and conceptualizations of those technologies reflect, intentionally or unintentionally, the cultures they were created in. And when they come to another sociocultural context, the technologies often bring with them these cultural and social ideologies and value systems.

But in many cases, a culture which imports a new technology from another does not just adopt the technology unchanged along with the ideologies and value systems embedded in it but instead adapts it so that it fits into its own cultural values, cultural ways of thinking and behaving, and so on. The goal of this chapter is to document differences between American and Japanese uses of Internet-based technologies, and to understand these differences as a process of adaption of technologies developed in one culture to be more appropriate for the other.

When new technologies are developed, they carry with them certain idealizations on the uses as well as conceptualizations of them. But examinations of how people actually use those technologies in situations often reveal multiple realizations, most of which are quite different from the idealizations (Bruce and Rubin, 1993). In most cases, such realizations in actual situations have emerged from bottom-up in grass-roots activities, not given from top-down in an authoritative way. Authoritative idealizations and actual realizations often conflict with each other, which results in those realizations developing in "hidden" places. Such hidden literacy practices reveal important aspects of our social and cognitive natures.

In the first section of this chapter, we look at two examples of Japanese culture importing literacy technologies from other cultures. From these two cases, we support the position that literacy and communication technologies are adapted, not adopted. In the following section, we analyze differences in e-mail discourse among Japanese and among Americans to show that uses of e-mail technologies are culturally grounded. In the third section, we consider differences of literacy practices on the Web in Japan and in the United States. Through these case analyses, we conclude with discussions on the importance of our framework for conceptualizing the relationships between technology and literacy.

A word of caution is needed to point out that any culture should not be regarded as a monolithic entity. There is certainly a great variety in uses and conceptualizations of the Internet and other literacy and communication technologies among users of the Internet both in Japan and in the United States. In this chapter, we discuss typical or salient features of the Internet uses in Japanese and American culture. Of course there are many cases where we can see people behaving in different ways than that which we describe here. The goal of this chapter is to demonstrate that there are some essential phenomena characteristic to different cultures in literacy and communication technologies.

Literacies in Japan: distinctions between adopting and adapting literacy technologies

Japanese letters

Japan has a rich history of importing foreign literacy technologies and adapting them to enrich literacy practices. An important historic example is the importation and adaption of the Japanese-writing system. In spite of major differences between the Chinese and Japanese languages, Japan imported Chinese characters for writing, then adapted them into quite a different orthographic system. The current Japanese language uses three different systems of characters.

The first system is called "kanji," the set of logographic characters that originated in China. Kanji characters are now used mostly to write nouns and verb roots, and other content words in the Japanese language. For several centuries after Japan imported Chinese characters, they wrote Chinese sentences instead of Japanese sentences by using those characters. Therefore, writing was used only in limited situations, mostly on formal occasions. Lay people did not use writing in everyday situations. But literacy gradually became used widely and the inconvenience of writing Chinese characters became salient. This led to the development of new ways of writing Japanese sentences using Chinese characters and later the development of new characters.

A kanji character can be read with its Chinese pronunciation or it can be "read" by saying the Japanese word corresponding to it in meaning. For example, when the kanji character meaning "wave" 波 entered ancient Japan, it could be read as "pa"[1] which was the Chinese word having the meaning "wave," or it could be read as "nami" which was the Japanese word meaning "wave." This is similar to an English speaker's reading "etc." as "and so on" or "e.g." as "for example." The first kind of readings are called "on-yomi" while the second are called "kun-yomi." A new way of denoting sounds of Japanese words was developed using the Chinese character meaning "wave" for another word which had a sound "pa" in it (for example as the first letter for "pana" 波奈). See Figure 6.1.

There are many kanji characters which have the same or similar "on-yomi," and initially different characters were used by different people to denote the same Japanese sounds and words. But they were gradually standardized. In addition, those characters were simplified. Kana characters, original Japanese characters denoting Japanese syllables, were created in this way. Each kana character represents a vowel or a syllable (a consonant followed by a vowel), with the exception of "n" which consists of a kana character though it is a consonant.

There are two kinds of "kana" characters. One is called "hiragana." These characters were made by transforming kanji characters so that several strokes in original kanji characters were written continuously as one stroke and some strokes were omitted. For some time after hiragana characters were created, they were supposed to be used only by women. In the Heian period (between the tenth and twelfth centuries) many literary pieces were written by Japanese women using hiragana. One notable genre of literature in this period was the literary diary. Essay-like literature in the form of diaries flourished in this period. On the other hand, men at that time were

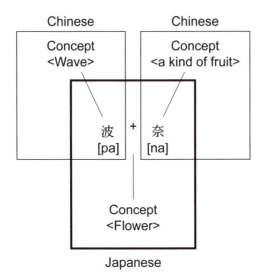

Figure 6.1 Adaptation of Chinese characters to Japanese use

supposed to use only kanji characters. One male writer named Ki-no Tsurayuki wrote a literary diary called "Tosa Nikki" ("The Tosa Diary") in 935 by using hiragana, but he pretended (or had to pretend) to be a woman to do so.

In current Japanese writing, only portions of sentences can be written in kanji. For one thing, many words are known only by sounds, not in kanji. Many words which originated in Japan have no kanji. Also, hiragana letters are added to Chinese characters to show their Japanese declension. Japanese adults write and read several thousand kanji characters, but of course it takes time to learn such a large number of characters. Thus children use fewer kanji characters in their writing than adults. Because kana characters denote sounds (syllables), Japanese children's literature is written using hiragana. When readers do not know kanji characters, they can use hiragana. But if adults use too many kana in their writing, they are regarded as childish. This cultural perception is one of driving forces to push children to learn kanji literacy (Hatano, 1995).

The third series of Japanese characters are called "katakana." Most words originating in western countries are written in katakana. Katakana characters were derived from parts of kanji characters. When Japanese men used only Chinese characters in writing, they often wrote small letters beside Japanese sentences as supplementary notes to help in reading them. For example, declensions were often added in small letters so that Chinese characters could be read in Japanese contexts. In writing these small letters, they came to omit parts of those Chinese characters for simplifications. Katakana characters were developed in this way.

As you can see from this description of how hiragana and katakana were born, these two systems of syllabaries in Japanese were used differently from the start. Hiragana characters were used mostly by women to write diaries, poems, literary works, and so on, while katakana characters were used mostly by men to supplement official texts, imported Chinese writings, and so on. Until the end of the Second World War, most authoritative documents were written with kanji and katakana, instead of kanji and hiragana. Katakana had long been regarded as authoritative, official, and masculine compared to the more casual and feminine hiragana. Hiragana and katakana now have different functions but do not have status- or gender-related differences.

In this way, the characters used in the Japanese language, which are essential technologies for literacy practices in the Japanese culture, originally came from the Chinese language and culture, but the current forms of Japanese characters are the result of adaptive processes that progressively modified foreign technologies to fit into another cultural context.

New literacy practices among Japanese youths: pagers

Recently, many new technologies for writing and communication have been developed, including word processors, computer networks, satellite TV, cellular phones, and pagers. Most of these have originated in the United States. But as these technologies entered Japanese culture, they have created new literacy and communication practices different from the US counterparts as well as from those in Japan before these technologies. Some of these technologies have created new forms of literacy in the Japanese culture.

For example, pagers were initially used in the United States in 1958 and they were imported to Japan ten years later. The pagers used at that time were called the "TP-type" (tone-only pager), which were very simple, beeping when someone called phone numbers for specific pagers. These were used almost exclusively in the business world. Employees working outside their offices were given pagers by their companies so that they could be called to make calls back when necessary. For twenty years or so, this technology saw almost no advancement.

But since the 1980s many functions have been added to pagers. For example, in 1982, a new type of pager was devised with two different tones. A pager of this kind made a tone when someone called a certain number, and another tone when someone else called another number for the same pager.

The most notable feature devised was the capability of displaying numbers on pagers, which is called the "NP-type" (numerical pager). This function was added so that people could tell what number to call back. And in the business world, this type of pager is used exactly in this manner. But Japanese youth showed great creativity in developing new literacy activities by using the NP-type pagers. They communicate with their friends who have a pager with this capability by pushing numbers on touch-tone phones. They conduct telecommunications with friends by using pagers!

For example, if you get a message "39," it means "thank you." If a message "88951" appeared on your pager, your friend is waiting for you to come. What are the secret codes behind these numbers? In Japanese the number 3 is read as "san" and 9 is read as "kyu." The English sound "th" does not exist in the Japanese language and when a Japanese speaker pronounces the "th" sounds in English words they usually use "s" or "z" as approximations. So, "39" can be read "san-kyu" which can be associated with the English phrase "thank you." For "88951," readings of numbers 8, 9, 5, 1 are "hachi," "kyu," "go," and "ichi" respectively when they are read by themselves. But when these numbers form phrases, they are read in many different ways. The number 8 is sometimes read as "ya," 9 is sometimes "ku," 1 is sometimes "i," and so on. So, what does "88951" mean? In this "code," the first 8 is read as "ha," from the first letter of "hachi." The second 8 is read as "ya," another reading of the number 8. The number 9 is read as "ku." The number 5 is read as "ko," the unvoiced sound of "go." The number 1 is read as "i." So the phrase "88951" is read "ha-ya-ku-ko-i." And "hayaku" means *early, soon, quickly* and so on. "Koi" means "come" (in commands or orders). So "88951" means "come quickly." These may sound very complicated, but many Japanese high-school and undergraduate students enjoy communicating with friends by using this method.

This technology together with methods of coding messages created new literacy practices among young Japanese people. The technology itself (the feature of displaying numbers on pagers) was not originally designed for this kind of literacy activity for young people. Its original aim was to make business contacts more convenient. But young people found a new way, quite different from the original intended purpose, to use this technology and made it an integral part of their culture.[2]

In Japanese culture, people often read numbers to make sense of random sequences of digits. For example, many butchers have their store phone numbers ending with "0298." Zero "0," can be read "o" from its similarity of the English alphabet "o." The numbers, 2, 9, and 8 can be read as "ni," "ku," and "ya" respectively from Japanese readings of these numbers. So "0298" forms a "meaningful" Japanese word "o-ni-ku-ya" which means "butchers." This way of playing with numbers to make sense is well established in the Japanese culture. In the same way, young Japanese people feel comfortable with, and even enjoy, playing with numbers on pagers.

This use of pagers among young Japanese people is a good example of how new technologies can create new literacy practices. Exchanging short messages with special codes using numbers is an innovative use of NP-type pagers.

In the United States, there are also some ways of using pagers outside of the originally intended contexts. For example, pagers have been banned in some US schools because they have been used in drug dealing. The perception of pagers among educators in the United States is thus related to crimes with which they do not want their students to be involved. Some Japanese schools prohibit their students from bringing pagers to schools too, but for quite a different reason. They do so to prevent the students from being engaged in enjoyable little conversations all the time.

Some English words can be displayed by using numbers. Children sometimes play with hand calculators to type 14 and look at it upside down to read it as "hi," for example. And this way of using numbers to "write" messages is slowly entering young people's culture in the United States. But American ways of communicating by numbers seem in most cases quite different from the Japanese way of making sense out of series of numbers. The American culture does not have as strong a cultural practice of reading numbers to make meanings as in Japan. There are some code tables to use numerical pagers to make meaningful messages in the United States, but many codes are just random assignments of numbers to messages. However, some codes have developed which draw upon cultural knowledge (Motorola, 1998). For example, "1040" means "You owe me big time," a cultural reference to the US tax form 1040, the form that individuals fill out each year to pay their federal income taxes. Or "1701," which means "live long and prosper," a reference to the ship number of the Starship Enterprise, whose science officer Spock used that phrase. Two codes drawn from the telephone system in the US are "911," which means urgent," and "411" which is a request for information. The "911" code is the number typed into many US telephones to get emergency help; "411" is the number for directory assistance.

In spite of the differences discussed above in literacy activities related to pagers and numbers, we can see some important characteristics in uses of communication technologies in the United States and Japan. For one thing, communication media help form and establish certain discourse communities. A pager is an important medium for communication among young people in Japan, while it is sometimes a tool for drug dealing in the United States. In these two cases, the same tool is used for quite different purposes. But the tool has a common function in both. It separates insiders and outsiders. Those who share the tool are insiders while those who do not are outsiders.

Summary

This section has looked at two examples of bringing foreign-made writing and communication technologies into Japanese cultures. These two cases have important similarities.

The processes of importing these technologies can be regarded as those of adaption, rather than those of adoption. "Adoption" implies using something which is created by another in the same manner intended by its developers. In the two cases described in this section, however, the Japanese culture "adapted" what was created in another culture in ways different from its use in the original cultural contexts. Instead, it has modified the uses as well as the conceptualizations of them in the process of taking them into the culture.

Modifications in such adaptation processes emerged in grass-roots practices among lay people in a bottom-up fashion, not in a way imposed top-down. In many cases, different subcultures use the same technology in quite different ways, each of which is deeply grounded in the context of the subculture.

Literacy practices in e-mail on the Internet

In this section, we will discuss two facets of literacy practices that differ between Japanese and American uses of e-mail. The first one concerns the ways that people state their identities (names and affiliations) in e-mail. The second one concerns the use of emoticons in electronic mail. Differences in e-mail represented in these two aspects of discourse features show how the same communication medium is used differently in different cultures.

Moran and Hawisher (1998) stated "when we argue that e-mail is a new medium, developing its own rhetorics and languages, we mean that although new, it is intimately related to its ancestors. In its gene pool are all former and current modes and styles of human communication, written and spoken" (pp. 80–1). And those "ancestors" are culturally grounded. In this section we demonstrate how cultural ancestors are related to current e-mail rhetoric in different cultures.

Self-identification in e-mail

E-mail is one of the most widely used functions of the Internet. On e-mail people use more colloquial styles than in postal mail. E-mail communication has some elements shared with postal mail as well as with telephone conversation.

Letters sent through postal mail have certain conventional formats. For example, English letters often start with "Dear . . .," and end with "Sincerely yours," or "Yours sincerely." Similar patterns can be found in Japanese letters. For example, many letters start with "Haikei" and end with "Keigu." And it is usual that some seasonal greetings are at the beginning of letters.

But e-mail messages are usually more colloquial than postal letters both in the United Stated and Japan. Many US messages start with "Hi, how are you doing?" or something like that, which is more similar to telephone conversations than written letters.

Many Japanese people start their e-mail messages by stating their own names and affiliations, like "This is Sugimoto @ U of Tokyo" (杉本@東京大学です). A sample of a Japanese e-mail message is shown in Figure 6.2. This may be a reflection of Japanese ways of communication and Japanese culture, for social affiliations and statuses are often important in communications in Japanese culture. Even when they have their names and affiliations in their signatures at the end of e-mail as well as their names together with their e-mail addresses and their domain names which indicate their affiliations in many cases in the headers at the beginning of messages, they often feel uneasy if they don't mention their names and affiliations at the beginning of the message bodies.

It is interesting to compare this custom of starting e-mail messages among Japanese users with that of US users. Table 6.1 shows an analysis of how people write their names and affiliations in messages posted to newsgroups. We randomly selected 50 messages from 8 groups, 4 each from Japanese and US newsgroups. As you can see from this table, it is very rare for Americans to start their e-mail with their own names. It may be because they feel it is enough to write their names at the ends of messages. Or it

X–Sender: tanaka@xx.yamada-u.ac.jp
Mime–Version: 1.0
Date: Tue, 21 Jul 1997 19:43: 16 +0900
To: taku@p.u-tokyo.ac.jp
Subject: 8/13
Status: 0

田中@山田大学です。

8/13 の会議ですが、
何時頃までかかるんでしょうか・・・
宿泊の手配が必要かな？と思って。

田中太郎 (Taro TANAKA)　　E-mail : tanaka@xx.yamada-u.ac.jp
山田大学教育学部
College of Education, Yamada Univ.
〒 321-1122　山田市弥生 3250　Tel. 0864-21-4321 (直通)

Note: The meaning of the message body is:
　　　 This is Tanaka @ Yamada University.
Regarding the meeting on 13 Aug.,
what time can I expect it to be over?
I wonder if I need to make a hotel reservation.

Figure 6.2 A sample e-mail message in Japanese

Table 6.1 Name and affiliations in e-mail messages

	US				Japan			
	alt.books. reviews	k12.chat. teachers	rec. humor	rec.travel .usa-canada	fj. books	fj. education	fj. jokes	fj. travel
Name at beginning					13	20		1
Name + affiliation at beginning	1	2			8	6		2
Name at end	31	8	21	23	2	13	34	
Name + affiliation at end	1	21		2			1	1
Name both at beginning and end					1	3		
Name + affiliation at beginning and name at end						1		

may be because it is easy for them to find the "From:" line in the headers to identify the senders of messages. But it is more interesting that only in special cases do Americans give their affiliations in e-mail messages except in signatures at the end of messages.

Table 6.2 shows how many people use "signatures" in their messages in the same samples used above. More people in Japan use signature files in their messages than in the United States, but the use of signatures is not different between the two cultures.

This way of starting Japanese e-mail messages may have developed because e-mail headers have many lines with Roman letters, some lines which make sense but with other lines that make no sense to ordinary people. So it is very hard for Japanese people to find the "From:" line among the header.

Another explanation of this way of starting Japanese e-mail is that this custom originated with e-mail, chat and bulletin-board communications in "*paso-kon tsushin*" (literally, personal computer communication). "*Paso-kon tsushin*" is network communication using commercial Japanese network-service companies (similar to America Online or CompuServe in the US). These services started their operations in the 1980s and had been growing in popularity until displaced by the Internet. These network companies now offer Internet connections but still many people enjoy their forums and

Table 6.2 Use of signature files in e-mail messages

	alt.books. reviews	k12.chat. teachers	rec. humor	rec.travel .usa-canada	fj. books	fj. education	fj. jokes	fj. travel
no. of sig files	11	7	16	12	36	29	28	10

continue using information services provided by them. In the Japanese "*paso-kon tsusin*" world, it is the custom that users communicate with each other by using pen-names, or "handle names" as they call it. In the headers of e-mail messages as well as postings on bulletin boards, only nonsense strings of alphabetic characters and digits (user IDs) appear as the identities of the senders. So senders state their handle name at the beginning of their messages so that readers can identify them. Even though readers do not usually know who this person is in real life, they can identify the user in the online world. Handle names or nicknames are much easier to read and remember than strings of random characters and numbers. So it is natural (or at least they feel it is) that they want to give their own names at the beginning.

Anyway, it is not clear where the custom of giving names and affiliations in the form "(name)@(affiliation)" at the beginning of e-mail messages came from, but there are possible sources of this custom in pre-existing Japanese culture related to communications using technologies.

It is interesting to note that there are at least two writing formats that use this format of forefronting name and affiliation. One is the "letterhead" used in formal paper-based business letters and memos, which usually contains the name and institutional affiliation of the writer. The other format is formal writing such as this very chapter, which puts the authors' names right at the beginning after the title. There are no differences between using these formats in business and formal writings in both Japanese and US culture, probably because names and affiliations are regarded as essential in these cases in both cultures. But in less formal situations, and in the situations where it does not appear to be essential to share affiliations at first, like some kinds of face-to-face, telephone, and e-mail communications, the use of affiliations are different in these two cultures.

When US e-mail technology entered Japanese culture, it did so with the habit of forefronting names and affiliations. That habit was associated with the e-mail medium, based on the Japanese communication culture. In this way, e-mail has been adapted, in the sense discussed in the first section of this chapter, to the Japanese culture.

Emoticons in e-mail messages

In e-mail communications people sometimes use "emoticons" to add emotional flavor to their written texts. In e-mail communications without non-verbal cues, people often overreact and express their emotions too strongly. So-called "flaming" may become a problem in newsgroups and list-serves. Emoticons, as defined earlier, are simple character sequences that express emotions and are intended to soften the tones of written messages, thus, avoiding unnecessary confrontation and arguments (Sproull and Kiesler, 1986). Both Japanese and US emoticons are intended to have this same function.

143

But many emoticons are different between the two cultures. The basic smiley is :-) in the US. The basic smiley is (^_^) in Japan. Both of these represent, through Roman characters, a smiling face. The most obvious difference between these two emoticons is that while the US smiley is rotated to the left, the Japanese one is upright. Many people who first see the US smiley have to be told that it is a sideways face.

There is another, more interesting difference between these two emoticons, which most people who know both these emoticons are often not aware of. According to an American English dictionary (Random House, 1991), to smile means "to assume a facial expression usu. indicating pleasure, favor, or amusement, but sometimes derision or scorn, characterized by an upturning of the corners of the mouth." The American smiley emoticon represents exactly the smile in this definition with an "upturning of the corners of the mouth." But the Japanese smiley emoticon has a straight mouth. Many Japanese use a variation of the standard Japanese smiley emoticon, which is just (^^) without a straight line in the middle, which does not have a mouth at all. So it is not smiling in the American sense.

A generally accepted Japanese translation of the English word "smile" is "hoho-emu" (in the verb form). Etymologically, "hoho" means "a cheek" and "emu" means "smile." So literally, Japanese people smile with their cheeks. But the Japanese emoticon (^_^) does not seem to smile with its cheeks. Apparently it smiles with its eyes. How is this so? One explanation is that Japanese people actually smile with their eyes. There are some phrases in Japanese whose meanings are similar to "smiling," like "me o hosomeru" (literally "narrow one's eyes") and "me ga waratteiru" (literally "one's eyes are smiling"). Another explanation is that in many cartoons and animations (manga and anime) smiling faces are depicted as having ^ ^ shaped eyes. Of course facial expressions in cartoons are exaggerated, but they are often reflections of the surrounding cultural realities. At least it can be said that Japanese people perceive this shape of eyes as part of smiles.

In this way, even though these two cultures have emoticons with a similar function in e-mail communications, they are quite different in their shapes. Both originated from their own cultures.

There is another interesting aspect to Japanese uses of emoticons. The most frequently used Japanese emoticon is (^_^;) or (^^;) which has "cold sweat" on the side of its face. Ways of using this "cold sweat" smile reflect Japanese styles of communication. The most typical use of emoticon (^_^;) or (^^;) is when Japanese writers are afraid they are saying something too strongly. It is an expression of the Japanese cultural value of modesty in communication.

Table 6.3 shows the result of an analysis of uses of emoticons on netnews groups both in the United States and in Japan. We chose four news groups in Japan on a variety of topics ranging from education (fj.education), books (fj.books) to jokes (fj.jokes) and travels (fj.travel). We chose

144

Table 6.3 Use of emoticons in e-mail messages

	USA				Japan			
	alt.books. reviews	k12.chat. teachers	rec. humor	rec.travel .usa-canada	fj. books	fj. education	fj. jokes	fj. travel
total no.	**0**	**5**	**5**	**0**	**12**	**20**	**0**	**15**
:-) "smiling"			1		1	5		1
:) "smiling"		3	1					
:-("sad face"		1						
:("sad face"		1	1					
;-) "wink"		1						1
;) "wink"		1						
?-("questioning"						1		
^^ "smile"					2	4	1	
^^; "smile with cold sweat"					6	7		4
(^.^;) "smile with cold sweat"								8
(-.-;) "silence with cold sweat"								1
^^;v "smile with cold sweat and 'v-sign'"								
m(__)m "apology or thanks"					5			
[;^J^] "a variation of the 'cold sweat' smiley"					1			
^<>^ "smile with open mouth"					1			
(^^)y "smile with smoking"						1		
(?_?) "wondering"						1		
(;;) "crying"						1		
(_o_) "I'm sorry . . ."								1

four news groups in the United States on similar topics (k12.chat.teachers, alt.books.reviews, rec.humor, and rec.travel.usa-canada). From messages posted on each group during a one month period, we randomly selected 50 messages. And we counted the numbers of emoticons appearing in those messages.

From this analysis, it is evident that some of the Japanese writers used "American" emoticons, such as :-), ;-) and so on, but most Japanese use Japanese emoticons instead of American ones. On the other hand, no Japanese emoticons appear in the US messages. Even though some books collecting emoticons published in the United States list one or more of Japanese emoticons (for example, Sanderson (1993) lists (@@) as "You're kidding!" and (^^)y~~~~ as "smoking"), it does not seem that they have yet entered American cyberculture. Also, we can see more different kinds of emoticons in Japanese messages than in the US messages. Japanese people use many different emoticons having cold sweat (;), v-sign (v), and so on beside smiling faces.

Uses of emoticons in these two cultures are thus quite different. The general function of emoticons are similar, but the specific forms and uses differ. Emoticons were originally born in the United States but those unique to Japanese culture have emerged. Uses of emoticons are strongly grounded in the communication styles of each culture.

Literacy practices in the Web

Biases in reading Web pages

The Web is a huge network of information. We are able to access information from the other side of the globe very easily. But do we really read text from other cultures in the way the authors intended? Can we say that we read the same text on the Web with the same meanings? There are three main ways of accessing information on the Web: following a link from another page, using a search engine, and typing in an URL directly. Each of these three ways has a potential to mislead readers (Sugimoto, 1997a, 1997b).

When following a link from another page, the reading of the linked page is contextualized by the previous page. So the same Web page may have different meanings depending on what paths the reader has taken in coming to it. In this sense, each page of text is not neutral on the Web. Each page does not necessarily convey the meanings intended by its authors, since the path to the page provides a context for sense making. This is complicated by the fact that users can make a link to any page on the Web in any way they like. In conventional media, meanings are constructed through interactions between authors and readers. But on the Web, meanings are constructed between authors of pages and those who make links to those pages on the one hand, and readers on the other. Authors cannot control who can make links to the pages they have created.

For example, one of the authors of this chapter has been working on a project developing Web-based materials for learning English as a second/foreign language. The site has a collection of magazine-like articles written for language learners with hypertextual links to vocabulary explanations as well as to related readings. There are many links (over 150 outside links) to this site. As expected, most of them are from sites related to language learning, for example from pages entitled "ESL Homepage," "Resources for language learning," and so on. People who visit this site following links from these pages read articles there to practice reading English as a foreign or second language. This is the use the creators of this site intended.

But there are also different kinds of links to some of the Web pages of this site. For example, one article on this site is about the O. J. Simpson case and the issue of domestic violence. There are two links to this article from outside this site. One is from the "O. J. Links" page <http://lrs. ed.uiuc.edu/Impact/articles/Domestic_Violence/DomViolence.html>. This page is a collection of links to Web pages related to O. J. Simpson which are categorized into "information, humor, fan pages, articles, books, commercial links, and opinion polls." Those who follow a link from this "O. J. Links" page to the O. J. article on the ESL site will have quite a different context than that which ESL learners have. Another link to this same article is from a page titled "Stop Domestic Violence Web Resources" <http://www.isis.aust.com/domviolence/ webresourses.htm>. People who come to the O. J. article on the ESL site from this page would have yet another kind of context.

About one tenth of the links to this ESL site are not related to language learning, but to the subject matter content of one of the articles at the site. Besides the pages related to O. J. Simpson and domestic violence mentioned previously, health-related sites, a page on Arnold Schwartznegger, pages collecting links to Web pages on environmental issues, and so on are among those pages having links to articles at the site. This means that as many as 10 percent of links to this site may create understandings of information at this site that are substantially different from the original intent of the authors.

The second way of accessing information on the Web is by search engine. In this case, the page has a very different contextualization. The context is that you used a search engine, the key words you used in the search, the expectations and framework you had when running the search, and so on. In this case, understandings may be based on the framework and knowledge the reader brings to reading it in ways only weakly influenced by the intention of the author of the page.

A poor design or structure of information on a site may increase the possibility of readers having trouble in understanding the site properly. For example, if a Web page you happened to arrive at by using a search engine did not have a link to its overview or introductory page, it would be very difficult or sometimes impossible for a reader to obtain information on the nature of the site or the page. The chances of the readers having misunderstandings or lack of sufficient information of this nature will be substantial especially when readers and authors belong to different cultures or communities.

The third way of accessing information on the Web is by typing in the URL of a Web page received from someone else, a magazine, an ad, or somewhere else. The contextualization of the page will depend on how you got the URL. The context for a Web page reached in this way will be yet different than for the pages reached in other ways.

Burbulus (1998) problematized the apparently neutral character of a "link" and suggested that we "concentrate more on links – as associative relations that change, redefine, and enhance or restrict access to the information they comprise." Considering the issues of how our readings of information on the Web are affected by links, we cannot say that information on the Web is neutral in any sense. Readers can too easily comprehend information differently from the original intents of the author.

One important implication is that conceptualizations of links may not be the same across cultures. Burbulus (1998) lists different kinds of links on the Web. Given that our readings of Web pages are highly influenced by how we have accessed it (especially what links we have followed to reach it), cultural differences in the interpretation of links can affect our readings as well as the whole literacy practices on the Web.

Self-expression on the Web

There are a few studies which have investigated the motivations and purposes of making "home pages" or personal Web pages both in Japan and the United States.

Kawaura and Shibanai (1997) conducted a survey of those who had personal Web pages on a Japanese commercial network provider between mid-April and May in 1996. They had 211 e-mail responses to their study. The answer that most respondents selected was "my own way of sending out information" (78.7 percent). It is followed by "easy way of sending out information" (67.8 percent), "just wanted to try it" (67.3 percent), "wanted to get responses from others" (36.5 percent), "interpersonal relations with strangers" (32.2 percent), "it is in fashion" (27.5 percent), and "wanted others to know myself" (22.3 percent).

Another study was done by Kawakami *et al.* (1996) of users of another Japanese commercial network provider in August and September of 1996. Among 3,358 respondents, 839 persons (about 25 percent) had personal Web pages. Major purposes they gave for having Web pages were to "publish messages and opinions" (47.1 percent), "for business use" (43.4 percent), "exchange information about my hobbies" (38.9 percent), "sending out information" (33.7 percent), "appreciate my own existence" (18.5 percent), "don't want to be behind the age" (16.7 percent).

A similar study was done in the United States by Buten (1996). He conducted a survey in May 1996 of Internet users who had their own personal Web pages in Pennsylvania. "Expressing myself" was at the top of the answers from the respondents (49 percent), which was followed by "studying and practicing HTML" (48 percent), "communicating information to myself" (43 percent), "sending information to those strangers who share interests" (34 percent), "serve as bookmarks" (32 percent), and "advertise myself" (24 percent).

These studies used different categories, so it is not easy to compare them. But it is clear that Internet users who have their own personal Web pages both in Japan and the United States often have a similar motivation, "self-expression."

Japanese people are often described as less assertive and less good at expressing themselves than people in the US. But the Web has attracted public attention in Japan as a medium for ordinary people to "publish" their personal writings to the world. It is interesting that by using the Internet, Japanese people have shown an eagerness to express themselves similarly to people in the United States. But there are some differences between the two cultures in how they express themselves.

For example there are many "diary" pages in Japan in which ordinary people write their daily personal happenings and thinking and put them on the Web to tell such things to the world. More than 10 percent of the users of a commercial Internet provider in Japan had their diaries on the Web (Kawaura and Shibanai, 1997).

Diaries are personal things in nature and are generally not shown to others. Hassam (1993) summarized the features of diaries in the following way:

> *Narrator*: The diary is a first-person narration in which the narrator is also the protagonist; the recording is therefore from the narrator's point of view.
>
> *Narration*: The diary is composed of regular dated sections corresponding to the time of composition; it has thus a fragmented narrative structure and is non-retrospective.
>
> *Addressee*: The diarist is writing for himself or herself, the resultant style being abbreviated and containing semantic gaps.
>
> (Hassam, 1993, p. 21)

It appears that many diary Web pages in Japan share most features Hassam mentioned in regard to narrator and narration. But in terms of addressee, we can assume that Japanese Web-diarists are not writing for themselves, but to show their writings to others.

There are some diary-related literacy practices in Japan in which diaries are actually written to show to others. One is the Japanese tradition of literary diaries. As mentioned earlier, literary diaries as a genre of litera-ture flourished as early as the tenth century in Japan. In western countries, literary diaries began appearing in fifteenth century, but have never been a major literary genre though there are some English and American diary novels.

Another line of Japanese tradition related to diaries are so-called "*Koukan Nikki*" (*Koukan*: exchange; *Nikki*: diary). This practice is popular especially among Japanese school girls. Two or a few persons share a note in which they take turns making entries to describe daily happenings, thoughts, and so on. This is a diary in the sense that they write about daily activities and ideas, but it is different from a diary in the ordinary sense in that it is not written by a single person, but instead is exchanged and shared. In these "exchange diaries," young Japanese girls create literacy forms quite different from the school-taught authoritative literacy (Honda, 1996). It is comparable to various "hidden" literacies American adolescent girls practice in many situations (Finders, 1997), although it is much less common for American youths to exchange diaries.

As can be seen from these practices related to diaries in Japan, not just writing diaries but also sharing them with others in some way has been part of Japanese literacy culture for a long time. One interesting fact is that not many of those who have personal diary pages on the Web in Japan had a previous habit of keeping diaries (Ikeda *et al.*, 1997). An interaction between the cultural ground and the new communication technology may have prepared them to keep and publish diaries on the Web.

An interactive version of this chapter

After writing the initial drafts of this chapter, we wanted to obtain some feedback from people. Traditionally this would be done with paper-based media – copies would be xeroxed, marked on the front as "Draft," and circulated informally to friends and colleagues. The Web version of this literacy practice is to save a word-processed paper as HTML and make it available informally on the Web as a linear Web page, with feedback being sent back by readers as e-mail to the authors.

We were interested in exploring more interactive formats on the Web, and so we worked with James Buell at the University of Illinois to develop a simple "interactive paper" format, using the Web as a "front-end" to a database <http://lrsdb.ed.uiuc.edu:591/whitepaper/s-l.html >. Readers had the opportunity to respond to each paragraph, to see the responses of others, and to respond to the comments of others.

In an earlier draft of the paper, we documented the culturally specific ways that numeric codes were used in Japan to communicate using numeric pagers, but we did not specify any similar patterns in the United States. Feedback by several readers pointed out this shortcoming, and motivated us to research the use of pagers in the US, leading to our documentation of pager codes in the US that drew upon cultural aspects of American culture.

Other comments took the line of argument in quite a different direction, drawing parallels to differences in the structure of e-mail between the US and Japan and differences in when business cards are handed out (at the start of a face-to-face interaction in Japan, at the end in the US). In this case, the commentary was very interesting, but could not be incorporated into the chapter given its scope. So we found that this interactive mechanism expanded the range of feedback on draft versions, but that not all comments were helpful for the chapter itself.

This kind of interactive feedback also raises important intellectual ownership issues – if someone provided a substantial commentary that we wanted to include in the chapter, would we make that person a contributing author? What about the status of people who offer more general suggestions, that lead to changes in the chapter, but who did not supply the text? How much of the notion of intellectual ownership is culturally bound and how much differs across different cultures? One of the main advantages of studies like those in this book is that not only do cultural comparisons allow us to see better elements of each culture, but cultures become more visible under the rapid changes brought about by new communication technologies. By studying how each culture uses a new technology, we gain a better understanding of each culture and a better idea of how best to use the new technologies.

Conclusion

In this chapter, we have looked at a variety of cases of using information and communication technologies. A culture which has imported a technology creates new ways of using it which are quite different from those practiced in the culture the technology originally came from, ways that are deeply grounded in the culture which adapted it. Substantive as well as subtle variations and differences rooted in cultural differences are often observed in ways of using and conceptualizing a technology. Through these cases, we conclude that if we look carefully at any literacy practice in actual contexts, the processes of using information and communication technologies will be the result of adaption rather than adoption. People's literacy activities in everyday situations using those technologies are embedded and grounded in their sociocultural contexts.

The Internet is a powerful medium for international and intercultural communications. Language barriers are the most obvious obstacle to mutual understanding. But we tend to overlook more invisible and subtle barriers, which result from the cultural embededness of literacy practices on the Internet. Communications and literacy practices on the Internet have cultural ancestors. If we ignore these, then any mutual understandings are in danger.

One aspect of the cultural embededness of Internet literacies is that a great variety of literacy practices, many of which have been "hidden" in everyday cultural practices instead of "authoritative," "official," and "school-related" ones, have emerged in cyberspace. Internet literacies open up a window to our cultural-practices-related literacy, both with these new communication technologies and also with more conventional media.

Acknowledgements

We would like to thank Cindy Selfe and Gail Hawisher for their excellent work as editors, the anonymous reviewer from Routledge for helpful feedback, and all the people who provided interactive feedback to our Web-based interactive paper format for this chapter. We'd like to thank Chip Bruce and Nick Burbules for helping us think about these issues.

Notes

1   Japanese pronunciations have changed over time. The syllable "ha" in modern Japanese used to be pronounced as "pa" in earlier times. For example, the Japanese word for "flower" is currently pronounced as "ha-NA," but in earlier times it was pronounced as "pa-NA."
2   In the late 1990s, the prices and charges for cellular phones dropped drastically, which led many Japanese young people (including college and high-school students) to carry them instead of beepers. But still many Japanese youth use beepers to communicate with each other. Some people carry both cellular phones and beepers. There are even cellular phones with the added function of beepers available on the market in Japan. This shows that beepers are still in demand by young Japanese people, not for financial reasons, but for more social and cultural reasons.

References

Bruce, B. C., and Rubin, A (1993) *Electronic Quills: A Situated Evaluation of Using Computers for Writing in Classrooms*, Hillsdale, NJ: Lawrence Erlbaum.
Burbulus, N. C. (1998) "Rhetorics of the Web: Hyperreading and critical literacy," in Snyder, I. (ed.) *Page to Screen: Taking Literacy into the Electronic Era*, New York: Routledge.
Buten, J. (1996) "The First World Wide Web Personal Home Page Survey," [online], available at <http://www.asc.upenn.edu/usr/sbuten/phpi.htm>
Finders, M. J. (1997) *Just Girls: Hidden Literacies and Life in Junior High*, New York: Teachers College Press.
Hassam, A. (1993) *Writing and Reality: A Study of Modern British Diary Fiction*, London, Greenwood Press.

Hatano, G. (1995) "The Psychology of Japanese Literacy: Expanding 'the Practice Account,'" in Martin, L. Nelson, K. and Tobach, E. (eds) *Sociocultural Psychology: Theory and Practice of Doing and Knowing*, New York: Cambridge University Press.

Honda, M. (1996) *Kokan nikki: Shojo tachi no himitsu no purei rando* [Exchange diary: A hidden playland for girls], Tokyo: Iwanami Shoten.

Ikeda, K. (ed.) (1997) *Nettowakingu komyuniti* [Networking Community], Tokyo: University of Tokyo.

Kawakami, Y., Tamura, K., Uchida, H., Tabata, A., and Fukuda, M. (1996) *A Report of an Internet Online Survey*, available at <http://www.ntv.co.jp/bekkoame/> [in Japanese]

Kawaura, Y. and Shibanai, Y. (1997) "Netto ni bunsan, netto de linku" [distributed on the Net, linked with the Net], in Ikeda, K. (ed.) *Nettowakingu komyuniti* [Networking community], Tokyo: University of Tokyo Press.

Moran, C. and Hawisher, G. E. (1998) "The Rhetorics and Languages of Electronic Mail," in Snyder, I. (ed.) *Page to Screen: Taking Literacy into the Electronic Era*, New York: Routledge.

Motorola. Pager Codes (1998) "Motorola Develops List of Codes for Ingenious Messages Using Numeric Pagers," [online], available at <http://www.spirit.mot.com/MIMS/MSPG/Press/PR960327_17755.html>

Sanderson, D. (1993) *Smileys*. Sebastopol, CA: O'Reilly & Associates.

Sproull, L. and Kiesler, S. (1986) "Reducing Social Context Cues: The Case of Electronic Mail," *Management Science* 32: 1492–1512.

Street, B. V. (1995) *Social Literacies: Critical Approaches to Literacy in Development, Ethnography and Education*, New York: Longman.

Sugimoto, T. (1997a) "Comprehension Difficulties due to Lack or Shortage of Contextualization Information in Reading Information through the World Wide Web," paper presented at the Annual Meeting of the American Educational Research Association, Chicago, IL.

Sugimoto, T. (1997b) "Cognitive Difficulties and their Resolutions in Comprehending Information through the Web," paper presented at the 7th European Conference for Research on Learning and Instruction, Athens, Greece.

READING SIDEWAYS, BACKWARDS, AND ACROSS: SCOTTISH AND AMERICAN LITERACY PRACTICES AND WEAVING THE WEB

Sarah Sloane and Jason Johnstone

A web, I hear, thou hast begun,
And know'st not when it may be done –
(Michael Bruce, "Weaving Spiritualized")

Writing is often contested terrain. Tracing the provenance, circulation, and reception of any substantive writing provokes questions that come to be debated fiercely by cantankerous critics, thoughtful theorists, and other curious readers. However, Scottish writing – and the signs that constitute the visible traces of its practices in manuscripts, codex books, and computers – has a history of particularly sharp debates about who wrote what for whom. What does it mean to be original? What is the relationship between personal identity and public performance of that self? Many Scottish writers, critics, and publishers between the seventeenth and twentieth centuries have been involved in colorful debates about textual ownership, intellectual property, plagiarism, and copyright. A close reading of Scottish literary history reveals that some Scottish writers have borrowed freely and feverishly from writers beyond their country's borders. Starting with William Drummond of Hawthornden (1585–1649),[1] some Scottish writers have been experts at writing the unacknowledged translation, assembling a pastiche of other writers' work, and cobbling together the unattributed bricolage, or what Rebecca Howard has called, in another context, "patch-writing" (Howard, 1995). When we take a historical overview of Scottish literacy practices and events, we find a composing method that often relies (sometimes inordinately) on an expert hand that splices together the works and ideas of other writers, a hand whose only real genius is a capacity for the artful cut and paste. When the circulation of Scottish texts is amplified by the Internet,

154

it is no surprise that new questions about textual origins arise. Specifically, reading Scottish daily newspapers (and watching Scottish readers read about the United States) on the Web reveals a new dimension of literacy practices, practices both familiar and newly evolved.

Readers' responses to contemporary Scottish writings such as daily newspapers grow more querulous and snarled as those readers encounter locally grounded texts like daily newspapers online – and as the constituencies of readers grow more multicultural, multimodal, multilingual, and postmodern. Web-based texts such as newspapers in general threaten modernist definitions of literary value and force anew a postmodern appreciation for the breadth and diversity of literary form and meaning. Scottish Web-based newspapers in particular offer a new site to chart a familiar dynamic: how at the center of some Scottish composing processes and some critical evaluations of Scottish texts is a nervous looking outward beyond the borders of Scotland to determine worth, quality, and form of compositions, critical responses, and even Scottish identity.

Critical readers of Scottish newspapers on the Web today are likely to find themselves interacting with online reporting that reveals cross-cultural dynamics of power and national identity as much as it relays the news. Large circulation of newspapers like that enjoyed by the *Scotsman* does little to alter that paper's essential grounding in a sometimes provincial Edinburgh, a smallish city hungry to be the capital of a new Scotland, the Saltire waving behind every printed word. Other online newspapers like the *Shetland News* force an appreciation of how a region's size and power may be amplified when a paper's readership swells to include North Americans and other national peoples. What, for example, do Americans make of the obituary of Captain John Westwood Hay of Delgatie, a colorful fellow who "died peacefully in his sleep on 6 September, just five days after the momentous referendum which showed that his fellow Scots, even the Shetland awkward squad, had at last come round to his way of thinking?" Or a description of "feathered serial killers," rare local birds called Bonxies or the Great Skua, who are wiping out whole colonies of kittiwakes? And a feature called "Get the fish prices, laddie!"?[2] The speed, efficiency, and cost of Scottish newspapers delivered on the Web allows a wide, international readership to participate in Scottish local traditions as well as larger national debates.

Again, we acknowledge that all writing is often contested terrain, and certainly many national literary traditions could be understood in the same terms as we have here introduced. Appropriating others' words for one's own use is a time-honored authorial practice. However, we propose that Scottish writers are particularly keen to borrow ideas, words, and other signs from neighboring countries and cultures for a number of reasons specific to their culture, including reasons both geographical and ideological, such as the size of Scotland's territory and population, as well as its uneasy relations with England and English ideas about education, style, literary worth, and critical taste. And we posit that some North American readers like to appropriate signs of Scottish identity like a knowledge of fish prices in Shetland. In this chapter, we will explore how a particular aspect of Scottish literacy practices, *borrowing*, is transposed and transfigured into some reading and writing practices undertaken about and by Scottish people "reading the news" on the Web.

By taking a perspective both social and semiotic, we can see the Web as a mechanism for the transmission and reception of signs, especially cultural signs; and when we study the transmission and reception of cultural signs at a particular social site, the daily newspaper, we see a Scottish tradition of borrowing transmuted into a new medium, and with a new profile. This new borrowing, as it emerges in our personal reading patterns, has been both cross-cultural and nostalgic, as we discuss below.

Historical background

William Drummond of Hawthornden's borrowings are among the earliest examples of a Scottish ambivalence about the nature and worth of home-grown words, an ambivalence expressed more recently in the critical responses to Ian Hamilton Finlay's poems written in Glaswegian dialect, or the furor surrounding the granting of the 1994 Booker Prize to the Scottish writer James Kelman's novel, *How Late it was, How Late*. Often accused of plagiarism (literally, the kidnapping of words belonging to someone else), Drummond read and rewrote in English, the French and Italian literature lodged in his personal library. A dubious process of "imitation," Drummond's efforts yielded work in the forms, phrases, and, occasionally, poems translated whole cloth that were invariably attributed by Drummond to himself alone. Defended by the critic Edwin Morgan as a writer who was simply participating in the Renaissance tradition of imitation, Drummond's authorial practice nonetheless can be seen as an early Scottish example of "patch-writing," or reading with intent to kidnap words. In this famous case, Drummond appropriated the ideas and phrases of some of the best of seventeenth-century continental poetry.

In the eighteenth century, too, at least in the literacy practices of key figures in the Edinburgh Enlightenment, the circulation of written ideas about taste, elocution, the sublime, and even the history of the English language was such that very similar themes and phrases surfaced in the writings of Lord Kames, Adam Smith, Hugh Blair, and William Greenfield (Sloane, 1997). That circulation of ideas among the Edinburgh *literati* today would be characterized at best as an unacknowledged collaboration and at worst as plagiarism. We might also include here, in our brief survey of Scottish borrowers, the nineteenth-century compositions of Walter Scott, which relied heavily on the oral stories and myths circulating in the Scottish Borders, and George Macdonald, whose *Lilith* matches closely in conception and plot the work of C. S. Lewis's *Narnia Chronicles,* composed decades later. In the twentieth century, the Scottish poet Hugh Macdiarmid rewrote poems by Robert Burns to reflect contemporary ideas of Scottish identity, and informationist poets reshuffle materials lifted from computer manuals, scientific treatises, and the like. Most recently, two Scottish poets had their poems "raided," their words and forms kidnapped, in this case by a Cornishman, Alan Kent, in a case that has provided entertaining reading in the *TLS,* the *Scotsman,* and other newspapers.[3] Certainly, one strand of the rich tapestry that comprises Scottish writing is a tradition of writers borrowing words, ideas, and themes from beyond its borders.

Scottish writing is rich, diverse, and has multiple preoccupations and perspectives. When this strand is transposed onto the Web, we can observe and answer more completely the question of how cultural values are embedded in any writing.

Method

The two authors of this chapter well demonstrate the cross-cultural character of some Web-based readings, and we study our experiences in reading about Scotland in Web-based newspapers as an image of how two readers' literacy practices are shaped by their own idiosyncratic national, ideological, and cultural locations. We explore how our own behaviors and responses as readers on the Web reveal a dimension of online literacy practices being framed by cultural context.

In this chapter we look at how we have read two current events – the 11 September 1997 Scottish Home Rule Vote and the 26–28 September 1997 Ryder Cup Competition – covered by newspapers published on the Web. We believe that the patterns of our own responses to Web-based versions of the *Scotsman,* the *Glasgow Herald,* the *International Herald Tribune,* as well as the *Dallas Morning News* reveal our own regional location, cultural biases, and ideological bases. By putting these Web-based newspapers and our own readings of them under scrutiny, we uncover one small part of the fluid picture of how the Web connects and crosses cultures, dispositions, and positions. Further, by seeing our readings in the historical context of debates about national identity, educational policy and practices, and literacy education in the United Kingdom and the United States, we are beginning to realize how the Web spurs and blurs understandings of national identity and cultural pride.

The first half of this chapter offers a general description of Scottish literacy practices and events and focuses on Scottish political, economic, educational, and historical contexts of the simple act of reading a newspaper online. The second half of this chapter offers our readings of online newspapers and suggests an interpretation of our own readings. Ultimately, we attempt to connect the two halves of the chapter, speculating how the thick description of Scottish literacy events inflects the authors' own idio-syncratic, culturally-based negotiations of reading online newspapers including the *Scotsman,* the *International Herald Tribune,* and the *Dallas Morning News.*

Desire for news that maintains our sense of identities drives our reading patterns on the Web. We speculate that Sarah's readings might best be characterized as nostalgic or "looking backwards," and Jason's as paratactic or "looking sideways," and as more broadly international. While we do not offer our own readings or processes of using the Web as representative of American or Scottish readings in general, we do see our readings and subsequent analyses as moving towards the development of a critical category in understanding how cultural identity is formed, fractured, and reinforced by reading practices. We believe that the way we follow national stories in online newspapers published on the Web fits into a Scottish pattern of borrowing ideas, themes, and words written outside its borders, and an American pattern of seeking meaning and authenticity in the traces of self we find in some Web-version of an ancestral homeland. We see our nostalgic and paratactic readings as fitting into a strand of the literacy practices of Scottish readers and writers composing over the last four hundred years, albeit in a different material.

In general, we have found that reading about current events in Scotland on the Web complicates the ways in which we define national interests, boundaries, and identity. When we consider how national context affects composition and interpretation, we are in a good position to start exploring how newspaper articles about Scotland or read from Scotland on the Web foster literacy practices familiar in kind but new in their particulars. We notice that the Web allows the import and export of general *cultural* knowl-edge, and that that binational, cross-Atlantic exchange of cultural knowledge contributes to a kind of reading that might well be called "patch-reading" on the screen. Patch-reading, we propose, might be considered a counter-point to Howard's (1995) patch-writing, and the term is designed to capture the essence of this new activity of hand and eye: splicing together stories and meaning across the Web.

Authors' profiles and theoretical stances

In the field of literacy neither theory nor practice can be divorced from their ideological roots.

(Street, 1995, p. 45)

Sarah Sloane offers her reading of the Home Rule Vote and the news stories leading up to that vote as an example of an American's "nostalgic" reading, or a reading "backwards." She sees her own readings in the context of her personal longing for Scottish identity and a national longing for history, background, and heritage. Jason Johnstone offers his reading of the Ryder Cup Competition as an example of how he uses the Web to follow sporting events outside of Scotland; he acknowledges the shift in his own Web-reading practices when his flesh-and-blood location shifts radically from his national location, that is, when he finds himself hungry for news of Scottish sports and players during his year studying abroad in Tacoma, Washington. Johnstone's readings might be characterized as reading "side-ways," as Web-based readings that allow him to shuttle back and forth between the United States and Scotland, understanding his national iden-tity primarily in terms of sporting events and their outcomes. In both cases, the co-authors of this chapter are "reading across" the Atlantic Ocean in an attempt to find and redefine their understanding of the signal elements of Scottish identity.

Obviously, we approach writing this chapter as two people arriving from very different cultural experiences. Sarah Sloane is an associate professor of English at the University of Puget Sound whose primary training is in rhetoric and composition, and whose research interests include eighteenth-century Scottish rhetoric. She lived in Edinburgh, Scotland from 1979–1981 (following her senior year at Middlebury College) as a Thomas J. Watson Fellow writing poems and stories for blind children. She has spent parts of the last five summers in Scotland. Sarah continues to read with avid interest any Scottish fiction, poetry, news, politics, and aesthetic theories, in books and libraries, here and abroad, and on the Web. Jason Johnstone, whose home institution is Aberdeen University, was an undergraduate exchange student at University of Puget Sound for the 1997–1998 academic year. A joint major in philosophy and English, Jason came to America for that year, he admits candidly, to see American sports firsthand. He also studied for two years for an applied bio-sciences degree at Glasgow Caledonian University; and at the University of Strathclyde, he studied English, Scottish history and politics. During his junior year at University of Puget Sound, Jason took a year's set of courses in philosophy and English, including coursework in the history of ethics, ethical problems, and American literature. At the time of this writing, Jason is back at Aberdeen and studying four contemporary Scots poets (Crichton Smith, Leonard, Dunn, and Lochhead) and looking forward to his spring courses on Romantic and Renaissance Scotland. Someday, Jason hopes, he might teach philosophy at a university while writing on the side.

The theoretical stances of the two primary authors of this chapter are informed by Brian Street's 1995 publication, *Social Literacies*, quoted at the beginning of this chapter. In particular, we are interested in the ways that cultural studies, literacy studies, and studies in rhetoric and composition might usefully converge in an analysis of how readers and writers use the Web. Brian Street's intelligent synthesis of Hoggart's *The Uses of Literacy* (1957) connects Hoggart's work to the ultimate aims of the Centre for

Contemporary Cultural Studies (the CCCS was founded by Hoggart in the late 1950s), and the theories that underlie Street's own research. Street explains that Hoggart was interested in exploring "how separate texts/ rituals/ institutions interrelated in a 'whole way of life'" (p. 58). Street sees Hoggart's *The Uses of Literacy* as,

> an attempt to "read" intuitively the cultural meaning of that period in British society from the inside; to see especially how change was being lived through and lived out in the "felt" experiences of men and women in the society; and to define the impact of the new mass media and the more contemporary modes of feeling which they expressed, on the cultural attitudes, sentiments, values and traditions of working class life and experience.
>
> (Publicity for CCCS, 1978, p. 19, quoted in Street, 1995, p. 59)

The ways in which Street and the Centre defined "culture" is helpful to our study, and we note the Centre's definition of culture because it describes the site of our own efforts – particularly in its inclusiveness. According to Centre publicity, "culture" is best understood as:

> the lived experience, the consciousness of a whole society; that particular order, pattern, configuration of valued experience, expressed now in imaginative art of the highest order, now in the most popular and proverbial forms, in gesture and language, in myth and ideology, in modes of communication and in forms of social relationship and organisation.
>
> (Publicity for CCCS, 1978, p. 19, quoted in Street, 1995, p. 59).

By connecting studies in literary critical theory and anthropological approaches and ideas, Street reminds literacy researchers of the vital importance of considering not just literacy *per se*, but the content and ideology of literacy events and practices (p. 71). We follow Street in our assumptions, methodology, and critical stance.

The participation of Jason and Sarah together in this study is crucial because each brings different strengths to the study. Jason is a native Scotsman who understands the culture as an insider; Sarah is able to bring her academic expertise to understanding some of the assumptions and literacy practices Jason describes. By working together, they hope to avoid what Brian Street characterizes as the "'if I were a horse approach' to other cultures"(1995, p. 75). Street uses Sir James Frazer as a prime example of a researcher practicing this flawed approach:

Frazer's psychological insight, in which he prided himself, was often at fault, largely because he thought that he could understand very foreign beliefs quite out of their real contexts simply by an effort of introspection. He and others of his time had something of the approach of Sherlock Holmes in the work of his near-contemporary Conan Doyle: "You know my methods in such cases, Watson. I put myself in the man's place, and having first gauged his intelligence, I try to imagine how I myself should have proceeded under the same circumstances."

(Lienhardt, 1964, p. 27, quoted in Street, 1995, p. 76).

As Street explains later in his discussion of Walter Ong's tendency to assume the "if I were a horse" thinking, "the basic problem here is that if the observer has no first-hand experience of the people whose thinking he is trying to replicate imaginatively, then in effect the account becomes a reflection of the writer's own culture and own thinking" (1995, p. 150).

Finally, this chapter also takes the perspective that within the social practices of reading and writing we will find embedded (if not entrenched) cultural ideas and values. We find Street's argument persuasive that within the "current writing practices and pedagogy in American schooling" for example, there is evidence not of instruction in "neutral learning skills" but in "deep levels of cultural meaning and belief" (1995, p. 111). We acknowledge that our critical stance, finally, is influenced by our own entrenchment in academic practices, communities, and discourses. We try our best to heed Street's plea and thus to understand the Web not as a neutral information delivery system, but as an apparatus that conveys cultural position and insiders' knowledge as much as it conveys the words of particular peoples.

The whole ball of wax: demographics, politics, educational history, computer usage, newspaper usage, and languages of Scotland

Introduction

All Scottish literacy practices and events exist, of course, in a context, and today's images of Scotland on the Web exist in particular demographic, political and national, and historical contexts. We posit that those contexts are apparent in Web discourse in ways both visible and invisible – and of course, it is the invisible in which we are most interested. In other words, we acknowledge that the elements of Scottish identities are a rich mix, and we speculate that when the Web conveys the signs (and distortions) of Scottish identities, it does so in ways that extend beyond the visible images and symbols, the bits and bytes that comprise traffic on the Web. We suspect that Scottish identities are assembled on the Web in ways that are as incomplete and haphazard as the compositions assembled by professors in Jonathan Swift's Grand Academy of Lagado. As readers may recall, in this academy, professors turned the handle on a 20-foot square frame that contained all the words of their language in different moods, declensions, and tenses strung on slender wires stretched across the frame. By turning the handle, the professors were able to arrange parts of sentences occurring by chance, and those sentences were assembled into books that became part and parcel of the scholarly knowledge of the Academy of Lagado (Sloane, 2000). Of course, even as these sentences were assembled and printed, the far more interesting question is what on earth was going on in the minds of these so-called professors. Why did they so trust and elevate in status the words revealed on a frame that sounds like a giant abacus, a low-rent Web? What does Swift reveal about contemporary scholarship in his colorful image of professors blinkered by convention and blind to the limits of the ways in which they discover knowledge? And how apt is this metaphor to the ways in which we study the pastiches that comprise reading on the Web today?

When we identify the demographic, political, and historical contexts surrounding all written compositions in Scotland, and we look at patterns of computer use, habits of reading newspapers, and the representation of Scottish languages online and offline, we are better prepared to study how the Web facilitates and inhibits the formation of Scottish identities in our own readings. We can see how we read the words churning on the Web. Finally, because of its overarching importance, we wish to restate one point: we recognize that Scotland's peoples are diverse in identity, point of view, literacy, and computer knowledge, and we do not intend to blur these differences in sweeping generalizations. On the contrary, we wish only to contextualize our own two reading practices on the Web to see how this new information delivery system might affect the way we see ourselves and assemble our own senses of Scottish identity.

Demographics

Scotland is a country of 77,167 square kilometers with a population of about 5.1 million. It is simultaneously a member of the United Kingdom, the Commonwealth, the European Union, the Council of Europe, the Western European Union, and NATO. The country is currently under the governance of Prime Minister, the Right Honourable Tony Blair (b. 1953) and Scottish interests in the government are represented by the Secretary of State for Scotland, the Right Honourable Donald Dewar (b. 1937). In May 1999, elections will be held to elect a new Scottish Parliament, an election that is expected to place more Scottish Nationalist party members than Labour party members in parliament (see, for example, Hoge, 1998, p. 3).

Politics

Street (1995) helps us see that all Scottish literacy practices are undertaken within the cultural context of an uncomfortable union with a dominant partner to the south (England) for almost four hundred years. A brief summary of some of the salient moments in that relationship must include the following. In 1603, James VI of Scotland (son of Mary, Queen of Scots) succeeded to the throne of England as James I – and thus effected the Union of the Crowns of England and Scotland. In 1707, The Act of Union was passed, in which in principle the two parliaments were "united" and in practice, Scotland was granted representation in the British Parliament. A 1979 referendum on whether to create an elected Scottish assembly was defeated, but the proposal to create a Scottish legislature with limited taxing authority passed on 11 September 1997 by 74 percent (Hoge, 1998, p. 3). Again, a new Scottish parliament, to be elected in May 1999, will have law-making and taxing powers over all domestic matters.

Histories

The Web's implicit assumption of shared cultural values and a neutral appara-tus of disseminating ideas begins to falter when we look at it through Scottish eyes. In particular, the political and ideological contexts of literacy events in Scotland since the Act of Union have been dominated by crude generalizations about the commonality between the Scottish and the English – and characterized by a sustained attempt by educational bodies, govern-ment, and even churches, to minimize differences while at the same time asserting English ways of talking, writing, and reading as the model to which Scots must aspire.

We can see the historical roots of this English attitude of superiority in the decades immediately following the implementation of the 1707 Act of Union. In the aftermath of uprisings against the English in 1715 and 1745, the University of Edinburgh appointed the first Regius Professor of Rhetoric and Belles Lettres, Hugh Blair, to help train men destined for the clergy or the bar in how to use the English language properly. Literacy events and practices in eighteenth-century Scotland were clearly affected by the dominant discourse patterns streaming in from the south: Blair and his successors used examples from contemporaneous English journals (the *Spectator,* the *Tatler,* and others) to educate their students in how to write and speak; Lecturers Adam Smith, Thomas Sheridan, and Hugh Blair gave public courses of lectures on "good taste" and "the sublime" which relied on examples drawn from English poets (Milton, Pope), artists (Sir Joshua Reynolds), and writers (Addison and Steele). Thomas Sheridan's (an Irishman, ironically) lectures on elocution and James Beattie's books on unwitting Scotticisms were designed to help educated Scotsmen and women rid their language of unwanted Scottish rusticisms; Samuel Johnson railed against the Scots, as is well known, teasing his biographer Boswell with the remark that he knew Boswell could not help coming from Scotland. Even today, in many literary and critical discussions of British literature, English writers are cited, discussed, emulated, and applauded at the expense of the Scottish, the Welsh, and the Irish. The occasional reversal of this relationship, as in Scotsman James Kelman winning the 1994 Booker Prize, is often met with English incredulity.

Histories of the relations between Scotland and the United States

Scotland and the United State, too, have had significant cross-pollination of political ideas, intellectual traditions, and educational policies over time. In America alone there are eight Aberdeens, eight Edinburghs, and seven Glasgows (McCrum and McNeil, 1987, p. 127). Three of the original signers (Benjamin Rush, John Witherspoon, and James Wilson) to the American Declaration of Independence were native-born Scots (Horner, 1998, p. 3). In addition, several critics (Horner, 1998; Turnbull, 1986) have demonstrated the deep undercurrent of principles of the Scottish Enlightenment in the early documents and recorded statements of the framers of the US Constitution. In Turnbull's terms:

> the spirit that infuses many of the central doctrines of Congress, from 1774–1787, is in peculiar harmony with the legal, philosophical and moral teachings of Hutcheson, Reid, and Kames; whose views in turn reflect the historical and constitutional inheritance of Scotland itself.
>
> (Horner, 1998, p. 3, quoting Turnbull, p. 149)

The educational system that arose in the United States in the late eighteenth century was directly influenced by Scottish Enlightenment thinkers. For example, Hugh Blair's *Lectures on Rhetoric and Belles Lettres*, published in 1783 in Edinburgh, went into 130 editions and was adopted by several of the best universities, including Yale in 1785, Harvard in 1788, and Dartmouth in 1822 (Horner, 1998, p. 3). According to Kitzhaber, "In 1850, [Blair's lectures] were used in 20 of 43 American colleges and was in use at Yale and Williams until 1850 and Notre Dame as late as 1880" (Kitzhaber, 1990, quoted in Horner, 1998, p. 3).

Scottish Patterns of Computer Use

Patterns of Scottish representations on the Web show a tendency to subsume the Scottish under the English. Web domain addresses for Scotland are subsumed within "co.uk." ("English" is often used as a synonym for "British" as Crawford has painstakingly outlined in the introduction to his *Devolving*

English Literature (1992), and things Scottish are misnamed English.) And searches on the Web for information about Scotland lead to tourist caricatures of men in kilts drinking whisky or fishing for salmon, and listings of Lowlands bed-and-breakfast establishments where one might hunt pheasant, play golf, or drink a wee dram. The tourist marketing of Scotland to a wealthy American audience is enough to make this American, anyway, cringe.

According to the Office for National Statistics, in 1992, 19.1 percent of British citizens claimed to have a computer at home.[4] A more recent study (1996) of computer use in the United Kingdom summarizes the following statistics:

> PC penetration per household is 37% in the United States, 25% in the United Kingdom, and only 7% in Japan, although the Japanese market is growing rapidly. 20% of United States households have modemed PCs, compared with only 2% in the United Kingdom and 1.4% in Japan. There are 16 Internet hosts per thousand population in the United States, 12 in Sweden, 5 in the United Kingdom, and 1.3 in Japan. . . . Fewer than 300,000 British PC owners currently subscribe to either a Bulletin Board Service or have an account with an Internet Service provider. This represents a penetration of about 3% of PC owners.[5]

After one is done being amused by the serious-minded metaphor of "penetration," one might note the great disparity in the number of Internet service providers and access to computers between the United States and Great Britain. Internet cafés in America outnumber Internet cafés in Great Britain by almost three to one.[6] Further, many workaday Scottish people do not have any access to a computer. In the summer of 1997, there were three Internet cafés in all of Edinburgh, and none had facilities for printing from an Apple computer. Only one Macintosh computer was available for public use in the entire city, a city of more than half a million people.

Some Scottish schools are attempting to change this trend and to increase access to computers for children. In March 1996, St Andrews High School, Kirkcaldy in Fife, was announced as one of three European sites for an Apple Computer of Tomorrow (APCOT) environment (Sealey, 1996). In December 1996, the 1,100-pupil Linlithgow Academy was announced as the first secondary school in Scotland to be fully networked, "that is, linked to both a local area network and via a broad band cable band to the Internet." Linlithgow Academy, located in Scotland's central belt, has 120 computers, of which 80 were able to access the Internet through the Edinburgh University's gateway. According to one newspaper report, Ann Coles, the assistant head at Linlithgow, reflected that one motivation for getting the country's secondary schools linked up to the Internet is that she wants

Scottish pupils to have "technological entitlement" even as they learn first-hand the importance of "old skills" like "literacy" (Mackie, 1996).

As Scotland adds computers to its schools, administrators such as Ann Coles are curtailing certain practices on the computer:

> At Linlithgow, Ann Coles says, a lot of thought went into devising a culture of proper use of the Internet. The school has a "responsible use agreement," which staff and pupils sign and which covers areas such as accessing pornographic or racist files, creating and uploading computer viruses, using copyrighted material without permission, and sending threatening or obscene messages. The agreement also binds users not to waste time by looking for irrelevant information, playing games on the Internet and hogging the system.
>
> (Mackie, 1996, p. 4)

Embedded within this "responsible use agreement" are cultural ideas about freedom of expression, censorship, and access. In particular, the admonition against "using copyrighted material without permission" is worth noting.

Scottish patterns of reading newspapers

In 1996, in the United Kingdom as a whole there were 10 national dailies with a combined average circulation in June of 13, 202, 574; there were nine national Sunday newspapers with an average circulation of 15, 174, 032. There were also about 100 morning, evening, and Sunday regional newspapers, and 2,000 weekly newspapers (about 1000 of which are given away free) (Hunter, 1997, p. 1327).

The *Scotsman,* an engaging daily newspaper whose logo on both the paper and Web versions is a Scottish thistle, calls itself "Scotland's National Newspaper." First published on Scottish poet Robert Burns' birthday, 25 January 1817, it started as an eight-page, ten-pence, Saturday journal, selling 300 copies. In 1823 the paper became a biweekly, and by 1897 the Scotsman circulation had expanded to 60,000 copies daily. Hot-metal printing ended in 1987, and in 1990, the giant Web-offset Goss Colorliner press opened which can print "in full colour 48 broadsheet pages at 75,000 copies an hour." The *Scotsman* made its début on the Web in 1995 with its publication of "Edinburgh Festival and Fringe 1995," a guide to the Edinburgh Festival of Arts and Music. Currently providing an online edition free to all visitors, the cover page to the *Scotsman Online Edition* says in part:

> The online edition is updated Monday through Saturday at 8 am GMT and although the majority of visitors will be those that cannot buy the terrestrial product, everybody is welcome to *The Scotsman*

Web site. We will portray modern Scotland in all its complexity and since we want to improve and extend our output we need plenty of feedback from you. Hope you enjoy it. Bye for the moment.[7]

This opening message is interesting to us in two important ways. First, the metaphor of paper-based newspapers being "terrestrial" yields the inference that the Web-based newspaper is somehow "celestial," and we wonder whether such status is based on a vision that sees the Web as broader in reach, higher (and more heavenly), or more efficient. Second, the informality and friendliness of the "you-address" and its request for feedback are in a tone and form more epistolary than journalistic. Does this introductory statement hint at a rhetorical leveling, a tighter connection between writer and reader, never mind where that reader might be? Are Web-based versions of newspapers, like e-mail, slipping into a secondary orality? And is this invitation to correspond ultimately false?

The Scottish author's habit of borrowing can be seen in the cut-and-paste practices of journalists writing in the nineteenth century. According to the newspaper historians Munro and Cormack:

> In accordance with the practice of the time, reporting was haphazard, dependent on "borrowing" from London and contemporary Scottish papers under the "mutual appropriation system." Low and others noted with some amusement the "extraordinary puff" of 25 January 1811 in which it was claimed that the Review would carry material supplied by special correspondence "that will only be found in the London papers OF THE DAY FOLLOWING."

Munro debunks this claim in his history of the *Montrose Review*:

> In fact, an analysis of the supply of news to a variety of Scottish newspapers made by R. M. W. Cowan revealed that much of the private correspondence published in Glasgow and Edinburgh came from shared sources. "It seems almost certain," he wrote, "that some correspondent in London took cuttings from one or more of the London papers and expressed them daily to the Scottish cities for the general benefit of the press, ahead of the normal deliveries of the London papers in Scotland. This feature, therefore, was not an exclusive despatch but a late-news column of common information."
>
> (Munro, 1986, p. 17)

Munro also cites statistics showing that around 1836, the *Scotsman* estimated a readership of six to ten readers per copy (ibid.).

167

Scotland's linguistic contexts: makars and balloons,[8] flyting or flaming,[9] and extraordinary puffs[10]

One of the most interesting aspects of the intercultural representation of Scotland on the Web is the way in which Scotland's linguistic complexity is muted and distorted in websites. Scots Gaelic is spoken in the north and central counties of Ross, the Islands of the Hebrides, and on Skye. (It is also spoken in Nova Scotia, Cape Breton, and Prince Edward Island, Canada, and New South Wales, Australia.)[11] In the 1971 census, 50 percent of respondents who spoke Gaelic claimed they could also read Gaelic. Approximately 65,000 Scottish people speak Gaelic (compared with Wales's 500,000 Welsh speakers and Britain's 1.5 million Hindi speakers). In the past ten years, the number of Gaelic speakers has fallen off by 20 percent. According to a 1992 article in *The Economist,*

> Gaels argue passionately over the source of the language's decline. Some date the downturn from the compulsory teaching [of] English [starting] in schools in 1872, others from the banning of Gaelic after the 1746 Battle of Culloden, while the long-termists insist that the end began at the Battle of Harlaw in 1411.
>
> (*The Economist,* November 14 1992)

According to the 1991 census, Gaelic is spoken regularly by less than 2 percent of Scotland's population (*St Louis Post-Dispatch,* 28 September 1997).

When we consider Gaelic from the point of view of "language display," a term developed in Eastman and Stein (1993) and cited by Cormack (1995) to ground his interpretation of how Gaelic is presented within the Scottish media, we can see that semiotically, at any rate, Gaelic is a linguistic marker for Scottish nationalism. According to Eastman and Stein, "Language display is used to negotiate an identity in order to establish a broader conception of self in society', and it is thus 'symbolic rather than structural or semantic expression'", (quoted in Cormack, 1995, p. 270, referring to Eastman and Stein, 1993, p. 200). Cormack underscores his findings of "language displays" by his observation that, "In the Scottish context, Gaelic is frequently used in such displays to indicate 'real' Scottishness, even by speakers who know virtually nothing of the language other than the toast *Slàinte mhath* (Good health)." He notes, for example:

> At the Scottish Conservative Party's 1994 Annual Conference held at Inverness, prominent on the front of the stage (and therefore frequently featuring in news reports) were the words *Alba: Adhartas Gach Latha* (Scotland: Progress Each Day).
>
> (Cormack, 1995, p. 271)

Today, Gaelic also appears weekly in a column published by *The Scotsman.*

Scots dialect

Scots dialect, on the other hand, appears more frequently within ordinary Scottish writing, from the stories by Irvine Welsh to feature articles published in the *Scotsman*. In 1983, William Laughton Lorimer offered his translation of *The New Testament in Scots* using twelve different varieties of Scots dialect, and most Scottish-born people had no difficulty understanding it. (In the Lorimer *New Testament*, incidentally, only the Devil speaks Standard English (McCrum, 1987, pp. 144–145).) Scots dialects in general are divided into four principal groups of dialects, each group designated as such largely through geographical distinctions. Central Scots is spoken in the area throughout the west and south of the Tay, except for a small area in the Borders and East Dumfriesshire. According to several sources, it is the most widely spoken form of Scots. Northern Scots is the other main form (within which Northeastern Scots, spoken in the area north of Stonehaven and East of Inverness, thrives as a distinct dialect).[12] In addition, Island Scots (primarily based in the Orkney and Shetland Islands) and Southern Scots (spoken in Eastern Dufriessshire and in the Borders; known sometimes as the "yow and mey" dialect because of the way speakers add -*ow* and -*ey* to the end of words where other people would say -*oo* and -*ee*), are spoken.

Comments

These rich linguistic contexts to Scottish literacy sites, events, and practices (including reading newspapers on the Web), while not a primary focus of this article, allow us to see another aspect of what is lost and what gained by reading about Scotland on the Internet. While the Web permits a wider readership of minority dialects like Scots or Gaelic, at the same time, oral distinctions among speakers of different Scots dialects are erased by their visual uniformity on the screen. Further, the dominant discourses of the Web, primarily those of American English, run the risk of silencing the rich, interesting, but ultimately local dialects such as Gaelic or Scots. The Internet permits the wide dissemination of minority views and discourses, but if those discourses are not accompanied by the literacy practices necessary to interpret and vocalize them, Gaelic on the Web is in danger of becoming a general sign, a linguistic display, of Scottish heritage with no particular meaning. One of the questions Scottish Web-based newspaper prompts is this important one: to what extent is the Internet a system of export and to what extent import, when the users of this information delivery system are widely disparate in views, voices, numbers, and power?

Looking at the reading experiences of two readers might help answer this question.

Sarah Sloane's reading of the Home Rule Vote:
or Auld Lang Syne

- HAVE A TRIP ROUND THE WEB LOUVRE
- DISCOVER HOW MANY AMERICANS ARE PANTYHOSE FETISHISTS
- E-MAIL MADONNA
- LISTEN TO BILL CLINTON ADDRESS YOU
- BOLDLY GO TO THE STAR TREK PAGES
- SEE WHAT A HUMAN LOOKS LIKE IN SLICES
- FIND OUT WHAT YOU CAN DO WITH LEGO!
- GET ON SITE WITH 'BLUR' OR 'MASSIVE ATTACK'

(Advertising flyer for Cyberia,
"Scotland's First Cybercafé," 1997)

For the last four summers (1995–1998), I have spent some time studying eighteenth-century writings on taste and the sublime housed at the National Library of Scotland in Edinburgh. The pattern of my days in Edinburgh has been about the same each summer. I rise around nine, eat a simple breakfast (usually strong coffee, boxed orange juice, oatcakes, butter, and a yogurt) in a spartan short-term rental, and walk the mile or so, rain or shine, hail or sun, to the National Library of Scotland on George IV Bridge. On my way to the library I walk through the Meadows (one time through a Celtic technopagan festival) and past charity shops, banks, fruit stands, baked-potato venders, construction sites, and the churchyard where Regius Professor Hugh Blair is buried. After arriving and getting the books I had put on reserve the day before, I work in the library from about eleven until six or seven, when I step out to get a bite to eat nearby, or, if I can stand it, until about eight or nine, when the library closes for the night. Then I walk or ride the bus over to Hanover Street, to Henderson's, my favorite vegetarian restaurant in the world, where I eat dinner, and then head over to Cyberia, Edinburgh's oldest Internet cafe, to correspond with friends and family back home. Every evening I spend at least an hour in Cyberia. I sit at the front of the coffeeshop/Internet space looking out on Hanover Street, across to the gray brick of the buildings opposite. I answer e-mail, correspond with advisees and former students, write to family, friends, and colleagues.

In time I began to spot the other regulars in the café. My rough estimate is that about a third of the writers were American; I usually, but not always, was the oldest person in the café; and at least half of the users on any given day seemed to be foreigners. One young woman from India was there every time I was there for at least ten days, chain-smoking and writing, quarreling with an older Indian woman who hovered always behind her, offering suggestions which seemed frequently spurned. One day last summer, a group of American women huddled around MSNBC and CNN weather maps posted to the Web, trying to figure out whether a hurricane had struck their homes back in Florida.

These days, back in Tacoma, Washington, I sit in my office at the university and use my computer to access the Web and hook up to "the live videocam" at Cyberia. On my computer screen, I look out on the same view I used to have from my chair in Cyberia, the same dull gray brick of the restaurants opposite, the same cobblestone Hanover Street. I wonder how my view of this particular street is different when seen through a window rather than through a computer screen in North America. And I wonder why I am drawn to read the online newspapers and websites devoted to Scotland (from sites on Scotch to those on the Findhorn Foundation) in general.

The best explanation I can come up with is that my reading is governed by an impulse primarily nostalgic. Nostalgia's etymology is *nostos* for home, and *-algia,* meaning pain. The nostalgic reading is one that tries to reinforce and reassemble a sense of national identity and pride, that in my case understands Scotland as the native land, the birthplace, a source of an embarrassing and perplexing pride in my own mixed Celtic background. Geoffrey Nunberg notes the peculiar property of the Web to atomize and convey bits of information, across oceans and peoples. He explains, "[documents like those on the Web] are highly modular, amenable to extraction and reorganization, and are much easier to dislodge and decontextualize than print documents are, features that support the sense of corpuscularity and tranferability" (Nunberg, 1996, p. 125). It seems to me that my own readings are ones of extraction, motivated by wishing. And within the reorganizations fostered by my wistfulness, a hybrid, shaky, and blurred Scottish identity rises.

Let me be more specific about the character of my nostalgic readings. As I sat at my desk in Tacoma, I tracked the daily accounts of the debates about devolution in newspapers on the Web, I found myself invariably rooting for the positions of the Scottish National Party and understanding the dynamics of the question in the simplistic terms of underdog versus oppressor. I remembered a Scottish friend telling me in person (during the summer of 1997) that if Scotland ever gained complete independence there might come a day when the new Scottish government would proclaim that everyone within the borders of Scotland that day would automatically become a Scottish citizen. *I want to be there on that day,* I told my friend. And I still feel that way.

I am captivated by my memories of Scotland and am delighted by every new bit of evidence that my own ancestors are from Scotland, that Sloane was originally a Scottish name, that my grandmother was one of the MacBean's of the Highlands, that my love of the Scottish landscape might be more than just another American's longing for history and background, the "continuity from the past, from their dungheaps of ancestor worship

171

and wealth and what they call their heritage," as Victoria Glendinning's character Peter Fisher so eloquently calls this preoccupation with one's roots (Glendinning, 1995, p. 139). Finally, I find myself wondering as I undertake my "nostalgic readings" how much I am responding as my own cultural context has programmed me to respond. That is, is my nostalgic reading simply a counterpart to Nunberg's claim that "all information is a mode of reading" (1996, p. 123)? In the same way that Web-based news-papers encode patterns of reading (in page layout), establish hierarchies of worth (in size of headlines), and direct and deflect our attention towards particular "stories" (according to placement on the "page" and ease of access through hot buttons), have my own somatic habits of reading been encoded by a larger cultural narrative of nostalgia and yearning? I don't know. But when I read via the Web about Scotland's new parliament and the histories that lie behind this new institution, I am deeply engaged.

In the Queen's Speech on 15 May 1997, Prime Minister Tony Blair's Labour Party set out its plans to hold a referendum on Scottish devolution. As promised by the Labour Party, on 11 September 1997, Scottish voters will be asked to answer two question: Do you want a Scottish parliament? Should it have power to raise its own revenue? When a simple majority of Scottish voters voted "yes, yes," Scotland was on its way to having its own parliament for the first time in nearly three hundred years. American news-papers like the *Seattle Post-Intelligencer* picked up Sarah Lyall's news article in the *New York Times* the day after the Home Rule Vote and printed the following remarks:

> Seven hundred years after Scottish hero William Wallace routed England's forces at the Battle of Stirling Bridge, Scotland won a modern nationalist fight yesterday, voting to establish a Legislature of its own for the first time since 1707. The move, the greatest upheaval for Britain's unity since southern Ireland became the Irish Free State in 1922, stops short of severing Scotland's ties with the rest of Britain; Queen Elizabeth will still be head of state here, and Tony Blair head of government. But the new Legislature, which could start work as early as 2000, would have a budget of about $38 billion a year and a range of powers over every facet of Scotland's domestic affairs.
>
> (Lyall, 1997, p. 6)

According to several reports, "[w]ith votes in 18 of the 32 regions counted, 72.6 percent of voters backed a parliament, with most regions posting turnouts of more than 60 percent" (Lyall, 1997). Donald Dewar, the British secretary of state for Scotland, declared victory for Blair's policies.

In an opinion piece published about three weeks before the Scottish vote on devolution, the *Scotsman*'s Scottish political editor, Peter MacMahon, chastised the Scottish Secretary, Donald Dewar for his part in "an ill-tempered press conference." At one point, MacMahon acknowledges his readership directly with a wry Scottish rusticism that caught my eye:

> As we have known for some time – though it may be a shock to those who have been **furth of Scotland** of late – the new parliament will not be some kind of Strathclyde regional council "socialist supreme soviet." Thanks to the additional member voting system, Labour will not dominate, although it is likely to be the largest party.
>
> (MacMahon, 1997b)

As a reader located, indeed, "furth of Scotland," I was delighted to be instructed in what every Scottish schoolboy and girl already knew.

Peter Jones, the Scotland and North of England correspondent of *The Economist* also ventured an opinion piece about the upcoming referendum, a provocatively entitled "Less–less for yes–yes?" He refers to a former United States president for an image of the kind of campaign Scotland should at all costs avoid. He reminds readers of "Ronald Reagan, the born-again, astrology-guided fundamentalist zombie with a lively interest in Armageddon brought the world closer to disaster than most people realise . . .". Jones admonishes his readers to:

> Think only of the vacuous Hollywood liberals who endorsed Clinton, that beacon of virtue, or the luvvies for Labour who were recently spilling wine and platitudes on the Downing Street carpets, and you realise that entertainment is all that remains when politics loses its point. The ability to deliver a script convincingly matters more than the script itself. The impersonation of integrity – a Reagan specialty – becomes the only virtue. . . . Now, with something like dread, we hear that the pro-devolution campaign is assembling a star-studded cast to advance its cause.
>
> (Jones, 1997)

There is a part of me that greatly enjoys this sniggering at America's expense, and I am sure it is in part because I agree so heartily. However, what makes this reading of the Home Rule Vote discussions and outcome notable is that it took place on the Web, thousands of miles from the event itself, substituting the context of a university office for the immediate, real-time contexts of the sometimes heated debates that surrounded devolution. Further, digitized images, real-time video, and newspaper stories replete with hot links and decontextualized slurs on the United States political system substitute for real participation. It is all observer and no participation. It is the simulacrum and not the real. Maybe the Web helps politics become entertainment, after all.

When we think about our training in classical rhetoric and the Aristotelian notion of the importance of selection and arrangement, we see that one way to understand better the literacy practices of reading newspapers on the Web is to understand them as comprising three major processes of selection. First, the collaborations of writers and editors at the *Scotsman* and other newspapers constitute a selection of topic and treatment that is crucial. Second, the selection of material to post to a server and thus disseminate world-wide is constrained by economic resources, available computing technologies, and user access and competence. Third, and most important for our purposes, the reader selects journal, page, and topic to read on the Web always according to his or her interests, contexts, and cultural and ideological position. We find cultural signs where we look for them, and we look for them according to our needs.

Finally, we recognize that Sarah's nostalgic readings, or readings that look back to earlier Scottish experiences, are directed by search engines, recommendations of friends, and advertisements on the Web itself – all evidence that the Web's presentation of information is not necessarily innocent nor neutral. As Nunberg remarks about another information delivery system, the radio, we are remarkably naïve about the source of what we look at and listen to. In his example, Nunberg explains:

> You get into a rental car in a strange city, turn on the radio, and hear an announcer say that the Giants have been eliminated from the division race on the last day of the season; you accept what you hear without interrogating it, or without having to know anything more about the speaker, the program, or the radio station. You accept, that is, in virtue of the form of language that expresses it and the kind of document that presents it.
>
> (Nunberg, 1996, pp. 122–123)

Already, individual search engines lead Sarah to particular websites in patterns of suggested readings she is remarkably unquestioning in following. And as she pursues the nostalgic readings facilitated by the Web, she pays little or no attention to those elements of cultural situation or kairotic moment that are stripped away by the speed, efficiency, focus, and limits of the Web itself. Sarah treats the Web like an ossuary and wanders around it seeking the relief of memory in its transparent bones.

Looking for Hugh Blair's grave

in the last fickle Edinburgh light
shafts of sun burning down
the clouds dimming over
the tomb of Adam Fergusson

just past the sloped grass
of a bookseller's grave
the churchyard slope dappled
by wild daisy, shadow, light –

In fact, William Creech, the bookseller,
has the grandest stone we find,
its carved letters framing
an old message dark
under the thin coins of sun
falling from the fast
unpromising skies –

we can't find the stone
we are looking for
so we keep talking,
the Scottish woman
and her tall American friend
met by chance and plan
in this quiet graveyard thronged
by ghosts of the Enlightenment.

Alone in the graveyard
we walk, look, talk
about that crazy Russian artist
your brother married, the one
who paints portraits of dead fish,
each hanging carcass scaled and crepuscular –

the one painting she repeats
in stained glass and oils
is a fish strung from a leash
held by two nuns
the fish's otherworldly, mixed face
bearing a huge single eye
not quite live, but marking time
against our slow, gossipy walk
across brae, hummock, and stone.

And we find we are still looking hard
to find the one stone
that will release us
from seeking, wondering
whether the sagging, scaled clouds
will yield to our looking tonight.

Sarah Sloane

Jason Johnstone's reading of the 1997 Ryder Cup competition

Background

I became a Dallas Cowboys fan when I was six years old. My cousins, aunt, and uncle from America came to visit me in Ayr in 1980, and they brought me football jerseys, jackets, and socks – all sporting the colors and insignia of the Dallas Cowboys. I felt sheer excitement and jubilation to be wearing a Dallas Cowboys jacket to school, with the dark blue and the silver sleeves, the helmet stitched on the chest. I've got two pieces of the old tartan turf from the Dallas Cowboys old field (from when they replaced it with Texas turf). My cousin gave me the two $4'' \times 2''$ blocks because he knew I was a Dallas Cowboys fan. To have affiliations with a country that you could look at on a globe and a wall chart and see that it was so far away but to know that you had part of that place right there made me feel grand. It made me feel different, like an individual, to have this interest in American football.

Around 1984, when I was 10 years old, I began to read a football almanac published in America. The *American Football Almanac* is a small, thick book published each year which offered me my first chance to read about a sport that wasn't discussed in national Scottish newspapers. I devoured it, spent hours reading it, taking it to school, showing friends. When I think back on my sports-reading history, finding this book was momentous. At home in Scotland, soccer is the primary game that is covered by the newspapers. I've never liked reading about soccer, watching soccer, nor playing soccer. I find it extremely boring. Reading about American football was infinitely superior. American football is broken into plays in a way that makes it very interesting to watch. Soccer, on the other hand, seems interminable to me. The physicality of football is wonderful.

As soon as I got to Aberdeen University in 1996, I started reading about sports on the Web. My readings started by looking up nfl.com, nba.com, and the *Dallas Morning News*, online. (I saw the Internet addresses of nfl.com and nba.com on the sidelines of the games that I saw on TV, and I looked at those, too.) Since I had spent a summer at Dallas reading the *Morning News* every day, it was a pleasure to read it again at home in Aberdeen. It was familiar. And it gave me a perspective on the Dallas Cowboys that I thought was really objective.

Today, at University of Aberdeen, I have my homepage set to espn.com. Whenever I log onto the Web, I go first to espn.com, read the headlines, check out the main story, and then, in general, just see what's happening. When I'm in America, I take less off the Web because I can read about it in the local newspapers. At home, I look at the headlines, the main story, and then go off to the main section of nfl.com. At the beginning, I would

176

look at nba.com, nfl.com, espn.com, the *Dallas News,* and the *Sporting News,* for at least three hours each day. My eyes began to hurt and I started to get headaches. I put in an hour or two every day, then, and maybe two or three hours on the weekend each day. I looked for an overview of football and to fulfill my interests in basketball and hockey.

The Ryder Cup

In general, I don't read about golf nor watch it much. But the Ryder Cup is one of those events I feel I just have to watch. My father has played golf since he was eight, and I grew up watching every single golf event with him, sitting up late at night watching the Masters Tournament live with my Dad, eating cheese and crackers. I have been reading about and watching the Ryder Cup competition at least since I was 13 years old. I love the Ryder Cup competition because for Scotland to send its own player to this European competition is a big deal. It helps with Scottish pride. It's good for braggin' rights. In addition, the Americans often come over thinking they're just going to sideswipe the Europeans and knock them out on Day One. But in 1997 they came over and it was like "oh my goodness," and they didn't do so well.

The general history of the Ryder Cup is as follows. The first informal matches were held in 1921 in Gleneagles, Scotland during which match the British defeated the United States, 9–3. A second, unofficial, match occurred in 1926 before the British Open in Wentworth, England. Once again, the British triumphed over the United States with the score of 13.5–1.5. Samuel Ryder was present at this second match. According to many historical accounts of the origins of the Ryder Cup competition, the planning for the event we know today began when Samuel Ryder, an English nurseryman from St Albans in Hertfordshire, who made his future selling packaged seeds for a penny, had tea with various members of the British and American teams, including his personal golf tutor, Abe Mitchell. At this tea one of the British team members, George Duncan, suggested that Ryder should sponsor a trophy and establish regular matches between the two countries. Ryder agreed immediately and commissioned the design of a gold chalice which bears his name and Abe Mitchell's likeness on the top.[13]

The inaugural matches were held at Worcester (Massachusetts) Country Club in 1927 where the United States defeated the British 9.5–2.5. Since this historic first match the Ryder Cup has been held every two years except for the period 1939–1945 when the Second World War interrupted play. In 1973 the British team was extended to include the Republic of Ireland. Then, in 1978 it was decided that the Ryder Cup would be held between the United States and Europe.

Today the Ryder Cup is held over three days. In 1997 it was held between 26–28 September. The first two days consist of the foursome and fourball competitions while the final Sunday holds the singles competition. The foursome competition has four groups of two two-man teams playing alternate shot. That is, Player A plays the first shot and Player B plays the second. This pattern continues until the ball is in the hole. Players A and B alternate tee-offs so that each player tees-off an equal number of times. Fourball competition also has four groups of two two-man teams; however, the groups compete with the best scores. That is, Players A and B both play their own balls but only the best score from the hole is used to win the hole. The final day of singles competition has twelve groups of two one-man teams playing eighteen holes of match-play golf. (In match-play golf the player with the lowest score wins the hole.) To win the Ryder Cup a team must accumulate 14.5 points over the three days of competition. However, the defending team need only reach 14 points to force a tie and retain the trophy.

At the 1997 Ryder Cup Competition, going into the Sunday, it looked like the Europeans were definitely going to win. However, the American started to fight back in the singles. German's Berhard Langer secured the fourteenth point of the match and ensured that the Europeans would retain the Ryder Cup. However, it was Colin Montgomerie of Scotland who scored the final half point that clinched the victory for Europe. Listening to the Scottish media, one could imagine that Colin Montgomerie had single-handedly won the Ryder Cup for Europe.

The day after the Ryder Cup Competition, the *Electronic Herald's* website opened with a brief history of the Ryder Cup's most epic moments before turning its attention to the action of the day before. It reported on 29 September 1997 that "[t]he two men landed with the task of playing the deciding match were our own Colin Montgomerie and the most abrasive member of the American side, Scott Hoch." These remarks set the tone for the rest of the article. In describing both players' efforts at the last, we learn "Hoch drove into the left rough off the eighteenth tee, the American then pulled his second shot badly ... after colliding with what looked like more than one tree." This is in direct contrast to "Montgomery's enviable rhythm ... He split the fairway with a beautifully struck No. 3 wood ... [his] No. 9-iron approach was another thing of beauty."[14]

On the same day, the *Daily Record's* article informs us that "they [the US team] arrogantly called themselves the finest Ryder Cup fighting force ever to leave American Shores," and by paragraph four the American team have become "the Yanks." Eventually, the article returns to the praise afforded to Montgomerie with the remark that "it often looked as if he might be Man of the Match with 3.5 points out of a possible five. In the end, nobody could argue against that."

Finally, the *Scotsman* on the same day presents a very quiet, innocent image of the event over the course of the article. The description of Colin Montgomerie is "the big man with the accent of an Englishman, but the blood of a Scot." In contrast to the *Electronic Herald* they describe Scott Hoch as "a fierce opponent and, on a bad day, not the most friendly one." The match itself is not described in too much detail; instead the space is devoted to the mental attributes of the game as well as the emotions concerned:

> In the moment when mental toughness was paramount, the Scot guaranteed that the Ryder Cup will remain on this side of the Atlantic for another two years. The Americans were sent home to think again.

How many Americans are likely to recognize this final line from the Scottish National Anthem, "Flower of Scotland"? The original line being "and send him [Prince Edward's army] homeward to think again."

In general, the American Internet pages speak little of Scott Hoch's shortcomings and Brad's loss to Berhard Langer – both instead share a paragraph on page three (of three) in espn.com's coverage of the same day. espn and *USA Today* dedicate much space to the shortcomings of Tom Kite as captain and Tiger Woods, Justin Leonard and Davis Love III as major flops. Woods won the US Masters, Leonard won the British Open and Love won the USPGA yet the three could only muster one point out of a possible thirteen.

However, the American perspective is a lot more humble than the Scottish perspective. (One could say *rightly* so after the unwarranted confidence demonstrated by the US team.) Also, the pages of espn.com and *USA Today* attempt to shy away from the comments of Kite that the US lost the Cup as opposed to the Europeans winning it. espn.com quotes Kite as saying: "I honestly believe that the only reason we got beat is they knew the golf course and we didn't." Espn.com informs us that Ballesteros respectfully disagreed: "I think the European team won it." Espn.com's view is similar to that of Ballesteros: "[Ballesteros is] probably right. Europe played well Friday, dominated Saturday and won some early key matches Sunday."

Interestingly, Colin Montgomerie, the man who put the final nail in the American team's coffin, is absent from virtually all of the American coverage. His efforts are noted in just one line in espn.com: "Europe won the Cup on the last hole of the last match, when Montgomerie halved with Scott Hoch," *USA Today* does not dedicate much more space: "Scotland's Colin Montgomerie gave Europe the win by tying his match with Scott Hoch." As might be expected, Colin Montgomerie's heritage is not noted nor put in its European context.

On the other hand, also on the day following the match, the *International Herald Tribune* dedicates the majority of its three-page coverage of the 1997 Ryder Cup competition to an analysis of why the Americans lost. The opening page is almost entirely an investigation into why Tom Kite was such a bad captain, and the vast majority of the remainder of the article questions why the American superpowers of Woods, Leonard, and Love all failed to produce.

Indeed, the final quarter of the article is solely dedicated to Woods' failure. Their closing line highlights that they are looking from an unbiased objective "Rocca's 4-and-2 victory, as much as any other victory, decided the outcome of the Ryder Cup." There is no false belief in Colin Montgomerie's achievements and there is no belief that the Americans lost the Ryder Cup – it is only the *International Herald Tribune* which takes the time to praise where praise is truly due.

However, more interesting than the degree and kind of biases existing in the respective coverage of the Ryder Cup Competition by these four newspapers is my own reading of the event on the Web. My own literacy practices of reading about sporting events, fostered by my American cousins and my father when I was much younger, and sharpened by my Web readings at Aberdeen University, demonstrate a personal truth about how I approach the Web as a Scotsman. Specifically, as a Scotsman I use the Web as a place to get wider coverage of the sporting events in which I am interested. And I enjoy reading about American football and European golf from both sides of the Atlantic ocean.

Conclusions

In the heart of the Scottish Borders, in Tweeddale, 25 hectares of landscaped gardens known as the Dawyck Botanic Gardens offer visitors a look at trees and plants from the Pacific Northwest. Thanks to the efforts of nineteenth-century Scottish seed collectors David Douglas and F. R. S. Balfour, who visited Washington and Oregon states, extensive collections of North American conifers now crown this Scottish arboretum. It is amusing to some visitors from the Pacific Northwest to see hardy rhododendrons, mixed woodlands, and flowering shrubs that look just like those found at home. On the other hand, Scotch Broom, a widespread and invasive shrub commonly found in North America, was introduced by Captain Walter Colquhoun Grant to Vancouver Island in the Pacific Northwest in 1850. Grant, a recent immigrant from Scotland, had picked up some seeds from Hawaii from the British Consul. As many guides to native flora indicate, "[o]f the seeds he planted in Sooke, three germinated, and descendants of these three plants have subsequently colonized most of southern Vancouver Island" (Pojar and MacKinnon, 1994, p. 83). Any casual driver today along Interstate Route 5 between Tacoma and Seattle would be shocked to realize that much of that yellow broom sprang from just three successful seeds sown by a homesick Scotsman.

Discourse and language likewise invade, establish, spread, and cross-pollinate in countries far apart, but in ways often less visible. Yet the Web affords a window onto the ways in which language changes, accrues, and grows, shaping identities even as it offers a seemingly neutral portal to other countries. When Jason looks to the Web to learn what he can about American sports like football and international golf competitions like the Ryder Cup, his eyes and ears are reaching out and stitching together diverse accounts into a single story of identity, self, and preoccupation. When Sarah looks to the Web to revisit places, friends, and memories, she is engaged in a kind of patchwork discourse that is likewise partial, sometimes interstitial, and often illusory in the connections it creates.

While borrowing has been a central activity in Scottish writing over the last four centuries, thanks to the Web, "borrowing," patch-writing, and now, patch-reading, are becoming one of the signal gestures of late twentieth-century readers reading on the Web. That is, in a movement similar to William of Drummond's sideways glance at the Italian and French books on his shelves, Jason Johnstone is able to surf the Internet and study an event like the Ryder Cup from the points of view of several national and international newspapers. Jason's sideways glance is complemented by Sarah's looking backwards, using the Web to trace the latest events in a nostalgic narrative of lost roots or identity. Fully aware of the ironies of admitting to this naïve, nostalgic desire for Scottish land and identity, Sarah continues to use a computer to read the *Scotsman* online daily, to bid on used books about Edinburgh in online auctions, to plan her next research trip to the National Library of Scotland, to daydream about taking lessons in Gaelic on the Isle of Skye, to read up on Scottish women's events on "Quine Online." Borrowing accounts of local events and connecting them with our evolving internationalist perspectives reveals something new about how we assemble late twentieth-century identity.

In the cases of both Sarah's and Jason's readings, however, the central point to realize is not the directionality of their readings, nor the fact that those readings bridge two continents separated by an ocean, but how those readings illuminate the capacities and apparatus that is the Web. The Web not only connects me to you, it mingles bits of my words with bytes of yours, my account with your account, Scottish tales with American stories. Geoffrey Nunberg echoes our finding that information is somehow granular, manipulable, when encountered on the Web: "Unlike knowledge, which we often regard holistically, information is essentially corpuscular, like sand or succotash. It consists of little atoms of content – propositions, sentences, bits, infons, *morceaux* – each independently detachable, manipulable, and tabulable" (Nunberg, 1996, p. 117). But in addition to seeing what Nunberg has identified as part of electronic discourse in general, we see in particular that the Web stitches us and our experiences into an international community and a sense of self that is both illusive and allusive, incomplete and borrowed, organic, fecund, and ultimately uncontrolled.

The relationship between context and text has never been more complicated. It is clear to the two of us that the Web is not just a new site for well-rehearsed literacy practices and borrowings, for the exchange of languages, ideas, and identities; it is a sprawling, enormous, organic tissue of ideas, critical stances, and points of view that is never static nor innocent, and neither comprehensive nor predictable. When we read Scottish and American newspapers online and gratify our personal needs for heritage or sporting news, we can see how the Web enables the satisfaction of some of our desires. We don't yet fully comprehend, though, how that satisfaction is complicated by the pieces of culture and ideology less visibly conveyed by the Web, how the unexamined language or gesture conveyed by the Web results in shifts in consciousness or in any of the ways we understand ourselves. Ultimately, how the Web-based rituals of patch-reading – and all their accompanying erasures, elisions, and cross-cultural assortments of odd bedfellows – are incorporated into a reader's identity remains to be seen.

Acknowledgements

Much of the demographic information on Scotland was compiled with the help of Maureen Kelly, reference librarian at the University of Puget Sound. Scottish and American students, including especially Ashley Hardy, Alan Hughes, Andy Volk, and Emma Grundy were of great help in answering questions about their literacy practices. The assistance of all these participants and contributors is greatly appreciated, while the writers acknowledge, of course, that any errors in this essay are their responsibility alone. Correspondence concerning this article should be addressed to Sarah Sloane, Department of English, University of Puget Sound, Tacoma, Washington 98416, sloane@ups.edu; or Jason Johnstone, u01jnj@abdn.ac.uk.

Notes

1 See, for example, Edwin Morgan's essay, "How Good a Poet is Drummond?" wherein he examines the charges of plagiarism against Drummond within the larger context of "the Renascence doctrine of imitation" (Morgan, 1990, p. 58) and modernist notions of intertextuality. Lindsay's *History of Scottish Literature* also mentions William Drummond (1585–1649) in passing, noting his education in France as well as at Edinburgh and that he "had read widely in French and Italian literature, in both of which he amassed a considerable library" (Lindsay, 1992, p. 133).
2 http://www.shetland-news.co.uk/ [accessed on 11 December 1998, 2 pm PST].
3 See, for example, the *Scotsman*, 12 September 1997.
4 Office for National Statistics (ONS), United Kingdom. Standard of Living according to 1996 Edition. http://www.ons.gov.uk.ukinfigs/stats/stand.htm [Accessed on 12:00 PST December 11, 1998].
5 See the results published as "Superhighways for Education: The Way Forward," which can be accessed at http://www.tsoinfo.gov.uk/document/supered.supered.html
6 http://dir.yahoo.com/Business_and_Economy/Companies/Internet-Services/Internet_Cafes/Complete_Listing/ [accessed on 3:40 pm PST, 30 October 1998].
7 *Scotsman* Web page [accessed about 5 pm PST on 21 August 1997].

8 According to the *Collins Pocket Dictionary*: "**makar** (rhymes with *backer*): A **makar** is an old-fashioned or literary word for a poet, often used to refer to the major Scots poets of the 15th and early 16th century, such as Douglas, Dunbar, or Henryson" (p. 156); "**balloon:** A **balloon** is a Glasgow term for someone who is full of hot air and whose opinions, although loudly and frequently expressed, are regarded as worthless, [for example,] *A pompous balloon who drivelled on about 'mission statements' and 'human resources'*" (p. 12).

9 See, for example, Morgan's discussion and colorful examples of flyting in *Crossing the Border,* pp. 25–37. According to Morgan, "To flyte with someone or to have a flyting with someone is to engage in some kind of dispute or row, preferably in public, so everyone can enjoy it" (p. 25). Flaming, of course, is the slang term for the computer-based mud-slinging matches between correspondents, especially writers in chat rooms, newsgroups, and listservs.

10 An "extraordinary puff" is ill-founded hooplah surrounding the announcement of some novelty. For example, Munro uses the term to describe the reaction of realists to an announcement that a Scottish newspaper would carry original news that would be printed a day *before* it appeared in England.

11 http://www.sil.org/ethnologue/countries/Unit.html

12 According to the *Collins Dictionary*, Northern Scots is distinguished by two idiosyncratic habits of pronunciation:

> The most immediately obvious feature of Northern Scots is that the *wh-* at the beginning of a word is usually pronounced **f-,** for instance in *fit* (what) or *fite* (white). The vowel in *guid, school,* and *moon* is generally pronounced with an **-ee-** (as in English **heed**), but in the Northeast when this sound follows a hard g or k it is pronounced **-wee-** (*gweed, skweel*). All forms of Northern Scots frequently drop the initial th- in words such as *the, this* and *that*.
>
> (*Collins*, 1996, p. viii)

13 http://www.rydercup.com/10welc/ 1036gen.html [accessed 29 September 1997 4:55 pm PST].

14 http://www.theherald.co.uk/SPORT/sport1.html [accessed 29 September 1997 4:34 pm PST].

References

Anonymous (1992) "Soft-soaping the Gaels," *The Economist,* 14 November.

Collins Pocket Scots dictionary (1996) Glasgow: HarperCollins Publishers.

Cormack, Mike (1995) "The Use of Gaelic in Scottish Newspapers," *Journal of Multilingual and Multicultural Development* 16(4): 269–280.

Cowan, R. M. W. (1946) *The Newspaper in Scotland: A Study of its First Expansion, 1815–60,* Glasgow, Scotland.

Crawford, Robert (1992) *Devolving English Literature,* Oxford: Oxford University Press.

Crawford, Robert. (1997) "The computer and the painted Pict," *Times Literary Supplement,* 15 August, p. 4.

Crawford, Robert, (ed.) (1997) *Robert Burns and Cultural Authority,* Edinburgh, Scotland: Edinburgh University Press.

Crotty, Patrick (1996) "Battles in the Celtic Mist," [review of the book *The Poems of Ossian and Related Works*] *Times Literary Supplement,* 29 March, p. 25.

Cyberia Edinburgh Live WebCam! dewars.cybersurf.co.uk

Daily Record and Sunday Mail, Glasgow, Scotland, Devolution Chat Room; www.record-mail.co.uk/rm/devo/index.html

Eastman, C. M. and Stein, R. F. (1993) "Language Display: Authenticating Claims to Social Identity," *Journal of Multilingual and Multicultural Development* 14: 187–202.

Electronic Herald, www.cims.co.uk/herald/

espn.com; http://www/ESPN.SportsZone.com/golf.ryder97/nwqa

Gee, James Paul (1990) *Social Linguistics and Literacies: Ideology in Discourses*, Brighton, England: Palmer Press.

Glendinning, Victoria (1995) *Electricity*, New York: Little, Brown, and Company.

Harvey, Christopher (1994) *Scotland and Nationalism: Scottish Society and Politics 1707–1994*, 2nd edn, London: Routledge.

Hoge, Warren (1998) "Blair Finds Autonomy only Whets Scots' Appetite", the *New York Times*, 29 November, p. 3.

Hoggart, Richard (1957) *The Uses of Literacy: Aspects of Working-Class Life with Special Reference to Publications and Entertainments*, London: Chatto and Windus.

Horner, Winifred (1998) "Introduction," in Gaillet, Lynee Lewis (ed.) *Scottish Rhetoric and its Influences*, New Jersey: Lawrence Erlbaum Associates, Publishers and Hermagoras Press, pp. 1–16.

Howard, Rebecca Moore (1995) "Plagiarisms, Authorships, and the Academic Death Penalty," *College English* 57(7): 708–36.

Hunter, Brian (ed.) (1997) *The Statesman's Year-Book 1997–98*. London: Macmillan Reference Ltd.

International Herald Tribune; http://www.iht.com/IHT/TODAY/TUES/SPT/ryder.html

Jones, Peter (1997) "Less–Less for Yes–Yes?," the *Scotsman*, 21 August.

Lindsay, Maurice (1992) *History of Scottish Literature*, (2nd edn), London: Robert Hale.

Lyall, Sarah (1997) "Scotland Votes to Establish Legislature," the *New York Times*, 12 September, p. 6.

MacDonald, George (1996) *Lilith*, Grand Rapids, Michigan: Wm. B. Eerdmans Publishing Co.

McCrum, Robert, Crane, William and MacNeil, Robert (1987) *The Story of English*, New York: Penguin Books.

Mackie, Lindsay (1996) "The Fruits of Networking: How a Scottish School is Spearheading the Drive to get the Country's Secondary Schools Fully Linked Up," the *Guardian*, 3 December, p. 4.

MacMahon, Peter (1997) "Can Dewar Bring in the New Dawn?", the *Scotsman*, 21 August.

MacMahon, Peter (21 August 1997) "Dewar Promises that Powerful Panel will Screen All Candidates," the *Scotsman*, 21 August.

Morgan, Edwin (1990) *Crossing the Border*, Manchester, England: Carcanet Press Limited.

Munro, Donald (1986) "175 Years of the *Montrose Review*: Scotland's Second Oldest Weekly Newspaper," *Journal of Newspaper and Periodical History* 2(3): 14–21.

N.B. (1997) *Times Literary Supplement*, 5 September, p. 16.

The New London Group (1996) "A Pedagogy of Multiliteracies: Designing Social Futures," *Harvard Educational Review*, 66(1): 60–92.

Nunberg, Geoffrey (1996) "Farewell to the Information Age," in Nunberg, G. (ed.) *The Future of the Book*, Berkeley: University of California Press, pp. 103–138.

Office of National Statistics (1996) "The UK in Figures," http://www.ons.gov.uk/ukinfigs/stats/stand.htm [accessed on 12:00 PST 11 December 1998].

Pojar, Jim, and MacKinnon, Andy (eds) (1994) *Plants of the Pacific Northwest Coast: Washington, Oregon, British Columbia, and Alaska*, British Columbia: British Columbia Ministry of Forests and Lone Pine Publishing.

Quine Online – Scottish Women, http://www.quine.org.uk/

Riffenburgh, Beau, and Thomas, Ken (1992) *The American Football Almanac: The Official Handbook of the History and Records of the National Football League*, Seven Hills Publishing.

Rose, Mark (1993) *Authors and Owners: The Invention of Copyright*, Cambridge: Harvard University Press.

St Louis Post-Dispatch (1997) "College in Scotland tries to save Gaelic tradition," 28 September.

Scotsman, www.scotsman.com/index.html

Sealey, Mark (1996) "Classrooms Beyond the Year 2000: An Amazing Experiment in Teaching with IT, Soon to Start in Scotland," the *Guardian*, 5 March, p. 6.

Shetland News, www.shetland-news.co.uk

Sloane, Sarah (1997) "Borrowing Longinus: Visible Traces of On the Sublime in the Primary Authors of the Scottish Enlightenment, 1757–1809," paper presented at the International Society for the History of Rhetoric, Saskatoon, Saskatchewan, July.

Sloane, Sarah (in press) *Digital Fictions: Storytelling in a Material World*, Stamford, Connecticut: Ablex Press.

Street, Brian (1995) *Social Literacies: Critical Approaches to Literacy Development, Ethnography, and Education*, New York and Reading: Addison-Wesley Publishing Co.

Turnbull, A. (1986) "Scotland and America," 1730–90, in D. Daiches *et al.* (eds) *A Hotbed of Genuis: The Scottish Enlightenment*, Edinburgh: Edinburgh University Press, pp. 137–152.

USA Today, http://www.usatoday.com/sports/ccovmon.htm

Weinbrot, Howard D. (1993) *Britannia's Issue: The Rise of British Literature from Dryden to Ossian*, Cambridge: Cambridge University Press.

Part 3

LITERACY, CONFLICT, AND HYBRIDITY ON THE WEB

8

WEB LITERACIES OF THE ALREADY ACCESSED AND TECHNICALLY INCLINED: SCHOOLING IN MONTERREY, MEXICO

Susan Romano, Barbara Field, and Elizabeth W. de Huergo

The Internet is forever.

> (14-year-old male student, American Institute of
> Monterrey, Mexico)

On the Internet you can find Benito Juarez *and* Leonardo DiCaprio.

> (13-year-old female student, American Institute of
> Monterrey, Mexico)

Like some people think that all we do is farm and all that, so we can show them it's not true, we're into technology, too.

> (14-year-old male student, American Institute of
> Monterrey, Mexico)

I don't need to use Spanish search engines because everything I need is in English.

> (14-year-old female student, American Institute of
> Monterrey, Mexico)

Se puede considerar que el idioma inglés es básico para la red; ésta es una limitante para mi. ("You could say that English is basic knowledge for the Net; this is my limitation.")

> (eighth-grade Spanish teacher, American Institute of
> Monterrey, Mexico)

Knowing Monterrey

Grounding this essay are words like those above, written by students and teachers at the American Institute of Monterrey, Mexico, a bilingual school of high standing in this city. The students – nearly all Mexican nationals – attend class on two campuses, one situated in an upper-class residential

189

area and the other in a once-outlying colonial town now nearly adjacent to the city. Even if you are unacquainted with Monterrey, you may have heard that its terrain is both flat and mountainous, that its governing bodies are both conservative and innovative, that its residents perceive themselves as both provincial and international. All of these rumors are true, and in addition, this historically isolated city now serves all of Latin America as a center for telecommunications, international commerce, and technology education. Indeed no single image does justice to Monterrey.

If you approach the city by car from the north, taking either the *autopista* or the highway *libre*, you'll pass through miles of grasslands, Joshua-tree forests, and purple flowering sage before climbing and descending a mountain pass and eventually swinging on to the long artery leading from the outskirts of the city to its center. Along the way you'll find that stereotypes of the modern do not hold, for certainly Monterrey's high-tech side is not readily apparent to the average passerby. Those fiberoptic and coaxial cables supporting commerce, culture, and education are simply not visible from the road, where at each stop, energetic young men apply large dust mops to your car and scrape invisible insects from your windshield, even and especially if you shake your head "no."

Yet by the end of your stay in Monterrey, you'll have seen that both state and private university students read, write, and design with computers; you'll have glimpsed NAFTA's imprint on the city – J. C. Penney's, Sirloin Stockade, and Chili's; you'll have heard the history of entrepreneurialism and early technical education at Monterrey's original brewery; you'll have experienced state-of-the-art multimedia curating at the *Museo de Historia Mexicana*, where segmented video clips and meticulously composed hypertexts compete with traditional artifacts for your attention. Yet even the orange- and purple-plastered walls of *La Gran Plaza* and the *Tecnológico*'s giant geometrical landmarks (twentieth-century equivalents of Olmec heads) do not quite succeed in representing the power and complexity of this city. Monterrey's strengths in industry, in entrepreneurialism, in education, and in technology are not to be underestimated. No borrowed goods, these core components are proper to Monterrey culture.

Monterrey's ur-story of entrepreneurialism, for example, pre-dates the 1910 Revolution.[1] In the late nineteenth century, following the marriage of Isaac Garza to his business-partner's sister, Consuelo Sada, the newly united families founded a brewery and a dynasty. For one hundred years, the Garza Sadas and their descendants have gone about their businesses, becoming prosperous during the Porfiriato era and extending their economic reach before and after the 1910 Revolution until the 1980s, when the Mexican government reduced protectionist measures and forced upon the Garza Sada dynasty a reconsideration of kinship as the organizing principle for economic prowess. The Monterrey Group (as the Garza Sada coalition of entrepreneurs came to be known) currently competes on international turf. It must do so or perish. Leaning on its well-wrought business acumen, the extended family has responded to reduced regulatory protection by cutting losses, diversifying holdings, investing overseas, partnering with international corporations, and consenting to intrafamily competition for ownership in banking, breweries, glass, bottling, telephones, steel, petrochemicals, telecommunications, and finance (Palmieri and Dolan, 1995).[2]

Although alternatives to kinship-based business are indeed a historical novelty, cross-border commerce is not. Studies recently compiled by Mexican scholars, Mario Cenutti and Miguel A. González Quiroga (1993), document a number of thriving trade partnerships between Mexico and the US confederacy from 1820 through the confederate period and US civil war. Nor is the role that technical expertise plays in sustaining the economy aberrational within Monterrey culture. Indeed affinity with a range of technologies is "natural" in that the history of successful private enterprise in Monterrey is also a history of technical innovation. The production, bottling, and distribution of beer at *Cervecería Cuauhtemoc*, the first entrepreneurial undertaking of the early Garza Sada period, required glass for packaging, steel for bottle capping, cement for building, cardboard for packaging, and printing presses for advertising (Nichols, 1993). The need for ongoing technical innovation was eventually supported educationally, first with a short-lived, brewery-supported polytechnic school, and eventually with the founding of the *Instituto Tecnológico de Estudios Superiores de Monterrey* (ITESM), known as the *Tecnológico* or *Tec*.[3] Mexico's first-ranked post-secondary private institution, the *Tecnológico* was founded in 1943 by Eugenio Garza Sada (who was murdered by leftist guerrillas in a 1973 kidnapping attempt) and is one of some 200 private universities currently providing an alternative to public higher education.[4] Twenty-six campuses across Mexico and a newly erected (1997) virtual campus comprise the ITESM system and serve 75,000 students. Although for many years residents of Monterrey have demanded quality education for their children, the growing international reputation of a local technology institute, the recent displacement of Mexican telecommunications from Mexico City to Monterrey, the rise of global entrepreneurialism, and the associated influx of international human resources have augmented the need for quality, local pre-university training for Monterrey's resident youth.[5] The American Institute of Monterrey (AIM) responds to these changes and offers such training.

AIM was founded in 1968 by three experienced school teachers, Betina Elizondo, Alma Melo, and Betty Wagner. Dedicated educators, who did not think of themselves as business women, they did the unthinkable for women of their era: they rented a building on Hidalgo street, downtown, launched an elementary and junior high school, filled adjacent houses with classrooms and children, and, finally, relying on loans in the form of special fees recoverable upon each pupil's graduation, financed their own school building.

Elizabeth Huergo, daughter of founder Betty Wagner, is now Director. Huergo attended AIM as a child, witnessed its birth and growth, and currently enrolls her two sons there. She is one of three researchers undertaking this study.

Barbara Field is a second researcher. Field works for Simon and Schuster as sales representative for Latin America and is a 20-year veteran teacher and administrator in international schools. AIM is but one of her many clients. She resides in Monterrey.

Susan Romano, professor of English at the University of Texas at San Antonio, is a third researcher and primary writer of the study. When, during fall 1997, Romano began searching for sites appropriate for the Routledge global-literacies project, she visited AIM's website on the recommendation of Field and noted its corporate look, its all-in-English claim to be part of a "new infrastructure," its promise to grant its students contact with the world via access to state-of-the-art technology. Romano was startled by the Microsoft-cum-Gore-inflected language that similarly marks US discourses on technology and education and impressed by AIM's statement of educational philosophy: "We believe that effective learning is achieved when students are responsible for their own learning, achieving this through investigation, peer coaching, collaborative and cooperative means . . .". Coincidental to Romano's visit to AIM's website, we learned later, AIM students composing in HTML were planning a conference presentation about their Web projects before an international audience in Austin, Texas. Because the global-literacies project investigates the Internet writing practices of non-US Internet users, AIM seemed like a good bet to Romano and Field, and after some consultation, the three of us – Romano, Field, and Huergo – agreed to a collaborative project.

Now a study of electronic literacy as practiced by middle-school students belonging to a highly successful economic group may strike some as suspect. Literacy researchers, after all, typically study cultures whose literacies are considered inadequate for effective social participation or at best under development. When the topic "literacy" migrates from a disenfranchised culture to a dominant one, its study becomes less compelling. Yet if we consider that literacy ethnographers target for scholarly inquiry those sites where changes in literacy practices are afoot, then the American Institute of Monterrey is a choice site, for literacy education at AIM is both undergoing and causing significant change. And if we accept that changes in literacy practices are associated with reconfigurations of social relationships, then Monterrey's economically élite youth become an extremely important population for investigation, for they are future leaders of their country. The study of literacy and social change should not be confined, we argue, to worst-case scenarios of inadequate schooling in dysfunctional social sectors. The relationship of literacy to social change is best figured as sets of altering practices at all levels of society. Under this assertion, we argue for the importance of examining Internet literacy practices of the privileged as well as the disenfranchised. And this is what we have set out to do. To a tangle of stories associating Monterrey, Nuevo Leon, Mexico, with economic success, democracy, industry, technology, transnational capitalism, and quality education, we would add an account of literacy acquisition. Broadly conceived, our project initiates inquiry into the new literacy practices of the already accessed, already globally identified, already economically successful, and already technically inclined.

Creating methodology

Unable to undertake the sort of ethnographic study necessary for a rich construction of transforming literacy practices at AIM, we opted for a procedure affording us access to participants' *perceptions* of their Web literacies. Via a survey administered to nearly 200 students in the seventh, eighth, and ninth grades and to 120 teachers and administrators, we solicited information about computer purchases and family literacies, knowledge of computer applications, Web use at home and school, school instruction, favorite websites, and projected future uses. We asked participants to evaluate two websites (*Today* on HotWired and the European Union website) chosen by global literacies project editors Gail Hawisher and Cynthia Selfe and three websites of our choice: the American Institute of Monterrey, of course; *Preparatoria 15*, a public, college preparatory school also located in Monterrey; and *Oventic Aguascalientes II*, an Indigenous, bilingual middle school under construction in Chiapas.

The surveys were not administered in any way we may comfortably construe as uniform. We don't know, for example, whether in every case participants discussed answers among themselves; the occasional extreme uniformity of syntax and vocabulary for certain answers from certain groups suggests that, at least part of the time, students may have consulted each other or their teachers as to the best answer. Although we preferred that certain responses (specifically those evaluating the websites) be elaborated after group discussion, we have no way of knowing how "collaboration" was effected; in fact, not a single group answered the question specifically requesting group construction of evaluative criteria. Abstruse questions about "civic" life (a word with as little currency among Mexican children as among US children) did not prove useful. Most lamentably overlooked on our part was the provision of a strong Latin American website written in Spanish, whose inclusion would have provided an alternative perspective on students' overwhelming preference for English-language sites. Despite these lapses and irregularities, we have gathered a rich body of information accommodating a range of inquiries.[6]

Conflicting stakes: putting researcher heads together

As we set about elaborating the questions for our survey, we found ourselves at odds regarding the issues each believed our research should address. Huergo, responsible to the 975 students whose parents she consults in person at least once each year, is interested in documenting the phenomenal success of the technology project undertaken conjointly by AIM parents, faculty, and administration and in improving the services she offers her students and their families. Romano, a teacher and researcher of rhetoric and writing instruction, is more interested in what students do write than in what curriculum planners envision them writing. Field, who markets educational materials and trains teachers across a highly diversified Latin America, is interested in forecasting the needs of educators in her service area and in serving her clients well. Because of our differences, the questions driving our survey are formulated differently, depending on who speaks. Similarly, we tend to evaluate survey responses differently and our proposed courses of action, which we do not pursue in this study, go unaligned. We find, nonetheless, that our interests converge on several planes: the influence of schooling on literacy and the extension, development, and uses of literacy outside school environments. Drawing on these shared interests, we believe our research addresses the following questions:

- What is the role of school in promoting and guiding Internet literacy?
- What is at stake for Mexican children acquiring Web literacy and English literacy simultaneously?
- How does a culture closely aligned with and influenced by US culture represent and protect its differences?
- Do Monterrey schoolchildren "act upon" and adapt the new literacies to their own purposes, as social theorist Brian Street and others believe people do?
- Does AIM function as guardian of cultural values via its assignments and other measures associated with school literacy? How so and with what success?

The strengths and limitations of our survey questions extend beyond mere methodological considerations, permeating regions of difference between and among researchers that defy resolution. Ethically situated within Monterrey's cultural, social, and political value system, Elizabeth Huergo is entrusted not only with the provision of sound education in English and Spanish, math and science, fine arts and technology education, health and sports (and with the maintenance of a healthy balance among them), but also with upholding community values and social order. Ethically situated within her own field – rhetoric, writing instruction, and theories of discourse – Susan Romano regards school literacy with some ambivalence, wary of its power to marginalize thriving practices such as the *tejano* English widely spoken in Texas, wary of a teacher's power to narrow rather than broaden students' literate repertoires. Barbara Field's work with administrators, teachers, and children across differently financed and disparately staffed schools in Latin America compel her dedication to providing quality English education in countries seeking to enter the global economy. In this section and throughout, we offer fragments of our dialog. We hope our situatedness and individual stakes in the matter remain visible and hence informative for our readers.

Romano posits that given the long reach and connective capabilities of electronic communications technologies, quite possibly Web literacy educators might foster practices supporting a more equitable distribution of resources in Mexico. Ideally, in Romano's view, a distributed Web literacy would enable mutually beneficial connections between such economically disparate regions as Nuevo Leon in the far north and Chiapas in the far south, each region representing its economic and social complexities in ways leading to mutually beneficial actions. Yet when Romano wrote to Huergo and Field enthusiastically about subcomandante Marcos's use of the Internet to publicize social conditions of the disenfranchised in Chiapas, Huergo and Field were puzzled. "In Monterrey we don't emphasize Chiapas quite so much," replied Field, who lives in Monterrey. "Chiapas is important, but not a major topic of conversation."[7]

Pointing out that the University of Texas at Austin LANIC website, hub for US scholarship on Latin America, devotes an entire section to Chiapas and that articles about Chiapas are so commonplace as to have found their way into first-year composition essay collections in the US, Romano pressed Huergo and Field. "Can it be that YA BASTA, a website housing communiqués from Marcos, images of Indigenous women in combat fatigue, links to the Mexican daily *La Jornada*, and daily up-dates on affairs from 1994 forward, is not followed in Monterrey?" she asked. "Not really," replied Field and Huergo. "We do not know YA BASTA, at least not in the sense that you do." Huergo offered an explanation:

> We may visit such sites as YA BASTA to inform ourselves from time to time, but we do not follow them day by day. The matter of Chiapas, for us, is lumped together with other newsmaking issues in politics or economics. Chiapas is not known as a website, but rather as a political disruption, one of many troubled areas of Mexico. It has become for us a headache which does not go away.

"But Chiapas," responded Romano, offering the clichés of her discipline, "has powerfully engaged a global, on-line community certain that without the visibility afforded by electronic technologies, the Mexican government would have paid little heed to an impoverished group of Mayans." Huergo responded:

> It is interesting that you see the WWW as a catalyst for social justice. We [Monterrey Mexicans] see the WWW as a catalyst for development in *all* aspects of our country . . . [T]hrough communication with others throughout the world there will develop interdependence, which in turn, will bring growth and development. I would say that we view the WWW as a window to the world more so than a window among ourselves in Mexico, and that the Chiapas affair seen from the insiders' perspective is a combination of problems, stemming from all types of reasons . . . Chiapas is but one case of many in Mexico that tell of inequality and social injustice.

As our dialog demonstrates, we were looking through the windows of the Web right past each other. And dissatisfied with impasse, we came to agree that although Monterrey is no match for Chiapas in the matter of global storytelling, its leadership in the recent loosening of oppressive restrictions on Mexican media is a comparable story and one worth telling. In 1993, Alejandro Junco, editor of the Monterrey newspaper *El Norte,* took on the government (PRI)-sponsored print monopoly by successfully introducing into circulation in Mexico City the oppositional newspaper *Reforma.* The feat is best understood in historical context: twenty-five years ago President Luis Echeverría, unhappy with *El Norte* coverage of politics, reduced its allotment of newsprint by 80 percent, and even today it is possible for some to purchase front-page space in certain Mexico City newspapers (Palmieri, 1995). Departing from its initial conservative stance, *Reforma* currently features government critique from the left as well as the right, and recent accords with CNN and Microsoft ensure its continuing influence. Despite geographic, economic, political, and social disalignment, then, people in Monterrey and people in Chiapas have been about a common task: the breakdown of controlled information distribution.

Context

These matters clarified, we found it imperative to investigate and acknowledge the privileged position of the population of students whose literacy we study in order to indicate the degree to which they are not representative. Unlike the majority of Mexico's school-age children, AIM students enjoy the benefits of an extensive technology initiative, planned and funded by parents and carried out by talented and dedicated school personnel. Whereas AIM students' and teachers' Web literacies rely upon sustained training in English and computer technologies, the majority of Mexico's students have access to neither. To more fully contextualize our study, we offer the following demographic information taken from 1990 census data reported in the *International Encyclopedia of Education* (Reyes, 1994), from INEGI (Instituto Nacional de Estadística, Geographía e Informática) and from the University of California at Los Angeles Program on Mexico (Lorey, 1995); we situate our own sample of 200 privately educated, middle school-children among other children of their approximate ages.

According to 1990 census data, the total population of Mexico is 94 million. Children between ages 6 and 14 number 33 million. Of these 33 million children, 23 million finish sixth grade. Fifteen million children between ages 15 and 19 are in school. Of these 15 million, 12 million finish sixth grade and 6 million finish ninth grade (Reyes, 1994; Lorey, 1995; INEGI, 1999). In short, many of Mexico's schoolchildren are marginalized not only with respect to English and Web literacy, but with respect to the entire school curriculum.[8]

Because we consider carefully the role of bilingualism at AIM, we note that approximately five million people speak Indigenous languages in Mexico. One million of these do not speak Spanish. Approximately one hundred Indigenous languages are spoken in Mexico's rural areas (Reyes, 1994; Lorey, 1995), and 4 percent of Mexican students attend bilingual schools featuring one or more Indigenous languages as well as Spanish (Reyes, 1994). Literacy education for this sector of Mexico is surely more complicated than for AIM students. In order to participate in global, Web-supported conversations, for example, the Chiapanecan Indigenous people negotiate complex oral transactions among their many languages – Tzetzal, Tzotzil, Tolojobal, Mam, and Chol – even before negotiating that literacy terrain where Spanish, then English, then technical access come into play. Hence multilingualism is at issue not only for AIM students but for many Mexican youths at opposite ends of the geographic, economic, social, and political spectrum.

Because she understands the teaching of English as commerical and polit-ical as well as educational, Field provides insight into the mechanisms of social stratification among schools offering bilingual education. No public schools in Mexico purchase American-published textbooks, to Field's knowl-edge at this writing, and hence the teaching of American English and acculturation under American-style pedagogies remains largely in the hands of private educators.[9] Although AIM students expect to enter a global, English-speaking culture, students in other regions of Latin America will enter in-country professions for which a more limited bilingualism is advan-tageous. These students learn English in a more piecemeal fashion. Their schools do not have Internet access and few students are likely, for economic reasons, to have access from home.

More so than the vast majority of Latin Americans, then, American Institute children and school personnel are well positioned economically and geographically to respond to the digital revolution and its attendant educational demands. Yet both incipient internationalism and a Web-literate student population pose pedagogical challenges even for cutting-edge private schools. Although small, AIM's enrollment of international students tripled this year, and several new students speak neither English nor Spanish. The impact on AIM of this small shift is far-reaching: the student body and their families now must accommodate new cultural perspectives, quite difficult for a conservative society, and teachers must develop new pedagogies for children who speak neither English nor Spanish. Furthermore, down the road the role of textbooks as sole avenues to English proficiency will be significantly eroded by the Web, which provides an accessible, interactive, international learning environment. Indeed, our surveys demonstrate that AIM students are rapidly becoming not only more dexterous on computers and more savvy as Internet navigators than their teachers, they are practicing their English in ways that far exceed the boundaries imposed by the textbooks from which they traditionally work.

Reading our data: two theories

All participant situations acknowledged, we turn to the AIM students and to our interpretative task, relying on social theorists Brian Street and Ann Swidler for scholarship lending critical force to our study. Understanding literacy as neither communication device nor social problem, Brian Street argues that literacy is best understood as a social practice embedded in larger cultural phenomena. The "autonomous" theories of literacy he objects to, the very theories so easily naturalized among those of us participating in language education, propose that literacy is a "'technical' affair, independent of social context, a variable whose impact on human beings and society derives from some mysterious intrinsic power (1993, p. 5). Street proposes an alternative: literacy is acted upon by those who undertake it. In other words, people shape literacy, argues Street, not vice versa.

Street's argument persuades us to abandon such questions as "Are AIM students proficient in digital literacy?" and "How does Web literacy affect AIM students?" Instead, we ask "How do AIM students make use of their reading and writing in digital forms?" and "How do they understand and talk about their own practices?" and "How do they situate their Internet reading and writing within perceived social structures?" The introduction of a "foreign" literacy, such as Web literacy, into a school curriculum suggests that researchers (that's us – Romano, Huergo, and Field) ask the newly literate (the AIM students and their teachers) what they make of this new way of reading and writing.

The term "literacy practice," argues Street, refers not only to "the [reading and writing] event itself but [to] the *conceptions of the reading and writing process that people hold* when they are engaged in the event" (1995, p. 133, our emphasis). In this light, we may say that chat sessions, for example, are literacy events, high-intensity episodes of reading and writing, which are best defined by the chatters themselves, by their understandings of the repeated experience of chatting. In other words, we researchers might be tempted to call the chat sessions "healthy, productive" or, alternatively, "useless, dangerous" social interaction, and the students might call them something else. This "something else" is what we hope to tease out by way of the surveys.

Street holds all school literacies suspect, arguing that at given historical moments, they tend to marginalize thriving and socially serviceable literacies operating outside their reach. This negative view of literacy instruction problematizes what perhaps is the most attractive reading for Huergo and Field, a reading not to be taken lightly, and indeed worthy of inclusion in a Mike Rose collection of successful educational enterprises. The story goes like this: northern Mexico schoolchildren in a prosperous, parent-participative, private school undertake the addition of digital literacy to their already extensive print-based literacies. Data confirm success, owing in part to the quick reflexes and careful planning on the part of educators and parents responding positively and aggressively to changing times. And this story is indeed an extremely important part of our collective story, for our surveys document the tremendous influence that schooling has had on the literate behaviors of AIM teachers and children and their families. Nearly to a person, over 300 people profess indebtedness to AIM for getting them (and their families) started on the Web. The model AIM has implemented is worthy of emulation.

In fact, our research exposes Street's rather too rigid understanding of literacy hierarchies. Street juxtaposes school literacies exclusively with undervalued non-school literacies, yet we find that in the case of AIM, school-bred literacy practices spin off, so to speak, only to thrive outside the purview of school authorities and without their blessing. While fully attentive to the parent- and teacher-imposed goals for their reading and writing ("My parents want me to read the Web in English so that I can practice acquiring more vocabulary," writes one student), AIM students make ragged the boundaries between in-school and out-of-school literacies. Street is correct: they do "act upon" introduced literacy, turning it to their own purposes. Although AIM does not support global chatting, indeed prohibits it on school grounds, students report that global chatting is their favorite Web activity. Their new literacy enables them to escape the authority of school-based knowledge. On viewing the new AIM website for our survey, for example, some AIM students proved sufficiently well (Web)read, as we will see, to recommend changes in keeping with a set of standards derived from sources other than school.

We interpret these extensions and permutations of school literacy through the eyes of our second theorist, sociologist Ann Swidler, who, like Street, challenges academic and popular commonplaces – in this case commonplaces about culture. Culture is productively defined, she argues, not as a set of ideals that drive action but rather as a "repertoire or 'toolkit' of habits, skills, and styles from which people construct 'strategies of action'" (1986, p. 273). Thus responding to the question "What do you think you will use the Internet for in the working world?" students rummage in their toolkits for knowledge about the habits of working adults in their "culture." Our survey reveals that for AIM students, the work "tools" they'll use on the Internet when they become adults include buying and selling merchandise, pricing goods, trading stocks, holding meetings, talking to business associates, sending blueprints to employees, conducting business, finding out about other companies, interacting with others, translating important information, organizing themselves with information, making deals, predicting and preventing certain actions, and showcasing their work. We note the preponderance of commercial references (goods, merchandise, buying, selling, deals), and we note as well that organizing, predicting, and preventing are actions specific to people accustomed to gathering information before making decisions. In addition, a large majority of responses feature human interaction: talking, interacting, meeting. This repertoire of strategies defines "work" as relationship dependent. We speculate and confirm that to conduct business in Monterrey with or without the Internet is to construct networks, whether familial, local, or global. By Swidler's theory of culture and human behavior, then, "human interaction" and "business vocabulary and knowledge" are not goals or ideals students strive to attain or preserve; rather their "culture provides the tools with which [they] construct lines of action" (1986, p. 277). It follows, however, that students' intimacy with Monterrey's professional culture both enables *and limits* their responses to our question. We propose that Monterrey citizens not owning such tools may well construct alternative lines of action, when provided with Internet access, lines of action perhaps unavailable to AIM students.

Swidler distinguishes usefully, we find, between the role cultural phenomena play in "settled" times and in "unsettled" times. During settled times, she writes, we are tempted to perceive that values organize action quite effortlessly, for there is little disjuncture between belief and activity. During unsettled times, however, culture's role in reinforcing traditional strategies for action is complicated by its new role: composing new strategies for new actions (1986, p. 278).

On this matter, Huergo holds that Monterrey culture is clearly unsettled, and that technology has recently played a prominent role in its unsettling. During the 1980s the Monterrey citizenry came to own the largest number of satellite dishes per square mile in the world. *Regiomontanos*, as Monterrey citizens call themselves, began to perceive the devices they had purchased as media through which their pure and sane provincial culture had become corrupted by an alien culture introducing drinking, drugs, and sex. The

200

Internet is similarly perceived, despite belief in its economic and educational importance. It is not difficult, then, to imagine the strain on a culture that prides itself on its global connections yet is essentially provincial and conservative. Paradoxically, AIM families' sustained economic privilege is contingent upon a willingness to allow their children to venture out into a world where values, as well as styles, habits, and skills (cultural tools), are mixed, conglomerate, and under construction.[10] Guided by Swidler's theory, we find indications that parents, teachers, and students alike constrain action via tightened procedures ranging from restrictions on international chatting, controlled selection of appropriate websites, and perfectionist attitudes toward English-language skills.

Such "controls" over literacy, however, are instantiated more by practice than dicta. The responses of AIM teachers to our survey questions illustrate the meaning of practice. A large majority of AIM teachers persistently, across a range of survey questions, view the Web as purely educational. When asked to view and comment on two websites – HotWired and the European Union – nearly to a person teachers mulled over the appropriateness of each, not for their own edification or entertainment, but for that of their pupils: "Too advanced for my elementary students," some remarked, and "Good for the secondary students," wrote others, or, imposing school on extended family, "Good for my niece, who is studying European history." The ubiquity of such answers affirms that school culture provides "persistent ways of ordering action" (Swidler, 1986, p. 273). We are unwilling to dismiss our observation by recalling that the survey was AIM designed and AIM administered, for teachers' accounts of home uses of the Internet do not render additional repertoire. By ordering this new literacy within the structure of school, teachers efface the alternative: Web as global shopping mall replete with alien and dangerous cultural information and new cultural tools and habits.

In the sections that follow, we rely on Swidler's insights and Street's methodology to temper our teacherly urges to explain away student responses by educational logic. We have sharpened our abilities to listen closely to these children whose new strategies for literate and life action are in the process of shaping. We understand responses to our survey questions as culture-specific compositions of the meaning of Web literacy by students enrolled in a small private school in northern Mexico, toward the end of the twentieth century. We reminded ourselves not to seek uniformity across our student or teacher populations, for, argues Swidler, from similar cultural tool kits come overlapping and contradictory strategies. Happily, our respondents provide idiosyncratic as well as common combinations of strategies for reading on the Web. Had they not, their answers would indeed be puzzling.

The students speak: toolkits, repertoire, and languages of access

> I don't use Spanish language because I understand better in English.
>
> [seventh-grade male student]

By all reports, not a single student at the American Institute is anything but proficient in English. Of 190 student respondents to the question "How well do you read the English language and how well do you write it?" only one reports "poor" reading ability, and no one claims deficiency in writing. While nearly 8 percent are willing to occupy middle ground (the word in Spanish for "so-so" is *regular*), fully 92 percent rate their proficiency levels as "good" or "very good." Hence this population of students appears to consider English a given, a primary cultural tool and one they expect, not aspire, to employ. Indeed several students challenge the very appropriateness of such a question. The occasional bald response "Well, I study in a bilingual school" suggests that the question is considered naïve, even offensive.[11]

But when presented with a context for the *uses* of English and Spanish, when asked specifically about tools they reach for on the Web, students offer a more complex picture. When asked "When you search the Web, do you sometimes choose the Spanish-language option?", a little over one third of our respondents answered yes, they do use a Spanish option. This flexible, "multiple tools" approach to Web reading seems entirely predictable for a bilingual student population, especially given that *all* students (even the two international students) report Spanish as a first language, even in light of their near universal claims to English proficiency. More significant for global-communications researchers and educators is the tendency among about one-third of the respondents to arrange the two languages hierarchically, preferring English to Spanish, and the countertendency among fewer students to allow context to inform their communication strategies, choosing Spanish when appropriate. These latter students conceive multilingualism as repertoire, not contest.[12]

Most students provide careful reasoning for their "yes" and "no" answers (this reasoning a tribute, we think, to their teachers and to the educational philosophy of the school), and we have classified their reasons in order to examine the centering and marginalizing of the two components of communicative repertoire – English and Spanish. For example, respondents A and B below both participate in an ordering process that privileges English as the "better" language, even though one response is a "no" and the other a "yes."[13]

> *Student A*: No, I don't like to choose 'Spanish Language' because by reading in English I can learn more.

Student B: Yes, sometimes I choose 'Spanish Language' because I understand it better, but I prefer 'English Language' so I can learn more.[14]

Similarly, we divide the following four "no" answers into several camps, teasing out students' perceptions of the meaning of literacy from their answers:

Student C: No, because I understand better in English.

Student D: No, because I want (or I'm supposed) to practice my English.

Student E: No, because Web information only exists in English.

Student F: No, I didn't know a Spanish option existed.

Students who purport to understand "better" in English (C), along with those who believe that Web pages are written in English only (E and F), fuse Web-based literacy with English proficiency, thus creating by their definitions, beliefs, and practices what Street finds typical across societies – the hierarchizing of certain literacies and the marginalizing of others. According to these particular students, Spanish has dropped out of the useful repertoire of communicative action tools where the Web is concerned (although we must keep in mind that students are not necessarily reliable narrators, nor do we expect them to be). Students such as student A, B, and D, who use English on the Web to "learn," conceive of their Web reading as school literacy. By no means do we imply that students are naïve in their beliefs about language; quite the contrary, we follow Street and Swidler in allowing students to theorize from their experiences on the Web, noting that some, but not all, experience the Web as an English-only environment, and that some, but not all, experience the Web as a school exercise.

The "yes" answers and the proffered rationales and qualifiers confirm that students hold competing theories of language itself and of its strategic uses, some understanding literate behavior as a matter of proficiency in a dominant language and others as a matter of context and purpose. We again break the "yes" answers into two categories: "yes, only when" and "yes, when."

Student G: *Yes, only when* the project/assignment is for Spanish class.

Student H: *Yes, when* the project/assignment is for Spanish class. (our emphases)

Here both students G and H understand the question to be about school literacy and adapt their responses to school requirements. The "only when" responses (G), however, suggest that a fuller literate life is led in English, the "real" language of Web literacy, and that Spanish as a tool in the repertoire of communicative action tools is useful but marginalized. The "yes when" responses (H), on the other hand, mark their authors' understanding of languages as situation specific rather than hierarchical. For them, context dictates usage, even on the Web. We speculate that these latter students are best positioned for future global encounters, for they attend less to their own proficiencies and more to the social and linguistic demands of the moment. They practice, to use a rhetorician's vocabulary, *kairos* – the Greek expression associated with timeliness, opportunity, and discursive context. English is not a language of choice for these students; it is but one number chosen from a larger repertoire, one tool among many in the kit.

Overall, our survey responses indicate a strong tendency for Web literacy and literacy in English to converge, becoming nearly one and the same, and certainly this understanding makes sense given that in AIM school culture, English proficiency is required and given that students who are experienced Web readers do find most pages in English. Inevitably, however, English as preferred language, as the language of access, shapes perceptions of non-access languages, and Spanish for some AIM students is a non-access language. The common-sensical fusion of English literacy with Web literacy make the minority "yes when" answers all the more remarkable. We wonder what has made the difference for such students, how they came to *kairos* when others did not.

In a thin but interesting strand, several students find that "translations" into Spanish on some websites are not idiomatic, and they are disturbed by this tampering with their first language. Calls for correctness in Spanish-language usage alongside an insistence upon their own English proficiency partially confirm the notion of cultural unsettledness and lead to speculations we cannot pursue here. Were we to do so, we would explore along the lines suggested by Thomas P. Miller in *The Formation of College English: Rhetoric and Belles Lettres in the British Cultural Provinces.* Cosmopolitanism and its obverse, provincialism, argues Miller, are natural partners (1997, p. 11). Adoption of cosmopolitan culture (in our case, Internet/English culture) by individuals from strong local cultures (in our case, Monterrey's) necessarily entails a zealous preservation of those local languages.

Talking with strangers: child's play

There are many Pamelas in the world.
(seventh-grade female student)

They can't find you and they can't insult you.
(seventh-grade male student)

Many AIM students are experienced chatterers. "Chatting" is a term they themselves introduced (it was not on our survey), and they incorporated it into the survey in response to questions about pleasurable activities. Because chatting online entails writing, it encodes students' presence within Internet culture in ways that mere surfing or reading does not. Unfortunately, we did not foresee when we elaborated our survey the extent to which AIM students engage in chatting. Hence our questions were sorely inadequate, and we neglected an important component of our Spanish/English investigation by failing to ask what language students used for *writing* on the Web! Because many students report international chatting, we assume they use English, unless they confine chatting to Latin America and other Spanish-speaking countries, and we have a smattering of evidence to the contrary. We did ask, however, whether students had ever used pseudonyms and found that half the students regularly use pseudonyms or first-names-only when talking with strangers online. Their responses provide rich readings of Web culture as they experience it and contribute to it.[15]

AIM middle-schoolers see themselves as relaxed and savvy travelers in the global Internet community, but they travel carefully, for the most part, protecting from view what they perceive as "real" selves and attending to issues of security and safety through anonymity.[16] Most students set up an equation by which to figure their relationships with online strangers: security versus risk and "real" versus fictitious, where being "real" increases risk and being fictitious enhances security. The idea of protected identity among AIM students is highly naturalized, routine, a matter of course. And Huergo reports that teachers did at one time teach and enforce anonymity; more recently, the school administration restricts chatting to in-school networks, blocks pornography sites, and works to increase student awareness of these security measures.

That safety and security are important pieces of a Monterrey middle schoolchild's toolkit does not surprise us; indeed anonymity is likely to be an internationally available tool belonging to children everywhere, common to Internet culture, crossing many otherwise formidable racial, ethnic, and national boundaries. Yet the real versus fictitious distinction Monterrey students use with such aplomb does not quite satisfy them, and many take pains to parse identity with greater care than we did. Going far beyond the survey demands, some students made careful distinctions between pseudonymity and partial anonymity – between false names and first-names-only. We read this collective call for precision in questions of identity (anonymity, pseudonymity, partial anonymity) as evidently important to their understanding of Web culture, as crucial components of their careful forays out into dangerous but highly pleasurable and entertaining territory.

Indeed, students' very insistent attention to danger so prominently encoded in the terms "security" and "safety" belies the pleasure they derive from chatting. Of the varied responses to "What was your most satisfying experience on the Web?" the most frequent response was "chatting." Reports of human contact with strangers, of turning strangers into acquaintances and friends, and of success at these enterprises suggest that safety and security may be dead or dying cultural trappings unsupported experientially, yet habitually used as cultural repertoire. The "bad people" materialize in the surveys only as hearsay. Similarly, adherence to the value of anonymity as opposed to the practice of anonymity is negated by student reviews of school websites. We explore their demands for self-revelation and true words from real people below.[17]

The students speak: the family and the literacy machine

For projects, for fun, for us to learn more.

(eighth-grade female student)

Nearly to a person, teachers and students credit AIM with initiating their Internet activity. The enormously important role played by school in the formation of Web literacies is confirmed by Huergo's account of a school–family partnership both financial and educational to promote electronic literacies.[18] Hence when we asked students to say why their families purchased computers, we were not surprised to find nearly all listing school projects as one important reason. Entertainment, however, (often listed as "play" or "fun") challenged "school" as a purchasing rationale. And although many parents reportedly use the family computer for work, seldom was work listed as a primary reason for purchase.

Our questions about family-purchase decisions and uses provided students an opportunity to talk about computer literacies outside the context of school. We found it difficult to devise prompts sufficiently powerful to counter the school influence but were eager to investigate non-school literacies without diminishing the role AIM plays in family lives. Using questions about families and computers, we tried to resituate the students textually and rhetorically.

Educational purposes notwithstanding, students report that the computers in their homes now support multiple literacies. Alongside comments such as "for us to do our homework," they report the following:

My father keeps records of my mother's store.
My father saves memories of swimming tournaments.
So that we can get more information.
To help my mother with her kinder[garten].
So my parents can work at home.
So my family can do all of our works.
To make our life easier.
To get e-mails.

To check product prices.

To do my dad's business stuff.

To fill the needs of the family and especially for my mother for work.

For projects, sending mails, navigating through the Internet, using chat, writing, and playing.

For music listening.

To access encyclopedias.

For printing and scanning.

To fax.

To paint.

To do home page pictures and cards.

To talk to kids from another country.

Students reported all-too-familiar generational and gender differences in computer usage. First mothers, then fathers, are cited as the least frequent computer users. Twice as many mothers as fathers are reported non-users. Older siblings (in their thirties or forties) are usually classified as non-users as well. For the younger generation, however, usage is both mandatory and commonplace. College prep, university, and young professional siblings use the computer extensively for schoolwork and professional projects, while younger siblings use it heavily as well, for play and for homework.

Whereas we understand gendered parent behavior as a generational phenomenon, we interpret gendered student behavior cautiously, attentive to evidence that male students are more likely to consider themselves savvy computer users, but hopeful that our figures indicate positive change for female students. Of all student respondents, 40 percent name themselves as primary users of the family computer, yet of this 40 percent, two thirds are male and one third female. The pattern emerging from our small sample bears watching: whereas 33 percent of seventh-grade, self-identified primary users are female, and whereas a comparable 40 percent of eighth-grade primary users are female, only 25 percent of ninth-grade primary users are female. We hope what we see is not a pattern of dwindling interest in computer-based literacy among young women moving into adolescence, but rather a pattern of *increasing* female interest at early ages perhaps induced by their educational experiences.

I was looking for this actor and when he appeared I screamed with joy.

(seventh-grade female student)

To get at students' non-school-based literacies from another angle, we asked them what experiences on the Web had afforded them most satisfaction. While many expressed relief at fulfilling a school requirement ("finding what I needed to complete my assignment"), a majority listed chatting as their most satisfying experience: "Chatting internationally," "talking with friends in Sweden, Japan, Singapore," "making new friends." Yet disparate pleasures defied our attempts to categorize: watching videos on the Web, searching for music groups, buying a watch, getting information on basketball, seeing music groups and their instruments, e-mailing, the low-rider home page, the Titanic page, finding recipes, making designs for Christmas cards, finding phone numbers of friends in Florida and Italy, Brad Pitt, ballet topics, the 4,0000th visit to my own website, soccer, making my home page at geocities. We conclude that families' literate lives are far richer than a look at their schoolwork suggests and note the tendency to encode literacy practices within verbs "finding," "making," "chatting," "watching," "searching," and seldom "reading" and "writing."

Mexico and the Web: country, class, and new epistemologies

The question has no basis; Monterrey IS Mexico.

(eighth-grade female student)

Social classes are in person; you do not learn it from the Web.

(eighth-grade male student)

Left with little doubt that AIM students will be able players in the global, online culture of the coming century, we turn to questions closer to home. When asked to forecast Monterrey's role in the broader scheme of Mexico's progress, many students ignored the question, while some offered cultural commonplaces – necessarily and appropriately part of their cultural tool kits – about hard work, excellent schools, access to technology, and the advantages of being near the US border.

When asked about the potential social effects of online communication, they responded more carefully, offering analyses that reveal political differences as well as alternative lines of reasoning. Responding to a question about the effects of the Internet on the gap between socio-economic classes in Mexico, about half believed these gaps would narrow. Citing the power of information, the equalizing potential of anonymity, the educational potential of the Internet, and the political power afforded by free speech, about half responded along the following lines:

Question: Will the Internet narrow the gap between social classes?
Responses:

I think so because people can have more information.
Yes, because people can chat under anonymous.
Yes, because people will learn about economics.
There can be many rebellion sites calling for certain freedoms.

Less sanguine students offered opposing arguments both rational and political:

> Poor people have no Internet access.
> Almost all Internet users are from the higher class, which is completely wrong.
> The idea of freedom and democracy and Internet is "illogical."
> The question is irrelevant because people cannot buy a computer and with all the information nobody will read it.
> In a way that we have more knowledge than they and knowing computers and all, it is a big difference. I don't think it will help the causes of freedom and democracy because the Internet cannot do any single thing about it except, maybe, give us information.

Epistemologies of the young and very Web literate

Sites of excellence for my age require pictures and mail.
                                        (seventh-grade female student)

I would like to see the children while they are learning
                        (eighth-grade female student commenting on the
                                                Chiapas school website)

Still soliciting students' understanding of what it means and should mean for a Mexican citizen to read and write on the Web about Mexico, we took a different tack and asked for critical commentary about specific school websites in Monterrey and in Chiapas. In response to the question "What would give you a better idea of what this website is about?" many students answered with undisguised annoyance, complaining about the length of the assignment (they had six websites to analyze and possibly were asked to complete the exercise all at one sitting). Their irritation notwithstanding, the information we gleaned has proved rich in that even perfunctory answers evidence changing epistemologies. In other words, students were not satisfied with what had been offered them, for it was evidently not persuasive, and it was not persuasive, they say, because of the limited forms of representation offered by the site builders.

But before turning to student responses, we return to our own discussions regarding which websites students might usefully and appropriately examine. Unanimously we chose the AIM website, of course, but when it came to selecting others, our deliberations again turned political, coinciding as they did with President Zedillo's urgent request for a cessation of international interference in Chiapas affairs. As director of AIM, Huergo was particularly attuned to political sensitivities of the children's parents and to her sense of the political climate. We discarded the idea of having

209

children critique the presidential Web page, given the recent mandate, and wound up choosing three schools: AIM (The American Institute of Monterrey), *Preparatoria 15* (a government-sponsored preparatory school in Monterrey) and *Oventic Aguascalientes II* (the proposed Indigenous Jr. High School in Chiapas).

At first glance, many student responses seemed perfunctory and hence disappointing, no less so for the AIM site than for *Prepa 15* and the Chiapas school. A number of students registered surprise at the existence in Monterrey of a bilingual public school and comparable surprise that schools in Chiapas exist at all.[19] To our query as to how to improve each site we received a flurry of suggestions, and their collective responses offer strong evidence that students are careful connoisseurs of the new forms available to site designers. The following are representative of serious responses, although many students responded with a curt "nothing" or "it's fine."

> Chiapas needs a penpal feature.
> AIM needs a chatroom.
> More pictures and more children's opinions [AIM].
> Talk to people from Chiapas.
> I would like to see what the students think of their school [Preparatoria 15].
> First-hand student accounts [Preparatoria 15].
> Opinions of students studying there [Chiapas].
> Pictures of all the students [AIM].
> Their school projects [Chiapas].
> Children while they are learning [Chiapas].

By these comments, students propose standards for authoritative representation, insisting that sites include visual representations of the human inhabitants of these historically real places and that the words and work of the inhabitants be represented as well. Their answers suggest that the "what" of adequate representation should be human beings, and the "how" should be images of these human beings and representations of their speech or writing. Demands do not stop there: several AIM students request charts and graphs; others, we note, want interactive talk, not just posted opinions. Collectively, these suggestions demonstrate student understanding of the complexities of knowing in the digital age. Students are clear that knowledge, if believable, must come in multiple representational forms, that some forms are more necessary than others, and that it's not just about color and Java.

As Swidler predicts, strategies for action are not necessarily coherent or progressive. People do not sit down first to examine their cultural values and tools before they speak or act; rather, actions, including reading and writing, are pieced together spontaneously from a repertoire of habits on the one hand and from sets of newly available structures on the other. What's more, people come to value what these tools and structures enable them to do. Students' calls for images and talk demonstrate their knowledge and acceptance of structures they have experienced during their Internet wanderings. Strong calls for speech and writing from their peers in Mexico may seem logically inconsistent with students' near unanimous professions that English is the only valid language on the Internet. Yet by cultural logic, which according to Swidler entails a common-sense selection of available cultural tools adaptable to new situations, these statements exemplify students' adaptation of their new knowledge of newly possible means for knowing.

Indeed we find that contradictions provide the richest fields for our speculative analyses. By their answers to questions about anonymity and to questions about what's missing on given websites, AIM students position themselves in a field polarized by desires to know and the urges to remain unknown, a field where fear pulls at pleasure and dissimulation at revelation. Even as they demand more knowledge about people, they honor the impulse to remain themselves fictitious – "unreal" in online environments, unknowable. In demanding both truth and fiction in representation, they begin to get at the complexities linking literacy to knowledge in a global arena composed of a fluctuating population of strangers.

And who are we? The ambiguities of knowing

Like some people think that all we do is farm and all that, so, we can show them it's not true, we're into technology, too.

(seventh-grade male student)

The seventh-grade student who wrote the above statement understands the Web as a technology of positioning: his argument is not an argument against farmers but an argument against stereotypes, against inadequate knowing, against reducing an entire people to a single image. Extended, this comment becomes an argument that multiple forms of representation suggest multiple ways of being. Indeed, were we – Huergo, Field, and Romano – to represent these students speaking in chorus, we would purport to hear the following:

We take pleasure in the visual, [say the AIM students], we cross borders for our entertainment, we make computer-generated Christmas cards at home with our little sisters, we chat with bad strangers and protect ourselves with false names, we love these strangers, we believe in anonymity, we demand revelation from others and require their pictures and their words. We would like to see the faces and hear words of children in Chiapas as they learn.

If not farmers and if not beings willingly compressed into single images, who are these students and how do they position themselves in the world? They understand that the dynamics of knowing are complex; they subscribe to the strong mandate against being known even as they wish to know others; they prefer north-of-the-border leisure, they are savvy about social class divisions, they suspect that the Internet is no solution, they love the Internet. They know that the cultural tool kit at their disposal, which includes hardware, software, and English, is unusually powerful and hard to come by. They know that the contents of their tool kits separate them from others who will not know as they know. Boasting of their fine English even as they encode the features of second-language learning in their writing, they call out their favorite sites:

> NFL, Leonardo DiCaprio, Disney, Bluemountain, Crayola. We are still very young, not more than sixteen any one of us; we are not farmers; you may have our first names but not our real identities, for we travel incognito, pretending to speak little Spanish and fiercely protective of whoever would make bad translations, for we expect real writing from real people.

Revising and revisiting

When Romano first visited the AIM website in the fall of 1997, its corporate, educational language – the language of administrative missions – seemed strangely vacuous to her and the site slightly uncomfortable to read; Romano could imagine the administrators faxing and photocopying, the teachers entering grades in the computer, the children quietly seated before their books in neat rows, and the Web masters marking up approved texts. But the sense of chaos that is *school* was absent. In May 1998, toward the end of this writing, the AIM home page has been altered nearly beyond recognition. Currently photographic and iconographic images of children and school buildings dominate, and links to student projects are featured alongside the necessary administrative information.

"When we first created our home page," writes Huergo, "we wanted to let everyone know about our educational philosophy, but once we became more familiar with the World Wide Web, we realized that our site needed to be attractive in order to retain the attention of the parents, students, or teachers we hoped would visit the site." Appropriately, perhaps, for Monterrey culture, commercial interests are but a couple of links away from the AIM home page. Without straying too far, one connects with American Express, *Fidecomiso*, and commercial art galleries, the latter offering remarkable images representing the breadth and depth of Mexican culture. The effect is of submersion in all things modern, ancient, and very, very Mexican.

212

Certainly AIM has reconsidered its Web audience, replacing a controlled, administrative ethos with the child-directed and parent-inclusive look of "school" and, specifically, schooling in Monterrey, Mexico. The site does not tell all, as AIM students point out, but it's a fair start on representing the complex lives that students live in these times and the educational efforts to prepare them for the future.

How does an educational institution whose mission is to prepare students in English proficiency, to introduce them to the US and global cultures where many will further their educations and establish professional connections, and to provide the highest-quality technical education in a city steeped in a technical tradition consider the possible repercussions of its own success? How does an outward-looking, English-proficient, Web-savvy school population forge links with the complex entity that is Mexico? How indeed, when the new and necessary literacies supporting both school and pleasure, academic and lifeworld, are available in English and on the Web, when "English" and "Web" become so fused that "to read" means "to read in English"?

For educators who spend time teaching literacies, the real "find" among these pages is *Conoce Mexico Mi Pais* ("Get to Know Mexico, My Country"), a project built collaboratively by last year's ninth-grade students who, using raw HTML under the supervision of computer teacher *par excellence* Eva Ramírez, created Web pages for each Mexican state. These pages are not as polished as some of the other Web representations of AIM school work; they can be termed "display literacy" in that much of the textual work imitates the textbooks from which the information was taken. But they are clearly examples of work by students who are in the processes of learning to write in two languages using the Internet-supported forms that will become standard in their lifetimes. To all of us who love working with students over text, these pages are beautiful to behold.

Notes

1 A more accurate origins story may be found in *Fábricas pioneras de la industria en Nuevo Leon*, Monterrey: University Autónoma de Nuevo Leon, 1997.

2 From the *Wall Street Journal*, 30 September 1997: "In a huge transfer of ownership from Mexican to foreign hands, foreign multinationals have spent more than $7 billion in the past two years buying up stakes in everything free-trade advocates in and outside of Mexico, the sales represent the inevitable globalization of Mexican companies, which long hid their inefficiency behind protective tariffs and regulations. As those barriers are felled by the North American Free Trade Agreement and other accords, Mexican companies are increasingly exposed to global competitors and now may have little choice but to become a multinational or marry one. So far, a surprising number of Mexican companies are selling large stakes to foreign partners rather than expanding abroad. There are distinct reasons behind each sale. Some stem from issues arising as a new generation of the controlling family takes over, and others from financial needs

or changes in strategy. But generally, the goal is to become bigger, smarter and truly international companies as quickly as possible."

3 The *Cervecería Cuauhtemoc* had founded a polytechnic institute earlier in the century to train workers for the enterprise.

4 The *Universidad Nacional Autónoma de Mexico* (UNAM), the *Instituto Politécnico Nacional* (IPN), and the *Universidad Autónoma de Mexico* (UAM) – all public universities – were founded in 1929, 1937, and 1974 respectively. Initially, private universities were founded in response to regional demands for professional skills and instructional methods that were free from the socialist ideology prevalent at public universities in Mexico.

5 It should be noted that Monterrey's cultural identity is bound up in religious and political conservatism as well. Opus Dei, a conservative Catholic organization, is strong in Monterrey, and the *Partido de Acción Nacional* (PAN), conservative challenger to Mexico's long-ruling *Partido Revolutionario Institutional* (PRI), was founded in Monterrey.

6 We regret as well that the ninth graders who produced the *Conoce México Mi Pais* project had already graduated and thus were not available to participate in our survey. Their responses would have been invaluable, for we might have tracked the effects of experience in Web *writing* (as opposed to reading and information gathering) on student accounts of their Web literacies.

7 Internet watchers across the world became enamored with the case of Chiapas, where a small population of Indigenous residents spread their story across the world via electronic media. Subcomandante Marcos faxed communiqués in English and Spanish to the press, and world-wide dissemination proceeded via print and online technologies – newspapers, listservs, and Web pages. YA BASTA, a Web page built by an American college student, for several years provided the Web-literate world with a window on the political situation, suggesting that what we see on the Web is but the tip of an iceberg – a representation by someone – often Americans, often college students – of a complex of oral and literate activity far richer than the assemblage of images and texts on a Web page.

8 The 1917 Mexican Constitution mandates that basic education, which since 1992 is understood as primary and secondary (through ninth grade), must be available to all Mexican citizens (Lorey, 1995; Reyes, 1994), and today this education must address a school-age population which has risen from eleven million in 1950 to thirty-six million in 1990 (Lorey, 1995).

9 The *Universidad Autónoma de Nuevo Leon* system supports twenty-five college preparatory schools, only recently converting three of these to bilingual schools. Field does not yet supply these schools with textbooks, although Simon and Schuster alone sells US$4,000,000 in textbooks annually in Mexico.

10 Huergo notes that electronic media compete with additional unsettling forces. Some Monterrey citizens now question the wisdom of NAFTA, adapt to an unprecedented redistribution of political power (to the right in Monterrey and to the left in Mexico City), admit that the election of a conservative governor in Nuevo Leon has not solved many of the state's problems, and face the effects of an ever devaluing peso and other hardships associated with global, financial crisis.

11 Inappropriateness notwithstanding, questions about the teaching of English are of interest to us, and we gleaned from the surveys the following terms offered by the students naming the components of English instruction they found useful: reading, grammar, spelling, vocabulary, games and computer applications.

12 We anticipated that some students using a search engine such as Altavista would select a language under the provided menu, and that others would use the

all-Spanish search engines provided on AIM Web pages. The AIM website itself provides a collected list of Spanish-language search engines and e-mail applications (*Tarantula, Mex Master, buscar, búsqueda, correo electrónico, d a de baja tu e-mail*).

13 Although individual responses in this section are culled verbatim from our surveys, we use them to represent a large group of similar responses.

14 We have no sense, of course, of whether by "learn more," student A refers to "more" practice in English or whether her answer claims greater quantity of quality of information available on the Web in English, or both.

15 The "no, I've never used a pseudonym" responses remain ambiguous, reflecting either a decision to use "real" names or a lack of chatting experience altogether – we can't say which.

16 While one person anticipated a penalty for ultimate disclosure of his double identity, most students were comfortable leading dual-identity lives.

17 While most students indicated that their decisions to use pseudonyms were carefully considered, several students reported they had simply followed convention: "Everyone else does." These students afford us the luxury of catching in the act a new literacy practice settling into normalization. We found no significant gender differences associated with the use of pseudonyms.

18 Huergo writes:

> The implementation of computer-mediated learning began in the early 1980s, when the PTA so strongly desired that technology become an important aspect of their children's education that they created a revolving fund which is continually fed by a one-time, new-student entrance fee and dedicated to keeping pace with changing technologies. Not only were computer courses implemented for older students, but all teachers were trained in computer-assisted instruction, visiting computer labs weekly to learn software designed to enhance their teaching. The computerized report card emerged, and all teachers were required to input their students' raw grades, together with average formulas and weights, allowing mechanized grade tallies. The next step on our technological ladder was a giant one: the whole school was networked and Internet access implemented from our server, with dial-up access through our server provided our families as well. Teacher training was a primary concern. Teachers were required to check their e-mail daily, as well as to input homework assignments for their posting on the Net. Surfing the Web became part of a year-long training program so that teachers would become familiar with the vast array of resources suddenly at their and their students' disposal. At the same time, we promoted the evolution of the role of the classroom teacher from that of instructor to that of facilitator.

19 Education in English has only recently been introduced in government schools.

References

American Institute of Monterrey, (AIM) November 1998. www.aim-net.mx/mexico [accessed 09:33, 19 November 1998].

Cenutti, Mario, and Quiroga, Miguel A. González (1993) *Frontera e historia económica: Texas y el norte de México (1850–1866)*, México, DF: Instituto Mora, Universidad Autónoma Metropolitana.

INEGI (1999) http://www.inegi.gob.mx [accessed May 1999].

Lorey, David E. (1995, March–April) "Education and the Challenges of Mexican Development: Symposium: The Changing Structure of Mexico," *Challenge* 38(2): 51–55.

Miller, Thomas P. (1997) *The Formation of College English: Rhetoric and Belles Lettres in the British Cultural Provinces*, Pittsburgh: University of Pittsburgh Press.

Nichols, Nancy A. (1993, September–October) "The Monterrey Group: A Mexican Keiretsu," *Harvard Business Review* 168.

Schools for Chiapas * Chanobjunetik ta Chiapas * Escuelas para Chiapas, http://www. igc.org/mexicopeace [accessed 18 November 1998].

Palmieri, Christopher (24 April 1995) "Señor Clean," *Forbes* 155(9): 132–134.

Palmieri, Christopher, and Dolan, Kerry A. (1995) "A Tough New World," *Forbes* 156(2): 122–124.

Prepatoria 15 of the Universidad Autónoma de Nuevo Leon, July 1997, http://www.dsi.uanl.mx/rnnmsu/prepa15/ [accessed 19 November 1998].

Reyes, M. E. (1994) "Mexico: System of Education," in *International Encyclopedia of Education*, (eds) Husén, Torsten and Postlethwaite, T. Neville, Oxford: Pergamon Press, pp. 3792–3802.

Rojas Sandoval, Javier. (1997) *Fábricas pioneras de la industria en Nuevo Leon*, Monterrey, Mexico: University Autónoma de Nuevo Leon.

Street, Brian V. (1993) *Cross-Cultural Approaches to Literacy*, New York: Cambridge University Press.

Street, Brian V. (1995) *Social Literacies: Critical Approaches to Literacy in Development, Ethnography and Education*, New York: Longman.

Swidler, Ann. (1986) "Culture in Action: Symbols and Strategies," *American Sociological Review* 51: 273–286.

Torres, Craig (1997) "Foreigners Snap up Mexican Companies," *Wall Street Journal* 30 September, pp. A1, A12.

9

CYBERCUBA.COM(MUNIST): ELECTRONIC LITERACY, RESISTANCE, AND POSTREVOLUTIONARY CUBA

Laura Sullivan and Victor Fernandez

In his book on the social dimensions of print literacy, Brian Street explains that "control of the means of communication . . . relates to political and economic control" (1995, p. 95). Currently, the long-standing contestation of power between the US and Cuba now takes place in another arena – the Internet. This chapter examines the social, economic, and material conditions related to Cuba and electronic literacy, considering, for example: the history of state support of education and literacy, especially demonstrated in the postrevolutionary literacy campaign; socialism – its structure and goals; technological difficulties with the country's telecommunications infrastructure; the serious effects of the US embargo, particularly those manifested in the 1994 Helms–Burton Act; and the recent introduction of US dollars into the Cuban economy.

This chapter comes from the perspective of an American scholar touring Cuba – both virtually and literally – and from the perspectives of Cubans involved in Web production and consumption in Cuba, particularly that of Victor Fernandez, Web master of the electronic version of the Cuban newspaper, *Trabajadores* ("workers" in English).[1] First, we discuss the inadequacy of the application of stereotypes regarding print literacy to electronic literacy in Cuba, particularly in light of the class context involved. Second, we examine a particular instance of the unique nature of internally-directed Web production in Cuba, the InfoMed network. Third, we turn our attention to the way the Internet functions especially as a key medium of communications about Cuba to foreigners, beginning with an examination of the ideological conflicts manifested in websites about Cuba, and then focusing specifically on the examples of two of the most important Cuban websites designed for primarily foreign audiences: the "official website of the Republic of Cuba," CubaWeb, and the website of the Cuban newspaper

Granma Internacional. In the final sections of the chapter, we investigate website design techniques in more detail and explore power relations, including regional issues, gender differences, and economic positioning in the production and consumption of websites about and from Cuba.

Literacy stereotypes and class context

The stereotype that people in non-western (or "developing") countries are highly illiterate and therefore "lacking in cognitive skills," "backward," and "undeveloped" (Street, 1995, p. 13) and the corollary myth that "levels of literacy in a society ... correlate positively with any and all indicators of social and economic progress" (Street, 1995, pp. 74–75) do not apply to Cuba, which undertook an extensive literacy campaign after the 1959 revolution and continues to have a near-100 percent literacy rate to this day. Furthermore, Cuba currently enjoys this high literacy rate but not the supposed corresponding positive economic conditions, as it is a socialist country in a capitalist world, and as it is being crushed economically as a result of the US embargo, which is more accurately characterized as a blockade.[2]

The story of the postrevolutionary print literacy campaign forms the backdrop to this examination of electronic literacy in Cuba. In that effort, the Cubans did not assume that literacy is equivalent to "cognitive advance, social mobility or progress" (Street, 1995, p. 24). Instead, they recognized that "literacy practices are specific to the political and ideological context and their consequences vary situationally" (Street, 1995, p. 24). Because Cubans in charge of the literacy campaign understood that literacy is often used as a tool of colonialist/imperialist/capitalist social control, they wished to recontextualize literacy in order to use it subversively. Like the members of the Melanesian Cargo Cults,[3] the Cubans eschewed the autonomous model of literacy because they understood literacy's ideological nature and thus sought to use it towards their own ends. The same understanding and desire for recontextualization is at work in relation to Cuban electronic literacy today, though the current political and economic conditions differ from the immediate postrevolutionary period. In 1960, Cubans were working to collectively build a socialist society, fought for in a broad-based revolutionary struggle. In contrast, now Cubans are struggling to preserve their socialist state, and this effort has involved the introduction of at least a partial capitalist mode of economy.

Street notes that "lack of literacy is more likely to be a symptom of poverty and deprivation than a cause" (1995, p. 18). In the case of Cuba and electronic literacy, this direction of causality is particularly evident. The difficulties with spreading electronic literacy in Cuba are symptoms of poverty and deprivation, especially as direct consequences of the loss of financial support of the Soviet Bloc and of the devastating effects of the current US embargo.

Colonialism haunts the project of global literacy (Street, 1995, p. 15). "Colonial literacy" is that "brought by outsiders as part of a conquest" (ibid., p. 16) and "often . . . has involved some transfer of 'western' values to a non-western society" (ibid., p. 30). Street points to current neocolonial geopolitical conditions when he mentions that "at a structural level, [developing] countries are often economically dependent on the western economic order, through multinationals, export dependency, loans and aid" (ibid., p. 37). However, Cuba does not have the same relationship to the west, and to the US in particular, that other "developing" countries do. As a socialist country, Cuba is the last holdout in the US cold war, a thorn in the side of a government whose ideological position is one of automatic political, economic, and military antagonism with all non-capitalist countries. Thus, while Cuba is a "third world" country, it is not a site of capitalist expansion for the US.[4]

In other words, the traditional colonial literacy model outlined by Street fails to describe adequately the situation in Cuba, where, if anything, the US is trying to prevent the spread of electronic literacy. While the US government's blocking of the bringing of medical computers into Cuba by InfoMed USA and the Pastors for Peace in 1996 was clearly an attempt to prevent medical aid from being sent to Cuba,[5] the effort could also be read as an attempt to keep Cuba technologically deprived. These were, after all, old computers by "our" standards. Yet nonetheless the American government saw their successful delivery as a big threat. Moreover, there is also a double standard in the US government's policies, as the spread of computers and electronic literacy in Cuba is not universally opposed. As noted in the Cuban daily newspaper *Granma*,

> The US government gave $500,000 to the ultra-Right wing organization Freedom House to acquire computers and send them to individuals who agree with US anti-Cuba policies. At the same time, US authorities have spent nearly one million dollars to prevent the delivery of important humanitarian aid in the form of computers, which will be used to link Cuban hospitals and clinics, giving doctors and medical personnel life-saving, up-to-the-minute information.
> ("The Downing of the Planes: An Attempt to Provide Context",
> February 26, 1996)

Furthermore, unlike with print literacy and the dynamics outlined by Street (1995), the primary goal of the promotion of electronic literacy in non-western countries is not to cement ideologically a system of social control by a dominant power. Instead, the "global information highway" is advanced by transnational capital and western governments primarily to promote an entrenched consumerism, and to thereby ensure and increase markets for products. As noted above, the stereotypes about electronic literacy, as well as analyses such as Street's, construct the world in terms of traditional binaries: western–non-western; "developed"–"undeveloped"; "civilized"–"native"/indigenous societies. The capitalist–socialist (or capitalist–communist) divide is not mentioned. With the shift of Eastern Europe and the Soviet Union to explicitly capitalist economies, there is a pretense that the whole world is (or at least desires to be) capitalist. Cuba is precisely such a threat because it exemplifies a choice outside of capitalist ideology and negates this pretense, within which the proliferation of electronic technology and the building of the "global information highway" are seen as synonymous with the (desired and inevitable) global capitalist expansion ("Where do you want to go today?" – Microsoft).

Along these lines, James Brook and Iain Boal (1995) provide the picture left out of Street's approach to literacy: the dynamics of global capital. They analyze a March 1994 speech made by US Vice President, Al Gore, to the International Telecommunications Union in Buenos Aires, and point out that despite his appeals to "the democratic potentials of computer networks," Gore reveals the underlying agenda in claims such as "I see a new Athenian Age of democracy forged in the fora the GII [Global Information Infrastructure] will create" (Brook and Boal, 1995, p. xii). As Brook and Boal note, "Athens was an imperialist slave society, with democratic rights enjoyed only by a privileged few" (1995, p. xiii). The GII will ultimately "guarantee commodity flows without jeopardizing corporate, expert, and police control over communication" (1995, p. xii). Such structural intentions and conditions play vital roles in shaping the world of contemporary electronic literacy.

Cuba resisted the mandates of capital in their print literacy campaign: can they do the same with their electronic literacy efforts? Cuba's print literacy campaign is more aptly compared to that conducted by the Sandinistas of Nicaragua, since both occurred in the context of socialist revolutions and both were conducted as a means to empower people in a way different from that dictated by the logic of capital. Whereas typically literacy is not taught by western or colonial powers in order to develop critical thinking in the learners, but to increase social control by the dominant power (Street, 1995, p. 79), Cuba wanted to do the reverse with its literacy campaign, as the intent was to give people tools with which to think critically. Do Cuban educators and members of the Cuban government see the Web as a similar site for the development of critical thinking skills? Dominant ideology maintains that "literacy [is] the major source of western supremacy [and] scientific achievement" (Street, 1995, p. 119), yet Cuba's literacy campaign reworked this connection. Cuba used the western form of literacy, yet in their rejection of western purposes of literacy and capitalist ideological principles, they used literacy as a tool for scientific advancement for people, not for profit. The Internet is being mobilized in a similar fashion in Cuba. However, as we shall see, economic conditions presently prevent much of the desired spread of electronic literacy and these same have led to a less purely socialist approach to Cuba's electronic literacy and its presentation of information on the Web.

Cuba's computer history

Cuba provides an exemplary context in which to examine economic dimensions of electronic literacy. From the start of Cuba's relationship with the computer, economic and political conditions have been pivotal influences. As provided by Victor Fernandez, here is a brief history of Cuba's experiences with computers.

In 1960, a computer, Eliot 803, was installed at the University of Havana. The Center for Digital Research (CID) at the University of Havana played a major role in computer development in the 1970s, beginning with computers that were combinations of mini-computers and desktops, which were used in research, economic, and educational centers. French computers IRIS-10 and IRIS-50s were installed at this time as well. The first mainframe developed in the Soviet Union, built according to the standards of the Council of Mutual Economic Aid (CMEA), was also installed in the 1970s. Several machines were developed through this arrangement, with better and better systems supplied. In 1983, the first micro NEC came to Cuba; afterwards, the first IBM compatibles arrived. In 1983, remote access to databases via satellite was first made possible in Cuba, from Havana to Moscow and afterwards to some Eastern European cities, according to protocols signed by the countries who were members of the CMEA. Some free data from databanks in Western Europe were also available, and this service was extended to institutions all over the country. When the CMEA disappeared, these services were shut down, but new services came into being, such as e-mail.

From the start, computers were put to educational uses. In 1971, Havana University created the *licenciature* in Computer Science. Some years later, studies were offered in Systems of Automated Management and Electronic Computer Machines. Computer centers at the university were also developed. Now there are some classrooms dedicated to computer use. Middle- and primary-level education has also been involved with computers, as selected schools have received computers and instruction. Ten years ago, the Joven Clubs de Computacion were created, clubs designed for teaching and popularizing the computer primarily among young Cubans. In other educational centers, such as those for offices or investigation, some workers and investigators have received classes.

Economic hardship affects the current configuration of Cuban electronic literacy conditions. While almost all Cubans are familiar with *la computadora* and *la Internet*, most of them do not have any direct involvement with computers. One result of Cuba's economic struggles, particularly as influenced by the US embargo, is that Cuba lacks an adequate technological infrastructure to develop an entirely wired society. Thus, few Cubans have computers and of those who do, only workers at certain website-producing institutions, for example InfoMed, Cuba's medical network, have full access to the Web. Another aspect of Cuba's current socio-economic situation is the existence and continuing expansion of a second economy – one based on US dollars. This aspect, too, is reflected in the electronic literacy situation in Cuba, in which website workers, from HTML (hypertext mark-up language) specialists to graphic designers, are able to do freelance work on the side and thus earn some of the coveted dollar currency. One man who is in charge of the computer software for one of the online Cuban news publications explains that he can make as much money in one day from a freelance job that pays dollars as he makes in Cuban pesos in one month. So these workers involved with computers in Cuba have not only additional cultural capital, but more actual capital, than their non-wired counterparts.

The severe economic situation in Cuba means that at the present time there is not much money available for training people in computer skills, including those related to website production. According to David Wald of InfoMed USA (1998), of the computer clubs for training young people found throughout the country, the former Sears-Roebuck building in Havana is one of the major sites of computer training for young users. However, no Internet access is available at these sites. CubaWeb director Anibal Quevado (1998) reports that the government has just developed a plan for future education in electronic literacy. The government intends to computerize Cuban society through the implementation of its plan called "Informatizacion de la Sociedad Cubana." The ministry of higher education has already approved a budget of $1 million for computer education. Anibal asserts that "We don't have to take much time to teach the people – we have the ability to learn quickly and well." Several factors contribute to the speed and ease with which Cubans learn computer skills, including those involved in website production. First, the Cuban people are both highly literate and highly educated. Second, they are used to having to make do with little time or material objects in their learning situations. For example, paper and pens are both scarce items in Cuba since the implementation of the US embargo, so Cuban educational systems have had to contend with shortages of reading and writing materials for some time. And those who work on the websites produced in Cuba have had only short, intensive training periods. For example, Victor Fernandez received only one month of training in Canada for his work as Web master for the electronic version of a major Cuban newspaper. Third, there is a sense of urgency and pride involved with website production in Cuba. Orlando Romero (1998), the head of the design department for the electronic version of the Cuban newspaper *Granma Internacional*, declares that "In the world, the Internet is the most powerful communications force" and explains that at the start of the newspaper's online experience, "We began with a 386 VX and we would take the floppies of what we would produce by bicycle to the place that then made the website." As Orlando's story indicates, Cuban website producers demonstrate an intense dedication and willingness to learn under difficult conditions, as explored in more detail below.

The Cuban InfoMed website

The InfoMed network is an exemplary model for the Cuban state's position regarding the potential of the Internet for internal purposes of socially collective benefit. Begun in 1992, InfoMed is part of the CENIAI network (Center for the Automated Exchange of Information), the science ministry's network which facilitates the electronic mail "exchange [of] scientific information with other countries through its Internet connection in Canada" (Echevarria, 1996). InfoMed, "the computer network of the National System of Health Information of the Ministry of Health in Cuba," launched their website in February 1997 ("InfoMed, Cuba's Medical Network!"). Interviews with InfoMed's Web master, systems manager, information specialist and graphic designer in Havana revealed much about the detailed operation of Cuba's premier electronic network, and about the role of the Internet in Cuba in general.

InfoMed personnel point out that the issue of Internet access in Cuba is more complex than implied by the mainstream American idea that Cuba's government is heavily invested in restricting media access, including Internet access, in Cuba. The InfoMed network consists of the headquarters in Havana and labs in every Cuban province; doctors, nurses, and university faculty in the sciences have e-mail accounts and access to the InfoMed network, which provides health-related Web documents from throughout the world and connections to all Cuban websites. Restrictions on access are entirely related to the lack of a technologically advanced infrastructure. Without money to purchase more bandwidth and extra equipment, the InfoMed network is unable to support full Web access for all its users. In fact, at this point even 200 Cuban users surfing the Web would crash the InfoMed servers. The network is still very slow, although InfoMed workers are hopeful that the promised internal fully networked telecommunications system will be in place soon (yet for only half the island) and will speed things up.

InfoMed systems manager Augustin Magrans (1998) explains that foreigners who assume the Cuban government is anxious about the spread of non-communist ideas via the Web are ignorant about the actual conditions of the electronic world in Cuba. At this point, the Web itself is not the country's main problem along these lines. Instead, the Web masters of the country's most important institutional networks such as InfoMed must contend with a daily barrage of e-mail message spams sent to all Cubans on the Internet. The senders of these messages, Cuban exiles in the US, attempt to convince the receivers that they should condemn the revolution and embrace capitalist ideology.

Further, Cubans are familiar with the hegemonic ideological perspectives of the US as put forth by the American media, as Cubans have long been viewers of Hollywood films and, more recently, listeners of radio broadcasts from the US to Cuba. Cubans associated with InfoMed point to larger questions, and make clear that being a US citizen steeped in capitalist ideology already predisposes a certain point of view. They rarely think in terms of individualism and they are steadfast in support of their own ideological positions. Resisting the seduction of commodity capitalism, they explain that their greatest goal is to contribute to their country's advancement, in this case through the implementation of a network that connects all health care professionals in Cuba to each other and to the most important and up-to-date scientific information. I realized while listening to the InfoMed Web producers that I have no point of reference for the utterly complete separation of science and business. For most Cubans, these two arenas are antithetical. The InfoMed workers excitedly explain over and over how they want to bring services to the people, that giving others access to scientific information is necessary to continually improve their already excellent medical system. They predict that within a handful of years, all university students will have Internet access and perhaps most other Cuban citizens will as well.

The InfoMed electronic personnel I interviewed were impressed that I had used the Web to learn so much about the realities of Cuba. Again, the Web in Cuba is exceptional in this regard, and again in this way mirrors the progressive uses of print literacy after the revolution. While the Web in other countries may be used to contribute to the cementing of capitalist ideology by members of the dominant culture – government, business, or mass-media outfits, for example – the Internet as used internally in Cuba is not about indoctrination, but about social service. In fact, the correcting of misinformation about Cuba most frequently occurs on websites that are directed at a foreign audience. The Web may well be the key medium for disseminating correct information about the social, political, scientific, and technological realities of Cuba to the rest of the world.

Websites about Cuba

The Web foregrounds the operation of "power struggles between competing cultures" (Street, 1995, p. 126) concerning Cuba. Views of the website creators and viewers, both internal and external to Cuba, vary along a wide-ranging continuum of political perspectives. There are sites both pro- and anti-Castro/communism, and there are commercial and non-commercial sites (and some which are both). Furthermore, websites for/about Cuba(ns) are perfect texts to study "ideology [as] the site of tension between authority and power on the one hand and individual resistance and creativity on the other" (Street, 1995, p. 162). One corrective to Street's formulation here is important, though – resistance in the sense demonstrated by websites concerning Cuba, indeed perhaps on the Web in general, is not really individual, but collective in nature.

The collective quality of resistance promoted by websites about Cuba is best exemplified in the InfoMed USA/Cuba's Cuba Solidarity website, which provides a long list of links to many organizations and documents directly connected with various kinds of political action in support of Cuba, from the Cuba AIDS Project to Che Guevara's essay, "On Revolutionary Medicine," to the Cuban–American National Alliance. Cuba Solidarity features links to news sites, a section of links related to "Health and the US Embargo of Cuba," links concerning the "Background on the US Blockade Against Cuba," and information about links to other groups working in solidarity efforts for Cuba worldwide.

There are different perspectives and strategies employed in this most heated and vibrant representational battle in the cybertexts about Cuba. Some participants attempt to demarcate the lines of struggle along spatial and territorial lines. These people would like to see a clear boundary of cyberspaces for people on either side of the pro- or anti-communist position. For example, one writer to the "Guestbook" section of the Cuba Megalinks website complains about the lack of clearly demarcated boundaries in the cyberspaces regarding Cuba:

> Why don't we keep communists away from these freedom pages? We cannot write on their pages, why should they be allowed to use our vehicles of freedom? Do they really deserve to enjoy the liberties that the rest of the Cubans cannot? Don't they have enough with their own self-proclaimed revolutionary freedom?
>
> (Acevedo, 1998)

This comment comes from Gilberto Acevedo, a 37-year-old Cuban male who rates the Cuba MegaLinks site "Excelenticimo." Clearly, he sees this website as special and he would like to see that a separate ideological and discursive space exist for those with anti-communist sentiments.

While most sites about Cuba either contain a list of links to sites that share their ideological orientation, or a list that does not distinguish the political views of the linked sites, some sites acknowledge that sites about Cuba involve differences in political perspectives. For example, the website for Cornell University's Cuba Working Group, an organization that works for "an integrated program of teaching, research and scholarly exchange that would enhance mutual understanding of Cuban science, society and environment in a period of rapid transition," has a page that contains an annotated list of links to other resources and includes this entry:

Free Cuba Foundation/Fundacion Cuba Libre "provides up-to-date information on the situation inside Cuba focusing on the struggle for democracy and human rights." This organization takes what might be called a "conservative" view of Cuba, critical of Fidel Castro and socialism in Cuba.

Similarly, in the online article entitled, "Cuba on the Internet: Surprise! Cuba Has Internet, too," Vito Echevarria (1996) describes the CubaNet website and tells the reader that, "Because of the presence of Cuban exiles on this website, there is some material dedicated to the anti-Castro cause."

Producers of both pro- and anti-communist websites are interested in recruiting people to their "side" or "cause" and in providing resources and support to their ideological allies. In other words, both types of sites are invested in building collectivity, in bringing people together to try to effect change. And in their attempts to inspire others to action, these sites frequently give information about other organizations related to their cause or about ways to contact politicians to influence policy. For example, some sites provide addresses and phone numbers so that viewers can write or call in with their support of legislation such as the Humanitarian Relief Act, which will facilitate easing of the restrictions dictated by Helms–Burton.

Truth claims

Street draws our attention to "the variety of ways in which different media of communication are taken to signify the truth" (1995, p. 32), and websites about Cuba have in common their assertions that they are correcting misinformation. The nature of the Web allows us to see more easily the processes of ideological positioning inherent in all texts, as it is a place where one can view the whole spectrum of ideological views about a topic all at once. For example, one Web search for sites relating to Cuba turns up dozens of sites totally at opposite ends of the political and ideological spectrum. If with print literacy, "History . . . was being re-written to suit . . . purposes [of social control]" (Street, 1995, p. 66), with electronic literacy as manifested on the Web, there are highly visible, competing versions of history, as the various sites from and about Cuba demonstrate.

Although pro-Cuba websites tout, for example, the achievements of the revolution and the postrevolutionary literacy campaign, producers of anticommunist websites tell other stories. The latter sites are peppered with the buzzwords of western capitalism, such as "freedom" and "equality," and they deny the validity of Cuban claims about the greater existence of these states in Cuba than in "developed" countries. This ideological battle for power to describe the "real" Cuba is exemplified in an e-mail exchange with Ricardo Trelles (1998), the Web master of the anti-communist site for the Movimiento Humanista Evolucionario Cubano (Cuban Evolutionary

Humanist Movement). A request for information about print and electronic literacy in Cuba was met with this response which denies the politically radical version of Cuban history:

> Thanks for choosing us as part of your inquiry. We can even try to help you with your subject, because your questionnaire shows a complete lack of knowledge of even the most essential facts about our country . . .
>
> There isn't, and there hasn't been, any _social revolutions_ in Cuba. That is, if you understand by _revolution_ *accelerated progress*. Cuba is held hostage since 1959 by a gang of gangsters–demagogues, convinced that the Country is their private property, and that the Cuban people is their _human cattle_, to treat and take care of as such.
>
> (Trelles, 1998)

Trelles goes on to claim that the Cuban literacy campaign has never been successful and to deny the existence of the US blockade. He then concludes, "No wonder the phone system in Cuba is in shambles. No wonder you can't get an updated Cuban e-mail list. No wonder Internet services in Cuba are meager, strictly controled by the regime and not available for the common people. Thus, our Web site can hardly reach our people in the Island. But it is creating a very sound foundation for the new Cuba that we desperately need," (Trelles, 1998).

This example demonstrates how politically conservative producers of websites about Cuba view history as a contested category and see the Web as space to promote a capitalist version of the history of the Cuban revolution. Yet even a quick persual of websites about Cuba will give an inquisitive viewer a picture quite the opposite from the one Trelles paints here.

Producers of Internet sites from all ideological positions claim their sites provide a picture of the "real" Cuba. CubaNet is a right-wing website dedicated to bringing "democracy" to Cuba. The President of CubaNet, Jose Hernandez, responded to an e-mail request for information about Cuba and the Internet by positioning his organization as the provider of accurate information that is otherwise not available. He says,

> we are an organization dedicated to disseminate the work of the independent journalists in Cuba. The Cuban government does not allow these journalists access to the Internet – for that matter to any Cuban except its officers – so CubaNet obtains their information via phone calls and disseminate it through the Internet. As far as independent press, the role has been indirect although very important to them and the world wide audience interested in Cuba's realities.
>
> (1998)

First of all, the lack of universal Internet access in Cuba is a result of insufficient technology, not government restriction, as Hernandez asserts. Second, Hernandez's claim that CubaNet is providing scarcely available information about "Cuba's realities" is specious at best, especially given that the kind of information presented on websites such as this mirrors directly the American mainstream media's representation of Cuba as a horrific site of communist-inspired human rights violations, an assertion that is well contradicted by the documentation provided by left alternative media texts, as well as by experiences in Cuba.

In contrast, the Cuban website producers' claims to be filling an information gap are better substantiated. As explored in more detail below, the Cubans who produce CubaWeb, the online versions of *Granma Internacional* and *Trabajadores*, and similar sites, all have a clear sense that there is a great need to correct the misinformation about Cuba put out by the capitalist corporate mass media. This need is echoed in the sites produced by allies to Cuba, such as the Cuba Solidarity site, which includes a link that helps viewers write letters to members of the US Congress and which provides a copy of a sample letter that "counters some of the deliberate misinformation that the US Treasury Department is putting out" ("Send a Letter to . . .").

And in some cases in which this desire to correct misinformation is explicit, competing versions of "truth" are set one against the other. Here is one particularly rich example. On the "Cuba Health Care News" link from the Cuba Solidarity website, a site "devoted to providing news on developments in Cuba's uniquely resourceful health care system," one item featured is "Cuba: Insurmountable Paradox?: A Response to Linda Robinson's Article, 'The Island of Dr Castro," published in *US News and World Report*." In this article, author Julian Alvarez, a health care professional in Cuba, responds point-by-point to an article in the US media which compares Cuba and Castro to the novel, *The Island of Dr Moreau*. Alvarez explicitly outlines the stakes of such inaccurate coverage, beginning with the point that Robinson's text "could become a classic piece of misrepresentation of incontrovertible facts related to Cuban science and health care." Alvarez then enumerates the "genuine facts" about Cuban health care that are found in the *US News* piece, but follows this list by noting that these facts are accompanied by misrepresentations that paint a picture of "Cuban and the Cubans, our policies and our results, as an insurmountable paradox for US citizens." Alvarez intends to demystify this "paradox," and in so doing exposes the oppressive ideological framework that underpins the Robinson article:

> Robinson's focus is obviously based on paradigms of success in the United States (greater success means a better car and a larger house) that are not exactly ours (greater social recognition and pride in the achievements of our people). Therefore she highlights

the fact that our scientists go to work by bus or bicycle and that '50s Plymouths are still on the streets of Havana, without even mentioning that Cuba's gross domestic product dropped abruptly by 34 percent when our trade and credit relations with the Soviet Union and the Eastern European countries disappeared along with socialism in those states. Nor is it stated that throughout these 38 years of Revolution, Cuba concentrated all its efforts on offering every citizen, and in particular every child, an all-encompassing, free and equitable public health system and educational opportunities up to the most advanced level, through a nationwide and likewise free educational system. Nor does it state that the remainder of our spending was devoted to creating sources of employment and humanizing agricultural work, and that we never fell into the mortal sin of the poor countries, of attempting to imitate the consumer society created as a model by the United States. Neither did we commit the error of pouring our scant resources into extravagant articles or the luxury cars that Robinson would have liked to see on our streets.

After this scathing indictment of misplaced values and neglected information, Alvarez takes Robinson to task for incorrectly representing the medical system and priorities in Cuba, dismantling these falsehoods one by one. In the end, Alvarez returns to the larger ideological dimension of these two representations, taking on Robinson on her own terms:

> The image created in the article of policemen watching her front door can only be interpreted as a truculent tidbit aimed at deliberately twisting the truth. ... The Cuban scientific community, whose values are diametrically opposed to those which Ms Robinson tries to exalt in her article, is not ashamed of getting to work by bus or bicycle, or of living through the same difficulties as the rest of our people when there is a shortage of soap or deodorant ... our material well-being will be linked to that of our entire people, which will improve in line with our contribution to the national economy and to the solution of our country's major problems. We will help our country resist and overcome the almost all-powerful country which has not managed and will never manage to bring to its knees a people conscious of their duty and proud of their example.

This example shows the blatant misinformation about Cuba presented in the mainstream US media, and it also reflects the way the Internet is a site for intense representational battles, including those that involve the competing ideologies of capitalism and communism. There is no indication that Alvarez published this article in any other venue; more than likely, as the Cuba Solidarity site from which this text is linked is sponsored by Project InfoMed USA/Cuba, the piece was written specifically for posting on the Web. Thus, the Web provides a representational space heretofore not available to Cuban textual producers: the Web functions as a means to reach large numbers of people – including consumers of the mainstream US media – and gives Cubans who are wired a new opportunity to speak out in defense of the inaccurate portrayal of their country in these other venues.

Frequently, some websites about Cuba base truth claims upon elisions of information central to other sites' truth claims. For example, the Cuba Solidarity site about "Cuban Health Care News" contains links that describe the effects of the US embargo on health care efforts in Cuba, from the perspectives of organizations such as the American Association for World Health and the World Federation of Public Health Associations. The Cuba Solidarity site also includes a link to a site containing "Comments and Observations on the Seizure of Humanitarian Aid," a site which features documents that outline in detail the US government's seizure of computers that InfoMed and Pastors for Peace tried to deliver to Cuba for the Cuban InfoMed network. In an article of 5 February 1996, Project InfoMed's David Wald explains the real reasons behind the seizure:

> A national network of computers for disseminating medical infor-mation in Cuba is having a significant effect on the health care system of Cuba. It is precisely this genuine development which the US government wishes to stifle. It seeks to bring about a collapse of the Cuban government and, failing that, [to] keep Cuban devel-opment in a state of suspended animation, thereby proclaiming it a failed society.
>
> That is why our InfoMed computers were confiscated by the Treasury Department. It has nothing to do with the interests of the US people or its national security.

The website of "The Cuba Programs of Freedom House" stands in direct contrast to the sites of InfoMed USA and Cuba Solidarity. This site contains a link entitled, "Cuba Today" which is riddled with misspellings and typo-graphical errors, and which proudly declares that "Christopher Columbus discovered the island of Cuba in 1492." This site uses US government docu-ments as proof of its authority, such as an entry from the CIA World Factbook on Cuba, 1994, and the State Department's report, "The US Embargo and Healthcare in Cuba: Myth vs. Reality." This report's telling title reveals the contestation over representations of the "real" Cuba, a contest that is increasingly taking place on the Web itself. Yet the state department's report is directly misleading, claiming that, "The sad reality is that the healthcare available to the average Cuban has deteriorated because the Castro government has made a conscious choice to direct its increasingly scarce resources elsewhere." This false statement also belies the fact that Cuba's resources are "increasingly scarce" due to the policies of the US government. Further, the summary includes the "fact" that "The US has licensed over $150 million in humanitarian assistance" to Cuba since 1992, but this document can only promote such an assertion because it fails to mention the incident so prominently featured on pro-Cuba sites such as the InfoMed site – the American government's blocking of the delivery of medical computers to Cuba and the US customs officials' beating and incarceration of the non-violent members of InfoMed USA and Pastors for Peace who were attempting this delivery.[6]

The Cuban electronic press

Victor Fernandez details the history of the relationship between Cuban newspapers and computers. Before 1990, the national newspapers were edited daily, with one day off for each one, a rotating day of the week that alternated among the publications. These newspapers had 200,000 to 400,000 issues a year, each with between 12 and 16 pages. Other periodicals included newspapers of the Cuban provinces; magazines and newspapers from state institutions; the well-known magazine *Bohemia*, and other publications on cultural, scientific, economic, and political matters.

With the severe economic strain that came with the collapse of the Soviet Bloc and the ever tighter policy from the US, Cuban print publications had to be seriously limited. Many of the publications disappeared, and the editions of the newspapers were changed, with limited production. *Granma Internacional* began to be published on only five days a week, 8 pages each from Tuesday through Saturday. *Trabajadores* and *Juventud Rebelde* each published 16 pages weekly, and *Bohemia* became a biweekly publication. Editorial staff were greatly reduced, and in some cases, entirely eliminated.

The year 1989 saw the introduction of computers to the press. Word processors became available for newspaper writers, and a system for graphic simulation of developing pages was put into place. Typists, linotypists, and secretaries had to be reschooled in order to learn how to use the new computers. Eventually, they began to use 486 PCs and then Pentium processors, as well as Corel Draw and Corel Ventura for graphics. Word and Word Perfect programs were the word-processing preferences. Up until 1996, a photo process was used to produce the newspapers; from 1997, a digital process of editing and production of newspapers has been used. The last three years have seen a slow process of economic recuperation, and, as a result, some magazines have been resurrected or newly started, particularly those related to the new economic brand in Cuba, e.g., tourism.

In sum, the origins of the use of computer technology by the Cuban press came at the worst time, economically, for the country. Advances in both hardware and software have kept the newspapers increasingly reliant on computer technology for production. In these conditions, the Cuban press has gone on the Internet, with great success from the start. In 1996, *Granma Internacional* went online; in 1997, electronic versions of the national newspapers were begun. At the same time, websites were developed for NotiNet, the service for continuous information from Radio Reloj, the Agencia de Informacion Nacional, Prensa Latina, Radio Rebelde, and information services from TV. For the Cuban newspapers in particular, the Web provides a vital space for media communication. While paper subscriptions were low for these periodicals, and involved delays in the mail, these newspapers in their electronic form now receive millions of hits a month, reaching new audiences and overcoming technological and economic difficulties on a daily basis.

Granma Internacional

The Cuban Internet's primary function as a means to correct misinformation about Cuba is perhaps best exemplified in the website of the international version of the Cuban newspaper *Granma*.[6] This site reflects the importance of websites from news sources in the contest for representing the "real" Cuba on the Internet. Orlando Romero (1998), who oversees the design department for *Granma* online, explains that the site for *Granma* is the second-largest site originating in Cuba, and the digital international edition, in particular, serves a large foreign audience. Published in five languages – Spanish, English, French, Portuguese, and Dutch – the site was visited over 2 million times between 1 January and 1 May, 1998. Most Cubans do not have Internet access, so who are the viewers of this site? Orlando explains that,

> even the written version of *Granma Internacional*, which has been going on for thirty years now, is not directed at Cubans – it's directed at foreign readers. And we have subscribers in almost every country in the world. And we also have reprints in several different countries. We have a list of them all on the masthead – Brazil; Canada, in both French and English; Mexico; Spain – the main thing is that the readership in this case is foreign.

Orlando reveals the way that national pride enters the picture of Cuba's development of a Web presence when he asks rhetorically, "Since all the Latin American countries have newspapers on the Web, why can't the Cuban papers be on the Web, too?" Thus, Cuba's national newspapers, such as *Granma Diario* ("*Granma Daily*"), *Trabajadores*, and *Juventud Rebelde*, are all on line as well. Here we see that "the relationship between literacy, ideology, and nationalism" (Street, 1995, p. 107) is important to Cuba's electronic literacy, as it has been for its print literacy efforts as well.

This site is most effective in providing accurate information about Cuba, and in addition, about global politics in general. In terms of the former capability, *GI* originated when "there was a real need to get information out about Cuba's view of the situation when the airplanes went down in 1996," Orlando (1998) explains. Further, *GI* provides a much-needed stringently anti-capitalist and anti-imperialist perspective in its reporting of world politics.

Orlando (1998) reports that Cubans are sophisticated consumers of mainstream media texts and thus are not largely vulnerable to being persuaded to adopt an anti-communist stance from consuming texts on the Internet, should access become more widely available. He refers again to the island's technological limits and says,

> It is important to realize that Cubans have the highest educations. I can't say that people won't be affected – some will – but in general most will not. They have a sense of how things are in the world. For example, if I come across information in a news source such as *The Miami Herald* about incidents that have gone on here, I am skeptical about its accuracy, especially regarding incidents I have seen. If there was one stone thrown, the *Herald* will say there were 200, but I know their story is untrue.
>
> Cubans are very aware of the limitations. Amongst ourselves and foreigners, we constantly criticize what is going on. And so it isn't that these are new things – if Cubans read something negative about Cuba in the foreign press, they are very much aware of what's good and what's bad [information]. And that's why I say that what we do here is out of love. It's very much in that context. We are trying to present things that are true.

Cuba Web

While it might seem likely that there are only two sides to the information presented on websites from/about Cuba – capitalist and socialist/communist – there is a much more tangled picture here. The conditions of the political economy in Cuba are complex, and such complexity is reflected in the country's information economy as well. CubaWeb, Cuba's official government-endorsed website, is exemplary in this regard. It is unique among pro-communist sites in that it contains an additional layer of capitalist (not to be mistaken for pro-US) ideas. There are invitations of investment, tourism, commerce, and advertisements of goods for sale such as the *Encyclopedia of Cuba*. These elements parallel those found on the sites that encourage business and investment, except the latter are almost always explicitly anti-Castro and pro-"democracy." Perhaps CubaWeb embodies what *Atlantic Monthly* writer Joy Gordon (1998) calls "Cuba's Entrepreneurial Socialism."

Yet we must contextualize these moves of apparent commercialization, remembering Cuba's financial struggle, in part a result of the US embargo. Thus, for example, a closer examination of the "Quick Cash" Visa link/advertisement on the CubaWeb home page reveals the question "Send Money to Cuba?" in smaller letters, and the following explanation on the linked site: "the easiest, fastest, safest and most confidential way to . . . send money to your family or friends in Cuba." The Quick Cash site also explains that the Republic of Cuba authorizes their services, that these transactions are guaranteed to be secure, and that sponsorship of this system comes from Canadian banks. Here we have a microcosmic view of the political and economic situation in Cuba: the Cuban economy is struggling, suffering at the hands of the embargo; there is an air of distrust and suspicion between Cubans and the American government; Cubans in America are only recently allowed by the US government to send money to their family members who remain on the island; and Canada, in direct contrast to the US, is a major ally to Cuba in many ways, including financially.

CubaWeb team director Anibal Quevedo (1998) emphasizes that among websites, including the others produced in Cuba, CubaWeb is unique – no other website attempts to represent a whole country, and no other country has one "official" website. For example, he notes, there is no one US website that attempts to give a general idea of the whole country; as he says, "When you look at sites about the US, you are lost in a huge mountain of information." Anibal asserts that in their case, CubaWeb is "a website which gives as many possibilities as there are, regarding the world of Cuba. We say we're 'official' because we feature all the official media published in Cuba and because we follow the official policies of the country."

The story of the creation and evolution of CubaWeb is both fascinating and informative in relation to Cuba's economic position and the state of Cuban electronic representational efforts. In early 1995, a Canadian entrepreneur who was involved with a company working for the Web, Robert Sajo, came to Cuba and convinced the president of the Cuban business magazine *TIPS* to put the magazine on the Web. Anibal explains that from the start, there was a concern about the lack of information about Cuba on the Web:

> At that time, if you did an AltaVista search, you would find only two records for "Cuba." The information then was mainly coming from other parts of the reality, mainly from people from Miami. This is one of the most amazing things about the Internet – everybody has the space to say whatever they want. But there was little

information about Cuba and all the possibilities that Cuba had. So we started thinking about creating a Web page about Cuba.

There was no Internet linkage in Cuba yet. Sajo visited InfoMed to investigate their activities creating HTML, and he realized that there was no need to have workers in Canada overseeing the Cuban websites, that everything could be done in Cuba, by Cubans. Sajo saved the pages that would become the initial form of the Cubawebsite on a diskette and took them with him back to Canada. These first pages were run through servers in Canada and contained general information about the country and a few links about Cuban museums. Early efforts to maintain and develop CubaWeb were derailed when attacks on the site were made after the site's initial launch. Anibal mentions that firewalls and other virus-protection measures were not then available, and describes how people from Miami introduced viruses and destroyed two Canadian servers in the first week of CubaWeb's existence.

Sajo then obtained the cubaweb.cu domain and started using a secure server for CubaWeb. Yet there was still no Internet connection in Cuba itself. Anibal recounts the difficulties he and other Internet proponents faced during 1995:

> At the time, the Internet was seen as something subversive in Cuba. Most people didn't know even a word about the Internet. It was very hard to start convincing people working around the cities, especially here in Havana, knocking on their doors, and then when somebody appears at the door and you say, "I'm coming here to talk about the Internet" – Oh my God, I remember, that it was like being an evangelist, like in the Catholic church – no one wanted to know anything about it. It was the same with the Internet. If you knocked on the doors of some managers, saying you wanted to talk about business and the Internet, they would say, "It's not even on our minds today."
>
> ... We are an open country. There are a lot of frontiers and we are always in them. But the Internet is something new, and it is a pity, but our mentality, especially our official mentality, has not yet allowed open arms to new things. But this is not something that came from the sky – it came from a forty-year history of relations that comes not from good purpose.[8] They are serious and take decisions very slowly, not only the Cubans but also the people in charge of the government. The Internet is new and brings to the country many good things, but it can also bring to the country bad things.

In addition to these psychological barriers, there have been technological ones, and Anibal concurs that the main problem with the Internet in

Cuba has been the low bandwidth and slow speed. Thus, he relays, even with legal permission to connect to the Internet, Cuban companies do not have the present possibility of consistently good electronic performance.

After this rocky start, eventually the Cuban Web promoters convinced a few large companies, such as CubanaCan, the biggest tourist corporation in Cuba, to go on line with their offerings. More medium-sized companies joined in with websites. But, Anibal explains, "there was still missing information from the point of view of the people." Thus, in order for foreign Web viewers to "know a little bit of our reality, a little bit of our political point-of-view," they added the Cuban newspapers to CubaWeb. Significantly, the links to the Cuban media – newspapers and Radio Havana Cuba – are the first links featured on CubaWeb's listed links, preceding information about tourism, culture, and history.

The February 1996 downing of the planes flown by two US pilots was the catalyst for the serious development of CubaWeb, as it was for most of the other Cuban websites. In fact, it could be argued that this event mobilized Cuba's Internet development more than any other factor. Anibal relates how CNN ran a story about this incident that was televised before CNN Interactive existed on the Web. As a result, CNN told viewers at the end of its broadcast, "If you are interested in the Cuban side of the story, go to Cuba's official website at this URL." This CNN broadcast thus resulted in the Cubawebsite made by the Grupo Electronicao para el Turismo (GET/ Electronic Group for Tourism) being labeled the "official website" of Cuba – a connection that had not existed before. Now this Cuban company oversees this official site, and the workers are paid by the government. At that time, CubaWeb was run through servers in Canada, and GET paid for each hit on the site. The CNN broadcast resulted in 60,000 hits the following week, a number which greatly cost the Cubans.

Today CubaWeb is run off of three servers, and everything is administered in Cuba, an arrangement which is less costly to maintain. Clients such as *Granma* can go their virtual servers and update information each day. Between 50 percent to 60 percent of the traffic on CubaWeb is from the US and Canada, and the website currently receives five million hits a month. As Anibal exclaims, "The Internet is a very important [form of] media. Cuba never before had the ability to say what is really happening here" (1998).

Cubans involved in cyberspace understand that Cuba's battle with the US and its allies is not only economic, but also representational. The US government and media, whose ideology is reflected in right-wing organizations' websites about Cuba, paints a picture of Cuba as victim of a crazed dictator who deprives the Cuban people of the beneficent forces of the "free market" and the freedom inherent in the act of consumption privileged in commodity capitalism. CubaWeb responds to this construction of Cuba with two images, two visual and social representations of Cuba. First, Cuba is presented as *not* the "bad" place it has been made out to be. While these negative characterizations are not explicitly addressed on the Cubawebsite, they haunt its promotion of Cuba as a pretty place, one with a rich history and culture, a place "you" would want to visit and see. These interpellations of the potential tourist are countered with another image of Cuba, that of the country as a different place politically than has been represented by the western mass media. From the beginning, the Cuban presence on the Internet was envisioned as a means to counter misrepresentations about Cuba, which is why all of the sources of Cuban news – both print and radio – are linked to the Cubawebsite. These news sources provide both a picture of Cuba's socialist goals and achievements as well as a sharp anti-imperialist and anti-capitalist critique of global politics.

Cuba's desperate economic situation led to the government's decision to open up its economy to US dollars and to promote tourism as a means of raising capital. This context underlies CubaWeb's need to successfully promote Cuba as a desirable vacation spot. The "La Isla Grande" Ministry of Tourism series of links from the Cubawebsite features a "Gallery" link that gives the potential tourist viewer a slideshow series of images of Cuba. These images all seem to be from Havana, and there are no Cuban people highlighted in these color pictures. Ornate old buildings and sunsets are prominent. In contrast, the website of Dutch photographer Piet den Blanken contains a series of black and white photographs of Cuba which are much more intimate and feature many Cuban people, with titles such as "She Smokes a Cigar" and "In the Faces of Working Men You Can See . . ."

Given the economic dynamics of Cuba today, CubaWeb features a mix of capitalist thinking and methods and socialist content, a combination which involves contradictions. For one thing, advertising presumes a relationship predicated on exchange value. Advertising promotes the consumption of commodities, inherent in which, as Marx ([1867] 1990) makes clear at the start of volume I of *Capital*, is objectified labor. That is, intrinsic to the commodity form, unpaid objectified labor is congealed; thus, the process of exchange under capitalism, in which the value of goods is not in any direct way tied to their utility, is always supporting the exploitation of someone's labor that leads to the creation of surplus value and profit for the exploiters. In this way, it is not only strange to see advertising in a text promoted by the government of a socialist country, such as CubaWeb – it is also a contradiction in that advertising itself is antithetical to the socialist project. Cuba's exceptional situation of embracing (temporarily, they believe) some capitalist dynamics in part of the country's economy in order to stave off starvation imposed by the US embargo is demonstrated in this text, CubaWeb. The potential tourists who view this site are the potential consumers who must be wooed to come to the island and spend their precious dollars, as Cuba is desperate for hard currency to boost its economy. In this light, it is understandable that the Cubawebsite so prominently features information and links concerning tourism, flights, car rental, and the like. However, when one learns that 71 cents out of every dollar earned through tourism is ploughed back into the industry for items such as sugar packets which are perceived to be thought essential by western tourists, such wholesale use of capitalist advertising techniques by the Cubawebsite is disheartening. On the other hand, how could the Cubans entice most Web viewers to come and visit their country if they did not use ideas and formal techniques that come from the logic of capitalist tourism? In every aspect of the situation of Web production in Cuba, such contradictions arise, reflections of the political and economic contradictions in which Cubans currently live.

It is interesting that there is no encouragement of political allegiance or activism on CubaWeb. Perhaps, though, in a twisted way (at least from the perspectives of the governments of Cuba and the US), encouraging tourism is the most transgressive act a Cuban website can perform. Cuba is deemed an undesirable product by the American government and the mainstream media repeats this characterization in an unmediated way. Yet Cuba is now using the Internet to respond by saying, "Yes, our country is a good place, a worthy tourist destination." It's a self-commodification based on pride and desperation, though only the former comes through in the rhetoric of Cuban websites. It is hoped that the promotion of the Cuba of which they are proud will prevent the continuation of their desperate state. The Web is seen as a vital tool for performing the necessary self-promotion to attract western tourist customers to their shores.

Cuban website design

Websites about Cuba use the Web's combination of text and images in provocative ways. For example, the Cuba Solidarity website prominently features an image of a "sign in Havana, photographed in March 1997." The billboard is in Spanish, with the English translation below: "200 million children in the world sleep in the streets today. Not one of them is Cuban." Thus a billboard which was most likely originally directed at Cuba's own citizens (given the newness of tourism as a big industry there) is taken up as an image to show the rest of the world that Cuba has successfully avoided the homelessness endemic to capitalism.

The producers of Cuba's internally created websites also employ sophisticated strategies of textual design, as evidenced by both of the major Cuban websites considered here, CubaWeb and the online version of *Granma Internacional.* CubaWeb's initial page features a bold banner that says "CUBAWEB," in large letters, and "El Sitio Oficial de La Republica de Cuba" and "The Web Site of the Republic of Cuba" above and below "CUBAWEB." To the right of these words is an image of the sunset over the ocean in Havana, and the water shimmers in this animated GIF. Similarly, the website of *GI* displays fancy graphics and well-designed pages. The high level of technical skill displayed in these sites sometimes inspires incredulity in viewers when they discover that they are produced in Cuba. In fact, as *GI*'s head designer Orlando Romero (1998) relates, during their first months online, the newspaper received several e-mail messages asking them where the site was produced – New York? Washington? Miami? The writers were always shocked to learn that the site originates in Cuba. Orlando says, "We were forced to add a disclaimer at the bottom of the first page, explaining that the site is produced here." In this way, Cuba's websites negate the myth that economic "development" and electronic literacy go hand in hand.

In order to decide future directions for site design, Cuban website producers monitor viewing patterns. Here is one example. Of the many intriguing features of the Cubawebsite, the one about which I was most curious was an icon which appeared between my first visit to the Cubawebsite in April 1998 and my next visit to the site a month later – a baby's head. All the other icons on the Cubawebsite have an indexical relationship to their links in that the image leads the reader to information about that particular image. In other words, the image of an airplane links to the page that tells the viewer "How to Fly Inside Cuba"; the image of a car goes to the link with information about car rental in Cuba; the image of an LP record connects to the site on which Cuban music is sold; and an image of a hand holding up money connects to the QuickCash site. Yet the baby head is linked to "Cuba: La Isla Grande," a series of pages that feature lavish images and descriptions of the island (written solely in Spanish), pages created by the Ministy of Tourism of Cuba. I wondered if there were some cultural connection between the baby head and the content of these pages, so the baby head was one of my primary areas of interest during my interviews in Cuba. When I visited the *GI* offices in Havana, I noticed the dancing baby from the American television show, *Ally McBeal,* on one of the computer screens, but I was told the Microsoft screen saver has no relation to the CubaWeb baby head icon. (Imagine me trying to explain in halting Spanish the presence of this dancing baby on *Ally McBeal* – one of the many such comical moments I experienced while in Cuba.)

Anibal Quevedo (1998) describes the evolution of this element of CubaWeb:

> The story of the baby is very funny. We wanted to add a link here for things that were coming new. The designer, a second-year college student, had the idea of the head of the baby, and everybody was angry here. They thought it was not proper, but then I didn't decide anything. I let it remain for a while, to see the reaction of the traffic, and after two weeks I came back again to the head of the baby. It gave me a few ideas because of the e-mails that we were receiving, coming from that specific link. There was

something which was very important for us. First of all, when viewers looked at it, it was something completely different from the rest. And what we are depending on is that you click on it and you go directly to what we want to show you. So this is a technique that's very commonly used on the Net. Most of the time when you look at a banner, you can never imagine what is going to happen when you click on it. There is always some type of provocation that gives you the idea to click on it, to see what is after that. So that's why we finally let the designer put the baby head for all the new links that we are incorporating into the page. If you ask me why, I will tell you what – I don't know why. The statue of Oscar has become today that most famous award in the world regarding films – what does it mean? It means nothing. But it's an Oscar, and if you win an Oscar, you are one of the most famous people in the world.

This example shows how Cuban website producers use design and monitoring techniques to influence viewer experiences. I tell Anibal that though I was confused about the baby head, I was not only drawn to click on it as they intended, I also saw the baby head as a reflection of the playfulness of Cuba and its people. He is pleased and sums up, simply, "For us, a new website is like a baby." I tell Anibal about my university teaching in an electronic classroom, and explain that I have my students create politically radical websites, to which he responds, "Good," and laughs. He agrees when I say that there is some power to the link, that the link calls one as a viewer, arouses one's curiosity.

Power relations

Street notes that "The primary dimensions of this new power structure [resulting from literacy campaigns] involve hegemony of urban areas over rural, of men over women and of central elites over local populations" (1995, p. 37). Are power relations concerning website production and consumption in Cuba similarly configured?

Geographies of power: Havana hegemony?

The internal power relations that Street describes to some extent apply to Cuba's electronic literacy dynamics. For one thing, the city of Havana dominates the Web activity in Cuba, so there is certainly urban hegemony in the production of eletronic texts. The headquarters of InfoMed, the Cuban newspapers and radio stations, and Teledatos/GET, the company that produces CubaWeb, are all located in Havana. However, this trend reflects the larger way that Havana is a different world than the rest of the country in a general sense. In fact, the promotion of tourism and the US dollar economy is taking place primarily in Havana and is being strongly resisted by Cubans who live outside of the capitol city. Many of the Cubans outside Havana refuse to use US dollars or to accept any gifts bought with this currency.

Gender dynamics

While I went to Cuba with the impression that I would find the "boy's world" of cyberspace replicated in the sites of Web production there – something akin to what Sharon Traweek (1998) confronted in the Japanese astrophysics labs she investigated – I was shocked to discover that my question about gender differences was met with an initial lack of understanding and then with incredulity. Cuban website producers could not imagine that anyone would be surprised to find women so involved with computers and Web activities there. At InfoMed, one of the graphic designers is a young woman; at *Granma Internacional* two of the four workers involved with the production of the online version are women, both with young children at home, and one of these women is the director of the Web production team; and a woman is a key member of the CubaWeb team as well. According to Cuban website producers, more women than men are trained in science and technology fields, and the prevalence of women in technology is reflected in website production as well.

However, as with the Internet in general, there is a growing link between pornography and sex tourism in Cuba on the Web. Though I have been told there are Cubans who run dating services over the Web, I have only been able to track down externally produced websites that promote this service. One such example is the "Desiree's Guide to Sex in Cuba" link from the "Desiree's World Guide to Sex" site. This site reflects the way that the Internet is enabling the re-establishment of clandestine operations that were shut down after the revolution. Prostitution, and with it a racialist discourse, has resurfaced and is promoted on the Web.[9] Desiree's guide tells the potential tourist:

> The girls that are the easiest to find are usually black and from Oriente [outside of Havana]. I think the girls in the Dominican Republic, which are all mixed race, are more beautiful than these Cuban girls. But the black Cubans do not have the same dark complexions as the Haitians. There are also white girls, but they may be a little bit harder to find and there are fewer of them. Actually just about any un-married Cuban girl is available, many of them just don't know about it, until they make friends with a tourist.

241

The commodification of Cuban women is similarly exemplified in the "Cuba" link of the Foreign Relations website. Foreign Relations "features more than 7000 current personal photo profiles of beautiful foreign women . . . [who] are interested in meeting a kind, loving man for a serious relationship and eventual marriage" ("Foreign Relations International Introductions"). Male viewers are invited to "Browse or search through our website . . . to find many lovely ladies who share your interests and want to meet you." The website's search engine "allows [viewers] to search by country, religion, height, age and other features." The women featured on this site are clearly seen as commodities – on the pages describing each woman is a link that says, "Add to Order," reminiscent of the "Add to Shopping Cart" links provided by electronic bookstores. Cuban women are highlighted on this site. For each woman, the following information is provided: first name, age, Cuban city of residence, height, weight, short decription of interests and desires, education, marital status, religion, number of previous address requests by viewers, and the date on which her information was originally posted. Almost all of the Cuban women featured on this site seek "an honest, caring man" or a man who is "decent" or "loving." Of course, what is unmentioned in these descriptions is any desire to leave Cuba, though this dimension of this system of exchange is reflected in links describing "Fiancée Visas."

There is something quite pathetic and sad about the Cuban section of this site. While some of the women who are more stereotypically beautiful have received many e-mail requests from viewers, some of the other women have not yet received any, though their information may have been posted for several months. (My own ambivalance in relationship to such sites is evidenced in the fact that I feel sorry for the women who have not received any responses. More than that, though, I feel for the women who find them-selves living in a situation where they will sell their selves or their bodies to escape, or at least to help them survive financially.) Another website, "The World Sex Guide – Prostitution around the World," has a series of links about prostitution in Cuba, including many e-mail reports from men who have visited the country. The men detail how US citizens can work around the legal restrictions on travel to Cuba and they describe every facet of experience with prostitutes in Cuba, from locations, to prices, to what types of sex acts a visitor can expect to be able to experience.

Thus, while women enjoy a respected and equal status in terms of Web production in Cuba, the Web is still a vehicle that very much helps to perpetuate the objectification of Cuban women. The Cuban government is working to fight the rise in prostitution that has accompanied the intro-duction of the dollar economy into the country. But while the government is coming to view the Internet as a beneficial space for their project of economic repair, they are bound to be dismayed about the role of the Web in the promotion of prostitution and arranged marriages.

One phenomenon provides a bizarre counterpoint to the types of sites mentioned above, those that sell future brides or encourage prostitution in Cuba. On one of the major websites about Cuba, Cuba Megalinks, there is a series of links to the Cuban-American prisoners featured on Prison. Pen Pals.com. Each page features one American prisoner of Cuban descent, including his picture. Each prisoner has written a personal ad inviting women to write to him. Some of these men will mention their status as prisoners, referring to the crimes they committed or to their impending release dates. Some have unique links to the prisoner's poems or artwork. But in most other respects, these ads read like typical personal ads, putting a very strange twist on the commodification of bodies in cyberspaces about Cuba. For example, here is an excerpt from the ad for Andrew Murillo:

Hi there! It's me ... Andrew! I'm a young 24 year old who's currently single, and searching for friendship and possible companionship. Spent my youth in New York, lived in Florida for the past 12 years. Enjoy traveling and going to different destinations to see sights.

Am Cuban/American, white, 5'7", weigh 158 lbs., have hazel eyes, black straight hair, and a nice body to match. Enjoy parties and getting together with new friends. Like all kinds of music, concerts, animals, sports and other outdoor activities.

Have an outgoing personality that is sincere and enthusiastic, making the ordinary situation – extraordinary! Came to prison at the young age of 17 resulting from poor judgement. Definitely had time to mature, reflect and refocus on life. Have high expectations. Looking for someone to fill me in on what I've missed. Be released by Thanksgiving '98.

It is quite ironic that while the addresses of Cuban women are provided over the Web to an international audience of men who can shop for future wives, the addresses of Cuban men are given so that prisoners of Cuban descent can meet female pen pals and possible future lovers. Both women and men in these contexts are trapped and view their ads as a means to meet someone who can help them become free of their situations. The perpetuation of sexism over the Web is not exempted from Cuban Internet relations.

Class power: condoning and contesting capitalism

In general, the relationship between Cuba and the Web occurs within the context of the larger global battles between proponents of capitalism and those who seek a different way of organizing society. There are specific ways that this tension is manifested, though. First there are the sites which overtly address this tension. On the one hand, we find sites such as CyberCuba.com. The "About our company" link states in all seriousness, "'Yeehaa!, We're Texans!' . . . Pure Cuba Play Corporation is a Texas based for profit corporation. Cuba Yes! Marxism and Atheism No!" Another of the site's links, about the "Cuba Stock Exchange," more explicitly spells out this company's ideological position and purpose:

> "Preserving and Promoting Capitalism in La Republica de Cuba" Hopes and dreams versus Sales and Earnings . . . in a nutshell, the hopes and dreams of the Cuban people have not been attained by the totalitarian government intoxicated with Marxism. Sales and earnings, profit and loss, return on assets, earnings per share, free cash flow . . . all the reverberations of capitalism at work echoing throughout the island Christopher Columbus called "the most beautiful land" he had ever seen . . . Cuba.
>
> Utilizing our knowledge of past and, now, nascent capitalism in Cuba, we intend (when permitted by regulatory agencies) to offer securities through which US investors can participate in a New Cuba. Please Contact Us! for further information.

On the other hand, we have sites such as the Fidel for President Home Page, which acknowledges in tongue-in-cheek style the nature of the US government's stance towards Cuba. For example, reflecting the intense surveillance our government visits upon allies of Cuba, the "Committee to Help Elect Fidel" link encourages viewers to join their campaign with this prod: "Why delay the inevitable? The CIA already knows you're reading this, so why not go all the way?" Adam Reith, creator of the site, both plays off the viewer's position in a capitalist world and simultaneously critiques the capitalist system. In a link from the initial page, Reith invites viewers to "Satisfy your sick capitalist urges with the Fidel for President Catalog: Campaign t-shirts, bumper stickers and bubble gum cigars." (Elsewhere in the site, Reith explains that funds from the sales of these items go to fund the site itself.) On two pages, Reith includes this link: "Yow this is frightening! Send me back to the bosom of the bourgeois elite." The link from the Catalog page goes to the Microsoft Corporation home page, and the same link from the membership form page goes to a site called "The Spot" which features the daily journals of some young bourgeois Americans who share a beach house in Santa Monica. On the page featuring the initial "hate mail" e-mail message the site received, the last in a series of links at the bottom of the page says, "Wait a second! This guy's right on! To hell with this Fidel crap, give me real American values!!!" and sends the viewer to the website for Pizza Hut. Similarly, on the page that provides alt.smokers.cigars discussion list excerpts, Reith offers the viewer links back to previous parts of his site, or this link: "Holy cow! Cuban cigars shouldn't be worshipped; they're contraband! Does no one understand?!?!" which takes the viewer to the Right Side of the website, "est. March 1994 to counter the economic socialism and cultural Marxism out there on the Net." And lastly, at the end of the initial invitation for the viewer to join the Fidel for President movement, Reith gives the viewer the choice to go to the membership sign-up link or click on the following link, "No way! Newt is right; a capital gains tax cut will help working people! Communist–Marxist–Socialist–Fascist Cuba is a National Security Risk and besides, Fidel threatens my gender role! I'm outta here!" In a move that explicitly points to the values underlying the ideological battles between the US and Cuba – including those voiced on the Net – Reith has linked this statement to the website of the Internet Shopping Network.

The tensions between the philosophies of communism/socialism and capitalism are evident in the dynamics of Web production within Cuba as well. For example, there is a major connection to the Microsoft corporation. The website of *Granma Internacional* is created with Microsoft's Frontpage software, a fact proudly proclaimed on the site's initial page. And InfoMed's Web master, 23-year-old Ernesto Couso Artiles, happily wears various Microsoft-emblazoned T-shirts to work each day, and admits to heartily admiring Bill Gates. In fact, while reading over an early draft of this chapter, Ernesto flinched at the slam of the Microsoft slogan, "Where do you want to go today?" in the critique of capital's intent for the global "information highway." Yet, at the same time that Ernesto displayed these pro-Microsoft sentiments, he embraced a socialist politics at heart when he declared the conclusions drawn thus far in the draft, such as in the analysis of the contradictions inherent in CubaWeb, to be accurate.

All the workers involved with website production were asked about their own personal Web viewing habits and preferences. As these workers are, after all, the only people in Cuba who currently enjoy full access to the Web, it seemed reasonable to assume that, as such, perhaps their own viewing habits might foreshadow potential problems involved with increased Web access by other Cubans in the future. Yet this projection still relies upon the belief that perhaps there is some ideological contamination at work in their own relationship to the Internet. On the contrary, these workers use the Web mostly in conjunction with their jobs. As the leader of the team that produces CubaWeb, Anibal views websites mostly regarding marketing online (his favorite site is Wilsonweb). Similarly, one worker for the electronic dimension of the Latin press agency, Prensa Latina, often searches the Web for free software he needs for his work. So does InfoMed Web master Ernesto, who, one Saturday afternoon at the InfoMed offices, spent hours surfing the Web in search of a particular computer game to download, a game he wanted for his work with a group of children who have cancer.

The sheer reality is that these workers simply do not have the time to indulge in frivolous Web surfing. Lacking the surplus leisure time typically enjoyed by most American Web viewers, such as middle- and upper-class male college students, these folks spend ten- and twelve-hour workdays in their jobs as Web designers, editors, and hypertext writers. I was struck by the small groups who actually do the work on these websites. *Granma Internacional* online received over 2 million hits in the first four months of 1998, is published in five languages, and is updated daily – yet only *four* people do this work! Similarly, while the Cubawebsite receives 5 million hits a month and features extensive links, the team which produces this site is comprised of only five people. The offices from which these sites originate are small and slightly crowded, with tables of various sizes lined up along the walls and minimal décor or comfort – though most have air conditioners, rare throughout the country. These workers are aware that they could make much money performing their work in other countries, 3,000 to 4,000 American dollars a month in most cases, but they are committed to using their knowledge to further the political project of their country.

Conclusion

Street's understanding that regarding print literacy, "There is much research to be done yet on the actual relations between specific genres and the holding of power, financial and political" (1995, p. 140) also applies to electronic literacy, and this chapter is a contribution to this project, since it details some of the crucial power relations that underlie the production and consumption of websites from and about Cuba. This examination of the websites about Cuba, produced from within and without the country, reveals that electronic literacy in Cuba is as much about the electronic literacy practices of Web viewers outside of Cuba, as about those of Cubans living in Cuba. At this point, the primary players in the world of Cuba's electronic literacy are the Cuban producers of Cuban websites, the pro- and anti-Cuba/Castro producers of externally originating websites, and the mostly foreign viewers of all of these websites.

Moreover, as demonstrated in this chapter, the case of Cuba's electronic literacy compels us to historicize not only in terms of colonialism's legacy, but also in relation to the workings of global capitalism. And one of the central questions prompted by this investigation of Cuba and the Internet is this: as consumerism spreads in Cuba, will the capitalist approach to electronic literacy become more prevalent there? Or will the Cubans continue to be able to use the consumerism inherently promoted by the Internet to further their non-consumerist goals, to keep alive the socialist dimension of their state?

Acknowledgements

Thanks to Cindy Selfe and Gail Hawisher for including me in such an important and provocative project. I am also most grateful to all the brilliant and generous Cuban website producers who provided extensive interviews. And thanks to the *taxistas* "taxi drivers," who often waited patiently in the Havana sun for hours while I conducted interviews.

Notes

1   This chapter is the result of personal research on the Web, much e-mail exchange with the producers of many websites from or about Cuba, and in-depth interviews with Cubans most involved with website production in Cuba. One Cuban website producer, Victor Fernandez, the Web master for *Trabajadores*, wrote large sections of the chapter and commented thoroughly on the chapter as a whole. In every way, this chapter has been produced with great input from Cubans who work with the Internet, and thus the voices of those who speak from a close and intimate knowledge of the Cuban culture are featured prominently throughout the chapter. Much information as well as extensive direct quotes from the interviews conducted during a week-long trip to Havana are included. Additionally, the general shape of the chapter has been influenced greatly by the perspectives of the Cuban interviewees. Finally, the Cubans interviewed also commented on various drafts of this paper, and were invited (via e-mail) to add their input regarding the chapter's final form.

2   This chapter follows conventional usage and uses the term "embargo," though with the recognition that the embargo functions more in the fashion of a blockade. Blair Lopes, Canadian delegate to the 14th World Youth and Student Festival, describes well the true nature of the US policy towards Cuba:

> I learned that the embargo is more accurately called a "blockade." Besides imposing a ban on all trade with Cuba, it also pressures governments and businesses in other countries to withhold aid, trade, and technology from Cuba, and uses its clout in international lending institutions to prevent access to credit. The Torricelli Law, passed in 1992, tightens the embargo even further by making it impossible for foreign subsidiaries of US corporations to do business with Cuba, and by denying commercial ships access to US ports if they are carrying goods for Cuba. The blockade amounts to economic warfare and intervention in the affairs of a sovereign nation. It is a violation of international law and US treaty obligations. And it causes widespread shortages of food, medicine and fuel for eleven million Cubans.
>
> (Lopes, 1998)

3   "Cargo cults" are documented particularly in Melanesia during the early part of this century and occurred where local responses to European control of goods and resources took the form of cult movements attempting to commandeer this "'cargo' for the indigenous population" (Street, 1995, p. 77). Street argues that the uses of literacy by members of these cargo cults have been mistakenly judged as "irrational" by anthropologists who employ the autonomous model of literacy and asserts that the cults' use of literacy was predicated on an understanding of literacy's ideological nature. For more of Street's analysis of this phenomenon, see Street, 1995, p. 53–54 and Chapter 4, "Orality and Literacy as Ideological Constructions: Some Problems in Cross-Cultural Studies."

4   These dynamics are currently in flux, however. While Cuba has resisted capitalist economic modes for over three decades, recently the Cuban government
has officially endorsed the creation of a two-tier economy that allows the influx
of American dollars. Tourism and some investment ventures are being encouraged by the government in order to prop up their ailing economy. As evidenced
in some of the websites regarding Cuba, many US corporations are poised on
the brink of entering the Cuban economic scene if US policy toward trading
with Cuba changes significantly (or if the country itself is won over by capitalism
in total).

5   In January of 1996,

> agents of the US Treasury, along with other police forces took action . . .
> in California to seize a shipment of computers being brought to Cuba by
> [InfoMed USA and] Pastors for Peace to aid that country's online medical
> information system, and detained on criminal charges those who were
> bringing that shipment in to Mexico for transport to Cuba . . . the police
> action was conducted with extreme police violence, resulting in injury to
> many of those arrested, despite the full knowledge that all participants in
> the Friendshipment Caravan were explicitly pledged to non-violence.
>
> ("A Letter from The Catholic Worker")

6   Radio Havana Cuba conducted an interview with Blake Dunlap, the National
Co-Coordinator of Pastors for Peace, and reported his account of the violence
that occurred in this incident:

> After being blocked several times by the San Diego police, US Customs
> agents replaced the locks on the trucks with their own locks. Officials also
> totally shut down the bridge to all pedestrian traffic for most of the day.
> At approximately 4 p.m. local time, US Customs agents opened the backs
> of several trucks and began removing computers. Caravan drivers, who had
> formed a protective ring around the trucks, some even sitting on top of
> the trucks, were violently dragged away from their vehicles. Several cara-
> vanistas then attempted to carry the computers across the border on foot
> and were gang-tackled by as many as eight police officers at a time. The
> officers then violently wrenched the computers from their arms. Several
> people have been detained and several more have been injured. As many
> as 50 riot police with shields, helmets and billy-clubs moved into place,
> despite the commitment that caravan drivers have expressed to conduct
> themselves non-violently at all times. Fifteen squad cars and many uniformed
> and plain-clothed police from a number of law-enforcement agencies have
> converged on the border along with 19 tow-trucks. According to unclassi-
> fied government documents, this was a coordinated effort by US Customs,
> the Immigration and Naturalization Service, the FBI, California Highway
> Patrol and the San Diego Police and Fire Departments, who have been
> planning for weeks to seize the computers before they crossed the border
> to Mexico.
>
> ("Pastors for Peace Caravan Stopped")

7   *Granma* is the name of the ship that carried Fidel Castro back to Cuba to begin
the second, and successful, attempt at revolution in Cuba.

8   The relationship between Cuba and the US has long been troubled, and the
US has been violently aggressive towards the Caribbean country ever since the

revolution. For example, according to the autobiography of Robert McNamara, in the last few decades, the US has bombed Cuba over 1,600 times.

9   I am grateful to Jamie Owen Daniel for pointing out these dynamics.

References

"About Our Company," http://www.cybercuba.com/about.html. (27 May 1998).

Acevedo, G. "Guestbook Entry #6," 30 April 1998, Cuba Megalinks site, http://central.solarianet.com/guest/view.wex?gid=atreus (9 July 1998).

Alvarez, J. "Cuba: Insurmountable Paradox?: A Response to Linda Robinson's Article, 'The Island of Dr Castro,'" published in *US News and World Report* and included in "Cuban Health Care News," http://www.igc.apc.org/cubasoli/health.html. (28 June 1998).

Artiles, Ernesto C., personal interviews, 5 and 6 June 1998.

Brook, J. and Boal, I. A., (eds) (1995) *Resisting the Virtual Life: The Culture and Politics of Information*, San Francisco: City Lights.

"The Committee to Help Elect Fidel," link from the Fidel for President Home Page, http://www.imagesmith.com/imagesmith/fidel/); http://www.imagesmith.com/imagesmith/fidel/fidel_sign_up.html. (17 April 1998).

Cuba Megalinks, http://www.laker.net/nike/megalinks.html#tour. (17 April 1998) and e-mail on the guestlist of this site.

"Cuban Health Care News," http://www.igc.apc.org/cubasoli/health.html. (28 June 1998).

"The Cuba-pictures of Piet den Blanken," http://www.iaehv.nl/users.robr/blanken.html. (16 June 1998).

Cuba Programs of Freedom House, http://www.freecuba.org. (17 April 1998).

Cuba Solidarity website, http://www.igc.agp.org/cubasoli (13 June 1998).

"Cuba Stock Exchange," http://www.cybercuba.com/cubaexchange.html. (27 May 1998).

"Cuba Working Group Home Page," http://www.msc.cornell.edu/~plh2/cuba/. (17 April 1998).

"The Downing of the Planes: An Attempt to Provide Context," link from the Cuba Solidarity website, http://www.igc.apc.org/cubasoli/); http://www.igc.apc.org/cubasoli/planes2.html. (17 April 1998).

Echevarria, V. May 1996. "Cuba on the Internet: Surprise! Cuba Has Internet, too," *Boardwatch Magazine,* http://www.boardwatch.com/mag/96/MAY/bwm60.htm. (17 April 1998).

Fernandez, V., personal interview, 7 June 1998.

"Fidel Castro: Tough Enough for Washington, DC," link from the Fidel for President Home Page, http://www.imagesmith.com/imagesmith/fidel/); http://www.imagesmith.com/imagesmith/fidel/issues.html. (26 May 1998).

"The Fidel for President Catalog," link from the Fidel for President Home Page, http://www.imagesmith.com/imagesmith/fidel/); http://www.imagesmith.com/imagesmith/fidel/fidel_catalog.html. (17 April 1998).

"Fidel for President Home Page," http://www.imagesmith.com/imagesmith/fidel/. (17 April 1998).

Gordon, J. January 1997. "Cuba's Entrepreneurial Socialism," *Atlantic Monthly,* http://www.theatlantic.com/atlantic/issues/97jan/cuba/cuba.htm. (16 June 1998).

Hernandez, J. A., MD personal e-mail (31 May 1998).

"InfoMed, Cuba's Medical Network!" Link from the Cuba Solidarity website http://www.igc.apc.org/cubasoli/; http://www.igc.apc.org/cubasoli/infomed.html. (28 June 1998).

"Internet Shopping Network," http://www.internet.net/. (26 May 1998).

Lopes, B. "My Socio-Cultural Cuban Reality," http://www.hooked.net/~rlegates/blair.htm. (17 April 1998).

Magno, P. "A Letter from The Catholic Worker," Comments and Observations on the Seizure of Humanitarian Aid, http://igc.apc.org/cubasoli/seizure.html. (17 April 1998).

Magrans, A., personal interview, 4 June 1998.

Marx, K. ([1867] 1990) *Capital: A Critique of Political Economy*, vol. I, London: Penguin Books.

McNamara, R. S. (1996) *In Retrospect: The Tragedy and Lessons of Vietnam*, New York: Vintage Press.

"Microsoft Corporation Home Page," http://www.microsoft.com. (30 June 1998).

Movimiento Humanista Evolucionario Cubano (Cuban Evolutionary Humanist Movement) website. http://ourworld.compuserve.com/homepages/MHEC. (17 April 1998).

Murillo, A., personal ad. Prison Pen Pals.com., http://www.prisonpenpals.com/442014.html. (13 June 1998)

"Other Institutions/Other Resources," Link from the Cuba Working Group Home Page, http://www.msc.cornell.edu/~plh2/cuba/others.html. (17 April 1998).

"Pastors for Peace Caravan Stopped on the Border with Mexico," Report from Radio Havana Cuba, 31 January 1998, Comments & Observations on the Seizure of Humanitarian Aid, http://igc.apc.org/cubasoli/seizure.html. (17 April 1998).

"The Pizza Hut Home Page," wysiwyg://653/http://www.pizzahut.com. (30 June 1998).

Prison Pen Pals.com., http://www.prisonpenpals.com/442014.html. (5 July 1998).

"Prostitution in: Cuba," The World Sex Guide, http://www.worldsexguide.org/Cuba.html. (16 June 1998).

Quevedo, A., personal interview, 8 June 1998.

"The Right Side of the Web," http://www.rtside.com. (30 June 1998).

Romero, O., personal interview, 5 June 1998.

"Send a Letter to Congress!" link from the Cuba Solidarity website http://www.igc.apc.org/cubasoli/). http://www.igc.apc.org/cubasoli/conglett.html. (visited 17 April 1998).

Silverman, K. (19) *On Semiotics*, The Pierce reference comes from this book.

"The Spot," http://www.thespot.com/. (26 May 1998).

Street, B. V. (1995) *Social Literacies: Critical Approaches to Literacy in Development, Ethnography and Education*, London: Longman.

Traweek, S. (1988) *Beamtimes and Lifetimes: The World of High Energy Physicists*, Cambridge, MA: Harvard University Press.

Trelles, Ricardo, personal e-mail, 27 May 1998.

"The US Embargo and Healthcare in Cuba: Myth vs. Reality," link from the Cuba Programs of Freedom House website, http://www.freecuba.org; http://www.freecuba.org/scaife/ad.htm. (17 April 1998).

Wald, D., personal e-mail, 26 May 1998.

"Welcome to CyberCuba," http://www.cybercuba.com/. (27 May 1998).

10

"FLIPPIN THE SCRIPT"/ "BLOWIN UP THE SPOT": PUTTIN' HIP-HOP ONLINE IN (AFRICAN) AMERICA AND SOUTH AFRICA

Elaine Richardson and Sean Lewis

From very modest beginnings, hip-hop has grown into a cultural phenom-enon that has transcended boundaries, such as race, class, gender, and geography. Young people in places as diverse as New York, Tokyo, London, Seoul, and Cape Town, to name just a few, have embraced various elements of the culture. They listen to and enjoy the intricate rhymes and rhythms of rap music, and make up their own; they pop and glide in breakdance; they pop open a spraycan and create public works of art in graffiti; and they mix and scratch their way into the art of DJing. In addition, a number of movies, like *Beat Street, Wild Style, Krush Groove, Juice,* and *House Party* have centered on the hip-hop phenomenon. Even when the focus has not been on hip-hop, it has been represented in soundtracks, and backdrops of various movies, especially by directors like John Singleton and Spike Lee, and in television shows such as *New York Undercover* and *Homeboys in Outer Space.* Hip-hop has arrived in visual and audio media and has loudly announced its presence on the world stage.

The arrival of the Web saw the hip-hop movement extend its sphere of operation to embrace this new technology. The Web offers new opportu-nities and challenges to the hip-hop culture as a whole. Hip-hop has taken to the Web and uses it as a means of representing, preserving, critiquing, and controlling the images and issues of hip-hop culture. "Tha Elements," "Hardcore Hip-Hop," "Lil Flava's Hip-Hop Nation," "The Universal Hip-Hop Alliance," are just a few of the site names that signal some of the central issues of hip-hop, characterized most articulately in its struggle for survival, self-definition, and self-determination.

Hip-hop on the Web

As of the writing of this article, Yahoo had 573 site matches and 11 categories for "Hip-Hop;" AltaVista had 88,661 web pages. The US Department of Commerce in a 1996 study reported that Black Americans account "for 25 percent of all online spending and are more likely to buy online than white America."[1] Yet it is safe to say that that percentage represents a small part of Black America and an even smaller segment of the hip-hop community. Searching with the terms "South Africa > Hip-Hop" yields a significantly small number of sites. In a 1997 report, South Africa had about 500,000 Internet users and was expected to have 1,000,000 by the end of 1997. Most of these users represent the European minority that possesses the overwhelming amount of South Africa's wealth.[2] This signals the fact that although the Web is in South Africa still essentially a privileged domain, Black South Africans who identified most closely with the African-American experience of oppression and struggle appropriated the music and have created a strong online presence.

As space does not permit us to survey and discuss the complete range of the hip-hop sites, we have selected a few sites that seem to us to display the richness of online hip-hop culture. To our knowledge, every site that we have presented is owned or controlled by African-Americans and South Africans, with the exception of the discussion taken from a hip-hip newsgroup and graffiti.org/"Art Crimes." In the following sites, hip-hoppers from the selected American and South African sites "represent" what hip-hop is for themselves. They represent a general consensus of what hip-hop is to its constituents as well as some of the issues within not only hip-hop culture but also within diasporic subordinated cultures. The technology of the Web, itself, introduces new dynamics into the discourses on the Web.

One Web dynamic is the internationalization of Web discourses. Put another way, in many cases, the Web makes it difficult to determine race, class, and geographic profiles of the participants in the Web discourses. The site owner of "graffiti.org" put it this way:

> On the Internet no one knows if you're white. But my unscientific impression is that the online hip-hop scene is majority white, with a strong showing of Latino, Asian and Black participation. I think the minority participation is stronger in online hip-hop than in some other interest groups, because hip-hop is grassroots and multicultural In Real Life. Lots of kids find ways to get access just because their culture is doing something interesting and irresistible online. Many have started their own sites, and many of those folks are not white.
>
> (Farrell, 1998)

Farrell's comments highlight two things, namely, that the ethnic identity of Web participants is an issue, and that people within the culture identify strongly enough with the culture to make extraordinary effort to gain access to the Web discourses. What does emerge clearly from Farrell's comments, above, is that identity is a critical question in hip-hop culture. On the website, "Davey D's Hip-Hop Corner," Afrika Bambataa, in attempting to provide a definition of hip-hop, says: "how you act, walk, look, talk are all part of hip-hop culture" (Cook, 1996b). Identity, according to Bambataa is strongly related to acting, walking, talking, and appearance.

What the Web does is eliminate "act" and "walk," and, in most cases, "look." All that remains is "talk," in the form of writing on the Web. Hip-hop is represented on the Web through a literacy act which, at least on the surface and according to Bambataa, is not considered a conventional means of establishing and recognizing identity within hip-hop culture. Although lyrical skill is an essential element of hip-hop, an emcee must have the ability to keep the crowd hyped and control them with their oral delivery, immediacy, style, and street credibility, something that is at best hard to capture on cyberwalls. The average Web participants, who may well be white, must be careful to establish themselves as insiders. One characteristic of an insider is one who not only uses Black speech appropriately, but one who also recognizes that hip-hop's ideology is embedded in Black speech, which is by definition an alternative to official hegemonic discourses. According to Smitherman:

> Rap music is rooted in the Black oral tradition of tonal semantics, narrativizing, signification/signifying, the dozens/ playin the dozens, Africanized syntax, and other communicative practices. ... The rapper is a postmodern African griot, the verbally gifted storyteller and cultural historian ... [Rap artists] decry, for all the world to hear the deplorable conditions of the hood ...
>
> (1997, p. 4–5)

Hence, Black speech has been a traditional tool in the Black struggle for equality and self-definition. In the following discussion from Rebensdorf's (1998) study of hip-hop on the Internet, a White hip-hopper is criticized for his "overuse" of Black speech and "fronting." The first post is from the "fronter," the second from a "true" insider.

I'M FUCKIN LIVIN PROOF DAT WHITE PEEPS GOD MAD FLOW. IM A WHITE MC MYSELF AND WHEN EVA I RAP 2 WHITES BLACKS WHOEVA I ALWAYS GOT MAD PROPS IT DOESN'T MATTER WHAT FUCKIN COLOR YOU IZ IF YOU GOT SKILLS YOU GOT SKILLS BUT ME I'M PROBABLY WANNA PHATTEST MCS IN MY AGE GROUP MADA FACT IF

YOU WANNA HERE A BUTTER WHITE GROUP BE ON DA LOOK OUT
4 C.O.D. REPRESENTIN OUT A MASSACHSETTS SAPURB!
(Doug, 4 April 1996)

Anybody that types his messages with "4" instead of "for", "2" instead
of "to/too" "iz" instead of "is," compares his emceeing skillz with
his "age group" uses "wanna" instead of "one of the", "dat" instead
of "that", etc., is obviously FRONTIN HARD. Loose the front kid.
I don't give a fuck what you have to say, whether you're representing Massachusetts or kakalaka, If you have skills, you don't have
to post some bullshit retarded message on a newsgroup. If you are
really all that, people will recognize and realize.
(Quizativ, 5 November 1996)
[See http://clark.edu/~soan/alicia/rebensdorf.body.html]

In the above exchange a couple of points are central to our analysis.
Hip-hop Web discourse is a prime examples of vernacular literacy. Here,
vernacular literacy is meant in a sense close to that of Camitta (1993).
Vernacular literate behavior conforms to unofficial institutions, such as the
expressive ideology of hip-hop forms. This ideology is fundamentally
anti-hegemonic. Emceeing or rapping, the most verbal of the four pillars
of hip-hop, offers a different way of doing and seeing with words, and
alternative ways of achieving, such as getting "props" which is an alternative literacy for hip-hop. As shown by the "insider" above, props are
achieved by skills and street credibility. The "insider" flips the script on
the "fronter" by not using the surface features of Black speech such as
syntax and slang. Instead, he/she employs tonal semantics, "recognize and
realize," the rhyme pattern emphasizing the point that is being driven
home. By doing so, the "insider" demonstrates the central issue of hip-hop,
that hip-hop is more than the surface appearance of slang and style. It
is born from a culture of underground struggle and survival on a deep
level, no matter if the surface appears to comply with official dominant
discourses.

The internationalization of Web discourses is a result of hip-hop's appeal
to people of all ethnicities. The following thread from the website, "Support
Online Hip-Hop" is critical to our analysis of hip-hop on and offline.

[VeX aSSaSSin aka sHURiken]
[posted 11–25–98 09:22 PM ET (US)]

I don't know about ya'll but i'm really diggin theze white M.C's
like Eminem, 7L, Esoteric, Remedy, and El-p from Company Flow
to name a few. I'm black but I don't care what nationality you are
as long as you got Mic Skillz, even da Asian Culture is involved in
da culture they've actually been puttin down for yearz but there

overlooked as well. Theze kids don't get da recognition they deserve. What do ya'll think?

["Phuck Keepin it Real I keep it Right"]

[Unique]

[posted 11–27–98 05:35 AM ET (US)]

yo back in the day can't nobody say 3rd Base wasn't fully reppin it. That Cactus Lp strait up classic. Milkbone was nice too around 94 95. The ice ice baby guy sorta just killed it for most white rappers trying to come up. But if you go over to the UK they represent hip-hop culture better than we do here in the states. They embrace all facets of hip-hop, Graf, Djing, b-boying and Mcing. But if you got skills you got skills, no matter if you white black green or whatever

Superion7

[posted 11–27–98 10:56 AM ET (US)]

Yo Color doesn't bring out skills that's all I gotta say ... I know madd White Boy MC's that are representing to the Fullest, Most of Them I wouldn't even think were white ... For Example I know two Groups one's Called the Pride, the Other is Sons of Intellect they are Madd Dope ... Another MC I know calls himself Sev Statik, this Brother is Raw ... I think when Vanilla Ice came out it ruined it for White Rappers, because nowadays when you see a white boy on stage people are like, They Sound like Vanilla Ice, And It doesn't matter how phat they sound they'll still say that ...

RAZE

[posted 11–27–98 11:34 AM ET (US)]

BEING A WHITE EMCEE, I'VE NOTICED THAT WHITE RAPPERS ARE GETTING MORE OF THE RESPECT THEY DESERVE LATELY. LIKE MANY HAVE SAID EL-P .NON-PHIXON, EMINEM AND OTHERS ARE RIPPING ****

UP AND LOOK AT THE MOUNTAIN BROTHERS THEY ASIAN AND KEEPING IT REALER THAN MOST BLACK EMCEES. HIP-HOP STARTED IN THE BLACK COMMUNITY AND AS LONG AS WHERE HIP-HOP CAME FROM IS REMEMBERED THAN EMCEES FROM AROUND THE GLOBE COULD BE REPPIN TO THE FULLEST, AND NOTHINGS WRONG WITH THAT.

– – – – – – – – – – – –

WITNESS THE BIRTH OF EAST
COAST CANADAN HIP-HOP
VET CRU TILL 3000 **** 2000

jkeeler

[posted 12–09–98 04:34 PM ET (US)]

a lot of people talkin on this subject say that skills are skills, and color doesn't matter. I disagree to an extent. If a white rapper's got skills, but raps about culture, or an area, that he's not even from, then his hsit is wak. The same goes for black(or whatevercolor) studio gangstas, they as fake as anything and we all know it, even if they have skills. I guess I mean that skills and talent are not the end all of being good, or just average, content and reality have just as much power.

On whites emcees? Eyedea outta the Twin C's here in MN is dope. Representing Rhyme Sayers, Atmosphere, Dyno, etc . . .

(http://www.sohh.com/forum/Forum1/HTML/000045.html)

Several observations can be made from the above thread. First, although whites outnumber Blacks on the Web, they have been slow to catch on as insiders offline. This is in part due to the Vanilla Ice syndrome discussed above. Ice apparently was whack because he was not a true hip-hopper – one who really lives the hip-hop life and espouses and exemplifies certain hip-hop ideologies. He was fake in that sense. Second, true white hip-hoppers are not really white *per se.* To be "true hip-hoppers," they must develop an allegiance to hip-hop, that is, alternative/vernacular literacy. For this reason, it has been "natural" to see other people of color such as Asians and diasporic Blacks espouse vernacular discourses and their cultural manifestations because of colonial experiences, but the appeal for whites is at once beautiful and problematic. Regardless of the fact that most whites do not support white supremacist ideologies in theory, the majority of them comply in practice, however, unconsciously. How else could the system be maintained? Third, as discussed by the last poster above, some Blacks are fronters and fakers. Skin color does not qualify one as a true hip-hopper. Content and reality do. The reality appears to be that one cannot be at once "foreal" (for deep cultural development and concern the cultural developers, people) and "forplay" (for playing the official game whatever that game may be, race/white privilege, money, class etc). These are issues that are not easily resolved online or off, for hip-hoppers or for any of us.

That identity is a critical question in hip-hop is further borne out by the notion of "keepin' it real," that is, staying true to the culture, versus "sellin' out" or betraying the culture. This means that the literacy practices and literacy acts of participants in hip-hop discourses on the Web have to be identifiable with hip-hop culture. Because literacy practices are "inextricably linked to cultural and power structures in society" (Street, 1993, p. 7), they need to be examined in relation to the nature of hip-hop and the contexts in which this cultural phenomenon emerged. Thus, we will briefly examine the origins of hip-hop, in order to gain an understanding of why identity is such a critical issue within hip-hop, and how it is maintained on the Web.

The origins of hip-hop

> Hip-hop is an entire culture, a way of living, that was born in the BDX (Boogie Down Bronx) in the late 70s.
>
> (DJ Mass Dosage, 1996)

The statement above, taken from South African website "This Is It," is significant in a number of ways. It gives an indication of the place and time of the origins of hip-hop, as it is intended to do. But, more than that, it utilizes the insider abreviation, "BDX (Boogie Down Bronx)." The result is a palpable demonstration of the separate, insider subculture, which is hip-hop.

DJ Mass Dosage further summarizes the emergence of hip-hop thus:

> From these humble roots as a form of boasting over beats at parties, it moved into the parks of New York where DJs got involved behind turntables while the MCs experimented with rhyming to move the crowds. At the same time, graffiti and breakdancing, which were there from the beginning, started evolving. These four facets (rapping, D'jing, graffiti and breakdancing) are now represented under one unified banner called hip-hop.
>
> (DJ Mass Dosage, 1996)

Cook (1996b), of "Davey D's Hip-Hop Corner," provides a much more detailed, but essentially similar, narrative of the origins of hip-hop. However, where he differs is he also discusses various reasons for the emergence of hip-hop. One word that is repeated a number of times, in this regard, is "alienation." He makes the point that much of the impetus in the creation of hip-hop came from attempts to deal with the feelings of alienation of inner-city youth. According to him, they felt alienated from and marginalized by an older generation, by their conditions of poverty and other forms of economic deprivation, as well as by the discrimination, exclusion and ongoing subjugation of racism. Cook (1996) offers the following reasons for the emergence and growth of hip-hop; (our emphases).

- Hip-hop continues to be a direct response to an older generation's rejection of the values and needs of young people. (*Assertion of the value of their identity and culture.*)

257

- There are many kids out there under the belief that all they need to do is write a few "fresh" (good) rhymes and they're off to the good life. (*Aspirations to material well-being.*)
- Black radio was no longer languaging itself so that both a young and older generation could define and hear themselves reflected in this medium. (*Rejection of traditional institutions of culture.*)
- Point blank, hip-hop was a direct response to the watered down, Europeanized, disco music that permeated the airwaves. (*Rejection of racist discrimination and a media culture that promoted whiteness at the expense of blackness.*)
- The name of the game was to get props for rockin' the house. (*Search for esteem and being valued in the community.*)

What becomes clear is that hip-hop was one manifestation of the struggle of Black and Latino inner-city youth in America against various forms of alienation and marginalization. Hip-hop emerged from struggle and was born into it, but it emerged conscious of the struggle.

> Throughout history, music originating from America's Black communities has always had an accompanying subculture reflective of the political, social and economic conditions of the time. Rap is no different.
>
> (Cook, 1996a)

While the second part of Cook's statement above places rap (and by association hip-hop) within a specific political and cultural context of struggle, it also makes links between the emergence of hip-hop and other forms of music emanating from America's Black communities. Cultural critic and historian, Ferris-Thompson (1996), in "Hip-Hop 101" traces the origins of hip-hop to Kongo via Bronx Barbadians, Bronx Jamaicans, Bronx Afro-Cubans, Puerto Ricans, and North American Blacks living in the South Bronx, Fresno, and Los Angeles. Ferris-Thompson argues convincingly that there is a large Kongo influence on New World music and dance.

South African rap music emerged within the particular historical and material conditions of a South Africa, ravaged by apartheid, in communities that had been systematically dispossessed of their land, their language, their political rights, and their voice. Within the oppressive and repressive confines of apartheid, rap music enabled its practitioners to appropriate alternative cultural space, within which they could make real their resistance to the politics of oppression and repression. Haupt (1995) argues that the censorship and restriction of South Africa's apartheid past led to a "deterioration of the black urban music scene" and also created a "gap in the development of musical talent in the country" (p. 10). This gap was filled often by African-American and Caribbean music, which struck both emotional and political chords within South Africans. The rise of Black consciousness ideology made it possible for this music and other forms, such as theater to transcend their geographical boundaries, and their historical and cultural specificity, towards an expression of shared and unifying culture and conditions. Thus were the conditions created for Black South Africans to find their inspiration in African-American and Caribbean material, such as jazz, R&B and hip-hop. These borrowed and assimilated forms gave voice to those who had been rendered voiceless in the face of seemingly overwhelming opposing forces.

It is through these borrowed and assimilated forms, often, that Black South Africans were able to create alternative literacies to the hegemonic literacies of the apartheid state. The performance, production, distribution, reception, and interpretation of hip-hop music, as a literacy practice, is bound up in the ideological preconceptions that underpin them (see Street, 1993). In essence, then, following Street, music is about creativity, performance, and interpretation. But it is not only about these. Hip-hop music is also explicitly and implicitly about the structures and processes of a society, and the resistance to these structures and processes, with the means at hand. Hip-hop music is ideological, in the sense in which Street (1993) uses ideological, i.e. "where ideology is the site of tension between authority and power on the one hand and resistance and creativity, on the other," (p. 8), as well as ideological in the sense that it is often about consciously and explicitly propagating ideas that challenge or support authority, power and moral authority.

The major originating impetus of hip-hop, for both South Africans and African-Americans has been the need to carve out an alternative literacy. The assertion of a culture springs from a need by South African and US rappers to challenge the hegemony of white authority over all aspects of life. For African-Americans and Black South Africans, this authority was inevitably a European one.

Since the outset of western empire building and the enslavement of Africans, and throughout the African diaspora, literacy for Africans was intended as a two-edged sword. The one end was designed to cut Africans off from their culture and traditions, and their own and independent ways of living, thus making them more controllable, while the other was designed to deny them access to the western world to which they are introduced through literacy. The following two excerpts from South African history serve to illustrate both points.

> If we leave the natives beyond our border ignorant barbarians, they will remain a race of troublesome marauders. We should try to make them a part of ourselves, with a common faith and common interests, useful servants, consumers of our goods, contributors to our revenue. Therefore, I propose that we make unremitting efforts

to raise the natives in Christianity and civilisation, by establishing among them missions connected with industrial schools. The native races beyond our boundary, influenced by our missionaries, instructed in our schools, benefiting by our trade, would not make wars on our frontiers.

(Sir George Grey, Governor of the Cape in 1855 cited in Christie, 1991)

For the educated African there is no opening. He may be qualified to fill the post of a clerk, but there is no demand for such persons, or prejudice operates against persons of colour being so employed.

(Dale Langham, 1868 cited in Christie, 1991)

The Jim Crow era in the USA and the apartheid era in South Africa maintained these parallels in their respective conceptions of the functions of literacy. Woodson ([1933] 1990) explains that the general thinking about the education of Black people was that when they learned

to perform the duties which other elements of the population had prepared themselves to discharge they would be duly qualified . . . to function as citizens of the country . . . [However], [T]he poverty which afflicted them for a generation after Emancipation held them down to the lowest order of society, nominally free but economically enslaved.

H. F. Verwoerd, Minister of Education of South Africa in 1948 stated it more plainly: "There is no place for blacks in White South Africa, beyond certain elementary forms of labour" (Cited in Kane-Berman, 1978)

Education for Black children in both South Africa and the USA was neither free, nor compulsory. It was intended to separate Black children from the cultural and power structures of native society. Nowhere is this more dramatically represented as in the practice of refusing Black children, in South Africa, admission to the schools unless they abandoned (repudiated) their given names, and adopted, or were given a Christian name. This is even more powerfully and pervasively represented through the sustained Eurocentric view of the world, along with its myths of superiority and universality, which was the stock-in-trade of textbooks and curricula that were used throughout the African diaspora.

It is therefore not surprising that these imposed literacies were resisted from their inception. This resistance reached some of its most visible levels and forms of articulation in the Civil Rights Movements in the USA and the anti-apartheid struggles in South Africa.

There was an increasing realization, on both sides of the Atlantic Ocean, by both African-Americans and South Africans, that these imposed literacies were inimical to their social, cultural and political well-being.

Slowly but steadily, in the following years, a new vision began gradually to replace the dream of political power, – a powerful movement, the rise of another ideal to guide the unguided, another pillar of fire by night after a clouded day. It was the ideal of "book learning"; the curiosity, born of compulsory ignorance, to know and test the power of the cabalistic letters of the white man, the longing to know. Here at last seemed to have been discovered the mountain path to Canaan; longer than the highway of Emancipation and law, steep and rugged, but straight, leading to heights high enough to overlook life.

(W.E.B Du Bois quoted in Gates, 1988)

Hip-hop, as a culture which contains, at its center, an alternative literacy, has developed a distinctive character both because of its origins and its awareness of its origins, especially in its struggle, both for recognition and in revolt. Consequently, hip-hop discourses on the Web have been characterized both by their significant content, which revolve around a number of critical issues, and rhetorical devices.

Within the paradigm defined by Heath (1982, cited in Street, 1993), each hip-hop discourse on the Web constitutes a literacy event, that is, "any occasion in which a piece of writing is integral to the nature of participants' interactions and interpretive processes." These literacy events are characterized by literacy practices, in which the literacies of the participants are articulated through a number of very defined social practices, and are, in fact, transformed by these. The words below have been heretofore quoted, but are repeated again here to illustrate both a literacy practice and the transformation of received literacies.

Hip-hop is an entire culture, a way of living, that was born in the BDX (Boogie Down Bronx) in the late 70s.

(DJ Mass Dosage, 1996)

This excerpt asserts the hip-hop culture, as it challenges "structures of power and domination" (Street, 1993, p. 7). At the same time, it reinforces that assertion through the use of the vernacular of the culture "BDX (Boogie Down Bronx)."

Keepin' it real

To restate, a central issue of hip-hop, whether it be in the production of graffiti art, rap music, breakdance or scratching, is "keepin' it real vs. sellin' out." Hip-hop is at once an underground, non-mainstream form of empowerment for the disenfranchised, and, at the same time, a way out of the ghetto and into the mainstream. This somewhat schizoid character is acutely visible in hip-hop's participation in the music industry.

A common concern of hip-hop heads is that the music industry "sanitizes" the public image of hip-hop, by giving public airplay only to that which conforms to "standards of appropriacy" defined by a hegemonic literacy standard. Norfleet (1997) sums it up like this:

> Verbal musical practitioners (rap artists) hold a paradoxical yet symbiotic relationship with two realms: hip-hop culture and the commercial music industry. While striving to maintain social and ideological ties to the community ("keeping it real") most hope to reap the benefits of commercialization by becoming financially successful professional artists ("making money"). Nevertheless, insiders use the act of competitive musical performance as a means of separating what they consider to be the true purveyor of hip-hop musical verbal tradition ("the MC [emcee]) from one who merely "raps." (abstract).

Another chat-room discussion from the website "Support on Line Hip-Hop" explicates this problem:

> On 3/26/98 07:49 DEE JEKYLL wrote:

> Underground is about keeping it real and refuse radio airplay. To me, mc's like Nas or Jay-Z used to be underground artists but nowadays in hip-hop you have to be "radio friendly" if you wanna reach all audiences. This may be sad but this is good for hip-hop worldwide. Today the rap game is about money, it's sad but it's like that. Even Meth or Big Pun do guest appearances on R&B tracks and they're right!! To me, the goal of an artist is to get known all over the world. You may say I don't stay true to real hip-hop but you are the first ones to shake your ass over a Puffy track.[3] It's a choice: you get money and power but you are playa hated or you stay independent, poor but people say you stay true to hip-hop. What would you do?

> On 3/26/98 14:12 GForce wrote:

> Interesting points, Dee Jekyll. To me, they go right to the heart of what's wrong with hiphop. Do you stay "true to hiphop" with ugly, vulgar messages of violence and hatred toward women and all the other G's you gonna smoke, or do you become "radio friendly" by toning down that stuff and maybe putting out some positive messages about avoiding the Thug Life?
>   I think it's one of the fundamentals of hiphop that becoming radio friendly is considered selling out. The hiphop world established this standard by destroying Hammer, and you see it again

and again as anyone who broadens their audience and finds big success is attacked from within. Mainstream success – in terms of money and in terms of what you mentioned, getting your messages across to more people – is something to be avoided. This is self-limiting and self-defeating. It's part of the overall thug life self-destruction that makes hiphop an evil force throughout the land.

Jda9star on 3/28/98 wrote

See, here you're getting into something where you don't know what you're talking about. Positive/negative has nothing to do with underground/signed. Underground simply means that you aren't signed, you're doing this on your own, sellin tapes out the trunk of your car, whatever. Radio friendly doesn't necessarily mean positive. To be radio friendly, all you really need is a good beat and a clean version of your lyrics. There ain't got to be no positivity to it. I agree with you that mainstream success is not to be avoided, but you're way off in thinking that radio friendly = positive. I'm sorry, but Hammer[4] doesn't even have a place in this discussion, he's from a whole different time, a lot has changed. Your argument would at least carry some weight if you used a current example. For someone who admittedly doesn't listen to hip-hop, maybe you should stay in the background if you don't know what you're talking about, and stop trying to simplify everything into the same tired argument.

Peace.

The online hip-hoppers engage in conversations that get to the heart of the paradox of global African technological and commodified literacy. Should Black cultural producers strive to evolve their art forms and develop their art according to their own aesthetic ideals within the guidelines of their cultural values, or should the goal be to continue to internalize values of wealth and the valuing of non-human enterprises or material things that might bring with them a rejection of their own values? Cook (1996a) ["Davey D's"] makes the point that "Because rap has evolved to become such a big business, it has given many the false illusion of being a quick escape from the harshness of inner city life."

It appears that hip-hop tries to appropriate alternative space, within which the artists are able to realize notions of success. These notions range from uplifting the masses and providing cultural leadership to "getting props" or even simply "blowin' up the spot", that is, becoming a commercial success. Web commentators, such as DJ Mass Dosage, suggest that while they strive to ensure that hip-hop is about the elevation of a people, their notions of success more often than not conform completely to conventional, "capitalist" notions of success, manifested mostly through the accumulation of material wealth, status, and power. In a sense, the music is no longer produced by the young people themselves. It is "corporately orchestrated." (Tricia Rose, 1996 online) The music industry is controlled, by and large, by white men and green money, the commericialization and co-optation of Black culture, in many instances. The central issue is, in a sense, not race, but control of production, distribution, and profit, which often becomes conflated with race. Today's online hip-hop movement offers a way for hip-hoppers to control the production, marketing, and distribution of hip-hop.

Internal cohesion, external threat

An issue resurfacing from the exchange above between DEE JEKYLL, Gforce and Jda9star is that there is something that can be conceived of as "true hip-hop." This suggests that hip-hop contains a unifying system of beliefs that both transcends and informs the varying practice of hip-hoppers throughout the world. DJ Mass Dosage (1997b) tries to make this explicit.

> As a Hip-Hop purist who cares about this culture and wants to ensure that it continues to exist beyond the lifespan of all trends, I think that we should take what we have learnt in the past and use this information to come up with a set of rules. These rules can be used to spot DJs who may pose a threat to the culture and, if applied, will ensure that the commercialisation cycle described above does not inflict the damage that it has the potential to. So, I bring to you, "The minimum entry requirements for DJology 101" (a.k.a. "How to alienate yourself in a trendy crowd in 4 easy steps"):
>
> 1 Are you serious about your music? Do you have a love for it which you want to communicate to others by becoming a DJ? Do you intend to make a worth-while contribution to this culture which will benefit others/change their perceptions of the culture in a positive manner?
>
> 2 Do you know your shit? Do you have extensive knowledge (and critical insight) of your music (its origins, history, evolution, performers, etc.)?
>
> 3 Do you have skills? Do you know what to mix, and how and when to mix it? Do you try to evolve the artform in an original way?
>
> 4 Will you still be doing this in the future when the trend passes? When you no longer get paid to do it? When DJ'ing (and by extension you as a DJ) are no longer regarded as "cool"? When there is no fame or esteem associated with your position?
>
> (http://www.rucus.ru.ac.za/~hed/flip/wannabe.html)

At the same time, this continual pursuit of the pure culture also contains a suggestion of "internal cohesion, external threat" described by Paulston (1994) as a characteristic of the assertion of national (read cultural) identity. The greatest threat, or at least the most often cited is the commercial music industry, discussed above. This industry is not only responsible for the distortion, or "watering down" of hip-hop music through forcing artists to become "radio-friendly," DJ Mass Dosage (1997d) also holds them responsible for the violence and deaths that have come to plague the rap music industry.

> (Tupac, "Only God can judge me"); "fuck niggers, get money, fuck bitches, get money" (B.I.G., "Get Money"). This solves the riddle as to who is behind both Tupac and Biggies' deaths. Jealousy, greed, violence and the other evils that are destroying Hip-hop mentally are the same evils destroying the creators of the artform physically.
> (http://www.rucus.ru.ac.za/~hed/flip/enemy.html)

There seem to be two responses to this threat. DJ Mass Dosage would have those "who don't have anything positive to add to this culture as a whole and are only thinking of getting involved for *[their]* own personal gain", to think again. He wants to keep "fakers" out. Grandmaster Flash, one of the early rappers thinks about this issue differently:

> For anybody to say 'This is not hip-hop' or 'that is not hip-hop' is wrong. That is not the way the formula was laid down ... It was for the people who were going to continue this to take anything ... by all means necessary and string it along ...
> (http://www.daveyd.com/whatisflash.html)

Fenton (1998) of the website "360 Degrees" suggests, instead that "As hip-hop and rap music continue to grow in popular appeal, a distinct line is being formed separating true hip-hop from commercialized hip-hop. The former is reclaiming its historical legacy while the latter is, as with other genres of popular music, awaiting its eventual replacement with the hottest new music commodity."

Afrika Bambataa's conception of hip-hop as a "movement" is more active, thus likening it to a political or religious movement. If it is a political movement, it suggests that it is centrally concerned with the attainment of some form of empowerment, whether that be through liberation or conquest. The religious movement suggests that it has some proselytizing purpose, that is, the movement is geared towards winning more members to itself. The evidence suggests it is both. The hip-hop discourses on the Web are perpetually engaged in both trying to sell, as well as protect themselves from what are perceived as threats, both from within and without.

Paradox of diversity

Despite its assertions of a unifying culture, the quest for "true hip-hop" is caught in a paradox that is encapsulated in the words of Ralph Ellison (quoted in Gates, 1997) about jazz music.

> There is a cruel contradiction implicit in the art form itself. For true jazz is an art of individual assertion within and against the group. Each true jazz [*hip-hop*] moment (as distinct from the uninspired commercial performance) springs from a contest in which each artist challenges all the rest, each solo flight, or improvisation, represents (like the successive canvases of a painter) a definition of his identity: as individual, as member of the collectivity and as a link in the chain of tradition. Thus because jazz [*hip-hop*] finds its very life in an endless improvisation upon traditional materials, the jazzman [*hip-hop artist*] must lose his identity even as he finds it.

Thus, Grandmaster Flash denounces all efforts by various individuals and groups to limit the scope and range of hip-hop. He does not accept limitation of hip-hop by geographical region, or even by race. In this regard he is echoed by DJ Mass Dosage, who goes even further, and argues that the parochial chauvinism, sexism and homophobia that characterize much of the lyrics violate the principled essence of hip-hop. The essence of the message that emanates from hip-hop discourses on the Web is that hip-hop needs to continually evolve in order to stay fresh and new and build a positive culture.

This contrasts to some extent with the rap world offline. An East Coast/West Coast rivalry was implicated as the source of the very violent deaths of Tupac Shakur and Biggie Smalls, two popular hip-hop stars. However, it was also rumored that underworld figures called for the murders of both stars. In any case, this violence is being replicated in South Africa, with street gangs in Black townships of South Africa identifying with one or another. A huge mural of Tupac adorns the wall of a block of flats in Manenberg, a township outside of Cape Town, the territory of the Hard Living Kids, who terrorize and control that township.

Flippin' the script

Subversion, or flippin' the script on traditionally received conceptions of hip-hop, is the purpose of the South African website that provides us with another defining characteristic of hip-hop. DJ Mass Dosage writes that his (her?) purpose is to show the positive side of hip-hop, that hip-hop is not all about "guns, drugs, and hoes." This website is called "The Flipside." It is a monthly column that is a part of the Grahamstown, South Africa, Rhodes University, student newspaper, *Activate*. The newspaper is published online as a part of Rhodes University Computer Users Society aka "rucus." According to Mass Dosage, the reason that the website exists is to prove that "hip-hop is universal."

DJ Mass Dosage has his own notion of flippin' the script. He is concerned with managing, or changing public perceptions of hip-hop. That this is very necessary is clearly indicated in Fenton's (1998) "360 Degrees" description of the opposition to hip-hop.

> Throughout its formation, the various elements were at some time or another, deemed unacceptable. Graffiti artists faced jail sentences, break dancing became illegal in some areas, and rap music has been severely criticized for various reasons.
> (http://www.frymulti.com/~bfenton/politic/360.html)

However, the notion of flippin' the script runs much deeper than just perception management. Flippin' the script is the essence of hip-hop, and it is through this central literacy act that websites claim a place within the Web-based hip-hop culture. A closer examination of just one of the sites confirms this.

"Art Crimes: The Writing on the Wall"[5]

This American-based website shows graffiti from more than 130 cities around the world. It is an international site, and it is collaborative, so that people from anywhere can build on it and link up to it. Although an artfully bright graffiti-styled symbol next to the site's title is provocative, the title of the site "Art Crimes: The Writing on the Wall," evokes more curiosity about it because it is layered with meanings suggestive of some of the issues in hip-hop.

The title "Art Crimes" associates hip-hop with criminality. As explained on the "360 Degrees" website, one reasons for the graffitti on ghetto walls was because residents wanted to reclaim their neighborhoods. This was an attempt to appropriate their surroundings. Their painting of trains which traveled from one community to another was a kind of art in motion.

For their efforts they were denounced by respectable, law-abiding citizens, who felt outraged that their respect for property was not shared by these people who existed on the margins of respectable society. Many of hip-hop's pioneers were poor people of color. From the perspective of the "highly cultivated," or "those outside culture" (Mass Dosage, 1996b) it is a crime that they fashioned their "(deprived) experiences of nothingness" into "(debased) artforms" and cultural productions, redefining the possibilities and purposes of art and life.

267

The hip-hoppers of Art Crimes have therefore expropriated the term crime, and in the idiom of Gates (1988) have "vacated" the signifier and substituted it with a concept that moves "crime" from the margins to the center, and then gives it its props. This means that, while "art crimes" continue to keep non hip-hoppers at bay, with its conventional significa-tion, it elevates the act of graffitti writing and imbues it, even on the Net with an "in your face" attitude, thus capturing an essential element of graf-fitti in the world.

"Writing on the Wall," the second part of the title of the "Art Crimes" site, also functions on a number of levels. At one level, it is a description of the act of graffiti writing. On another level, "writing on the wall" has connotations of coming to the end of something; in this case, it appears that the writer is suggesting the end to the criminality of writing on the wall. Hip-hoppers have not changed the law. What they have done is come to "know and test the power of the cabalistic letters of the white man" (Du Bois, quoted above, p. 261). In composing this language to repre-sent itself to the world, the creators of this "graffiti" website are in effect inviting surfers and wannabees in beyond the wall of "debased artform," beyond the surface level wall, to get at the art or heart of graffiti. Site authors write:

> In many places, painting graffiti is illegal. We do not advocate breaking the law, but we think art belongs in public spaces and that more legal walls should be made available for this fascinating art form. Because it is so hard to get books published and to keep photos and blackbooks from being seized and destroyed, the Internet may be the best way to publish and preserve this infor-mation. Please get involved in the effort if you can. ... We also want to spread the word that this kind of graffiti, called "writing" is being done by artists, not by gangs ... [Writers] [m]ake the Internet work for you. Tell the world about your *zine* or your *art enterprise* ... hook up. Fight media with media ...
>
> (http://www.graffiti.org/index/story.html)

These "writers," "graffers," and "artists" are reaching out not only to repre-sent their work to those unfamiliar with the art form but to other "writers," "graffers," and "artists" who need to protect their work by putting it onto cyberwalls.

It is through the various literacy acts of subversion, or "flippin' the script" that Web-based hip-hop heads are able to most clearly demonstrate their shared identity with Emcees, Writers, B-Boys, and Djays.

On the Web, this reappropriation of a signifier is one such literacy act. It does not stand alone. The use of an in-culture vernacular and abbrevi-ated language has been discussed earlier in this paper ("BDX (Boogie Down

Bronx)"). A number of these various literacy acts of subversion are aptly illustrated in the review of Crucial Conflict's "Bone Thug" CD, from *On the Go* magazine, April–May, 1996.

> Crucial Conflict are phat fresh fly flow farmers that put some meat on the Thuggish Ruggish Bone. Good thing too, 'cause I gnawed on the Bone Thug ce all last year. (Really doe, "Hay" sparks a light on a very popular topic, weed. (Memo to all you rappers who don't rap about weed; Pride don't buy no gold front$, fool!) Many may rap about the diggity dank, but nobody ever rapped about chilling in the middle of a park and smoking, have they? PROPPPS to the Conflict for bustin' the new flavs! The B-side, "Showdown" is about violence that seems so real you'll pee your panties. I did! PROPPPS! If Pallas Records was a woman, she'd bare my children. PROPPS.

> (http://www.pallas-records.com/onthego.html)

The review, above, extols the virtues of the "Bone Thug" CD. The cut, "Hay" is praised for winning awards and for being both topical and innovative. The cut, "Showdown," is praised for its raw realism, which incidentally is one of the objectives of this group: "We try to scare people into not gangbanging by telling [them] just how rough it can be" (http://www.pallas-records.com/blackbeat.html).

Gates (1988) extensively discusses the process whereby Black people disrupt the signifier by a "shift in concepts denoted and connoted" (p. 47). This process of disruption and reappropriation is manifestly in evidence in "fresh fly flow farmers," "doe," and "gold front$." By this means, the hip-hop culture and community is signaling that it will define itself. It will no longer be defined by, and in terms of standard or official literacies, that have been imposed on them. In the contexts of both South Africa and the United States, this literacy act of subversion relates very directly to their histories of colonialism and slavery, and Jim Crow and apartheid respectively. A salient element of literacy histories of Blacks in the USA and South Africa has been the manipulation of literacy in order to denigrate and marginalize blacks, politically, economically, and even socially. Flippin' the script, or subversion, seems to have more profound significance within the hip-hop community on the Web, and we would venture, off the Web, than is allowed by DJ Mass Dosage.

Flippin' the script is also manifested in another significant feature of the in-culture vernacular, namely lexical innovation, seen in examples such as "phat," "diggity dank," "flavs." A few other significant literacy acts include the violation of taboos, such as "The B-side, "Showdown" is about violence that seems so real you'll pee your panties. I did!" and interjecting, or "shouting," for example "Hey Bone, you won 5 grammies at the PROPPPS awards. PROPPPS!", followed by appropriate interjections of "PROPPS!" throughout the rest of the text. This is reminiscent of the party shouts which are generally considered to have been the first form that this modern phenomenon, known as rap assumed.

These vernacular literacy acts, which include reappropriation, lexical innovation, violation of taboos, and interjection are all synonymous with and central to the verbal vocalization of lyrics in rap, which is perhaps the most audacious and wide-ranging in its subversion. It reappropriates and transforms language, rhythm, and rhythm. In addition, it defies the notions of personal creative property, and copyright through the technique of sampling, that is, taking bits of sound from other recordings, and using these in their own productions.

> Through sampling Emcees are able to subvert power relations through rhetorical tricks and other plays on language. It establishes an alternative to imposed hegemonic literacies, through the incorporation into musical production of various literacy acts, such as marking, loud-talking, testifyin', calling out, sounding, rapping and playin' the dozens.
>
> (Gates, 1987)

Conclusion

> The construction of literacy is embedded in the discursive practices and power relationships of everyday life: it is essentially socially constructed, materially produced, morally regulated and carries a symbolic significance which cannot be captured by its reduction to any one of these.
>
> (Rockhill, 1993, p. 171)

The emergence of hip-hop is certainly a socially constructed phenomenon "embedded in the discursive practices and power relationships of everyday life." Black youth in the United States, in the seventies had lost faith in the "American Dream," and were confronted, instead with the realities of institutional racism, poverty, crime, and drug-ridden inner cities. Massey and Denton (1993) show that racial segregation in the US is institutionalized by housing practices, joblessness, unequal schooling, and lack of adequate services to the Black underclass which is trapped in the ghettos. Cornel West argues that the USA

> is more and more a market culture dominated by gangster mentalities and self-destructive wantonness. This culture engulfs all of us – yet its impact on the disadvantaged is devastating, resulting in extreme violence in everyday life. Sexual violence against women

and homicidal assaults by young black men on one another are only the most obvious signs of this empty quest for pleasure, property, and power.

(1993, p. 10)

Hip-hop, that is, graffiti, breakdancing, rapping and DJ-ing, enabled African-American youth to find ways to both express themselves and value themselves. The fact that much of what they were doing was frowned upon by the "establishment," such as the language and the clothes, or even considered criminal, such as graffiti, gave it so much more value in a society where the "establishment" was seen as the reason for their continued marginalization and alienation. This anti-establishmentism became integral to hip-hop, and is manifested in many different ways, not least of all the pressure to continually evolve, or "bust new flavs."

On the Web, as in rap music, it is manifested most markedly in the various subversive literacy acts, discussed above.

The adoption of hip-hop in South Africa, by Black South African youth, emanates from a recognition that there are old ideas that need to be dethroned. The search for alternative ideas has had various outcomes for the youth of South Africa. One of these is the hip, tough, streetwise and in-your-face culture of inner-city African-Americans. Hip-hop rapidly grew beyond its geographical, and even racial origins and has grown beyond even the wildest imaginations of its originators.

Within and outside of the US we can observe the phenomenon of the Afro-Americanization of youth of all ethnicities and backgrounds. In Japan, you might see youth dressing with Malcolm X caps worn backwards; in Hawaii, you can hear youth rapping in Hawaiian Pidgin English; in South Africa, you can experience hip-hop of the Afrikaans, English, Zulu, and other flavas and it has appeal cross-culturally.

This phenomenal growth has not been all positive, however. The most oft-cited problem is the fact that the music industry is controlled by white men. This is discussed above. In addition, however, the major consumers of hip-hop artists are generally not part of the culture, and generally white. Fenton suggests that in America, as much as 70 percent of gansta rap is purchased by white suburban youth.

Cornel West offers an insightful analysis of the Afro-Americanization of white youth.

> The Afro-Americanization of white youth – has been more a male than a female affair, given the prominence of male athletes and the cultural weight of male pop artists. This process results in white youth – male and female – imitating and emulating black male styles of walking, talking, dressing, and gesticulating in relation to others. One irony of our present moment is that just as young

271

black men are murdered, maimed, and imprisoned in record numbers, their styles have become disproportionately influential in shaping popular culture . . . To be "bad" is good not simply because it subverts the language of the dominant white culture but also because it imposes a unique kind of order . . .

(1993, p. 128)

Cook (1992) argues that this emulation, albeit of surface features, is a very natural process by which humans (and animals) establish their identities. He refers to this as display, of which the main purpose is to establish and maintain identity. He says: "We display our identity by accepting somebody else's product, political programme, sporting prowess or art, rather than by making our own" (p. 148). Simple emulation of features of the subculture, often of some of the most contrived aspects that they have access to, such as the East Coast/West coast rivalry, would also fall within this category of display.

Hence, what has developed within hip-hop is a central imperative to "keep it real." On the Web, writers display through the use of the distinctive and subversive literacy acts of hip-hop, such as the reappropriation of language, lexical innovation, interjection, and violation of taboos.

In the various discourses around hip-hop on the Web, there are disagreements and even contradictions between hip-hop heads as to what hip-hop really is, and who should be recognized as part of the culture, or what is appropriately part of the culture. Hip-hop heads even contradict themselves.

Fenton's (1998) "360 Degrees" refers to KRS-One's preaching peace and unity and then rushing the stage at a PM Dawn concert, and to Tupac releasing two totally contradictory songs in "I get around" and "Keep your head up." Traces of the essence of hip-hop is evident in Web discourses. However, its elements can be traced to the heart of the culture wars as symbolized in Web discourse themes. Some of these are suggested above and include: "Keepin' it real"; "Internal cohesion," "External Threat;" "The paradox of diversity," and "Flippin' the script."

It is, however, in their literacy acts, which are driven by the dual imperatives of keepin' it real and flippin' the script, that we are able to find the defining essence of hip-hop on the Web. For hip-hop on the Web to stay real and continue flippin' the script, it can never allow itself to lose this character and become amorphised into an homogenous Web discourse that is not "embedded in the discursive practices and power relationships of everyday life."

Notes

1   http://www.nua.net/surveys/index.c. . .ew surveyandsurvey number=366andrel=
    no Nua internet surveys. "The *Nando Times*: Black America is Catching up in

the Move online," and "Black Americans not Being Left Behind on info Superhighway," <http://www.nando.net/newsroom/ntn/info/090007/info14_11516_noframes.html>

2   "Southern Africa: Slow But Steady Growth," in *Computerworld: the Network 25*, 29 September 1997, p. 24.

3   Puffy aka Puff Daddy is the rave of radio friendly hip-hop during the time of the writing of this article. He is criticized by some for being unable to produce any songs with original music or ideas, yet he's sold millions of units.

4   Hammer a.k.a MC Hammer is an example of a rap artist who was positive. He went back to his community and hired people whom he had grown up with, infused Christian ideals in his secular music, strove to be a role model for youth. He changed his image to fit in with the popularity of gangsta images and was rejected by other rap artists who attacked him for being too soft. Hammer went bankrupt.

5   http://www.graffiti.org/index/story.html

References

Bate, M. (1995) "Prophets of Da City", review, *Universal Souljaz* [online]. RUCUS: Rhodes University Computer Users Society [website]. Available at http://www.rucus.ru.ac.za/~eitan/poc.html

"Black America Is Catching Up in the Move Online," [online; accessed 11 September 1997]. The *Nando Times* [website]. Available http://www.nando.net/newsroom/ntn/info/090007/info14 11516 noframes.html

"Black Americans Not Being Left Behind on Info Superhighway," [online; accessed 9 March 1997]. The *Nando Times* [website]. Available http://www.nando.net/newsroom/ntn/info/090997/info14 11616 noframes.html

"A Brief History of Spraycan Art in Cape Town" [online; accessed 13 April 1998]. *Outcast '98: Cape flats online* [website]. Available http://www.outcast.co.za/spraytext.htm

Camitta, M. (1993) "Vernacular Writing: Varieties of Literacy Among Philadelphia High-School Students," in Street, B. V. (ed.) *Cambridge Studies in Oral and Literate Culture: Cross-Cultural Approaches to Literacy*, Cambridge: Cambridge University Press, pp. 156–175.

Christie, P. (1991) *The Right to Learn: The Struggle for Education in South Africa*, Braamfontein, South Africa: Ravan Press.

Christman, Robert (1983) in M. Marable (ed.), *How Capitalism Underdeveloped Black America: Problems in Race, Political Economy, and Society*, Boston: South End Press.

Computerworld: The Network 25 (1997) "South Africa: Slow But Steady Growth, 29 September, p. 24.

Cook, G. (1992) "Connected Text," in Cook, G. *The Discourse of Advertising*, London: Routledge, pp. 146–166.

Cook, D. 'Davey D.' (1996a) "Is Hip-Hop Culture Black culture?" [online]. *Davey D's Hip-Hop Corner* [website]. Available www.daveyd.com/blckculture.html

Cook, D. 'Davey D.' (1996b) "Afrika Bambataa's Definition of Hip-Hop?" [online; accessed 23 September]. *Davey D's Hip-Hop Corner* [website]. Available www.daveyd.com/whatisbam.html

DEE JEKYLL (1998) "SOHH Global Forum!" [online]. *Support Online Hip-Hop* [website]. Available http://sohh.com/cgi-bin/forum.cgi?Hip-Hop

DJ Mass Dosage (1996) "The Need for a South African Musical Revolution," *The Flipside* [website; accessed 4 August]. Available http://www.rucus.ru.ac.za/~hed/flip/revolution.html; "Hip-Hop: The 4 Chambers," *The flipside* [website; accessed 26 August]. Available http://www.rucus.ru.ac/za/~hed/flip/chambers.html; "Respect Where Is Due," *The flipside* [website; accessed 10 August]. Available http://www.rucus.ru.ac.za/~hed/flip/contradiction.html

DJ Mass Dosage (1997a) "The Enemy Within," *The flipside* [webside; accessed 21 March]. Available http://www.rucus.ru.ac.za/~hed/flip/enemy.html

DJ Mass Dosage (1997b) "Everybody Wanna Be . . ." *The flipside* [website; accessed 14 May]. Available http://www.rucus.ru.ac.za/~hed/flip/wannabe.html

DJ Mass Dosage (1997c) "3000," *The flipside* [website; accessed 2 August]. Available http://www.rucus.ru.ac.za/~hed/flip/3000.html

DJ Mass Dosage (1997d) "Divisional Calculus," *The flipside* [website; accessed 22 August]. Available http://www.rucus.ru.ac.za/~hed/flip/calculus.html

DJ Mass Dosage (1997e) "The Fifth Chamber: Knowledge of Self," *The flipside* [website; accessed 1 October]. Available http://www.rucus.ru.ac.za/~hed/flip/self.html

DJ Mass Dosage (1998) "Mindless Music for the Masses or Real Hip-hop? The Choice Is Yours [online; accessed 30 March]. *RUCUS: Rhodes University Computer Users Society* [website]. Available http://www.rucus.ru.ac.za/~hed

Dyson, M. E. (1996) *Between God and Gangsta Rap: Bearing Witness to Black Culture*, New York: Oxford University Press.

Farrell, S. (1994) "Graffiti Q & A," [online]. *Art Crimes: The Writing on the Wall* [website]. Available http://www.graffiti.org/faz/graffiti questions.html

Farrell, S., (1998) e-mail/personal communication, 14 April.

Fenton, B. "Political Opposition of Hip-Hop," *360 Degrees* [website]. Available http://www.frymulti.com/~bfenton/politic/360.html

Ferris-Thompson, R. (1996) "Hip-Hop 101," in Perkins, W. E. (ed.) *Droppin' Science: Critical Essays on Rap Music and Hip-Hop Culture*, Philadelphia: Temple University Press, pp. 211–219.

Gates, H. L., Jr. (1987) *Figures in Black: Words, Signs, and the "Racial" Self*, New York: Oxford University Press.

Gates, H. L., Jr. (1988) *The Signifying Monkey: A Theory of Afro-American Literacy Criticism*, New York: Harvard University Press.

Gates, H. L., Jr. (1997) "Defining the Vernacular," in Gates, Jr., H. L. and McKay, N. (eds) *The Norton Anthology of African American Literature*, New York: W. W. Norton & Co., Inc.

Gforce (1998) "SOHH Global Forum!" [Online]. *Support Online Hip-Hop* [website]. Available http://sohh.com/cgi-bin/forum.cgi?Hip-Hop

Haupt, A. (1995) "Rap and the Articulation of Resistance: An Exploration of Subversive Cultural Production During the early 90s, with Particular Reference to Prophets of da City," unpublished MA thesis, Bellville, South Africa: University of the Western Cape.

Jda9star. (1998) "SOHH Global Forum!" [online]. *Support online hip-hop* [website]. Available http://sohh.com/cgi-bin/forum.cgi?Hip-Hop

jkeeler (1998) "SOHH Global Forum!" [online]. *Support online hip-hop* [website]. Available http://sohh/com/cgi-bin/forum.cgi?Hip-Hop

Kane-Berman, J. (1978) *Soweto: Black Revolt, White Reaction*, Johannesburg, South Africa: Ravan Press.

Marable, M. (1983) *How Capitalism Underdeveloped Black America: Problems in Race, Political Economy, and Society*, Boston: South End Press.

Marley, B., and the Wailers. (1980) "Redemption Song," (recording), in *Uprising* (album), London: Island Records.

Massey, D. S., and Denton, N. A. (1993) *American Apartheid: Segregation and the Making of the Underclass*, Cambridge, MA: Harvard University Press.

Norfleet, D. M. (1997) "Hip-Hop Culture" in New York City: The Role of Verbal Music Performance in Defining a Community (Rap Music)," unpublished doctoral dissertation. New York: Columbia University.

Paulston, C. (1994) *Linguistic Minorities in Multilingual Settings: Implications for Language Policies*, Amsterdam: Benjamins.

Probst, P. (1993) "The Letter and the Spirit: Literacy and Religious Authority in the History of the Aladura Movement in Western Nigeria," in Street, B. V. (ed.) *Cambridge Studies in Oral and Literate Culture: Cross-Cultural Approaches to Literacy*, Cambridge: Cambridge University Press, pp. 198–219.

Raze (1998) "SOHH Global Forum!" [online]. *Support online hip-hop* [website]. Available http://sohh.com/cgi-bin/forum.cgi?Hip-Hop

Rebensdorf, A. (1998) "'Representing the Real' Exploring Appropriations of Hip-Hop Culture in the Internet and Nairobi." Available http://clark.edu/~soan/alicia/rebensdorf.body.html [accessed 20 May 1998].

Reder, S. M. (1987) "Comparative Aspects of Functional Literacy Development: Three Ethnic American Communities," in Wagner D. A. (ed.) *The Future of Literacy in a Changing World*, Oxford: Pergamon Press, pp. 250–270.

Reder, S., and Wikulund, K. R. (1993) "Literacy Development and Ethnicity: An Alaskan Example," in Street, B. V. (ed.) *Cambridge Studies in Oral and Literate Culture: Cross-Cultural Approaches to Literacy*, Cambridge: Cambridge University Press, pp. 176–197.

Rockhill, K. (1993) "Gender, Language and the Politics of Literacy," in Street, B. V. (ed.) *Cambridge Studies in Oral and Literate Culture: Cross-Cultural Approaches to Literacy*, Cambridge: Cambridge University Press, pp. 156–175.

Rodney, W. (1974) *How Europe Underdeveloped Africa*, Washington, DC: Howard University Press.

Rose, T. (9/12/96) "African-American Art and its Audience," Mellon Fellowship symposium [online]. *Washington University in St. Louis* [website]. Available http://www.artsci.wustl.edu/~afas/vis/fall96/5rose.html

Smitherman, G. (1997) "The Chain Remain the Same: Communicative Practices in the Hip-Hop Nation," *Journal of Black Studies* 28(1): 3–25.

Street, B. V. (ed.) (1993) *Cambridge Studies in Oral and Literate Culture: Cross-Cultural Approaches to Literacy*, Cambridge: Cambridge University Press.

Superion7 (1998) "SOHH Global Forum!" [online]. *Support online hip-hop* [website]. Available http://sohh.com/cgi-bin/forum.cgi?Hip-Hop

Toop, D. (1991) *Rap Attack 2: African Rap to Global Hip-Hop*, (2nd edn), New York: Serpent's Tail.

Unique (1998) "SOHH Global Forum!" [online]. *Support online hip-hop* [website]. Available http://sohh.com/cgi-bin/forum.cgi?Hip-Hop

VeX aSSaSSin aka sHURiken (1998) "SOHH Global Forum!" [online]. *Support online hip-hop* [website]. Available http://sohh.com/cgi-bin/forum.cgi?Hip-Hop

West, C. (1993) *Race Matters*, Boston: Beacon Press.

275

"What We're Doing and Why" [online]. *Art Crimes: The writing on the wall* [website]. Available http://www.graffiti.org/index/story.html

Woodson, C. G. ([1933] 1990) *The Mis-education of the Negro*, Trenton, NJ: Africa New World Press.

CONCLUSION: INVENTING POSTMODERN IDENTITIES: HYBRID AND TRANSGRESSIVE LITERACY PRACTICES ON THE WEB

Gail E. Hawisher and Cynthia L. Selfe

> I prefer a network ideological image, suggesting the profusion of spaces and identities and the permeability of boundaries in the personal body and the body politic. "Networking" is both a feminist practice and a multinational corporate strategy – weaving is for oppositional cyborgs.
>
> (Haraway, 1991)

> Feminism constructs not one but many identities, each one of which, by their autonomous existence, seizes micropowers in the world wide web of life experiences.
>
> (Castells, 1997)

Web literacies and the transformation of identity

The chapters that comprise this volume describe literacies born of, and marked by, their particular cultural, linguistic, historical, and geographic roots in Hungary, Greece, Australia, Palau, Norway, Japan, Scotland, Mexico, Cuba, South Africa, and the United States, but the chapters also describe literacies that clearly transcend, deny, or resist these specific geopolitical locations by, and through, their presence on the Web.

This dynamic tension between localness and globalness, takes us beyond the simple – if appealingly coherent and modernist – narrative of the global-village as described in the Introduction to this volume. The messy complexity – and the oftentimes contradictory nature – of these new literacies suggests, instead, a more complicated postmodern vision. This new vision recognizes online literacy practices not only as responses to the disintegration of conventional world-views, world orders, and social formations based on a

277

modernist framework, but also as an important primary means of creating and expressing identities in changing postmodern landscapes.

To explain these new identity formations and their connection to online literacy practices in this conclusion, we draw not only on specific examples from chapters that comprise this collection, but also on additional work by Manuel Castells (1996, 1997, 1998) that deals with the transformation of identity in the information age, by Donna Haraway (1991) whose concept of cyborg agency suggests a blurring of traditionally gendered and politicized identity boundaries, and by Hawisher (1998) whose study of international women Web spinners illustrates the hybridity with which identities are marked and enacted on the Web in contemporary contexts.

The rise of the information society and the transformation of primary identities

According to Manual Castells (1996, 1997, 1998), the traditional sources which humans use to build their identities – those that contribute a sense of self, community, and understanding of the world through literate practices – are shifting dynamically in these tumultuous times, along with many other conventional social institutions and practices.

Although ethnicity and nationality have offered traditional bases for meaning and the construction of identity throughout a large part of history, the impulse to ground ourselves primarily in such identities is changing as the historically and geographically determined nation state itself gives way to what Castells (1996) calls the "network society" (p. 21) and the information age. High-speed global communication networks – built around overlapping systems of computers, television, fax, and telephones that form a transnational web of information technologies – have been directly linked to the spread of multinational capitalism, and, thus, to the establishment of multiple and overlapping *transnational* authorities for economic and political affairs (Castells, 1996). Such transnational patterns serve, in turn, to supplant or undermine some state-controlled economic regulatory systems and systems of political allegiance by establishing multiple and overlapping global authorities for economic and political affairs, as well as by extending people's understanding of political, economic, and social roles beyond the physical borders of their home countries.

In addition, the rise of global information networks, Castells (1996) notes, has also been linked to additional changes that are equally significant. Among these, for example, is the rise of global criminal and terrorist organizations that use networks not only to exchange information about the strategic movement of law enforcement troops and the best ways to construct home-made bombs, but also to share self-published hate manuals and to distribute news of their successful terrorist activities. Castells also links the rise of the networked society to the increased activities of fundamental religious and political systems. These groups construct increasingly defensive and communal identities to reinforce the boundaries of belief systems threatened by the "destructuring" of familiar social organizations and the "delegitimization of institutions" that characterize the information age (Castells, 1996, p. 3). The changing networked society and the process of globalization that characterizes it, Castells (1998) contends, has been linked, as well, to a complex process of economic polarization and the expansion of both poverty and "extreme poverty" (p. 133) that threaten to marginalize "whole countries and peoples" from information networks – including the inhabitants of sub-Saharan Africa and the rural areas of Latin America and Asia, Blacks in the inner cities of America; and exploited child laborers in urban enclaves around the world. Further, Castells contends, the developing economic and political dynamic of the network society serves to attach such individuals and groups to an intergenerational cycle of misery, extreme poverty, and crime.

For Castells, power in the network society becomes "diffused in global networks of wealth, power, information, and images, which circulate and transmute in a system of variable geometry and dematerialized geography" (1997, p. 359). "[T]he new power," Castells (1997) argues, "lies in the codes of information and in the images of representation around which societies organize their institutions, and people build their lives, and decide their behavior" and adds simply that peoples' minds are the new sites for this power (p. 359). Power, in this system, is a function of the struggle around society's cultural codes, and it is a power that relates directly to identities. As Castells puts it, "Identities anchor power in some areas of the social structure, and build from there their resistance or their offensives in the informational struggle about the cultural codes constructing behavior . . ." (1997, p. 360).

What does this all have to do with literacy practices and instruction? In this electronic environment of rapid and disturbing social change where conventional social formations and institutions are being deconstructed, personal and group identity – as expressed through language and literacy practices – is, in Castells' words, "fast becoming the main, and sometimes the only source of meaning. . . . People increasingly organize their meaning not around what they do but on the basis of who they are, or believe they are" (Castells, 1996, p. 3), and they define their primary identities in their everyday literate practices within the networked society.

But there is also a deep-seated and disturbing irony associated with the nature of defining identity in the networked society – as Castells (1997) observes, many people and groups end up formulating their identity both within, and in resistance to, electronic networks, both within the system of the networked society and in resistance to it. In other words, while a great deal of identity primary formation now happens online – in electronic literacy exchanges on e-mail, bulletin boards, electronic conferences, and websites – much of it is motivated, ironically and paradoxically, by such

279

factors as a personal or group resistance to the problems generated by technology: for instance, by a reaction against the growing economic inequities generated by multinational capitalism as it flourishes in the new global networked environments, or by a reaction against the "primacy of technology for technology's sake" (1997, p. 358) that continues to characterize citizens' lives in developed or developing countries, by a reaction against the international and national criminal networks supported by the global information systems, or in resistance to the "diffusion of power" (1997, p. 359) that the globally networked society threatens. Often, these new identities are based on shared language, shared history, shared culture, or shared political interests – elements that help some groups formulate new "local" communities within the "global" setting of cyberspace.

This is a world in which conventional identities are challenged dramatically and fundamentally by the "placeless logic" (p. 358) and dizzying change associated with the new information age, and yet one in which citizens must nonetheless assemble online in electronic environments in order to facilitate the diffusion of their ideas, to participate in productive political involvement, and to extend their own "possibilities for interaction and debate" (p. 350).

Cyborgs and blurred identities on the Web

In many respects, Castells' arguments echo those of Donna Haraway (1991) in *Simians, Cyborgs, and Women: The Reinvention of Nature*. In this work, Haraway suggests turning to a politics of cyborgs and to cyborgian identities, which call themselves into existence as "hybrids, mosaics, chimeras" (p. 177), in part to escape traditional gendered roles and in part to invent new politicized subjects capable of acting productively and boldly in a changing world that continues to be shaped and mediated by technology. More than a blend of human and machine, Haraway's cyborgian identities also cut across national and geopolitical borders as they communicate with and within computer networks and grapple at all levels with what it means to be embodied beings in an information-rich technological world.

Cyborgs – in forming their identities within and through computer-based environments – transgress boundaries and present "dangerous possibilities which progressive people might explore as one part of needed political work" (p. 154). For Haraway, geopolitical identities no longer satisfy in a world where we must act not out of "natural identification" (p. 174) but only out "of conscious coalition, of affinity, of political kinship" (p. 174). We note that Castells' (1997) political identities are similarly (re)constructed out of collectives of subjects who share linguistic, cultural, or political aims and who see new forms of productive action as possible in electronic spaces. Such collectives, or what Castells (1997) would call the "collective social actor," build new identities out of their shared life projects and expand "toward the transformation of society as a prolongation of this project of identity as in the . . . example of a post-patriarchal society, liberating women, men, and children, through the realization of women's identity" (p. 10).

For Haraway (1991), too, the cyborg has powers capable of (re)constructing and transforming the postmodern, personal yet collective self. She contends that the "slightly perverse shift" (p. 154) to cyborg imagery might better enable us to vie for meanings, "as well as for other forms of power and pleasure in technologically mediated societies" (p. 154). She goes on to argue that written literacy practices are the technologies of choice for cyborgs, given that writing, historically, has enabled "others" to tell their stories. For Haraway, "the play of writing is deadly serious" (p. 175). Through writing and building effective affinities, she would have cyborgs "act potently" (p. 181) to change the world.

Online hybridity and other lessons from international women's websites

In Castells' notion of transformative identities and Haraway's concept of cyborgs, we find hints about the postmodern nature of the online literacy practices described in the chapters of this collection – and we see why the modernist narrative of the global village seems increasingly inadequate to the task of containing, explaining, or representing postmodern identities (either collectively or individually) as they are constructed through the literacy practices the authors describe.

A third source of information about the overlapping formations of literacy and identity in the postmodern world comes from one of the author's examinations of international websites created by feminist Web spinners. In her examination of these sites, Hawisher identifies at least one additional element – that of hybridity – to shed light on the ambiguities and contradictions associated with online identity formation, literacy practices, and globalization.

At the feminist sites, women construct identities that cross national and ethnic boundaries and that enlist gender as a basis for *hybrid* identities. No longer fully defined by history or geography, the identities the Web spinners carve out for themselves are multiple – at once Russian, European, or Latina but participating, too, in the marketplace economy of the Web dominated by Americans. In examining the websites, Hawisher argues that Web-based literacy practices, in McCongahy and Snyder's words (this volume, Chapter 3), "transform, rather than simply reproduce, particular social and cultural formations" – exploring from Castells's and Haraway's perspectives, how expanded identities expressed and enacted in, and through, online literacy practices contribute to transformations of the very societies in which individuals participate.

Hawisher (1998) examines three sites – two Russian and one German – at least in terms of the author's/designer's country of origin. In all three cases, however, the postmodern identities of the site's authors and content quickly overflow the conventional geopolitical. A useful case study of this claim is offered at "Russian Feminism Resources",[1] a website created and maintained by Elena Leonoff (see Plate 11.1).

On entering the site, readers encounter a variety of choices: links for versions in English or Russian, a list of conferences, organizations, personal home pages of Russian women (mostly college students now living in the United States), and even a category for "anti-feminist views." One link leads viewers to a list of feminist Web pages in what the Leonoff calls "other post-communist states." Nineteen countries are listed, extending from Albania to the Ukraine, with a variety of women's resources and the following note:

> This is a very brief, selective list . . . if you want more, please visit
> the Network of East–West Women for an extensive list of women's
> groups in Central/Eastern Europe and the FSU [former Soviet

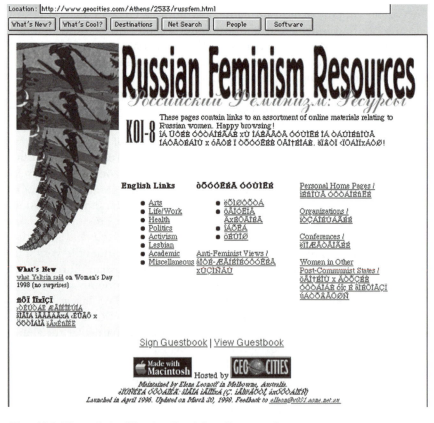

Plate 11.1 The website "Russian Feminism Resources"

Union], with e-mail addresses. The Center for Civil Society International also has a good women's page with lots of links. If you need general information about the countries in this region, visit the Institute on East Central Europe at Columbia University, which provides a heap of info sorted by country.

Links from this point include "Women for Women in Bosnia," which, when accessed, informs us that the site has changed its name to "Women for Women"[2] to better publicize the genocide occurring in Rwanda and the rape of an "estimated 250,000 to 500,000 women" in 1994.

Thus, a site, that at first glance seems mainly concerned with "Russian Feminism Resources" and even "Women in Other Postcommunist States," is articulated with a program aimed at women in Africa, which has an Advisory Board and Board of Directors who include women (and a few men) from different parts of the world – among them, US Senator Barbara Boxer; Amnesty International's Jodi Longo; Grameen Bank's Muhammad Yunus; Women for Women's founder and president Zainab Salbi; and Bernice Sandler, a well-known American academic and feminist. This site enlists the aid of other technologically rich inhabitants of the world by fusing what Haraway would call "outsider identities" (1991, p. 174), calling upon some of the insiders of the world to lend their identities to the cause, and finally collectively acting on the plight of the Rwandan women.

To complicate matters further, Elena Leonoff, who is of Russian descent, does not live in the former Soviet Union – rather, she lives in Melbourne, Australia, where she maintains the website with the services of GeoCities, a commercially viable American company that offers free personal home pages and e-mail addresses, all for the cost of allowing it to post advertisements on

*Plate 11.*2 "Some words from one of our sponsors . . ." (The pop-up marquee at the website "Russian Feminism Resources")

subscribers' pages. Every time readers access a web page at Elena's site, a marquee pops up (see Plate 11.2, "Some words from one of our sponsors . . ."), advertising everything from CDs, to American BankCards, to realtors, to body fitness opportunities, and more.

Other websites in the sample are characterized by similar hybrid identities involving gender, nationality, and other political and economic realities.

In analyzing sites like "Russian Feminism Resources," Hawisher attempts to build on and extend the work of scholars such as Donna Haraway and Anne Balsamo, linking the concepts of *cyborg* identities and *hybridity* in online communication environments. The cyborg women represented in these Web pages use online literacy practices to transgress against conventional national boundaries, to achieve multiple goals, and to construct cyborgian, hybrid identities in the process of practicing online literacies. As Homi Bhaba (1994) has suggested, "the display of hybridity – its peculiar 'replication' – terrorizes authority with the ruse of recognition, its mimicry, its mockery" (p. 115).

The concept of hybridity yields additional insights when applied to Castells's questions (1997) about the (re)construction of identities – from what, by whom, and for what are they constructed (p. 7). The women who compose these sites are very aware of the ways in which others view their extended gender and ethnic identities, and they also bend and shape these views to construct even more complicated hybrid identities online. Their purposes in constructing the identities are complex, as Elena Leonoff's work indicates. In the "Russian Feminist Resource site," for instance, Leonoff ostensibly announces her wish to share information that women who have an interest in Russian feminism might find useful. Yet her linked home page, entitled, "Get a Life," reveals more of her hybrid thinking:

> Ahhh, the de rigeur Narrative
> of Self page! This is where
> you get to sticky beak into the
> life of the blushing designer
> of this little web-corner.

> In a nutshell: I'm genetically
> Russian, born in San
> Francisco in 1996, raised in
> Melbourne, Australia; have
> been a chemistry student, a
> philosophy student, a
> librarian, a web designer.

> I live alone in a bedsitter with
> a view, a fat tabby called

Emma, my Purr Mac and six
bookcases. Most interesting
recent experience: spending
Jan–Feb 1998 in Tver,
Russia. Yes, it was cold.

I really can't cope with writing
a resume for myself on this
page . . . Welcome to
decontextualized
information.

Learn to like it.

If you like what I like, if you
like the way I like what I like, if
you hate what I like, if you
know any better ways of
getting a life, if you really
want to see a picture of my
cat . . .

E-mail me!

Technologically and educationally privileged, Elena and the other women involved in this study of websites write themselves online in sophisticated ways. As practiced and narrated in these Web pages, feminism takes on multiple identities that embrace cultural specificity and globalized culture all at once and in complex and, sometimes, contradictory ways.

As Castells argues, "in an interrelated world where people and experience travel and mingle," there is a "hyperquilt of women's voices [spreading] throughout most of the planet" (p. 137) Rewriting their identities through inscribing and linking Web pages, the women hint at what the Web is and is becoming – not a global village, but rather a shifting landscape of individual and collective identities, one inhabited by individuals situated in specific historical and cultural contexts, cyborgs who read the "Webs of power" and who have the potential to write new kinds of postmodern identities based on "new couplings, new coalitions" (Haraway, 1991, p. 170) and new literacy practices.

Online literacy practices, transgressions, and hybridity

We began this collection with a discussion of the global-village narrative and a reminder of the potency that this story exerts in shaping a contemporary vision of literacy practices on the Web. But the cracks and fissures in this story, as the preceding discussion and each of the chapters in this collection suggests, are becoming increasingly evident and powerfully insistent – the spread of global consumerism and multinational capitalism, and colonialism associated with investments in the global information infrastructure, the regional and national increase of poverty and the spread of transnational crime. The global-village narrative, it is becoming clear, simply will not work for much of the world in the next century – it is too reductive, too western, too colonial in its conception.

And so, what do the chapters in this collection suggest about an alternative vision of the Web, one more specifically and accurately reflective of the postmodern struggles with identity, nationality, ethnicity, and language threaded throughout the collection? The concept of blurred identities that we have presented from the work of Manuel Castells and illustrated with the examples of international women's websites offers a starting point for an alternative perspective to the global-village narrative by observing that identities built on the traditional foundations of nationalism, culture, race, and ethnicity are multiplied and freely transgressed through literacy practices in electronic landscapes. Working from these starting points, we can add, as well, the perspective of cyborgian hybridity, drawing on the work of Donna Haraway (1991), Anne Balsamo (1996), and Hawisher (1998) – all of which suggest a merging of traditionally uncombined (or uncombinable) parts with a tolerance for – and, more than that, a valuing of – difference and diversity.

The chapters in this collection provide particular examples of how identity formation and online literacy practives are inextricably linked and overlapping on the Web. As the Web establishes itself as a site for this dynamic mix of globally and locally situated identities, its value as a postmodern landscape emerges – it is a space defined, in part, by a tension between contestation and resolution, stasis and change, localness and globalness, single and multiple identities. And it is a malleable landscape that is charted by the moment, continually revealed in a changing topography of literate exchanges among humans. It's within this complex landscape of identity formation, expression, and politics that we must begin to understand the forces and influences shaping the literacy practices mentioned in this book.

Many of the conflicting forces growing out of the simultaneous move toward the global network society and the need to stay rooted in particular cultures are foregrounded in the stories of Web literacies presented in the chapters of this collection: the Greeks' penchant in the literacy environment of the Web to value English over other languages as the major linguistic medium of exchange and their concomitant fear that English might rob them of their cultural heritage of polylingualism; the 14-year-old Mexican student's eschewing Spanish search engines in favor of the English, which she says provide her with everything she needs online, yet the necessity of using the Spanish word *conocer* ("to have an understanding of") to describe Mexican students' and teachers' relationship with the Web; the Norwegians' strong sense of nationalism but nevertheless the recognition that when it comes to popular culture English is always "in the air"; the fact that 174 websites in Australia focus mainly on Indigenous topics yet only 61 percent of them demonstrate any sort of Indigenous involvement; and, in Palau, the obligatory western imperative to use two names instead of the customary Palauan single name so that children now sport their father's first name as a surname, which often causes mistaken identities.

All these examples speak to current conflicts in how we multiply – and continually reconstitute – our own identities through online literacy practices, and how we come to be known by our literate exchanges with others. No longer, for example, is identity constituted solely through nationality or ethnicity. The identity of Hungarian, Scots, American, or Palauan; of Black, Pacific Islander, or Hispanic no longer suffices in an isolated form; maybe it never did but certainly not today. The chapters in this collection indicate that individuals who use the Web are multiply defined – as Pacific Islanders living in America who choose to meet, identify, and correspond with native-born Palauans; as hip-hoppers located differentially in South Africa and America who share common roots in race and a taste for a transnational music that supports radical social redefinition; or as Indigenous Australians linked to the Aboriginal Youth Network in Canada; the citizens of the Great Sioux Nation; and the people of Tibet.

And even these multiply defined ethnic and national identities, these local–global hybrids, are insufficient to the task. As Castells (1997) argues, ethnicity in the Information Age is a "source of meaning and identity to be melted not with other ethnicities, but under broader principles of cultural self-definition, such as religion, nation, or gender" (p. 53). He goes on to state that "Ethnicity does not provide the basis for communal heavens in the network society, because it is based on primary bonds that lose significance, when cut from their historical context as a basis for reconstruction of meaning in a world of flows and networks, of recombination of images, and reassignment of meaning" (p. 59). For Castells, ethnic roots have become "twisted, divided, reprocessed, mixed, differentially stigmatized or rewarded, according to a new logic of informationalization/globalization of cultures and economies that makes symbolic composites out of blurred identities" (p. 59). This concept of "blurred identities" may prove valuable to readers trying to make cumulative sense of the literacy practices and chapters in this volume – especially because it refers to the ways in which literacy practices and literacy values overlap with the politics of identity and internationalism.

In combination, the concepts of blurred identity, transgressions, and hybridity suggest a distinctly postmodern redrawing of the Web landscape.

This redrawing admits to the increasingly global identity of the Web, but denies the colonial erasure associated with the global village as a formation that serves the interests of highly technologized nation states in the west. In place of the global-village narrative, the combined constellation of blurred identity + transgressive cyborgs + hybridity suggests an alternative landscape – one that is dynamic, unstable, and peopled by individuals and groups who form and reform according to multiply defined identities, constituting "planetary villages" or "imagined communities" (Deibert, 1996, p. 199). These shifting collections of individuals (many of whom belong to many more than one such group) are characterized by literacy practices and exchanges which cut across traditional national, cultural, and ethnic boundaries, but who also retain both cultural specificity and a value on difference.

This alternative vision of the Web, as Deibert points out, seems to provide a much better fit with the postmodern character of the Web:

> [C]ertainly the postmodern decentered self with multiple identities resonates with the demassification of imagined communities and the enmeshment of sovereign states in multiple layers of authority. And the latter seems especially to "fit" the postmodern sense of juxtaposition and superimposition, and nonlinear, pastiche-like orderings of space as characterized by Foucault's notion of "heterotopia . . ." And the recognition of "difference" and hyper-plurality . . . suggest that the emerging architecture of world order is moving away from territorially distinct, mutually exclusive, linear orderings of space toward nonlinear, multiperspectival, overlapping layers of political authority. Likewise, modern mass identities centered on the "nation" are being dispersed into multiple, nonterritorial "niche" communities and fragmented identities.
>
> (1996, p. 201)

It is important to point out, however, that the fragmentation associated with postmodernity is not an *end* point of the conflicts and transgressions reflected in literacy practices on the Web; fragmentation does not tell the whole story. The postmodern identities represented in the literacy practices we see in this collection also generate a productive hybridity, new meanings and identities continually assembled and reassembled though language and literate exchange.

In sum, the alternative vision we offer within these pages celebrates the dynamic capacity of transgressive identities that are generated within, and through, literacy practices on the Web. This vision, as the chapters of this collection indicate, recognizes the ongoing influences of traditional geopolitical contexts, but maintains a value on cultural specificity; it argues against a romanticized vision of global oneness, but for the continuing redefinition of ethnicity and difference in unstable, self-defined literacy communities; it resists the official literacies that Brian Street (1995) connects to the ongoing reproduction of illiteracy, poverty, and racism, while admitting the possibility of hybrid and multiple literacies that share the blessings of diversity and difference. It is with these hopful signs – and with the expectation of ongoing discussions of literacies on the Web – that we offer this collection for the consideration of readers and scholars entering the next century.

Notes

1   http://www.geocities.com/Athens/2533/russfem.html; 30 June 1998
2   http://www.embassy.org/wmn4wmn/ 1 July 1998

References

Balsamo, Anne (1996) *Technologies of the Gendered Body: Reading Cyborg Women*, Durham: Duke University Press.

Bhabha, Homi K. (1994) *The Location of Culture*, New York: Routledge.

Castells, Manuel (1996) *The Rise of the Network Society*, Malden, MA: Blackwell.

Castells, Manuel (1997) *The Power of Identity*, Malden, MA: Blackwell.

Castells, Manuel (1998) *End of Millennium*, Malden, MA: Blackwell.

Deibert, Ronald. J. (1996) *Parchment, Printing, and Hypermedia: Communication in World Order Transformation*, New York: Columbia University Press.

Haraway, Donna. (1991) *Simians, Cyborgs, and Women: The Reinvention of Nature*, New York: Routledge, pp. 149–181.

Hawisher, Gail E. (1998) "*Feminist Transgressions on the World Wide Web: International Connections,*" paper presented at the Conference on Rhetoric and Composition: Multiple Literacies for the 21st Century, October 1998, University of Louisville, Louisville, KY.

Selfe, Cynthia L. (1999) "Lest We Think the Revolution is a Revolution: Images of Technology and the Nature of Change," in Hawisher, Gail E. and Selfe, Cynthia L. (eds) *Passions, Pedagogies, and 21st Century Technologies*, Logan, UT: Utah State University Press.

Soja, Edward W. (1996) *ThirdSpace: Journeys to Los Angeles and Other Real-and-Imagined Places*, Cambridge: Blackwell.

Street, B. V. (1995) *Social Literacies: Critical Approaches to Literacy in Development, Ethnography and Education*, London: Longman.

Zone 451, <http://www/iconn/ca/zone451/issue08/verticles/ve08bab2.html> [accessed 23 July 1998].

INDEX